Significant Contemporary
American Feminists

Significant Contemporary American Feminists

A Biographical Sourcebook

Edited by
JENNIFER SCANLON

Greenwood Press
Westport, Connecticut • London

Library of Congress Cataloging-in-Publication Data

Significant contemporary American feminists : a biographical
  sourcebook / edited by Jennifer Scanlon.
        p.   cm.
    Includes bibliographical references (p.   ) and index.
    ISBN 0–313–30125–5 (alk. paper)
      1. Feminists—United States—Biography—Dictionaries.
    2. Feminism—United States—Bio-bibliography—Dictionaries.
    I. Scanlon, Jennifer, 1958– .
    HQ1412.S56   1999
    305.42'0973—dc21   98–22899

British Library Cataloguing in Publication Data is available.

Library of Congress Catalog Card Number: 98–22899
ISBN: 0–313–30125–5

First published in 1999

Greenwood Press, 88 Post Road West, Westport, CT 06881
An imprint of Greenwood Publishing Group, Inc.

Printed in the United States of America

The paper used in this book complies with the
Permanent Paper Standard issued by the National
Information Standards Organization (Z39.48–1984).

10 9 8 7 6 5 4 3 2 1

Copyright Acknowledgments

The author and publisher gratefully acknowledge permission for the use of the following material:

"Who Said It Was Simple" copyright © 1973 by Audre Lorde, from UNDERSONG: Chosen Poems Old and New by Audre Lorde. Reprinted in the U.S. and Canada by permission of W. W. Norton & Company, Inc. Reprinted in the UK and Commonwealth by permission of Abner Stein.

The lines from "Del otro lado" by Gloria Anzaldúa, copyright © 1994. From COMPANERAS: LATINA LESBIANS edited by Juanita Ramos. Reproduced by permission of Routledge, Inc.

From BORDERLANDS/LA FRONTERA by Gloria Anzaldúa, copyright © 1987. Reprinted with permission of Aunt Lute Books.

From THINKING OUT LOUD by Anna Quindlen. Copyright © 1993 by Anna Quindlen. Reprinted in the U.S. and Canada by permission of Random House, Inc. Reprinted in the United Kingdom and its territories by permission of International Creative Management, Inc. Copyright © 1993 The New York Times.

The lines from "Snapshots of a Daughter-in-Law," copyright © 1993, 1967, 1963 by Adrienne Rich. The lines from "Planetarium," copyright © 1993 by Adrienne Rich. Copyright © 1971 by W. W. Norton & Company, Inc. The lines from "The Burning of Paper Instead of Children," copyright © 1993 by Adrienne Rich. Copyright © 1971 by W. W. Norton & Company, Inc. from COLLECTED EARLY POEMS: 1950–1970 by Adrienne Rich. Reprinted by permission of the author and W. W. Norton & Company, Inc.

The lines from "Diving into the Wreck," from THE FACT OF A DOORFRAME: Poems Selected and New, 1950–1984 by Adrienne Rich. Copyright © 1984 by Adrienne Rich. Copyright © 1975, 1978 by W. W. Norton & Company, Inc. Copyright © 1981 by Adrienne Rich. Reprinted by permission of the author and W. W. Norton & Company, Inc.

The lines from "Inscriptions," from DARK FIELDS OF THE REPUBLIC: Poems 1991–1995 by Adrienne Rich. Copyright © 1995 by Adrienne Rich. Reprinted by permission of the author and W. W. Norton & Company, Inc.

The lines from "Getting Down to Get Over" and "Ah Momma" from THINGS THAT I DO IN THE DARK by June Jordan. Copyright © by June Jordan. Reprinted by permission of the author.

Every reasonable effort has been made to trace the owners of copyright materials in this book, but in some instances this has proven impossible. The author and publisher will be glad to receive information leading to more complete acknowledgments in subsequent printings of the book and in the meantime extend their apologies for any omissions.

CONTENTS

CONTENTS

PREFACE

This work provides biographical, analytical, and bibliographical portraits of fifty contemporary U.S. feminists. These women have served as catalysts in the developing feminist movement, drawn on their various identities to help define this and other social movements more broadly, and struggled to advance feminism in ways that would be both personally fulfilling and politically efficacious. Each of their stories serves as an inspiration to readers interested in the power of one, and collectively they provide a portrait of the range of motivations, activities, and accomplishments of feminist thinkers and activists today.

Each essay contains three parts: a biographical portrait of the individual, including information about education, family life, and early activism; an analytical discussion, highlighting the person's accomplishments and her relationship to U.S. feminism; and a bibliographical section that contains a selective list of publications by the subject and writings about her and her work. The bibliography at the end of the book offers readers an extensive listing of works about second and third wave feminism in the United States.

Significant Contemporary American Feminists: A Biographical Sourcebook goes to press in 1998, the thirty-year anniversary of many defining moments in civil rights, antiwar, and feminist politics. It is one of many publications that, with the distance of three decades, further attempt to explore those times and those movements. As part of the chronicling of that era, this work suggests that historians as well as other scholars examine the multiple roles women have held and the ways in which movement politics have been influenced by individuals with varieties of identities and affiliations. In other words, the history of the 1960s and beyond can become a history of individuals with multiple identities and of organizations that, consequently, overlap in significant ways. Not surprisingly, as this work demonstrates, feminist women can be found in every element of that history.

A work of this type faces an immediate criticism: it highlights the few and disregards the many. Although featuring a very selective group of women might seem to mirror too closely the "great men" method of organizing knowledge, it accomplishes several important goals: countering the tendency to write women out of movement histories; making connections between the personal and the political in individual life histories; and providing us with useful insights about many contemporary women who have, in their work and lives, dedicated themselves to positive social change for women. Admittedly, a work such as this could easily include hundreds of subjects rather than fifty. Nearly every reader will be able to point to a contemporary activist who ought to have been included. However, this work is meant to be highly selective rather than inclusive, and the editor hopes that other works will follow to fill in the gaps, provide other perspectives on what makes a feminist "significant," and add to the body of knowledge about women and social movements.

The difficult task of selecting individuals for inclusion was made somewhat easier because of the participation of the advisory board: Nedda Albray, Rosalyn Baxandall, and Jo Freeman. Unfortunately, several of the women they felt should be included are not. Early-movement women, in particular, who made a lasting impression but left little behind in the way of biographical information have been left out: they include Ti-Grace Atkinson, Catherine East, Lois Gibbs, Carol Hanisch, Kathy Sarachild, Margaret Sloan, and Johnnie Tillmon. Many others arguably belong here as well. Nevertheless, this book offers readers insights into the lives and work of an impressive group of American women: thinkers, active agents, leaders—truly significant contemporary feminists.

The contributors to this volume include activists and academics, women and men whose interests in feminist movements come from personal experience, scholarly interest, and, sometimes, bitter struggle. I offer thanks to all of them as well as to those who, after much preliminary research, found that they could not complete essays on the subjects assigned to them because there was not sufficient information available.

INTRODUCTION

This book provides the reader with compelling stories of individual women's lives, collective feminist struggles, and the possibilities of feminist social change. It highlights the lives and work of a group of fifty contemporary women who, engaging with feminism, provide the assurance that women can and do change the worlds they live in. As the media and politicians continually marginalize women's issues and minimize women's complaints, feminists maintain their determination to formulate and put into practice agendas about reducing the violence of sexism, racism, heterosexism, and the other forces that continue to oppress people in and outside the United States. This collection of essays pays tribute to many of those individuals and to their struggles.

The history of the second wave of feminism in the United States demonstrates the potential for serious social change as well as for seemingly intractable divisions among women. From the start of the women's movement, women embraced feminism for different reasons and from different positions. Race, social class, sexual orientation, and religion, among other identity factors, influenced individual women's perceptions of, and relation to, the feminist movement. In fact, three distinct groups of women formed the early second wave: the governmentally appointed members of the Kennedy Commission on the Status of Women, whose charge was to examine all aspects of women's conditions and status in the United States; grassroots organizers like those who emerged from civil rights and New Left organizations to form the Combahee River Collective, Redstockings, and many other feminist groups; and the discontented middle-class and educated housewives documented in Betty Friedan's *The Feminine Mystique*.[1]

Since then, great numbers of women and men with multiple other identities have engaged with this movement, struggling to define it and themselves in relation to it. They have taken a variety of actions in the name of feminism, naming and claiming identities and experiences. Yet their efforts have collectively been identified as second wave feminism—and collectively identified as having made a difference. For that reason they are grouped together in this book. The work and inspiration of second wave feminists have led to what some are calling a third wave, young women born into, but defining, feminism on their own terms. They all have a place in these pages.

If anything ties feminists together, it is, as Gloria Steinem reflects on looking back, freedom of choices. "The greatest gift we can give one another is the power to make a choice," she writes. "The power to choose is even more important than the choices we make."[2] In the name of feminism, women make very different choices about personal, social, and political change. They work independently at times; at other times they leave safe spaces to enter into coalitions. They try to rebuild existing institutions in more people-friendly ways; they also try to envision and build new institutions devoid of oppression. They find unsettling, at best, some of the choices of their sisters; they struggle to defend their sisters' right to choose. They try to learn from the errors that mark their own collective past; they make mistakes again and again. They truly struggle as they engage with feminism. As a consequence, the stories that mark these pages are filled with insight, humor, rage, contradiction, and inspiration.

A brief timeline of events from the 1970s, 1980s, and 1990s reveals the diversity of issues that contemporary U.S. feminism has raised and responded to. In one year, 1972, Shirley Chisholm ran for president of the United States; Ms. magazine premiered, selling out its first issue within eight days; the media responded to Ms., with Harry Reasoner's predicting on national television that the new publication would run out of things to say within six months; Sally Priesand was the first woman ordained as a rabbi; Title IX was passed, eliminating sex bias in federally funded programs; the National Conference of Puerto Rican Women was founded; and Congress sent the Equal Rights Amendment (ERA) to the states for ratification. To respond to feminism in the 1970s, as now, one had to engage with the pressing questions of politics, economics, culture, race, religion.

Ten years later, 1982 witnessed the fruits of many people's having undergone that engagement with feminism. Some were eager to declare the movement dead: Phyllis Schlafly, for example, celebrated 1982 by holding an end-of-ERA bash, and the New York Times coined the phrase "postfeminist generation."[3] However, feminist organizing and feminist accomplishments were also plentiful: Wisconsin passed the first state lesbian and gay rights bill; the first black women's studies anthology, All the Women Are White, All the Blacks Are Men, But Some of Us Are Brave, was published; the Older Women's League held its first national convention; and Ms. magazine published its tenth-anniversary issue.

The same struggles to define feminism and to declare it a lost cause or a revolution in process carried on into the 1990s as well. In 1992, the Los Angeles Times reported that "feminists have killed feminism."[4] In the same year, however, the National Organization for Women celebrated its silver anniversary with a diverse and growing membership, and in what was called Anita Hill's revenge, political candidates Carol Moseley Braun and Lynn Yeakel garnered votes for national office by exposing and opposing U.S. senators who had backed Clarence Thomas' appointment to the Supreme Court.

As the decade, century, and millennium wind to a close, feminism is alive and well in the United States, contrary to media declarations of its imminent demise. However, feminists still speak with no single voice and concern themselves with no one agenda. As they battle to end discrimination against women and children on a variety of fronts, feminist individuals and organizations continue to struggle with internal issues of race, sexuality, and class. Feminism remains an ideology many measure themselves against, often finding either it or themselves lacking. Feminism is in process, adjusting to, and incorporating issues of, identity, efforts toward coalition work, and the results of its own legacies as a movement.

The women profiled in this work stand as examples of feminism in action. Playwrights and politicians, grassroots organizers and scientists, poets and theologians, they put into practice a determination to engage with the world around them in ways that benefit women's lives. In and outside organizations, they help frame debates, link women's voices, and make the world a more just place. Their promise, as it links them together in this collection, is this: contemporary feminism is a movement worth engaging with, challenging, and furthering. There is truly a future in feminism.

NOTES

1. See Sheila Tobias, *Faces of Feminism: An Activist's Reflection on the Women's Movement* (Boulder, CO: Westview Press, 1997), 71–92.

2. Gloria Steinem, "Foreword," *To Be Real: Telling the Truth and Changing the Face of Feminism*, ed. Rebecca Walker (New York: Anchor Books, 1995), xxvi.

3. "Twenty Years of the Women's Movement," *Ms.* 3, no. 1 (July/August 1992): insert.

4. Ibid.

Significant Contemporary
American Feminists

BELLA ABZUG
(1920–1998)

Mary L. Ertel

Bella Abzug is most often remembered for her outspokenness on women's issues, peace, and civil rights issues, her flamboyant hats, and the three terms she served in the U.S. Congress (1970–1976). However, her work as a lawyer, peace activist, civil liberties advocate, and political organizer extends either side of that period of her life. And, from 1990 until her death, she expanded her efforts to an international area, working on environmental issues and efforts to bring social and economic justice to women of developing nations.

Bella Abzug was born in New York City on July 24, 1920, to Russian-Jewish immigrant parents, Emanuel and Esther Savitsky. Emanuel died when Bella was thirteen; Bella said Kaddish in synagogue every day for a year, a ritual restricted traditionally to males.

Bella Savitsky commuted from the South Bronx to Hunter College in Manhattan, earning a bachelor of arts degree in 1942. At Hunter, she was elected student body president and addressed an assembly with First Lady Eleanor Roosevelt. Refused by Harvard Law School's males-only policy, she was one of six women to attend Columbia University Law School, receiving her law degree and attaining admission to the bar in 1947. Abzug has honorary degrees from Hunter College, Hobart College, and Manhattanville College.

Just prior to graduating from Hunter, Bella Savitsky married Maurice M. Abzug, stockbroker and novelist. They had two daughters, Eve Gail and Isobel Jo. Maurice endorsed Bella's work and activism. Their marriage, described by Gloria Steinem (1996) as a partnership of love for politics, dancing, life's pleasures, and each other, lasted forty-two years. Bella wrote of their marriage and how she was coping with her grief over the loss of Maurice in the first issue of the remodeled Ms. in 1990.

Bella Abzug entered private law practice in 1947. She instigated her practice of wearing hats to let judges know she was a practicing woman lawyer, rather than the secretary many assumed any woman to be. She specialized in labor law and civil liberties, defending victims of the McCarthy communist witch-hunt and indigent southern blacks. Gloria Steinem notes that Bella Abzug "slept in a bus station—while pregnant with the first of her two daughters—because no hotel would accommodate her" (Steinem 1996, 63).

Abzug was a founder of Women Strike for Peace and its executive director from 1961 to 1970. She was exceedingly vocal in demanding withdrawal of U.S. military presence from Vietnam. She was a lifelong advocate for less military spending and more spending on the social ills that plague the poor, especially women.

In 1970, Abzug was elected to the first of three terms to the House of Representatives, the first Jewish woman to attain this position. She documented her first two years in Congress in a diary-type work, *Bella! Ms. Abzug Goes to Washington*. Here, she said of herself:

I am an activist. I'm the kind of person who *does things* at the same time that I'm working to create a feeling that *something can be done*. And I don't intend to disappear in Congress as many of my predecessors have. My role, as I see it, is among the people, and I am going to be *outside* organizing them at the same time that I'm *inside* fighting for them. (5)

As chair of the Subcommittee on Government Information and Individual Rights, Abzug conducted hearings on illegal and covert activities by federal government agents. This resulted in the landmark Freedom of Information Act, a "Government in the Sunshine" law giving citizens access to government records. Her best-known accomplishments in Congress, however, had to do with the status of women. In 1971 she cofounded, and became first chair of, the National Women's Political Caucus (NWPC). She helped found the Congressional Caucus on Women's Issues and introduced the first gay rights bill to Congress. She was appointed by President Ford as first chair of the National Commission on the Observance of International Women's Year (1976) and organized the first (and only) federally funded National Women's Conference in Houston (1977).

Abzug gave up her congressional seat in 1976 to run for the U.S. Senate from New York state (the first woman to do so), losing narrowly to Daniel Patrick Moynihan. She ran unsuccessfully for mayor of New York City in 1977 (again, the first woman to do so) and again for Congress in 1978. Her losses in these races, however, did not deter her from being active in public life. President Jimmy Carter appointed her cochair, with Carmen Delgado, of the National Advisory Committee for women but dismissed her in the "Friday Night Massacre" after she and the committee were critical of cuts in funding for women's programs. Abzug then returned to private law practice while continuing an active public life. She coauthored *Gender Gap: Bella Abzug's Guide to Political Power for American Women* with Mim Kelber (her congressional executive assistant) in 1984.

From her days in Congress right through to her recent death, Abzug worked extensively with the United Nations (UN) on women's issues and environmental issues. She participated in the UN's Women Conferences in Mexico City (1975), Copenhagen (1980), and Beijing (1995). Environmental concerns extended from her concern for women. In 1991, Abzug gave the opening speech at the World Women's Congress for a Healthy Planet, urging women's political empowerment and increased role in decision making. Along with Mim Kelber, Abzug was cofounder and cochair of the grassroots political action organization Women, U.S.A. Fund, Inc., and its program Women's Environment and Development Organization (WEDO). She remained active in the United Nations, where, with enormous energy and disarming humor, she engaged in many issues affecting women's lives.

Bella Abzug was known for her feistiness, her loud, outspoken presentations, and, as mentioned before, her flamboyant hats. She was outspoken as a child when she advocated for a Jewish homeland and against anti-Semitism; she remained outspoken throughout her life. Abzug was frequently criticized by the media as being too forceful, yet her ability to build bridges led colleagues to name her as one of the three most influential members of Congress during her stay there.

Abzug made it a policy to carry with her in Congress an anti–sex discrimination statement, which she introduced—and encouraged others to introduce—with any bill she could. She introduced many bills; in the 92d Congress alone, Abzug, along with Martha Griffiths, a representative from Michigan who was considered the senior fighter for woman's rights in Congress, introduced more than twenty bills pertaining to women, including those on abortion rights, Social Security, establishing credit for women, extension of minimum wage to domestic workers, and prohibitions against the use of "Miss" and "Mrs." by the federal government. These and new bills, including provision of comprehensive child care, were reintroduced into the 93d Congress. Although she was unable to forge major legislative victories, Abzug did accomplish one of her most pressing goals: establishing women as a political force in the United States. Through her work against the Vietnam War and for a peacetime economy that promoted social justice, the National Women's Political Caucus, and the Equal Rights Amendment, Abzug remained in the forefront of American politics.

In the 1970s and early 1980s, the Equal Rights Amendment was the focus of the women's movement. Abzug noted: "The ERA became the heart and soul of the contemporary women's peaceful revolution, with its quest for equality and economic justice. It was the legal bedrock on which all other changes were to be inscribed" (Abzug 1984b, 18). This summarizes her approach. While she did not fit the model of an establishment woman, Bella Abzug wanted to work within the institution for positive change toward equality for American women.

The National Women's Political Caucus (NWPC) was formed in July 1971 by a group including Bella Abzug, Gloria Steinem, Betty Friedan, Shirley Chisholm, and Patsy Mink. NWPC's goal was to get more women in public office, by election and appointment, and to work in both political parties, along with independent feminists, to get women and women's issues more attention in the political arena. One of NWPC's projects was the Women's Education for Delegate Selection (WEDS). As a result of numerous state conferences on delegate selection, spearheaded by Abzug and Gloria Steinem working with the McGovern arm of the Democratic Party, the percentage of delegates who were female increased from 13 percent in 1968 to 40 percent of those attending the Democratic National Convention in 1972. (The Republican effort brought an increase from 17 percent to 29 percent.)

Bella Abzug was strong in her support of gay rights, which caused some friction between her and other feminist leaders. An escalating series of events involving lesbian feminist leaders came to a head when Kate Millett admitted her bisexuality. This produced a scathing attack in the media, including *Time*, of the women's movement's lesbian connections. Betty Friedan, seemingly fearing the presence of outspoken lesbian leaders, resigned from the Women's Strike Coalition (which supported Millett) over this issue. By contrast, Abzug sent Kate Millett and the coalition a message of support. Indeed, strong public support from numerous feminists turned the issue around and significantly put the movement back on course. The relationship between Bella Abzug and Betty Friedan, however, remained difficult. Friedan had originally supported Abzug's run for Congress, but they disagreed on the lesbian issue. Friedan wanted NWPC to unite women to elect women in general and to organize strength around what she saw as women's issues; she was upset over the coalition of the poor, blacks, women, youth, and gays and lesbians Abzug and Gloria Steinem were organizing in the McGovern campaign and in political life generally. Abzug was aware of these differences. "She [Betty] seems to think we should support women for political office, no matter what their views, and we don't. I feel our obligation is to build a real political movement of *women for social change*. I don't think we're at a level where we have to fight to get just *any* woman elected" (Abzug 1972, 160).

Abzug remained strong and outspoken in her public posture. For this, Friedan called Abzug and Gloria Steinem "self-styled radicals in the caucus leadership" (Friedan 1977, 230). She accused them of taking alienating positions and seeking personal political power, not realizing that if they gained power for themselves, they gained it for the movement. Ideological issues aside, this disagreement was, in significant part, a struggle about who would be acknowledged by feminists, the media, and the power brokers as head of the women's movement. Ultimately, Abzug and Steinem prevailed. Bella Abzug, highly visible because of her position and activities in Congress, continued to relentlessly campaign for woman's rights.

Some feminists have criticized Abzug for being mainstream, a liberal feminist. Betsey Stone, for example, views the situation of NWPC—including Abzug's role in it—in a critical light. Stone notes that, among other things, NWPC's candidates always ran for office under the label of a traditional political party, failed to confront the issue of abortion in 1972 in an effort not to hurt the chances of the Democratic Party, and failed to take on what she felt was the true enemy of women, capitalism. Indeed, the Socialist Workers Party (SWP) denounced both Bella Abzug and Shirley Chisholm as capitalists and opportunists of feminism (both Stone and the SWP position are cited in Ginette Castro's *American Feminism*).

Regardless of the criticisms she faced within and outside the movement, Abzug continued her work. She and Patsy Mink drafted a bill providing for a public, government-funded conference in every state and territory to discuss women's issues and send delegates to a National Women's Conference. This constitutional convention for women was in contrast to the original Constitutional Convention, made up of all men. The purpose was for women to come together and propose changes in laws and government procedures that were barriers to their equality. Though it passed with a lesser budget and too late for the convention to be held in bicentennial 1976, it did pass. A Women's Year Commission, including Bella, was appointed by President Carter to organize the event.

The convention, held in Houston, involved 15,000 participants and 2,000 voting delegates. The conference was more representative by race, class, and age than was Congress; its procedures were significantly more open than those of Congress. Participants deliberated and passed legislation that was then sent on to Congress and the president. The Houston Conference was, ultimately, about empowering women.

After unsuccessful campaigns for Senate, mayor of New York City, and another House run, Bella Abzug turned her attention elsewhere. She wrote (with Mim Kelber) *Gender Gap: Bella Abzug's Guide to Political Power for American Women*. Crediting the feminist movement for empowering women, Abzug acknowledged the disparity in voting patterns of women and men, urged increased awareness of women's issues, and discussed ways to improve the position of women through the legislative process.

Ultimately, Abzug turned her attention to women worldwide, with increasing involvement with the United Nations, Women, U.S.A. Fund, Inc., and WEDO. WEDO is a worldwide network designed to put forth a feminist agenda and give women power within the UN. One agenda item is gender balance in all commissions of the UN. WEDO also performs the important function of analyzing every UN document for its impact on women, lobbying at the UN, and monitoring government action in the implementation of programs.

In her most recent work, *Women: Looking beyond 2000*, Bella Abzug noted how closely women in the developing world are tied to the environment. She detailed the extensive involvement of women in growing and gathering food and how environmental problems particularly impact the position and work of women. She called upon women to become aware of how their purchases can affect the practices of industry. Abzug called on women internationally to make connections and empower themselves to work actively to resolve environmental problems of the world.

In 1994, Bella Abzug was inducted into the National Women's Hall of Fame in Seneca Falls, New York. The same year, she was given a Medal of Honor by the Veteran Feminists of America. In 1996, she was *Ms.* magazine's Woman of the Year, with a tribute written by longtime friend Gloria Steinem, who acknowledged Bella "for acting locally and globally on behalf of women, peace, and justice."

Bella Abzug died in March of 1998, at age 77, from complications following heart surgery. President Bill Clinton was among the many who paid tribute to Bella Abzug at her death. Like many who will remember her, Clinton noted her tireless voice and passionate efforts on behalf of women in the United States and around the world.

WORKS BY BELLA ABZUG

Ed. Mel Ziegler. *Bella! Ms. Abzug Goes to Washington*. New York: Saturday Review Press, 1972.
"Bella's Eye View of Her Party's Future." *Ms*. 2 (April 1974): 64–65.
"Womanpower! A New American Doctrine." *Redbook* 146 (February 1976): 34+.
With Mim Kelber. *Gender Gap: Bella Abzug's Guide to Political Power for American Women*. Boston: Houghton Mifflin, 1984a.
———. "How to Win with the Gender Gap: Three Scenarios for the '84 Election" (excerpt from *Gender Gap*). *Ms*. 12 (March 1984b): 39–42+.
"Martin, What Should I Do Now?" *Ms*. 1, no. 1 (July/August 1990): 94+.
"Raising Our Voices." *The UNESCO Courier* 45, no. 3 (March 1992): 36–37.
"Empowering Women: Opening Speech at the World Women's Congress for a Healthy Planet." *Women's International Network News* 18, no. 1 (Winter 1992): 16+.
Et al. "On Globalizing Gender Justice." *The Nation* 61 (September 11, 1995): 6+.
———.*Women: Looking beyond 2000*. New York: United Nations, 1995.

SOUND RECORDINGS

Should Abortions Be Legal? Bella Abzug vs. Ann Toland Serb. By Bella Abzug and Ann Toland Serb. San Diego: Greenhaven Press, 1977.
Women's Lib (National Women's Political Caucus). By Betty Friedman, Gloria Steinem, and Bella Abzug. Encyclopedia Americana/CBS News Audio Resource Library, 1971.

WRITINGS ON BELLA ABZUG

"Abzug Makes the Heart Grow Fonder." *Village Voice* 39, no. 50 (December 13, 1993): 19.
Alpern, D. M., and P. Malamud. "Bella vs. Pat." *Newsweek* 88 (September 6, 1976): 16.
"Bella." *Newsweek* 76 (October 5, 1970): 28–29.
"Bella Abzug." *Ms*. 5, no. 1 (July/August 1994): 46.
"Bella Abzug." *Nation* 261, no. 7 (September 11, 1995): 230.
"Bella and Bill." *Newsweek* 79; no. 37 (May 8, 1972): 37.
Brozan, Nadine. "Chronicle." *New York Times* 144, 49896, November 30, 1994: B8.
Castro, Ginette. *American Feminism: A Contemporary History*. New York: New York University Press, 1990.

Faber, Doris. *Bella Abzug*. New York: Lothrop, Lee, and Shepard, 1976.

Faison, Seth. "A Well-Known Hat Bobs at Women's Conference: Acclaim for Bella Abzug." *New York Times*, September 12, 1995, A3.

Felner, Julie. "Lipstick and Lesbians." *Ms.* 6, no. 3 (November/December 1995): 85.

Friedan, Betty. *It Changed My Life: Writings on the Women's Movement*. New York: Dell, 1977.

M. Kelber, "Carter and Women: The Friday Night Massacre." *Nation* 228 (February 3, 1979): 97+.

J. L. "Abzug Applauded at Global Forum." *Earth Island Journal* 7, no. 3 (Summer 1992): 22.

O'Reilly, Jane. "Womanifesto." *Nation* 255, 3 (July 20, 1992): p. 77–78.

Ruben, Barbara. "Bella Abzug: Giving Women a Voice." *Environmental Action Magazine* 24 (Summer 1992): 12–15.

Steinem, Gloria. "Bella Abzug." *Ms.* 6, no. 4 (January/February 1996): 62–63.

Toolan, David S. "Earth Day with Bella, Barry and Friends." *America* 172 (May 12, 1995): 2–3.

PAULA GUNN ALLEN
(1939–)

Gönul Pültar

Paula Gunn Allen, a self-identified Native American feminist woman poet/author and scholar, was born in 1939 in Cubero, New Mexico, to a Laguna-Sioux-Scottish mother and a Lebanese-American father, both of whom were native New Mexicans.

After attending schools in Cubero, San Fidel, and Albuquerque, New Mexico, Allen entered Colorado Women's College. She eventually received a B.A. in English at the University of Oregon in 1966 and an M.F.A. in creative writing at the same university in 1968. She received a Ph.D. in American studies, with an emphasis on Native American studies, from the University of New Mexico in 1975.

While still a graduate student, Paula Gunn Allen started teaching and at the same time published her first book of poems, *The Blind Lion* (1974). In 1978 she received a National Endowment for the Arts Creative Writing Fellowship; and in 1980–1981, she was awarded a postdoctoral fellowship at the University of California at Los Angeles (UCLA) in the Native American Scholars Fellowship program to study Native American women's writings. In 1983 she edited *Studies in American Indian Literature: Critical Essays and Course Designs*. Her only published novel to date, *The Woman Who Owned the Shadows*, also came out that same year.

Such varied work has led her to a dual career of a published poet/creative writer and a full-time academic. After teaching for a number of years at the University of California at Berkeley, Allen is currently professor of American Indian studies, as a member of the English Department, at UCLA. These bare facts fail to underscore, however, that, in Allen, both pursuits are colored and sustained by feminism. Allen's feminism is itself, in turn, unequivocally colored by lesbianism.

It is impossible to pinpoint when Allen became a feminist, because, as Donna Marie Perry rightly points out, Allen's Native American heritage empowered her, as a woman, to speak. Growing up in a matriarchal culture, she was not limited by gender, as her white sisters normally are. She grew up surrounded by medicine women (Perry 1993, xiv). Then, while in high school, Allen discovered Gertrude Stein, who influenced her as an author. "I couldn't have found the rhythms I found in *The Woman Who Owned the Shadows*, which I borrowed from legend," she explains, "unless I had Stein's rhythms inside me. She fractured the language, which then enabled me to do that in my way" (Perry 1993, 11).

Although Allen is currently active in the women's movement in the United States, her contribution to the feminist movement must be viewed essentially through her writings. She is a poet, a novelist, an academician, a scholar, a critic, and a much-sought public speaker. But Paula Gunn Allen is more than just that: she has the unique ability to merge her interests and reach multiple audiences. She has successfully combined her skills as a creative writer with the methodology she has acquired as a scholar to expose and celebrate Native American culture in articles and books that range from theoretical writings and original studies to collections comprising contemporary stories and transcriptions and translations of traditional tales. Allen has also played a role in the emergence of ethnic studies in universities and multiculturalism in literature studies. She is one of the most articulate and prolific present-day Native American authors and scholars.

However, what is striking is that Allen is a "Native Americanist" from a feminist standpoint. Her treatment and examination of Native American themes and issues are posited within a feminist framework. They could have been expressed and/or formulated only within the boundaries of feminist epistemology. That makes Allen important for feminism and signifies her specific contribution to U.S. feminism.

As a feminist author and scholar, Allen achieves two goals through her texts. One has to do with lesbianism. She bestows respectability to it, first, by proclaiming that she, a well-known personality, is a lesbian; second, by celebrating it in her poems and other texts; and third and most importantly, by explaining that lesbianism as well as male homosexuality have always been present in Native American societies. Precontact Indian societies had a "gender-designation" that differed from that of the whites and that of contemporary U.S. society. Allen explains in *The Sacred Hoop: Recovering the Feminine in American Indian Traditions*: "As an example, the Kaska of Canada would designate [one] daughter in a family that had only daughters a boy. . . . She would dress in male clothing and would function in the Kaska male role for the rest of her life" (Allen 1992, 196). Gender roles and sexuality markers were less rigid.

For Allen, lesbians and homosexuals were ritually and socially valued tribal members, with special respect and honor accorded to them. Their status was altered as a result of colonization. Same-sex relationships, accepted as normal in precontact Indian societies, became frowned upon as traditional tribal values came to be exchanged for white Christian values, within the whites' overall attempt at obliterating Native American culture. The devalorization of same-sex relationships was part and parcel of efforts to dismantle the matriarchal setup of Indian nations with a view to disrupt and weaken these societies. Thus, for Allen, a return to, and espousal of, Native American culture and values would also mean a revalorization and rightful celebration of homosexuality in general and of lesbianism in particular, since women play such an important role within Native American societies.

That brings us to Allen's second goal: the reinstatement of woman's place in Native American societies and, consequently, in U.S. society by revisiting these worlds in her writings. Put very simply, Allen explores the gynocratic nature of precontact Indian societies: they were gynocentric, matrifocal, and matrilineal (inheritance of rank through the maternal line), a situation that is the inverse of male-dominated, patriarchal societies.

AnaLouise Keating writes that "by describing preconquest North American cultures as gynocentric, Allen revises previous academic interpretations of Native traditions and attempts to enlist all U.S. feminists" (Keating 1996, 101). Allen herself has explained that "what I'm really attempting to do is affect feminist thinking. Because my white sisters . . . have given the impression that women have always been held down . . . but I know that's not true" (in Keating 1996, 101).

White colonizers deliberately broke down this woman-centered social system, Allen argues in *The Sacred Hoop*, because they saw that "as long as women held unquestioned power of such magnitude, attempts at total conquest of the continents were bound to fail. . . . [T]he invaders have exerted every effort to remove Indian women from every position of authority, to obliterate all records pertaining to gynocratic social systems, and to ensure that no American and few American Indians would remember that gynocracy was the primary social order of Indian America prior to 1800" (Allen 1992, 3).

Allen concludes that the "physical and cultural genocide of American Indian tribes is and was mostly about [the white invaders'] patriarchal fear of gynocracy" (Allen 1992, 3). She finds, moreover, that "Western studies of American Indian tribal systems are erroneous at base," as they are conducted from a "cultural bias of patriarchy," or they "recontextualize" Indian tribal features "so that they will appear patriarchal" (Allen 1992, 4). So, an orientation toward traditional Native American values must perforce entail women's empowerment among American Indians, which obviously will benefit all American women in the long run.

However, Allen does not stop at that. What she has in mind is not political power only—or not anymore, as her scholarly and personal interests take a turn. While the 1980s saw her as a champion of the Native American cause both as a scholar and as a poet/creative author, the 1990s have brought about a shift in Allen's thinking and theorization. In *Grandmothers of the Light: A Medicine Woman's Sourcebook*, she introduces the term "cosmogyny" (Allen 1991, xiii). What she now envisages is no less than a cosmos ruled by women. For Allen, in the beginning was Woman: Woman is the creatrix; God is female.

Allen sees Woman as creatrix not only in a biological sense but also as the creator of the universe, which she creates by thinking: woman creates the world by thinking it. She is a spirit that pervades everything and creates everything. However, Woman (or any of the various names she has in the different Indian nations) is not limited to a female role, and seeing her merely as a fertility goddess is wrong as well as demeaning. Woman is the supreme Spirit, both Mother and Father to all creatures. To address a person as "mother" is to pay the highest ritual respect. The primary potency in the universe is female.

Thus, according to Allen, the "degynocratization," as she calls it, of American Indian nations has meant much more than territorial loss, political defeat, or homicide pure and simple (Allen 1992, 38). It has meant spiritual loss that goes far beyond the destruction of cultures and traditions. The enormity of it does not need elaboration. It follows that women's empowerment, involving a spiritual dimension, becomes all the more indispensable.

As Keating points out, Allen's writings are not descriptive but performative (Keating 1996, 4). Allen is not interested merely in exposing the wrongs of the past or presenting archival studies, except to write in response to what she learned in her own pueblo from her mother or her grandmother. Her writings are the laying bare of an agenda for the future, and they have a definite function, both extraliterary and extrascholarly.

Paula Gunn Allen's writings fall into two categories, literary and scholarly, although in some cases, as in her rendering of traditional Indian tales, this division proves to be arbitrary since much effort that can only be called creative goes into it. First, though, are her creative writings, which comprise her poems, which she has been publishing since the early 1970s, and her novel, *The Woman Who Owned the Shadows*. This is a beautiful experimental novel, poetical prose more than anything else, that can withstand the accusation that ethnic women authors are not sufficiently innovative, being too preoccupied with content to attend to form. It has the merit also of encapsulating almost all the precepts that Allen professes in her nonfictional books. Her celebration of lesbianism, very much part of her feminism, is there; and her female deities are alive, much more than they are in the theoretical writings. Allen's major feat in this novel, however, is to have exposed powerfully, in fictional terms, the conflictual situation of a woman caught between the exigencies of two cultures, with the female protagonist's predicament as a half-breed functioning as a potent metaphor.

Allen's second batch of writings, her scholarly work, may, in turn, be divided into two. First are her collections of Native American literature by women. She seems tireless, almost self-effaced in her desire to promote this literature, whether stemming from oral tradition or written by other women writers, as she does in *Spider Woman's Granddaughters: Traditional Tales and Contemporary Writing by Native American Women*. Then there are what must be called her theoretical writings, although she professes to discuss in them a teleology that has been existent on the American continent since time immemorial. Allen advances in *Grandmothers of the Light* that the Native American spirituality and myths she exposes and discusses in that book have guided female shamans, the medicine women, "toward an understanding of the sacred for centuries," as the blurb on the back cover records it. For some, this may seem the antipode of serious scholarship, not because collecting such material is not in and of itself scholarship, which it is, but because the "spiritual" concepts and precepts thus promoted seem to be outside the realm of rationality, in the sense that Western epistemology understands it, whether phallocentric or not.

Thus, Allen's ideas could have been expressed only from a feminist viewpoint and within a feminist framework. In this she makes her greatest contribution to U.S. feminism, since feminist studies and feminist criticism are viable, it has been said, only insofar as they prove to be indispensable for critique and reappraisal, societal or otherwise.

Paula Gunn Allen is at present busy teaching, writing, and speaking. But it is already evident that through her disruption of the conventional image of womanhood and her introduction of a totally novel and forceful mythography, she is inventing a tradition and imagining a community for the future. It is too early to tell to what extent her performative writings will be consequential in the long run for U.S. feminism—or for U.S. society, for that matter—and what shape her ultimate contribution will take. Yet, as she always puts at the end of her texts, as if to announce her continued presence, *nos vemos*.

WORKS BY PAULA GUNN ALLEN

The Blind Lion. Berkeley, CA: Thorp Springs Press, 1974.
"Mythopoetic Vision in Native American Literature." *American Indian Culture and Research Journal* 1, no. 1 (1974): 3–13.
Coyote's Daylight Trip. Albuquerque, NM: La Confluencia, 1980.
A Cannon between My Knees. New York: Strawberry Press, 1983.
Ed. *Studies in American Indian Literature: Critical Essays and Course Designs.* New York: Modern Language Association of America, 1983.
The Woman Who Owned the Shadows. San Francisco: Spinsters Ink, 1983.
"Answering the Deer: Genocide and Continuance in American Indian Women's Poetry." *Coming to Light: American Women Poets in the Twentieth Century.* Ed. Diane Wood Middlebrook and Marilyn Yalom. Ann Arbor: University of Michigan Press, 1985, 223–232.
"Whose Dream Is This Anyway?" *Literature and the Visual Arts in Contemporary Society for USA 20/21 Number Two.* Ed. Suzann Ferguson and Barbara Groseclose. Columbus: Ohio State University Press, 1985, 95–122.
The Sacred Hoop: Recovering the Feminine in American Indian Traditions. Boston: Beacon Press, 1986; with a new preface, Boston: Beacon Press, 1992.
Skins and Bones. Albuquerque, NM: West End Press, 1988.
"Who Is Your Mother? Red Roots of White Feminism." *The Graywolf Annual Five: Multi-Cultural Literacy.* Ed. Rick Simonson and Scott Walker. St. Paul, MN: Graywolf Press, 1988, 13–29.
"Lesbians in American Indian Culture." *Conditions* 16, (1989): 84–106.
Spider Woman's Granddaughters: Traditional Tales and Contemporary Writing by Native

American Women. Boston: Beacon Press, 1989; Ballantine Books edition, New York: Fawcett Columbine, 1990.

Grandmothers of the Light: A Medicine Woman's Sourcebook. Boston: Beacon Press, 1991.

Voice of the Turtle: American Indian Literature. New York: Ballantine Books, 1994.

Song of the Turtle: American Indian Literature, 1974–1994. New York: Ballantine Books, 1996.

Life Is a Fatal Disease: Selected Poems, 1964–1994. Albuquerque, NM: West End Press, n.d.

WRITINGS ON PAULA GUNN ALLEN AND HER WORK

Hanson, Elizabeth I. *Paula Gunn Allen*. Boise State University Western Writers Series, no. 96. Boise, ID: Boise State University, 1990.

Keating, AnaLouise. *Women Reading Women Writing: Self-Invention in Paula Gunn Allen, Gloria Anzaldúa, and Audre Lorde*. Philadelphia: Temple University Press, 1996.

Moss, Maria. *We've Been Here Before: Women in Creation Myths and Contemporary Literature of the Native American Southwest*. Münster, Germany: Nordamerika-Studien, 1993.

Perry, Donna Marie. *Backtalk: Women Writers Speak Out*. New Brunswick, NJ: Rutgers University Press, 1993.

GLORIA ANZALDÚA
(1942-)

Judith Richards

Tejana-Chicana, *Mexicana*, *india*, lesbian, feminist, and *mestiza* (mixed race), scholar, writer, and activist, Gloria Evangelina Anzaldúa sometimes refers to herself as *Patlache*, the Nahuatl Indian word for lesbian (Marie 1994, 11). These plural and overlapping descriptors of her identity correspond to the border-crossing discourse, ethics, and politics that constitute her writing.

Born and raised in south Texas of Latino parents whose own ancestors were of European and American Indian descent, Anzaldúa experienced from an early age the contradictory dynamics at work in the socialization of ethnic minority and girl children. Contact with Anglos in the school setting— where the speaking of Spanish was prohibited and her family was ridiculed because of their poverty—served to silence her voice and conflict her sense of self: "The ancient dances beaten back inside her,/the old song choked back into her throat" ("Del otro lado"). Initially figuring in Anzaldúa's life as sources of pain and dislocation, the hybrid cultural mix that was her heritage and the geo-political fact of the Mexican–U.S. border, a "1,950 mile-long open wound/dividing a *pueblo*, a culture,/running down the length of my body,/staking fence rods in my flesh" (Anzaldúa 1987, 2), coalesced in her consciousness as the site from which to resist oppression and construct a new identity in *mestizaje*. Her "constellated self" claimed a home on the "thin edge of barbed wire," the site from which she took into her own (writer's) hands "the transformation of my own being" (Anzaldúa 1983, 200). For Anzaldúa, the Borderlands (capitalized) represents a third reality that overrides the either/or rules of border politics. It is a cultural and psychic location where she owes allegiance only to the self she is becoming rather than to one specific community, ethnic, or gender group. The Borderlands is both an uneasy site, where "you are the battleground/where enemies are kin to each other; /you are at home, a stranger,/ . . . wounded, lost in action/dead, fighting back," and a test of endurance, "To survive . . . you must live sin fronteras/be a crossroads" (Anzaldúa 1987, 194–195). In an overarching sense, the metaphor ultimately embraces a prophetic stance: "I span abysses" (Anzaldúa 1987, 200).

Anzaldúa's own experiences of school, family, and community life shape her current thinking on self and knowledge, pedagogy and writing. Forced to speak the languages of mainstream society and lacking the confidence shared by those whose schooling was more thorough than her own, she recalls, "[I] majored in English to spite, to show up, the arrogant racist teachers who thought all Chicano children were dumb and dirty" (Anzaldúa 1983, 165–166). Frustrated by double standards for male and female children in her home and Latino community, Anzaldúa left for college in her late teens, needing to "find myself/buried under the personality that had been imposed upon me. . . . Nothing in my culture approved of me" (Anzaldúa 1987, 16). The first in her family to go to college, she worked her way through the academic system, earning her B.A. from Pan American University in 1969 and her M.A. in English and education at the University of Texas (UT) in Austin in 1972. Unable to convince her adviser that feminist studies and Chicano literature were legitimate areas of study, she left the doctoral program in comparative literature at UT and moved to the University of California in Santa Cruz, where she began teaching and studying in 1988, and passed her doctoral exams in 1991. Presently, she is engaged in several writing projects and does lecture tours.

Anzaldúa's central contribution to contemporary feminisms is her articulation of the complex nature of issues called into question by the feminist movement since the late 1960s and by its more recent postcolonial counterpart. Her groundbreaking examination of the ways race, class, and sexual preference must be components in feminist analysis revealed gaps in Anglo-feminist theories where gender alone was the overriding category of study. In addition, Anzaldúa called critics' attention to colonized subjects' tendency to internalize and replicate their discriminatory realities and to the androcentric focus of ethnic political movements. From her *mestiza* location in the Borderlands, itself intersected by lesbian issues, Anzaldúa constructs the model of a synthesized self whose components represent the sum of many oppressed communities. Fluid, borderless, and yet cognizant of its various origins, this configuration challenges Anglo and male constructs of her identity as a woman, lesbian, feminist, and Latina (Torres 1992, 271) and establishes a revolutionary optic through which all cultural and academic discourses must be examined.

The centrality of autobiographical experience in Anzaldúa's work corresponds to her use of the personal as an analytical category. Her own border crossings into Anglo society, the academy, the workplace, writers' groups, and lesbian communities have taught her that oppressive relationships have never been rigid or easily identifiable (Perry 1993, 10). Deconstructing the historical sources of oppression, she uncovers the multiple factors that intersect and shape gender as a facet of identity and notes that the women's movement's failure to take race, class, and sexual preference into consideration has perpetuated discriminatory analyses and relationships. On the other hand, Anzaldúa observes that racism is not just a white phenomenon (Anzaldúa 1987, 209) and laments schisms that have arisen among the women of color she works with (Anzaldúa, "En Rapport" 1990). Again speaking from the Borderlands, she theorizes the self without boundaries as a means of mitigating simplistic (binary) thinking and subject-object, self-Other dualisms that constitute the cornerstones of patriarchal thinking.

Anzaldúa's model of the Borderlands as a situating context for women of color has become an important analytical and discursive component across academic disciplines as well as in public forums. In *Philosophy and Feminism. At the Border*, Andrea Nye praises "Hispanic philosopher" Gloria Anzaldúa's elegant and passionate defenses of the subject's multilevel consciousness, noting particularly her use of *mestizaje* to rearticulate the monolinguality of Western philosophy, structural linguistics, and intellectual analysis (Nye 1995, 75). Likewise, writer Sandra Cisneros claims *Borderlands/La Frontera* as the book that most influenced her life (1996 National Hispanic Heritage poster), and Sonia Saldívar-Hull commends Anzaldúa's impact on the traditions of the Chicano community, where she has forced homophobes to see their own prejudices (1991, 213).

One of Anzaldúa's principal roles in the feminist movement is that of anthologizer and editor. In the late 1970s, her unhappy experiences with the Anglo-dominated Feminist Writers' Guild, where she found herself playing the role of interpreter for all women of color, and a token voice at that, led to the creation of *This Bridge Called My Back: Writings by Radical Women of Color* (edited with Cherríe Moraga). In this collection, the writers sought to expose the racism in the women's movement, to share information among women of color, to encourage writing among women of color, and to make their texts available to a broad reading audience. A groundbreaking representation of multifaceted feminist subjectivities, the book's central metaphor—the "bridge"—called attention not only to the isolation of women of color and working-class women in the women's liberation movement but also to their role as colonized subjects, on whose bodies empires were built and sustained and whose (nonacademic) labor continues to privilege some women over others. At the same time, the bridge is a touchstone for women of color, a political viaduct through which they consciously build alliances between the fragmented portions of their selves and between each other. More than a decade later, when preparing to teach a women's studies course at the University of California in Santa Cruz, Anzaldúa created the necessary sequel to *Bridge*, whose title maintains the concepts of embodied oppression and knowledges—*Making Face, Making Soul—Haciendo Caras*. Both anthologies strive to challenge and unsettle readers accustomed to mainstream texts, to teach them to read in a nonwhite manner.

An important dimension of bridge building in Anzaldúa's work is the examination of the connection between negative attributes assigned to women's nature and the cultural and historical narratives that reinforce them. She identifies a direct link between the omission and/or falsification of women's histories and the acculturation of the female subject through shame, guilt, and self-hatred. During her undergraduate and graduate studies, the absence of academic courses dealing with the breadth of her cultural heritage led Gloria to do her own research on the historical roots of Latinos in the Western Hemisphere. This recuperated knowledge constitutes the first part of the autobiographical volume *Borderlands/ La Frontera: The New Mestiza* and provides a basis for the identity politics through which she seeks to understand dynamics in contemporary Latino cultures. Exploring the roots of cultural narratives in American Indian mythologies, she "discovers" sources of modern women's denial of their sexuality and self-expression in blended Aztec and Spanish misogynies: the Aztec's desexing of the principal Nahuatl goddess and the Spaniard's reinforcing of dichotomized models of women's nature through sacralizing of the virgin and denigrating the sexual female self. Originally intended to provide background material for the poems in its second half, the historical revisionist chapters of *Borderlands/La Frontera* have become an essential component of Anzaldúa's work and message.

In Anzaldúa's most frequently anthologized essay, "La conciencia de la mestiza/ Towards a New Consciousness" (Anzaldúa 1987), she outlines a new mythos on which to build an unfettered, proactive identity in the present and the future. This consciousness is of the Borderlands, nurtured in alienation, the product of a "racial, ideological, cultural and biological cross-pollenization" that engenders a female model for the development of an identity that can creatively embrace global difference. The "new *mestiza*" rejects the concept of a unified and stable self, a paradigm unable to interact with the world. Instead, it works to develop a tolerance and an aesthetic for contradiction and ambiguity. "I am cultureless because, as a feminist, I challenge the collective cultural/religious male-derived beliefs of Indo-Hispanics and Anglos; yet I am cultured because I am participating in the creation of yet another culture, a new story to explain the world and our participation in it, a new value system with images and symbols that connect us to each other and to the planet" (Anzaldúa 1987, 80–81).

The journey motifs in Anzaldúa's writing allow her to meet with, and mediate for, the Other—both within herself and in the world. Through the bridge and border-crossing practices, the subject develops, in interaction with the Other, a questing persona that crisscrosses uneasy cultural and political territories, "wades through" uncharted areas, and explores the borders between different components of the self as sites of creativity that strengthen—rather than limit—the perspective she calls the "new *mestiza* consciousness." Claiming the Borderlands as a positive point of departure for the future interaction of subjects and communities, Anzaldúa explores models through which women (and other marginal subjects) can change the world. The paradigm she finds useful is "nos/otras," the feminine "we," a subject pronoun that contains "nos" (us) as an object pronoun and "otras" (others) as both an adjective and a subject pronoun. Together, object and subject interact in a manner that allows both women of color and white women to see the "other" in themselves, see themselves as "other," and begin to see themselves as the "other" sees them.

The multigenre and dialogic form of Anzaldúa's work is the aesthetic counterpart of the border-crossing dynamic. The essays in Borderlands/La Frontera,
themselves interlaced with poetry and lyrics from popular corridos, or ballads,
were written to provide a context for the poetry that constitutes the second half
of the book. This aspect of her texts and her use of writing as a component of
political activism are means through which she identifies and challenges Anglo
feminism specifically and the academy in general. As Torres notes, Anzaldúa's
intentional interruption of traditional autobiographical constructs challenges the
reader's own expectations of a text that works according to Western logic (Torres
1991, 284). Additionally, even Anzaldúa's sentences can unsettle the reader who
anticipates being led directly to conclusions (Moraga 1993, 152) rather than
being forced to take the process of transformations into her or his own hands.

Other key concepts in reading Anzaldúa are the eponymous "making face,
making soul" images through which she substitutes traditional, abstract philosophical concepts with those of her own experience—"face," "mask," and "in-
terface." Face masks disguise pain and shame, protect the truth, and create a
space for challenging abuse—for "getting in someone's face." Between the inner
and outer layers of the face, the vulnerable self and the public mask, is the inter-
face, the evolving identity giving support to the self in process. Ultimately, "making face" alludes to self-respect and human dignity.

Anzaldúa's hobbies include reading dyke detective writers, who "make the
most radical departure from the hard-boiled [misogynist] detective," and science
fiction, "escapist trash" that helps her deal with tension produced by oppression
(Perry 1993, 39). In addition, she enjoys painting and increasingly uses picto-
graphs as the basis of lecture material to emphasize connections between the
physical and intellectual components of women's voices. The text of Donna
Perry's interview with Anzaldúa includes the drawing "Con los ojos y la lengua-
pluma en la mano izquierda" (With eyes and tongue-pen in the left hand), in
which the face sketched depicts a mouth and tongue that are also a pen, alluding
to the interaction between seeing, knowledge, speaking, and writing, in a self-
reflective and activist manner.

Readers can find Anzaldúa's early writing in the journals Trivia, Third Woman,
IKON, and Sinister Wisdom. She notes that before Borderlands/La Frontera came
out, publishers might have found her multigenre and code-switching style difficult to categorize. Despite early difficulties with Chicano publishing houses, Arte
Público now distributes Borderlands/La Frontera. She enjoys working with alternative presses run by feminists and lesbians and frequently acknowledges the
importance of their support. This Bridge Called My Back won the 1986 Before
Columbus Foundation American Book Award, and Borderlands was selected as
one of thirty-eight best books of 1987 by Library Journal.

WORKS BY GLORIA ANZALDÚA

Books

With Cherríe Moraga, eds. *This Bridge Called My Back: Writings by Radical Women of Color*. Watertown, MA: Persephone Press, 1981; Latham, NY: Kitchen Table: Women of Color Press, 1983.

Ed. *Making Face, Making Soul—Haciendo Caras: Creative and Critical Perspectives by Feminists of Color*. San Francisco: Aunt Lute Books, 1990.

Short Stories

"El Paisano Is a Bird of Good Omen." *Cuentos: Stories by Latinas*. Ed. Alma Gomez, Cherríe Moraga, and Mariana Romo-Carmona. Latham, NY: Kitchen Table: Women of Color Press, 1983.

"Life Line." *Lesbian Love Stories*. Ed. Irene Zahava. Freedom, CA: Crossing Press, 1989.

"Ms. Right, My Soul Mate." *Lesbian Love Stories*, vol. 2. Ed. Irene Zahava. Freedom, CA: Crossing Press, 1991.

"A Tale." *Word of Mouth: Short-Short Stories by Women Writers*. Ed. Irene Zahava. Freedom, CA: Crossing Press, 1991.

"La historia de la Marimacho." *The Sexuality of Latinas*. Ed. Norma Alarcon, Ana Castillo, and Cherríe Moraga. Berkeley, CA: Third Woman Press, 1993.

Essays

"Speaking in Tongues: A Letter to Third World Women Writers" and "La Prieta." *This Bridge Called My Back: Writings by Radical Women of Color*. Ed. Anzaldúa and Cherríe Moraga; foreword by Toni Cade Bambara. First edition, Watertown, MA: Persephone Press, 1981; second edition, Latham, NY: Kitchen Table: Women of Color Press, 1983.

"The Homeland, Aztlan/El Otro Mexico." *Aztlan: Essays on the Chicano Homeland*. Ed. Rudolfo A. Anaya and Francisco A. Lomelr. Albuquerque, NM: Academia/El Norte, 1989.

"Bridge, Drawbridge, Sandbar or Island: Lesbians-of-Color Haciendo Alianzas." *Bridges of Power: Women's Multicultural Alliances*. Ed. Lisa Albrecht and Rose M. Brewer. Philadelphia: New Society, 1990.

"En Rapport, In Opposition; Cobrando Cuentas a las Nuestras" and "La conciencia de la mestiza: Towards a New Consciousness." *Making Face, Making Soul—Haciendo Caras: Creative and Critical Perspectives by Feminists of Color*. Ed. Anzaldúa. San Francisco: Aunt Lute Books, 1990.

"Metaphors in the Tradition of the Shaman." *Conversant Essays: Contemporary Poets on Poetry*. Ed. James McCorckle. Detroit: Wayne State University Press, 1990.

"To(o) Queer the Writer—loca, escritora y chicana. *Inversions: Writing by Dykes, Queers and Lesbians*. Ed. Betsy Warland. Vancouver: Press Gang, 1991, 249–264.

"People Should Not Die in June in South Texas" and "El dia de la Chicana." *Infinite Divisions. An Anthology of Chicana Literature*. Ed. Tey Diana Rebolledo and Mariana Rivero. Tucson: University of Arizona Press, 1993.

Poetry

Borderlands/La Frontera: The New Mestiza. San Francisco: Aunt Lute Books, 1987.
"Del otro lado." *Companeras: Latina Lesbians (An Anthology).* Ed. Juanita Ramos. New
    York: Latina Lesbian History Project, 1987.
"Nightvoice" and "Old Loyalties." *Chicana Lesbians: The Girls Our Mothers Warned Us
    About.* Berkeley, CA: Third Woman Press, 1991.

WRITINGS ON GLORIA ANZALDÚA AND HER WORK

Literary Analysis and Criticism

Freedman, Estelle B., Barbara C. Gelpi, Susan L. Johnson, and Kathleen M. Weston, eds.
    The Lesbian Issue. Essays from SIGNS. Chicago: University of Chicago Press, 1985.
Keating, AnaLouise. *Women Reading. Women Writing. Self-Invention in Paula Gunn Allen,
    Gloria Anzaldúa and Audre Lorde.* Philadelphia: Temple University Press, 1996.
Lugones, Maria. "On Borderlands/La Frontera: An Interpretive Essay." *Hypatia* (Fall
    1992): 31–38.
Moraga, Cherríe. "Algo secretamente amado." *The Sexuality of Latinas.* Ed. Norma Alar-
    con, Ana Castillo, and Cherríe Moraga. Berkeley, CA: Third Woman Press, 1993.
"1996 Visionaries." *Utne Reader* 65, no. 4 (March–April 1996).
Nye, Andrea. *Philosophy and Feminism. At the Border.* New York: Twayne, 1995.
Quintana, Alvina E. "Beyond the Anti-Aesthetic: Reading Gloria Anzaldúa's *Borderlands*
    and Maxine Hong Kingston's *The Woman Warrior.*" *CHICANA (W)RITES on
    Word and Film.* Ed. Maria Herrera-Sobek and Helena Maria Viramontes. Berkeley,
    CA: Third Woman Press, 1995.
———. *Home Girls. Chicana Literary Voices.* Philadelphia: Temple University Press, 1996.
Randall, Margaret. "Una conciencia de mujer." *Women's Review of Books* (December
    1987): 8–9.
Saldivar Hull, Sonia. "Feminism in the Border: from Gender Politics to Geopolitics." In
    Criticism in the Borderlands: Studies in Chicano Literature, Culture, and Ideology. Eds.
    Hecter Calderon and Jose Saldivar. Durham, NC: Duke University Press, 1991.
Torres, Lourdes. "The Construction of the Self in U.S. Latina Autobiographies." *Third
    World Women and the Politics of Feminism.* Ed. Chandra Talpade Mohanty, Ann
    Russo, and Lourdes Torres. Bloomington: Indiana University Press, 1991.

Biography

Davidson, Cathy N., and Linda Wagner-Martin, eds. *Oxford Companion to Women Writers
    in the United States.* Oxford: Oxford University Press, 1995.
Green, Carol H., and Mary G. Mason, eds. *American Women Writers.* Vol. 5: *From Colonial
    Times to the Present Time. A Critical Reference Guide.* New York: Ungar, 1993.
Kamp, Jim, ed. *Reference Guide to American Literature.* Detroit: St. James Press, 1994.
Marie, Jacquelyn. *Gay and Lesbian Literature.* Detroit: St. James Press, 1994.
"Gloria Anzaldúa." Torres, Hector A. *Dictionary of Literary Biography.* Vol. 122: *Chicano
    Writers,* 2d series. Detroit: Gale Research, 1992.

Interviews

Hernandez, Ellie. "Re-Thinking Margins and Borders: An Interview with Gloria Anzaldúa." *Discourse 18. Theoretical Studies in Media and Culture*, nos. 1 and 2 (Fall
and Winter 1995–1996).

Perry, Donna, ed. *Backtalk. Women Writers Speak Out*. New Brunswick, NJ: Rutgers University Press, 1993, 19–42.

Unpublished and untranscribed conversations with Gloria Anzaldúa. By Judith Richards,
September–October 1996.

Recording

This Bridge Called My Back: Writings by Women of Color. Los Angeles: Pacifica Tape Library, 1983.

FRANCES BEALE
(1940–)

Marina Karides and Joya Misra

Frances Beale is a powerful feminist, civil rights activist, and freelance writer who was among the first to suggest that the intersection between race, class, and gender is critical to a full understanding of social problems. Beale was born in Binghamton, New York, to an African American/Native American father and a Jewish mother. With her parents and her three brothers, she grew up in a small community in the Binghamton area, which was home to fewer than 500 black families. After her father's death from cancer in 1955, Beale's mother moved the family to Queens, New York. In Queens, Beale began her lifelong activism within the African American community.

Beale's parents, Charolete Berman and Ernest Archer Yates, both played an inspiring role in her life and taught her to challenge injustice. Berman, member of a Russian/Polish family of secular Jewish immigrants, was herself a member of the American Labor Party. Later in her life, Berman returned to college and became an ardent feminist. Yates was the first member of his family to attain a college education, with the help of his siblings, parents, and a baseball scholarship, although limited job prospects led him to work as a truck driver. Berman and Yates first met when Yates was driving between Binghamton and New York.

From an early age, Beale was exposed to the richness of her African American heritage, with books like Langston Hughes' *Pictorial History of the Negro People*. She was also influenced by her African Methodist Episcopalian Zion church, where she sang in the choir and was particularly inspired by biblical stories of the Israelites' freeing themselves from Egypt's oppression. Beale rejected religion after her father's death, but she attributes her basic sense of morality and justice to her early experiences in her church.

Beale's family also helped shape her choices and values. Beale's mother's family remained supportive of communist ideals after emigrating to the United States. One family tale recounts her grandfather's being caught stealing supplies for an underground newspaper from the printing press he worked for. Her aunt's story of survival in Nazi Germany during World War II also deeply affected Beale's perception of the world. All the women in this aunt's family were deserted by the family's father, who escaped Germany with his son. Her aunt's story first showed Beale how the devaluation of women can threaten their lives.

Beale was also raised with a close relationship to her father's family, who provided a model of a supportive and close-knit family. Within this family, however, Beale became conscious of the limits placed on women and recognized both male privilege and the oppression women face. One aunt consistently reinforced stereotypes about the importance of women's subservience and the higher value of lighter-skinned blacks and straight hair. Yet these experiences helped Frances Beale develop her feminist and antiracist consciousness, as she rebelled from these strict gender and race norms.

Frances Beale began college at the University of Wisconsin, Madison, and completed her degree in history at the University of Paris at Sorbonne. She met and married her husband, and they moved to France in 1960. Her daughters, Anne and Lisa, were both born in France. During this period, Beale developed connections to the black expatriate community and became involved in the movements for African liberation, which included many women activists. Through these experiences, Beale gained a more international perspective.

Returning from France in 1967, Beale became politically active in the Student Nonviolent Coordinating Committee (SNCC). As SNCC began to disintegrate, Beale formed the Black Women's Liberation Committee and served as its New York coordinator. Since women were important forces in liberation movements in Africa, she argued that women's oppression should be overturned along with racism and colonialism. In 1970 she wrote "Double Jeopardy," first published in Robin Morgan's *Sisterhood Is Powerful* and the most anthologized essay in the early years of the movement. Recognizing that African American women shared many problems with other women of color, Beale and several other women founded the independent Third World Women Alliance (TWWA), which drew women from African American and Puerto Rican backgrounds together into a larger women's liberation movement.

TWWA worked to develop a consciousness of the overlapping effects of class, race, and gender on women. For example, TWWA's journal, *Triple Jeopardy*, put forth an all-encompassing platform in favor of twenty-four-hour child care, equal pay for equal work, and an end to gender-biased laws and regulations, as well as many other changes necessary to address the terrible impact of racism, sexism, and classism on American women. TWWA was involved in various political and social action movements, including the Project against Sterilization Abuse, founded to protest the indiscriminate sterilizations being performed on women of color without their consent. As part of this drive, Beale testified about sterilization abuse to the New York City Council, which subsequently passed an ordinance requiring informed consent before sterilizations.

Beale worked for the National Council of Negro Women from 1967 to 1976, where she began her journalistic career by editing their newsletter, *Black Women*, and worked on their "Woman Power" project. Beginning in 1972, she taught as an instructor of women's studies and black studies at the City University of New York—Richmond. Additionally, she became active as a freelance writer, writing for a number of magazines, newspapers, and journals, including *The Guardian*, which she managed for a time. In 1981, Beale moved to the Bay Area and began working for the Disability Rights, Education, and Defense Fund. Between 1984 and 1986 she was an associate editor of *Black Scholar*, and in 1990 she helped found *Frontline* (now *Crossroads*), a radical newspaper devoted to issues of domestic and international politics. She contributes frequently to various newspapers, newsletters, and journals. For the last ten years, she has been a legal assistant for the American Civil Liberties Union (ACLU) in northern California.

Divorced for a number of years, Beale maintains a close relationship with her mother and daughters. Her daughter Anne is a successful pediatrician with two children, Naimia and Djavan, a column in *Essence*, and a forthcoming book on black children's health. Beale's daughter Lisa is an environmentalist who presides over the National Natural Gas Association. Beale has developed a greater appreciation for nature since moving to the West Coast and also enjoys experimental theater and jazz.

Beale "became a radical because she was a woman" (Karides 1996). Rather than giving in to the pervasive white, male, middle-class privilege in U.S. society, her strong feminist, antiracist, and class consciousness has led her to engage in political activism and fight for justice and equality for all.

Among the important feminist voices that emerged during the 1960s, Frances Beale's has been one of the strongest in the black feminist movement against capitalism, racism, and sexism. Throughout her career as a freelance journalist, Beale has pointed to the triple oppression that poor black women face and the importance of black men and women working together to develop a better society. More than twenty-five years before the refrain of "class, race, and gender" was made commonplace, Beale argued that these are the most important frames for understanding the world.

Like others in the feminist movement, Beale critiques the limited definitions for masculinity and femininity in U.S. society, which suggest that only men should be primary members of the workforce. This model oppresses women, devaluing their abilities and contributions to society. Yet, Beale's contribution to feminism takes this critique further by examining the problems faced by women of color. She shows that the white, middle-class model has never been applicable to African American women, who have *always* been a part of the workforce. Yet, because black women *have* jobs, they have been accused of stealing jobs from, and emasculating, black men. Beale vehemently argues that black women did not create this situation and do not benefit from their increased participation in the workforce. Capitalism, not black women, has caused black men's oppression. As she remarks, "It is fallacious reasoning that in order for the Black man to be strong, the Black woman has to be weak" (Beale 1975, 344).

While some black activists might believe that African American women have already been liberated, Frances Beale proclaims, "Let me state here and now that Black Women in America can justly be described as a 'slave of a slave' " (Beale 1975, 343). She shows the many ways that black women continue to face oppression, not only from whites but from men, including black men. To black activists who have suggested that black women can contribute to the revolution only by "making babies," Beale argues that African American women can and have made important contributions to struggles for independence, although stereotypes and misconceptions have concealed these efforts. Beale evokes leaders such as Harriet Tubman, Ida B. Wells, and Ella Baker to illustrate the prominent role African American women have played in struggles against racism. To black activists who suggest that feminism interferes with the "real struggle against racism," Beale responds by showing that the feminist struggle against women's oppression is a crucial part of black activism, while black activism is similarly crucial to the feminist movement. Black women, in particular, are aware of the work that must be done because their exploitation is more radical than that of any other group. Their perspective can help create a movement with the potential of overturning the oppressive aspects of U.S. society. If a social movement is to be successful, Beale argues, "We need our whole army out there dealing with the enemy, not half an army" (Beale 1970, 344).

A central argument in Beale's writings is the need to "throw off the yoke" of capitalist oppression through grassroots social movements that include men, women, and children (Beale 1970). Addressing both the feminist and the civil rights movement, Beale suggests that sexism and racism are difficult problems that must be related to the central feature of oppression: capitalism. Capitalists use racism and sexism to increase profits, by separating workers and keeping them from joining together as a class. Beale describes the labor movement in the United States and shows how race and gender have been used to divide workers and weaken the movement. Both black workers and women are exploited, paid less for the same work, and relegated to low-paying and dead-end jobs. But this exploitation is felt doubly for black women.

Beale paints a varied picture of the feminist movement in the United States. She has been critical of the white women's liberation movement, particularly insofar as white women have avoided dealing with racism and capitalist oppression within their movement. In the 1970s, Beale criticized the white movement for focusing on "male chauvinism" without realizing that it will take a radical restructuring of society to overturn sexism, racism, and classism. By focusing on men as "the enemy," Beale suggests the white women's movement has missed much of the point of *liberation* (Beale 1975). While Beale agrees that sexist beliefs detrimentally affect women, she believes that chauvinism is the symptom, not the cause, of the disease. Although privileged, white, middle-class women may feel that their battle is won when men treat *them* as equals, Beale argues that the black women's struggle requires a much greater commitment to change:

If the white groups do not realize that they are in fact fighting capitalism and racism, we do not have common bonds. If they do not realize that the reasons for their condition lie in the system . . . then we cannot unite with them around common grievances or even discuss these groups in a serious manner because they're completely irrelevant to the Black struggle. (Beale 1970, 351)

While the women's movement of the 1960s and 1970s was primarily composed of white, middle-class women, Frances Beale suggests that it gave women "a new way of thinking about themselves and the world they lived in, and included at least some members with an active left-wing and civil rights agenda" (Karides 1996). Both class and race have become less apparent in the contemporary feminist movement. As a result, Beale sees the current feminist movement as a single-issue, legal-strategizing campaign that "strays from the true path which is the struggle for the liberation of all the people" (Beale 1975, 9). The perspective of women of color could help refocus this movement, since "Black women view the question of women's liberation through the prism of their racial and class status" (Beale 1985a, inside cover). Rather than focusing on the interests of white, heterosexual, middle-class women, Beale suggests that the feminist movement should, instead, set forth "an agenda that speaks to the least of us" (Karides 1996). The women's movement must recognize that a living wage for all workers and quality child care and schooling for all children are *women's* issues. As she argues, "the liberation of women cannot be separated from the liberation of society" (Beale 1975, 9).

Beale suggests that we must create new institutions and a new society centered around equality rather than oppression. Every man, woman, and child must be politically conscious and involved in this transformation. By joining together, Beale believes that we can create a society in which every person is valued, and sexism, racism, and capitalist exploitation have been vanquished. Beale's voice remains strong, as she encourages black men and women to work together and to build alliances with others in order to make the world a better place to live. Her radical approach to society's problems continues to come down to a basic, core principle: we must challenge this oppressive capitalist, racist, and sexist system as a whole. Beale suggests that movements that fight against racism or sexism alone are simply accommodating oppression if they do not address the exploitative nature of capitalism. Instead, we must conceptualize the interconnections between these three forms of exploitation and develop a unified and strong movement that can attack this system at its root. Beale's vision pushes us all forward and allows us to see the future as it is meant to be.

WORKS BY FRANCES BEALE

Beale has contributed numerous pieces to publications for the last thirty years; this list contains a few representative pieces.

Double Jeopardy: To Be Black and Female. Detroit: Radical Education Project, 1970a. (Also included in Robin Morgan, ed., *Sisterhood Is Powerful: An Anthology of Writings from the Women's Liberation Movement* [New York: Random House] and Toni Cade, ed., *The Black Woman: An Anthology* [New York: New American Library]. Page numbers cited in text refer to Morgan's volume.)

"Slave of a Slave No More: Black Women in Struggle." *Black Scholar* 6, no. 6 (1975): 2–10.

"Let's Unite to Stamp Out the Klan." *Black Scholar* 11, no. 4 (1980): 2–8.

"U.S. Politics Will Never Be the Same." *Black Scholar* 15, no. 5 (1984): 10–18.

"Black Women and Feminism." *Black Scholar* 16, no. 5 (1985a): inside front cover.

"United Nations International Women's Conference in Nairobi, Kenya: A Black Scholar Report." *Black Scholar* 16, no. 2 (1985b): 2–3.

With Ty DePass. "The Historical Black Presence in the Struggle for Peace." *Black Scholar* 17, no. 1 (1986): 2–7.

"Making History." *San Francisco Chronicle*, December 25, 1994a, Sec. REV, p. 1, col. 1. (Review of *Long Walk to Freedom: The Autobiography of Nelson Mandela*.)

"South Africa's Long Road to Freedom." *Black Scholar* 24, no. 3 (1994b): 7–10.

ADDITIONAL SOURCES

Karides, Marina. Interview with Frances M. Beale, October 7, 14, 1996.

RITA MAE BROWN
(1944–)

Julie A. Davies

As a writer, Rita Mae Brown prefers to be considered without the obvious mod-ifiers "lesbian," "feminist," "activist." In the context of the second wave of fem-inism, however, she plays a complex, critical, and often controversial role. Abbott and Love, the writers of the pivotal 1972 text, *Sappho Was a Right-On Woman*, dedicated their work to Rita Mae Brown "for starting it all." In retrospect and in many ways, it appears they were right.

Rita Mae Brown was born in Hanover, Pennsylvania, on November 28, 1944, to eighteen-year-old Juliann Young. After a brief stay at a Catholic orphanage, she was adopted by Ralph and Julia Ellen Brown of York, Pennsylvania. She was a bright child who later became an excellent student. Even in primary school, though, her working-class background and values would come up sharply against those of the middle and upper classes. When Brown was eleven, she moved with her family to Fort Lauderdale, Florida.

She was an excellent and popular student, but disclosure of her lesbianism in her final year of high school resulted in harassment by classmates, parents, and teachers and the loss of many friendships. On scholarship to the University of Florida, Brown excelled academically and was a member of Delta Delta Delta sorority. Again, as in high school, her penchant to be outspoken had dramatic results. In 1964, she became active in the civil rights movement and also dis-closed her lesbianism. What followed was far more dramatic than the earlier shunning. She lost her scholarship and was forced into daily therapy with the university's psychiatrist.

Without her scholarship, she could not afford to stay. In the summer of 1964, Brown left Florida and went to New York City. She found work waitressing and won a scholarship to study English at New York University (NYU). She earned a B.A. in 1968 and went on to study filmmaking at the School of Visual Arts.

Her outspoken nature and activist leanings found ready, though not always permanent, homes amid the politically and socially conscious New York climate.

While still a student a NYU, she became a gay activist and was one of the founders of the Student Homophile League of NYU and Columbia. Women's issues and lesbian oppression, however, were not a priority with this group, and Rita Mae Brown moved on to what she thought would be more receptive arms.

As a member of the New York chapter of the National Organization for Women (NOW), Brown experienced the first of a series of challenges to her particular brand of activism, both in style and in content. For openly questioning NOW's resistance to acknowledge the issues of class and sexuality, she was quickly no longer welcome. Her insistence on the open inclusion of lesbians in the women's movement was the precipitating factor that led to the now-famous "Lavender Menace" quote by New York NOW leader Betty Friedan.

In 1970, Brown resigned from NOW and joined the recently formed, radical feminist group Redstockings. With roots in the urban New Left, Redstockings was certainly more radical than NOW but not especially welcoming to Brown's rural, working-class, "immediate" style of political action. She found them to be more concerned with constructing ideology than with confronting real issues. Brown's suggestions that connections needed to be made with working-class women and with lesbians were largely disregarded. It was time to move on.

Rita Mae Brown's next move had far-reaching consequences, both for her own life and for the lives of generations of American women. She was determined to organize lesbians for open political action. The first meeting, held at her apartment, drew thirty women. Successive meetings drew more. Initially reclaiming the name "Lavender Menace," one of their memorable collective acts was an uninvited piece of guerrilla theater disrupting the Second Congress to Unite Women in May 1970. They held the floor for over two hours and presented a now-famous position paper entitled "The Woman-Identified Woman." They received significant support, and the final act of the congress was to adopt the resolutions presented by the Lavender Menace (more officially known as the Radicalesbians). These straightforward resolutions affirmed and validated lesbianism by redefining it as a political choice and therefore legitimately established within feminism. Rita Mae Brown was fast becoming a recognizable figure on the women's movement stage.

Always intent on being a writer, Brown was, throughout her New York years, continuously writing for underground papers as well as holding jobs as copywriter or proofreader in commercial publishing. In 1971, her first work of poetry, *The Hand That Cradles the Rock*, was published by New York University Press. With a title that revisions a time-worn phrase into an active assertion of women's power, the pieces in this slim volume clearly express Brown's radical views of patriarchal oppression. It is a mistake to consider Rita Mae Brown's career as a feminist/activist to be separate from her career as a writer. The two are consistently intertwined.

When personal, more than political, problems began to affect the solidity of the Radicalesbians, Brown decided to accept an invitation to join the growing lesbian movement in Washington, D.C. Self-identified as a southerner, Brown adds in her recent autobiography that she felt more comfortable in "this north-ernmost of Southern cities" (Brown 1997, 250). In May 1971, she cofounded with Charlotte Bunch a lesbian commune called the Furies Collective. Originally referring to themselves as "Those Women," they began a newspaper in January 1972 that they named *The Furies*. Through publishing, the Furies came to be nationally recognized. The work of Rita Mae Brown and Charlotte Bunch from this period continues to be considered seminal work in lesbian-feminist theory. In addition to their writings, the Furies were a constant presence at meetings and conferences, where they insisted on the inclusion of lesbian issues as essential to any feminist event. The positive and lasting legacy of the Furies was that lesbians found a voice and a place in American politics and culture that reached far beyond the bounds of Washington, D.C., and that continues to this day.

Internal discord rather than ideological changes led to Rita Mae Brown's break with the Furies. She moved back to her apartment with her beloved cat, Baby Jesus, and decided to write a novel. Her first and most enduring work of fiction was initially rejected by mainstream presses. Daughters, Inc., a small feminist press in Plainfield, Vermont, published *Rubyfruit Jungle* in 1973. With little but word-of-mouth advertising, the book sales were overwhelming—so over-whelming that a small press like Daughters couldn't keep up. With Brown's permission, they sold the rights to Bantam Books in 1977. *Rubyfruit Jungle* re-mains in print and is considered to be the classic coming-of-age lesbian novel. The heroine, Molly Bolt, was, in many ways, how Rita Mae Brown would later describe herself in *Starting from Scratch*, "southern, poor and rebellious" (Brown 1988, 14). In a much quieter appearance, 1973 also saw the publication of Brown's second volume of poetry, a work much more personal than political, entitled *Songs to a Handsome Woman*.

Between 1973 and 1977, Rita Mae Brown taught writing at Vermont's God-dard College and at the Women Writers Center in Cazenovia, New York. Essays that she wrote between 1969 and 1975 were collected and published in 1976 under the title *A Plain Brown Rapper*. Her activism is acknowledged in these early essays, as is her eloquent insistence that lesbianism, as well as racism and classism, must be addressed before genuine change can occur. When examined in the context of the period, they are an insightful chronicle of very exciting times. Occasionally dogmatic, but often marked with her trademark humor, these essays provide excellent information about the early days of the feminist movement and a prelude to her future work. The year 1976 also marked the appearance of Brown's second work of fiction. *In Her Day*, like *Rubyfruit Jungle*, was somewhat autobiographical in nature. However, instead of concentrating on one central character and plot, in this work Brown's multiple characters and story lines ap-pear to be an attempt to address the interconnectedness of women—a kind of fictional sisterhood. While this work was received as somewhat awkward and obvious, it nonetheless set the stage for what would become Brown's successful, multidimensional style.

The 1977 purchase of *Rubyfruit Jungle* by Bantam Books opened doors to the

mainstream press and public, and for the first time Rita Mae Brown was financially comfortable. Her next novel, a sort of sweeping, modern, southern epic,
was released to a large and welcoming mainstream audience. Published in 1978,
Six of One was also an alternate selection for the Macmillan Book Club and the
Literary Guild of America. This work is a very successful marriage of history,
humor, and the complexities of women's lives. Brown makes very clear her feeling
that an understanding of history and politics is essential for human development.
With its multiple narratives, *Six of One* unfolds for the reader the lives of indi-
vidual women in the context of history. Rita Mae Brown had become, perhaps,
America's most famous lesbian. In the same year, she moved to Charlottesville,
Virginia.

Events of the following year, 1979, would prove to only increase this fame or,
more appropriately, notoriety, for this was the year that Rita Mae Brown began
a lesbian relationship with celebrated tennis star Martina Navratilova. Their two-
year, much publicized relationship fell prey as much to the overwhelming homophobia of the press and the world of professional tennis as to intrinsic
differences between the two women. Following the breakup, Brown moved briefly
to Los Angeles and worked as a scriptwriter for television and film.

The novel that she wrote during her relationship with Navratilova was published in 1982. *Southern Discomfort* continues in the tradition of *Six of One* as a
southern novel with a historical setting. Divided into two distinct time periods,
1918 and 1928, this is Brown's first work to not include lesbian characters. Again
she weaves complex multiple narratives that occupy the southern cultural landscape. The characters unfold within a series of plots full of Brown's attention to
racism, class differences, and the politics of being female.

Brown returned to Charlottesville and in 1983 suffered the loss of her mother.
Julia Ellen Brown, or "Juts," as she was known, was the inspiration for several of
Brown's characters. Their relationship had been an enduring one, marked by
years of charged dialogue and mutual respect. The same year saw the publication
of *Sudden Death*, a novel exposing the underside of the world of professional
women's tennis. In her early essays, Brown is clear that physical strength and
health are essential for women to be psychologically and emotionally strong and
capable of survival. The strength and power of her fictional female characters
support this as well. In *Sudden Death*, however, we witness a commercialism of
sport that is never about women's well-being but, instead, about sponsors and
profits. Value is placed on pretty and feminine players, and any hint of lesbianism
must be suppressed.

In the following years, Rita Mae Brown worked again in filmmaking and script-
writing. The acclaimed documentary on the history of American homosexuality
Before Stonewall was narrated by Brown in 1985. The Stonewall riots in New
York City in the summer of 1969 had marked the beginning of the gay liberation
movement, precisely at the time that feminist and lesbian activism was gaining
considerable strength.

Rita Mae Brown claims to have always been interested in history, feeling that it is essential to know the past in order to understand the present and prepare for the future. Also intensely attached to the southern landscape, she spends considerable time doing background research. In addition to the loss of her mother and the end of the relationship with Navratilova, Brown lost a very dear friend, Jerry Pfeiffer, to AIDS and suffered the death of her beloved, seventeen-year-old cat, Baby Jesus. Her novel born of this emotional turmoil was a Civil War epic entitled *High Hearts*. Published in 1986, this saga follows the lives of those living in a small southern town during the devastating war years. As always, Brown is concerned with the issues of race, class, and gender and how they affect the lives of her characters. Though a period piece, *High Hearts* deals effectively with the timelessness of love, death, and politics.

In a shift back to nonfiction in 1988, Rita Mae Brown published *Starting from Scratch: A Different Kind of Writer's Manual*. As a former teacher of writing, Brown has a considerable interest in discussing the actual process of writing, as well as the possibilities of writing as a career. This manual is exceptionally readable and blends the account of her own career with practical and useful guidance for would-be writers. Also in 1988, Brown published the out-of-sequence sequel to *Six of One*, entitled *Bingo*, which brings the characters of the earlier novel into the present. Full of small-town, southern traditions and values as a backdrop, this work explores the connections and continuity of women's lives, as well as Brown's ever-present concerns for family, community, sexuality, and personal politics.

An enduring, collaborative effort began in 1990, when Rita Mae Brown coauthored her first book with Sneaky Pie Brown. Sneaky Pie is Brown's tiger cat, adopted at a Society for the Prevention of Cruelty to Animals (SPCA) shelter in 1982. Their first work, *Wish You Were Here*, was published in 1990 and was followed in 1992 by *Rest in Pieces*. These were the first works in a continuing series in the murder mystery genre. Set in the southern town of Crozet, Virginia, the sleuths solving small-town murders are Mrs. Murphy, a tiger cat, and Tee Tucker, a Welsh corgi. Criticized by her more serious audience as frivolous, these stories are, nonetheless, faithful to Brown's passionate devotion and respect for all animals.

While researching for her work on the Civil War, Rita Mae Brown became fascinated with some primary source material from an earlier period: the letters of Dolley Madison. Over the years, she continued to study Madison's writings as well as her husband's papers and other family documents. This led to the eventual publication in 1994 of *Dolley: A Novel of Dolley Madison in Love and War*. In this novel, Brown invents Dolley Madison's fictitious diary and unfolds the events of a well-known Revolutionary War drama through Dolley's writing. Based on facts from actual documents, this work is peopled with a cast of only true characters, and Brown provides for us a vision of history through the heroine's eyes.

In the years that followed *Dolley*, Rita Mae Brown continued to publish new entries to the collaborative mystery series. *Murder at Monticello*, published in 1994, was followed in 1995 by *Pay Dirt* and in 1996 by *Murder, She Meowed*. A new novel also appeared in 1996. *Riding Shotgun* featured an even more distant dip into history. The heroine, a single mother in the present day, time-travels to the year 1699 and in doing so learns the timeless nature of life and love.

November 1997 marked the publication by Bantam Books of Rita Mae Brown's memoirs. Entitled *Rita Will: Memoir of a Literary Rabble Rouser*, this is both an informative and entertaining work. In a series of loosely strung together chronological chapters, Brown unfolds the events of both her personal and political life. Beginning with her precarious birth and her boldly independent childhood, these essays proceed to link the series of events that took her from outspoken activist to perhaps the most famous, openly lesbian writer in America.

Alice Echols in *Daring to Be Bad: Radical Feminism in America 1967–1975* refers to Rita Mae Brown as "an important architect of lesbian feminism" (Echols 1989, 380). Her early work clarified the political definition of lesbianism and confronted the issues of race and class within the women's movement. Her essays remain intelligent, creative, and committed to critical social and political issues for women. The exciting period from the mid-1960s to the mid-1970s in America witnessed a tremendous blossoming of feminist consciousness and action. Rita Mae Brown was certainly an influential and important part of that history.

Feminist critics, however, all too often feel compelled to separate Brown's activism from her work as primarily an author of fiction. In reality, the two are truly inseparable. Her entire body of work and her public life as well have had enormous impact on women's place in American consciousness. Her humor, her passion for life, her lesbianism, her headline-making behavior, her strong women characters—all have had an effect on America's vision of women. Largely due to work like Brown's, which encompasses both theory and popular culture, feminism enters (sometimes through the back door) not only writing but film, television, art, and music.

SELECTED WORKS BY RITA MAE BROWN

Novels

Rubyfruit Jungle. Plainfield, VT: Daughters, Inc., 1973; reprinted 1977, New York: Bantam Books.

In Her Day. Plainfield, VT: Daughters, Inc., 1976; reprinted 1988, New York: Bantam Books.

Six of One. New York: Harper and Row, 1978; reprinted 1979, New York: Bantam Books.

Southern Discomfort. New York: Harper and Row, 1982; reprinted 1983, New York: Bantam Books.

Sudden Death. New York: Bantam Books, 1983.

High Hearts. New York: Bantam Books, 1986.

Bingo. New York: Bantam Books, 1988.

With Sneaky Pie Brown. *Wish You Were Here*. New York: Bantam Books, 1990.

———. *Rest in Pieces*. New York: Bantam Books, 1992.

Venus Envy. New York: Bantam Books, 1993.
Dolley: A Novel of Dolley Madison in Love and War. New York: Bantam Books, 1994.
With Sneaky Pie Brown. *Murder at Monticello.* New York: Bantam Books, 1994.
————. *Pay Dirt.* New York: Bantam Books, 1995.
————. *Murder, She Meowed.* New York: Bantam Books, 1996.
Riding Shotgun. New York: Bantam Books, 1996.

Poetry

The Hand That Cradles the Rock. New York: New York University Press, 1971.
Songs to a Handsome Woman. Oakland, CA: Diana Press, 1973.
Poems. Freedom, CA: Crossing Press, 1987.

Nonfiction

A Plain Brown Rapper. Oakland, CA: Diana Press, 1976.
Starting from Scratch: A Different Kind of Writer's Manual. New York: Bantam Books, 1988.
Rita Will: Memoir of a Literary Rabble Rouser. New York: Bantam Books, 1997.

SELECTED WRITINGS ON RITA MAE BROWN AND HER WORK

Books

Abbott, Sidney, and Barbara Love. *Sappho Was a Right-On Woman: A Liberated View of Lesbianism.* New York: Stein and Day, 1972.
Bunch, Charlotte. *Passionate Politics: Feminist Theory in Action.* New York: St. Martin's Press, 1987.
Bunch, Charlotte, and Sandra Pollack, eds. *Learning Our Way: Essays in Feminist Education.* Trumansburg, NY: Crossing Press, 1983.
Davis, Flora. *Moving the Mountain: The Women's Movement in America since 1960.* New York: Simon and Schuster, 1991.
Echols, Alice. *Daring to Be Bad: Radical Feminism in America 1967–1975.* Minneapolis: University of Minnesota Press, 1989.
Fritz, Leah. *Dreamers and Dealers: An Intimate Appraisal of the Women's Movement.* Boston: Beacon Press, 1979.
Kuda, Marie J., ed. *Women Loving Women: A Select and Annotated Bibliography of Women Loving Women in Literature.* Chicago: Lavender Press, 1974.
Morgan, Robin, ed. *Sisterhood Is Powerful: An Anthology of Writings from the Women's Liberation Movement.* New York: Random House, 1970.
Myron, Nancy, and Charlotte Bunch, eds. *Lesbianism and the Women's Movement.* Baltimore: Diana Press, 1975.
Rule, Jane. *Lesbian Images.* Garden City, NY: Doubleday, 1975.
Ryan, Barbara. *Feminism and the Women's Movement.* New York: Routledge, 1992.
Ward, Carol M. *Rita Mae Brown.* New York: Twayne, 1993.

Wandersee, Winifred D. *On the Move: American Women in the 1970s.* Boston: Twayne, 1988.

Articles, Reviews, and Interviews

Alexander, Dolores. "Rita Mae Brown: The Issue for the Future Is Power." *Ms.* (September 1994): 110–113.

Chew, Martha. "Rita Mae Brown: Feminist Theorist and Southern Novelist." *Women Writers of the Contemporary South.* Ed. Peggy Prenshaw. Jackson: University of Mississippi Press, 1984, 194–213.

Cruikshank, Cathy. "Lesbian Literature: Random Thoughts." *Margins* (August 1975): 16–18.

Fishbein, Leslie. "Rubyfruit Jungle: Lesbianism, Feminism and Narcissism." *International Journal of Women's Studies* (March/April 1984): 155–159.

Fleischer, Lenore. "Lenore Fleischer Talks with Rita Mae Brown." *Washington Post Book World*, October 15, 1978, sec. E, 2.

Fox, Terry Curtis. "Up from Cultdom—And Down Again." *Village Voice* (September 1997): 41.

Harris, Bertha. "Review of Rubyfruit Jungle." *Village Voice Literary Supplement* (April 4, 1974): 34–35.

———. "What We Mean to Say: Notes toward Defining the Nature of Lesbian Literature." *Heresies* (Fall 1977): 5–8.

Larkin, Joan. "Review of *In Her Day*." *Ms.* (April 1977): 4.

Marchino, Lois. "Rita Mae Brown." *American Women Writers*, vol. 1. Ed. Lina Mainiero. New York: Frederick Ungar, 1979, 257–259.

Maupin, Armistead. "Rita Mae Brown." *Interview* (February 1982): 50.

Stimpson, Catherine. "Zero Degree Deviancy: The Lesbian Novel in English." *Critical Inquiry* (Winter 1981): 363–379.

Zimmerman, Bonnie. "The Politics of Transliteration: Lesbian Personal Narratives." *Signs* (Summer 1984): 663–682.

CHARLOTTE BUNCH
(1944–)

Viki Soady

Charlotte Bunch, founder and director of the Douglass College Center for Women's Global Leadership at Rutgers University and 1997 inductee into the National Women's Hall of Fame, is a universally respected founder of the women's liberation movement. She is cherished by three generations of feminists for her integrity, idealism, warmth, and determined energy. From Selma to Beijing and beyond, as she has actively campaigned for the human rights and equality of women everywhere, her greatest theoretical contribution has been her evolving vision of the interconnectedness of militarism, racism, classism, homophobia, domestic violence, and the politics of hunger in the global oppression of women and children. Of her effective blending of activism with theory she wrote:

I have often been asked how I became a political organizer and writer. The short answer is that these activities most consistently engaged my imagination and energies over the years. They brought meaning and satisfaction to my life, and became what I needed to do to feel truly alive. Some call that a vocation, others call it survival, or see it as a career. For me, it has been all three. (Bunch 1987, 1)

Her quest for "meaning and satisfaction" in life had its fortunate beginnings in Artesia, a small town in southeastern New Mexico, where she was the third of four children born to professional and civic-minded parents. Her mother was a social worker who served a term as school board president; her father was a rural doctor. This secure, liberal, Methodist family was once named New Mexico's Methodist Family of the Year for its religious and social activism: "My parents were open-minded Methodists whose commitment to fairness and moderate politics often made them controversial" (Bunch 1987, 2). From her parents Bunch acquired the belief that good work can change the world. In her introduction to *Passionate Politics*, as part of her description of how her parents brought her east to attend Duke University in 1963 (B.A., magna cum laude, 1966),

Bunch recalls her growing involvement with the National Council of the Methodist Student Movement and her personal journey from a shy, unpolitical, naive person to civil rights protester and organizer of sit-ins from Selma to Montgomery, then on to Washington, D.C., to protest the Vietnam War. "I enjoyed combining what the university called the 'life of the mind' with life as an activist" (Bunch 1987, 3). Accordingly, her major went from religion, to psychology, to history, to political science and culminated in a senior essay addressing women in the Chinese Revolution. Nevertheless, as a student, Bunch remained strongly attracted to the spirit of love and peace within Christianity, cofounding the ecumenical University Christian Movement and serving as its national president from 1966 to 1967. Shortly after her marriage to James Weeks in 1967, she became a member of the campus ministry staff at Case Western Reserve University in Cleveland, Ohio (1968–1969), and published some of her earliest (1967–1973) pro-liberation and pro-lesbian writings in the *Motive*, a liberal Methodist journal that she eventually co-opted to feminist causes with the aid of its editor, Joanne Cooke, and Robin Morgan (see Bunch, Cooke, and Morgan 1970). Her religious roots also provided her first connections to global activism as she remained active in the World Student Christian Federation until its meeting in Ethiopia in the early 1970s.

Opting not to go to graduate school, Bunch affirmed her preference for social action by accepting a fellowship at the Institute for Policy Studies (IPS) (1967–1968) in Washington, D.C., an organization that, under the direction of Arthur Waskow, was designing policies and strategies to effect social change on racial questions. Here, for the first time, Bunch encountered sexism and marginalization in the workplace. Of this "aha" experience, Bunch wrote that "this was the place where I first confronted sex discrimination and patronizing attitudes toward women within social change groups" (Bunch 1987, 5). The strong suggestion that women were not politically serious led her to form a women's group at IPS with the help of Marilyn Salzman Webb, a fellow employee. This radical women's group became the D.C. arm of the women's liberation movement. Its agenda was feminist and antiwar. By the time of the protest at the Miss America Pageant in 1968, the Washington and Chicago groups combined comprised about 200 members.

Bunch accompanied her husband, a fellow student activist, to Cleveland for the years 1968–1969. At Case Western Reserve, she worked for campus ministries and for the causes of women's liberation among women who were particularly male-identified. She learned how to "organize new female constituencies utilizing street theater, provocative pamphlets, and public forums to reach women not already active politically" (Bunch 1987, 7). This aspect of her Cleveland years helped to prepare her for the communicative challenges of global activism, as did her encounters with the militant sexism of the Weathermen segment of the Students for a Democratic Society (SDS), a faction that originated in Cleveland.

By 1970, Bunch had resumed long-distance marriage and her work at the Institute for Policy Studies in D.C., where feminism was at last "catching on."

The women's liberation movement there was also growing, as a new council, Magic Quilt, was established to coordinate the different groups. Bunch became a part of the "Daughters of Lilith," a designation reserved for the veterans of the movement. Indeed, the tension between the radicals and conservatives within the women's movement was beginning to build. At the very time when the liberation movement was attempting to form a coalition with the National Organization for Women (NOW), which preferred to focus on equality, primarily in the workplace, and not upon peace and the cessation of imperialism, Bunch was called away to North Vietnam as part of the peace group to end the war in Vietnam. Furthermore, just as marches for equality began to unite the radicals with NOW, by August 1970 racism and homophobia were beginning to create new schisms.

Within this uneasy subtext, Bunch left her marriage in 1971 and came out as a lesbian, a decision that she describes as follows: "This was not a reaction against my husband but a response to the power of sexual self-discovery. . . . Lesbians were demanding recognition of our existence, of our contributions to the movement, and of the political implications of heterosexism for feminism" (Bunch 1987, 9). Her declaration was to force a final split in already divided ranks; the schism lasted for approximately five years until Bunch herself came to see that separatism and such open acrimony were not solutions within a movement best meant to battle against the sexual, economic, and social oppression of women.

The message of the separatists was, however, an important element in the ultimate achievement of equality; that is, somehow, the liberation of women had to include the freedom to make the decision to be a lesbian. In the context of her larger work, lesbianism has encountered much opposition from women globally and has won grudging acceptance largely because of the eminence and power of the rest of the feminist project. As Bunch expressed it in her essay "A Broom of One's Own" (first published in Bunch-Weeks, Cooke, and Morgan 1970), consciousness-raising is

learning to take pride and delight in our femaleness, rejecting the need to follow the feminine mystique or to copy men as our models; it is learning to trust and love each other as sisters, not competitors for male approval. It is deciding and redeciding each day that we will take control over our lives, create and support each other in alternative ways of living, and struggle together for the liberation of all women. (Bunch 1987, 30)

The decade of the 1970s represents a pivotal point in the extraordinary career of Charlotte Bunch. She began it as a confirmed separatist, pursuing largely domestic issues, then gradually committed herself to a more global focus, and ended the decade disavowing separatism in favor of coexistence and active cooperation. It was a time of extensive activity for her, regrouping and growth in which one can see all of the elements and issues of her current world-moving agenda beginning to coalesce. In 1971, she formed a new separatist group with Rita Mae Brown, Joan Biren, and others called the "Furies Collective," aimed at pursuing political and cultural analysis with a lesbian focus and base of power. The Furies Collective grew out of the editorial group of the *Motive*, the liberal, Methodist periodical that eventually ceased publication in 1973. Bunch describes this group as all-white, fighting various oppressions, and frequently colliding with each other. Her attendance at her last World Student Christian Federation Meeting in Ethiopia in 1973 reactivated her interest in global perspectives on women as she also visited such African countries as Kenya and Tanzania. Also pivotal was her resumption of her duties at the IPS, where she became the first woman to receive tenure in 1977. During this period, she also founded *Quest, a Feminist Quarterly*, intended to address issues of race, class, and sex inequality.

The years from 1975 to 1983 were marked by prolific collaborations and publications. Additionally, Bunch taught feminism at Sagaris, a summer institute in Vermont in 1975. Here, she discovered her great enthusiasm for feminist teaching and, as a result of the experience, coedited a book with Sandra Pollack on feminist education called *Learning Our Way* (1983).

Also in 1975, she began her fruitful connection with the United Nations' initiatives on women by encouraging the discussion of lesbian issues at the non-governmental tribunes in Mexico City, although she herself did not attend. She was, in fact, devoting her time to serving on the board of the gay male-dominated National Gay Task Force and was attempting to reach out to such organizations as NOW, the National Women's Political Caucus, and the American Association of University Women. Also in this busy year Bunch took the opportunity provided by a national women's conference to declare that she was no longer a separatist, having concluded that the progress of woman's rights depended on unity.

The healing of the breach began immediately. By the strength of her grassroots organizing at the state level, she and her supporters narrowly missed winning the approval of a pro-sexual preference, pro-lesbian plank at the Houston meeting of NOW in 1977, but the faction of the right wing nervously held its forces together.

The many peripeteias and political challenges of the decade exhausted Bunch emotionally and, by her own admission, left her in need of self-repair and new direction. She recognized that both the feminist movement and its leaders were in need of transitional changes and insights. Of this time, she stated:

I saw that my crisis also came from recognizing that I would never see the world change as much as I had hoped in my lifetime. I sought ways to adjust to that limitation without becoming cynical, giving up my visions, or no longer caring. (Bunch 1987, 15)

Since that existential crisis, caring has become the hallmark of Bunch's career as she has shifted the focus of her work from local to global feminism. She has applied the networking and consciousness-raising techniques of feminism's second wave to the causes of women everywhere. Since 1979, she has linked interest with such organizations as the Asian and Pacific Center for Women, the ISIS

Latin American and Caribbean Women's Health Network, the International
Women's Tribune Centre, and other groups that provide resources and communication service for women in developing countries. She has continued to
speak out on such provocative issues as sexual slavery and other forms of culturally sanctioned violence against women. She first brought these issues to the fore
during the regrettably placid decade of the 1980s by founding Interfem, a consulting firm, with Shirley Castley. This firm began by encouraging tribunals to
be held by nongovernmental organizations at the same time and geographical
locations as official world gatherings. Here women can talk, form coalitions, and
safely send their stories to the policymakers by making use of the same wave of
news-hungry media present for the government-sanctioned event.

In the 1980s her consultancy for women led to a heightened visibility for
lesbian and gay issues domestically; in 1982, she organized the National Gay
Task Force to conduct a huge rally in Central Park in sponsorship of disarmament
and nuclear freeze. At the international level, when disappointed by the reception of issues of lesbianism and human rights for women at the United Nations
(UN) Mid-Decade Conference on Women in Copenhagen in 1980, Bunch began
immediately redoubling her efforts for the UN End of the Decade on Women
Conference scheduled to be held in Nairobi in 1985. Although few governments
and nongovernmental organizations (NGOs) wished to finance work on violence
and abuse of women in the years between the conferences, her consultancy firm
enabled thirty women from twenty-four countries to meet in Rotterdam with
two-thirds of the delegates drawn from developing nations. As a result, a global
network was formed in 1983, and that network ensured the formation of many
strong coalitions on such issues as sexual slavery and lesbianism at the Nairobi
conference in 1985. Many critics agree that the feminist struggle renewed itself
as a result of Nairobi in 1985.

In the 1990s, as founder and director of the Center for Women's Global Leadership at Rutgers, where she also serves as a professor of urban studies at the
Bloustein School of Planning and Public Policy, Bunch has been able to provide
vast academic and electronic resources through which women everywhere may
tell their stories. Since 1990, the publications of the center have marked the
progress of global feminism as Bunch has coedited and encouraged writings by
African, Sri Lankan, and Japanese feminists, to name but a few of those nation-
alities who have found voice (see bibliography).

Even before Beijing, in June 1993, at the United Nations World Conference
on Human Rights in Vienna, Bunch and her coworkers were cited in the *New
York Times* as the "most effective lobby" present (*Women's Research Network
News* 1993, 12), where, as the result of three years of preparation, 950 different
women's organizations participated in the Global Tribunal on Violation in Human Rights held as parallel activities to coincide with the official conference.
Looking forward to Beijing, at Vienna, Bunch stated: "We want a final document
from the conference that says something about women's human rights because

that will legitimize our next step. But I think we've already demonstrated that a global movement exists" (ibid. 12).

Two years prior to Vienna, Bunch and the Center for Women's Global Leadership had forged the creation of that global movement by conducting a worldwide effort called "Sixteen Days of Activism against Gender Violence," which resulted in the gathering of half a million signatures from around the world in order to demonstrate how traditional definitions of human rights are inadequate and need to be expanded to include the concerns of women (Wong 1993, 11). After Vienna, in a publication edited by Bunch (see Bunch and Reilly 1994) in which accountability is demanded, thirty-three women from twenty-six countries committed to writing their lives as told at the Vienna Tribunal, stories of "infanticide, malnutrition, coercion, battery, mutilation, sexual assault, and murder suffered by women crossing national, cultural, religious, and ethnic boundaries" (Everitt 1996, 130). With such momentum gathering, the stage was set for Beijing.

At Beijing, Bunch was the keynote speaker on August 31, 1995, at the NGO Forum in Huairou. The messages that she sent on to Beijing resonate with the lessons and idealism learned from the second wave of the women's movement. Her speech was entitled "Through Women's Eyes" and began by addressing the "incredible failures of international policy in this century" that clearly demonstrate the need for women's input if change is to come. She spoke of how women can no longer be exploited for expediency's sake in the designs of the new global economies and of how fundamental religious forces serve inequality by keeping women in their place. Bunch also reprised and globalized her antiwar message, but peace also now refers to an inner tranquillity that will come with the cessation of prejudice and othering:

Whoever gets defined as the "other" in your culture, that is part of the way in which all of our humanity is destroyed. If we accept that any group is less than fully human and therefore deserves to have fewer human rights, we have started down the slope of losing human rights for all. And women especially should understand this. (Bunch 1995, 3)

As a true product of the 1960s, Bunch has not lost her vision of hope for change in her lifetime and is vibrantly spreading her message of love, justice, commitment, and activism through all her works, as the closing of her speech at Beijing makes evident:

So we put the UN and the governments on trial not only this week, but this year and this decade. We are participating now, we are watching, we are demanding, and we are here to see if this can become the arena of real participation where global governance and policies can be created with a human face that is both male and female and where all the diversity of both male and female can emerge. . . . We hope that they will allow us to participate and to lead. If they don't, we will take leadership anyway and show that the world can be better for all in the twenty-first century. (Bunch 1995, 6–7)

WORKS BY CHARLOTTE BUNCH

"A Broom of One's Own." Washington, DC: Women's Liberation Movement, 1970.

And Joanne Cooke and Robin Morgan, eds. *The New Women: A "Motive" Anthology on Women's Liberation.* Indianapolis: Bobbs-Merrill, 1970.

And Nancy Myron, eds. *Women Remembered: A Collection of Biographies from the Furies.* New York: Diana Press, 1974.

———. *Lesbianism and the Women's Movement.* New York: Diana Press, 1975.

Et al., eds. *Building Feminist Theory: Essays from "Quest."* New York: Longman, 1981.

And Sandra Pollack, eds. *Learning Our Way: Essays in Feminist Education.* New York: Crossing Press, 1983.

And Kathleen Barry and Shirley Castley, eds. *International Feminism: Networking against Female Sexual Slavery.* New York: International Women's Tribune Centre, 1984.

Passionate Politics: Feminist Theory in Action—Essays, 1968–1986. New York: St. Martin's, 1987.

Gender Violence: A Development and Human Rights Issue. New York: Attic Press, 1992.

And Niamh Reilly, eds. *Demanding Accountability: The Global Campaign and Vienna Tribunal for Women's Human Rights.* New York: United Nations Development Fund for Women (UNIFEM), 1994.

"Women's Rights as Human Rights—Toward Re-Vision of Human Rights." *Nivedini—A Sri Lankan Feminist Journal* 1, no. 2 (December 1994): 189–198.

"Through Women's Eyes: Global Forces Facing Women in the 21st Century." Center for Women's Global Leadership NGO Forum '95 on Women (Speech opening Plenary, August 31, 1995). http://www.feminist.com/cfwgl.htm.

Et al., eds. *Voices from the Japanese Women's Movement: Ampo Japan-Asia Quarterly Review.* New Brunswick, NJ: Center for Women's Global Leadership, Rutgers University, 1996.

"The Intolerable Status Quo." UNICEF Web Page *http://www.unicef.org/pon97/author5.htm.* 1997.

WRITINGS ON CHARLOTTE BUNCH AND HER WORK

Bader, Eleanor J. "Review of Passionate Politics." *Humanist* 49, no. 4 (July 1989): 45–46.

"Charlotte Bunch Makes News at Human Rights Conference." *Women's Research Network News* 5, no.2 (July 31, 1993): 12.

Everitt, Angela. "Review of Demanding Accountability: The Global Campaign and Vienna Tribunal." *Journal of Gender Studies* 5, no. 1 (March 1996): 130–131.

Hoffman, Nancy Jo. "Feminist Scholarship and Women's Studies." *Harvard Educational Review* 56, no. 1 (November 1986): 511–519.

Mantilla, Karla. "Thinking Locally, Thinking Globally." *Off Our Backs* 24, no. 3 (March 1994): 23.

Stuttaford, Genevieve. "Review of Passionate Politics." *Publishers Weekly* 231, no. 25 (June 26, 1987): 63.

Wong, Linda. "Women's Rights as Human Rights." *Sojourner: The Women's Forum* 18, no. 12 (August 31, 1993): 11.
Young, Iris Marion. "Review of Passionate Politics." *Signs: Journal of Women in Culture and Society* 5, no. 1 (Autumn 1989): 186–189.

PAT CALIFIA
(1954–)

Lisa Sigel

When Pat Califia came out as a lesbian in Salt Lake City in 1971, her involvement in the feminist movement began. She worked for woman's rights in Utah by founding a woman's center, editing a feminist newsletter, and fighting for state ratification of the Equal Rights Amendment (ERA). Upon moving to San Francisco in 1973, she began speaking on lesbian issues. By 1979, she worked at *The Advocate*, a national gay magazine, as an editor, columnist, and sex adviser. She has developed sadomasochistic community organizations and written and spoken on sexual politics, censorship, AIDS, gender relations, and sexual diversity. She currently lives in San Francisco, writes to support herself, and is working on an M.A. in counseling psychology at the University of San Francisco.

Pat Califia is a feminist advocate for lesbian sexuality, freedom of expression, safe sex, sexual diversity, and sexual pleasure. She writes pornography (generally, lesbian sadomasochistic pornography), gay sex columns, and politically oriented essays about sexuality. Califia focuses on sexuality because she believes that it is a major source of pain and discrimination in this society, even though it offers an arena for "adventure, risk, competition, self-display, pleasurable stimulation, and novelty" (Califia, *Public Sex* 1994, 151). The problems, discriminations, and abuses that attend expressions of sexuality, she argues, are matched by the capacity for sexuality to bring positive changes to people's lives.

Her most politically oriented work, *Public Sex*, takes up a number of unpopular causes and provides critical insight into why these ought to matter to feminists and nonfeminists alike. These causes include the problems of feminist censorship, the North American Man/Boy Love Association, safer sex in the world of AIDS, and the inclusion of leather, rubber, sado-masochism, and fetishism in the sexual vocabulary of women. Califia believes that American society must end the assignment of privilege based on adherence to moral codes and begin to deal honestly with pleasure (Califia, *Public Sex* 1994, 11). By emphasizing the right to pleasure in all its forms, she tries to create a "safe place," both physical and psychological, for differences in gender identity and sexual practices.

Califia's continued involvement with the feminist and gay movements in San Francisco between the 1970s and 1990s has taught her that assimilation within these communities can be as problematic as the moral control asserted outside them. She argues that patterns of sexual conformity placed on women—whether these come from the religious Right or the feminist community—hamper women's ability to define themselves. Communities working for change need to encourage diversity and support it in all its forms. "Decriminalizing sex and empowering women and queers would cause an explosion of decadence, perversity, dirty talking, intuition, fetishes, intelligence, sex toys, satire, makeup, promiscuity, blasphemy, celebration, bangles, art, nudity, weird hair, and political upheaval. For the first time we'd get to take a look at what's really inside the Pandora's Box of human sexuality" (Califia, *Public Sex* 1994, 152). Her agenda of empowering women and queers and of decriminalizing sex encourages the feminist community to broaden its political agenda to include a new range of people and behaviors. She sees sexual inequality as a root cause of women's broader inequality in contemporary American society and on that ground labels herself a feminist, regardless of her conflicts with any more limited definitions of feminism.

[L]et me explain why I still call myself a feminist. I believe that the society in which I live is a patriarchy with power concentrated in the hands of men, and that this patriarchy prevents women from becoming complete and independent human beings. Women are oppressed by being denied access to economic resources, political power, and control over their own reproduction. This oppression is managed by several institutions, chiefly the family, religion, and the state. An essential part of the oppression of women is control over sexual ideology, mythology, and behavior. (Califia, *Public Sex* 1994, 166)

Because she believes that sexuality is central to oppression of women and queers, Califia's fight to decriminalize and destigmatize sexuality has broad implications for social liberation.

While she believes that women need to be liberated as a group and considers herself a feminist, Califia also believes that feminist theories of sexuality are inadequate for understanding both heterosexuality and lesbianism. She particularly addresses theorists Adrienne Rich and Carroll Smith-Rosenberg, who have de-emphasized women's sexual lusts in favor of female homosociality. She believes their focus on women's sexuality as a nongenital, love-based, holistic emotion undercuts women's rights to pleasure. In many ways, Califia brings San Francisco-style gay liberation to women—both heterosexual and lesbian. "We have to fall in love with lust and defend it, claim it, and make it a source of affirmation" (Califia, *Public Sex* 1994, 22). Her insistence on sexual liberation comes from her own sexual tastes as a "leatherdyke," from her self-described position as an outlaw and sexual radical, and from her work as a sex columnist with *The Advocate*.

Claiming sexuality and defending the right to choose the circumstances of sexual intercourse have had a long history in the feminist community since the nineteenth century, when women began to separate sexuality from marriage through the free love movement and sexuality from procreation with demands for birth control. The development of new reproductive technologies that give women further control over their own bodies has allowed women to look for sexuality with or without procreation as they saw fit. Califia moves the agenda further by promoting lust in all its forms. Rather than accepting a defensive stance, where women and children need to defend their sexuality against encroachment, Califia creates an aggressive stance in which sexuality can be claimed as a basic right. The basic rights that she insists on include the right to give and receive pleasure and pain, to choose gender and the symbolic framework of sexuality, and to discuss all aspects of sexuality in the public realm. In taking this stance, Califia has positioned herself against antipornography activists Andrea Dworkin and Catharine MacKinnon, who believe that pornography and sexualized representations of women hurt women. Califia argues that rather than limiting pornography, feminists need more information about sexuality, more representations for and about women, and more overt pleasure. She believes that asking a patriarchal state to rescue women will only produce a stronger state that will work to keep women ignorant and defenseless. Likewise, rather than dichotomizing adults from children in an attempt to keep children safe in an unsafe world, Califia advocates providing rights, information, and mentoring for children.

Califia does not call for easy acceptance, and she does not receive it. While Califia's work has been reviewed in *The Progressive, The Library Journal, Cuir Underground,* and *The Women's Review of Books,* among others, these generally positive assessments of her writing mask Califia's problematic position within the feminist community. For example, Donna Minkowitz in *The Women's Review of Books* believes that though she "gets a few important specifics wrong, Califia may be one of the smartest and most principled writers really grappling with those issues" (Minkowitz 1995, 19). The few specifics at issue fall within the context of the "sex wars" that have openly split the feminist community since the Barnard Conference of 1982. While the contentious nature of the "sex wars" has occluded adequate assessments of Califia's work and led to discord within the feminist community, it has also added vigor to feminist theories. Califia's work has contributed to the growing theoretical complexity about sexuality in two areas: queer studies and the pornography debates.

Queer studies have tried to theorize sexuality and gender beyond male/female, heterosexual/homosexual divisions. Califia has received a mixed reception within the queer community, particularly among lesbian feminists. Califia states that deviations from hetero-normative sexual practices can constitute acts of resistance and liberation. Some theorists within the queer community agree. However, others have argued that Califia depends on male theories and practices that masquerade as transforming gender but that do not adequately address lesbian issues of queerness. Califia's fiction, her essays, and her political work have helped to energize queer studies, although the implications of her work are still under dispute.

In the pornography debates, Califia has been an active proponent in a war of words that has been taking place for over a decade. Catharine MacKinnon, Andrea Dworkin, and others have argued that Califia cannot be a feminist because, as a pornographer, she advocates the subordination of women. Califia has responded by stating that she will admit that "anti-porn leaders like Andrea Dworkin and Catharine MacKinnon are not the enemy—that we are all politically active women who want to make the world a better place. When pigs fly" (Califia *Public Sex* 1994, 107). On Califia's side and with Califia's help, organizations like Feminists for Free Expression (FFE), Feminist Anti-Censorship Taskforce (FACT), and the National Coalition against Censorship (NCAC) have written, argued, and lobbied against censorship on feminist grounds. On Dworkin and MacKinnon's side Women against Violence against Women, Women against Violence and Pornography in the Media (WAVPM), and Women against Pornography (WAP) have worked with the Canadian government, the Meese Commission, and American state and local governments to change the legal definition of pornography to materials that subordinate and encourage the subordination of women. The inability on all sides to find a workable middle ground has highlighted the centrality of sexuality to contemporary feminist thinkers. All sides believe they are fighting for the future of feminism.

Califia sees herself as battling the ignorance, shame, and prudery of American sexual culture. "We did not create this heritage of shame and hate. But shifting it from our shoulders is going to take the most enormous outpouring of sex-positive propaganda this world has ever seen" (Califia, *Public Sex* 1994, 22). Califia contributes frank discussions of both the mechanics and meanings of sexuality to the "outpouring of sex-positive propaganda." Her insistence on a frank discussion of hidden desires calls for a greater nuance in the analysis of sexuality. In this, she is also controversial and oppositional. She refuses to ally herself with feminists who believe that political liberation and political protection need to come before sexual liberation. Even though her insistence on nuance hampers theorizing about sexuality, Califia offers a basis for a broader inclusion of desire.

We should be wary of making broad statements about the worth or value of another lesbian's sexual style, especially if it involves behaviors we don't understand or have never participated in. No erotic act has an intrinsic meaning. A particular sexual activity may symbolize one thing in a majority culture, another thing to members of a sexual subculture or religious sect, and yet another thing to the individuals who engage in it. (Califia, *Sapphistry* 1980, 107)

Califia insists that sexuality is highly varied by context, by consensuality, and by the symbolic framework an individual brings to any erotic act.

While Califia argues for the highly varied and individual nature of sexuality, she does not retreat into a framework where any act is equally justified. Instead, she attempts to create an ethical basis for sexuality that rests on self-realization, responsibility, and mutual concern. She argues specifically for an understanding of sexuality that recognizes the distinctions between love and hate, sadomaso-chism and torture, self-exploration and self-loathing. Her ethical basis hinges on mutual consent rather than on false consciousness. She believes that individuals can knowingly enter into contracts, even if those contracts include the infliction of pain and humiliation.

In *Doc and Fluff*, Califia's lesbian science fiction novel, the protagonists explore a loving, sadomasochistic sexual relationship, while the antagonist provides a counterexample of brutality not based on a contractual understanding. Her vision includes a prophet of the Goddess who performs a just execution of the antag-onist, who both rapes and murders. " 'I take your life,' she said, 'in the name of everything living. You are a despoiler. You have squandered and ruined every good gift our Mother gave you' " (Califia, *Doc and Fluff* 1990, 289). Pleasure, regardless of the format in which it is found, is one of the "gifts" of being human. Califia argues that the ethical exchange of pleasure can and should be differen-tiated from coercion; coercion should be punished. However, when a contractual understanding for sexuality is respected, the pursuit of pleasure in all its forms provides its own justification and needs to be respected on that basis alone. "A sexual practice which provides mutual pleasure to consenting adults should not require any other justification. It is its own excuse and its own reason for being" (Califia, *Public Sex* 1994, 235). Implicit in this novel is the understanding that adults can be mature, responsible, and respectful of each other's needs if allowed to enter into mutually satisfying contracts. However, Califia does not address whether desire, as well as moralism, is socially learned. This question of the origin of desire becomes particularly important in her fiction because of the potency of the symbols she employs.

The buildup of meanings that Califia works with in her writings makes her ideas more, rather than less, explosive. Implicit in her fiction is the belief that the most culturally laden signs of power can be co-opted and used by women rather than against them. By confronting these signs and relocating them, she attempts to transgress the ways that power has been located in our society on the basis of gender, race, and class. For instance, the issue of rape has gained deep symbolic meaning in our culture. While Califia recognizes the seriousness of rape as an event, she also views it as a symbolic category that has been culturally laden with pain, pleasure, fear, sexuality, and powerlessness. Rather than deny the symbolic potential of rape, she co-opts it for that same symbolic potential. In "The Surprise Party," a short story from *Macho Sluts*, Califia takes the fantasy of rape seriously in all its regalia, which include figures of state domination (cops), physical domination (restraints, handcuffs, clamps), and phallic domination (penises, billy clubs, boots). She constructs the story as a staged, consensual scene in which the fears of, as well as the desires for, sexual force can be explored. However, acknowledging the sexual fantasy of rape can undercut the feminist position that rape is about violence, not sexuality. Califia's work demonstrates that rape can be a symbolic reservoir for both sexuality and violence. The lack of distinction between consensuality and force and the transgression of newly established boundaries of bodily autonomy can undercut the feminist position on these issues even as they provide sources of legitimation for women's desires.

Ultimately, Califia's work calls for the realization that sexuality is more varied and more potent than our society likes to acknowledge. Her fiction demonstrates that inequalities in power can be pleasurable and that this pleasure can be explored in ways that contradict, rather than reinforce, racial, gendered, and class-based systems of oppression. Califia insists that rather than try to force ourselves to accept a white-washed version of desire, we need to change society to fit our psychological and social variation.

WORKS BY PAT CALIFIA

Pat Califia is a prolific writer; this selection includes only her most important works and her collected columns.

Political Essays

"Sex and Madonna, or, What Do You Expect from a Girl Who Doesn't Put Out on the First Five Dates?" *Madonnarama: Essays on Sex and Popular Culture*. Ed. Lisa Frank and Paul Smith. Pittsburgh: Cleis Press, 1993, 169–184.
Public Sex: The Culture of Radical Sex. Pittsburgh: Cleis Press, 1994.
"Slipping." *Lesbian Words*. Ed. Randy Turoff. New York: Masquerade Books, a Richard Kasak Book, 1995, 207–229.

Sexual Advice Literature

Sapphistry: The Book of Lesbian Sexuality. Tallahassee, FL: Naiad Press, 1980; rev. and reprinted 1983, 1988.
Ed. *Lesbian S/M Safety Manual*. Denver: Lace, 1988.
Advocate Advisor. Boston: Alyson Books, 1991.
Ed. *The Sexpert*. New York: Masquerade Books, 1992.
Sensuous Magic. New York: Masquerade Books, a Richard Kasak Book, 1993.

Fiction

Macho Sluts. Boston: Alyson Books, 1988.
Doc and Fluff: The Distopian Tale of a Girl, and Her Biker. Boston: Alyson Press, 1990.
"Belonging." *Flesh and the Word: An Anthology of Erotic Writing*. Ed. John Preston. New York: Penguin, Plume Books, 1992, 173–188.

Melting Point. Boston: Alyson Books, 1993.

Ed. "It Takes a Good Boy to Make a Good Daddy." *Doing It for Daddy: Short and Sexy Fiction about a Very Forbidden Fantasy.* Boston: Alyson, 1994, 215–237.

WRITINGS ON PAT CALIFIA AND HER WORK

Few works are entirely about Pat Califia and her writing, but many scholars reference her work to discuss sexuality, sadomasochism, and anticensorship feminism. This selection includes some of the more thought-provoking works.

Bell, David. "Pleasure and Danger: The Paradoxical Spaces of Sexual Citizenship." *Political Geography* 12, no. 2 (1995): 139–153.

Bersani, Leo. "Foucault, Freud, Fantasy, and Power." *GLQ-A Journal of Lesbian and Gay Studies* 2, nos. 1–2 (1995): 11–33.

Creet, Julia. "Daughters of the Movement: The Psychodynamics of Lesbian S/M Fantasy." *Differences* 3, no. 2 (1991): 135–159.

Meyer, Carlin. "Sex, Sin and Women's Liberation: Against Porn-Suppression." *Texas Law Review* 72, no. 5 (April 1994): 1097–1201.

Minkowitz, Donna. "Pleasure Principles." *The Women's Review of Books* 12, no. 9 (June 1995): 19.

JUDY CHICAGO
(1939–)

Beatriz Badikian-Gartler

Judy Chicago was born Judy Cohen in the city she later adopted as her namesake. Her parents were involved in leftist politics, their house being the center for political activity in the neighborhood. As a consequence Judy Chicago grew up in a home filled with people of all races and a keen appreciation for human values, regardless of color, religious affiliation, or gender. Her father was a union organizer, and her mother worked outside the home, which gave Chicago a sense that she could be and do what she wanted. Two older female cousins, both in college and active intellectually, also provided positive role models for her. Because of her parents' left-wing politics, the family became a target of Federal Bureau of Investigation (FBI) harassment and questioning, ending in the McCarthy witch-hunts. In 1947 she began attending the Art Institute of Chicago. By 1948 her father had been driven out of the union and had to work as an insurance salesman. However, he began to get sick as a result, and Chicago would often find him home when she returned from school. His health deteriorated rapidly, and he died during an operation to remove an ulcer in his stomach. Chicago's adolescence was spent in long conversations and reminiscences about her father with those around her who had admired him. After high school, she attended the University of California at Los Angeles (UCLA) and lived with her mother's sister and husband, a childless couple, in Culver City. Her uncle's conservative views quickly clashed with Chicago's liberal ideas, prompting her to move in with a fellow art student. She graduated with a bachelor's degree in art in 1962 and, in 1964, received her master's degree from the same institution. By 1966 she had her first solo exhibition in Los Angeles at the Rolf Nelson Gallery and, in 1971, established the Feminist Art Program in the California Institute of the Arts in Valencia.

Judy Chicago went on to have numerous solo and group exhibitions of her work, to teach art for several years, and to receive a number of awards and grants from the Streisand Foundation, the Threshold Foundation, the Thanks Be to

Grandmother Winifred Foundation, the International Friends of Transformative Arts, the California Arts Commission, the Spertus Museum of Judaica, and the National Endowment for the Arts. She also received an Outstanding Woman of the Year Award from *Mademoiselle* magazine, a Woman of Achievement of the World Award from the Louisiana World Exposition, and the Vesta Award from the Los Angeles Women's Building.

Chicago resides in New Mexico but travels extensively with her exhibitions. Her most famous work, "The Dinner Party," is most recently on exhibit at the Armand Hammer Museum in UCLA under the title "Sexual Politics: Judy Chicago's Dinner Party in Feminist Art History." Curated by Dr. Amelia Jones, it examines the work's significance and features an accompanying art historical and critical catalog well as a third book about "The Dinner Party" by Chicago.

Judy Chicago played a pioneering role in the feminist art movement of the 1970s, founding the nation's first feminist art education program in Fresno, the Fresno Feminist Art Program, whose goal was to challenge the limitations placed on women artists. The students developed traditionally "masculine" skills such as negotiating business transactions and constructing their own studio space. Simultaneously Chicago encouraged her students to draw on their personal experiences for the content of their work. Extensive feminist consciousness-raising activities were also part of the curriculum during the first months of the program. Female sexuality became one of the most important topics addressed in the sessions as well as in the artwork. Collaboration among women constituted an essential component of the program as well. The students read feminist literature, researched the lives of women artists, and reached out to the community by publishing a magazine, *Everywoman*, documenting their activities.

In the fall of 1971, Judy Chicago and her students moved to California Institute of the Arts, invited by Miriam Schapiro. However, the facilities promised them had not been completed. The result was Womanhouse, an abandoned mansion that the artists transformed into a space where women could create as well as live their daily lives. Chicago was also instrumental in the development of Womanspace Gallery in Los Angeles, a cooperative dedicated to the exhibition and critique of women's artwork. She also helped establish the Woman's Building in Los Angeles, which has served as an important arts center and political base for women. However, her most famous artwork by far is "The Dinner Party."

Executed through the labor-intensive, traditionally feminine crafts of embroidery and china painting, "The Dinner Party" represents a monumental homage to women throughout history. It opened in 1979 in San Francisco at the Museum of Modern Art and drew record-breaking crowds of mostly female viewers. It also generated intense controversy among art critics and historians. With a team of 400 women and men, Chicago created thirty-nine handmade porcelain plates representing dinner guests, women ranging from prehistoric goddesses to Georgia O'Keefe. Each plate rested on a hand-embroidered runner executed in the needlework style of the honored guest's historical period. The triangular table rested on a porcelain floor where 999 names of other women were painted. The exhibition was complemented with documentary panels on the history of the project and the people who worked on it, brochures, and a book.

As much as general viewers loved "The Dinner Party," art critics criticized it as vulgar, crass, unworthy of exhibition. Conservative institutions, such as the Art Institute of Chicago and other museums, refused to exhibit the work. However, thanks to the efforts of grassroots women's groups, the exhibit traveled around all the major cities of the United States and five countries: Canada, Scotland, England, Germany, and Australia. During its fifteen exhibitions "The Dinner Party" has been seen by approximately 1 million viewers.

Feminist artists and writers in the 1980s also criticized "The Dinner Party" for its essentializing characteristics and its contribution to the ghettoizing of women's art. They claim that the focus on women's bodies and domestic themes reinforces the stereotypes of women as sexual objects and nurturing caretakers. More recently, however, a reassessment of early feminist activity has redefined the role works such as "The Dinner Party" played in strengthening women's sense of freedom and self-determination as well as laying crucial groundwork for later feminist activism. Since then, Chicago has completed other projects that address issues of sexual identity, power, and dominance in society.

From 1980 to 1985 she completed "The Birth Project," which consists of woven and embroidered images of childbirth. The works, presented in a series of 80 exhibition units, included documentation panels describing the intellectual, aesthetic, and human processes involved in the creation of the art. In 1986 Chicago returned to individual studio work and created her first noncollaborative project, "Powerplay." A series of drawings, paintings, weavings, cast paper, and bronze wall reliefs addresses the social construction of masculinity, exploring how definitions of power have affected the world in general and men in particular. Her interest in issues of power and powerlessness led her to "The Holocaust Project: From Darkness to Light." It premiered in 1993 at the Spertus Museum of Judaica in Chicago and is currently traveling across the country. With her husband, photographer Donald Woodman, Chicago spent eight years traveling, inquiring about, and studying the Holocaust. The work presents a series of images that combine her painting with his photography as well as stained glass and tapestry work designed by Chicago and executed by skilled artisans.

Judy Chicago's contribution to the feminist movement is invaluable. She rescued innumerable women from history's obscurity, where they had been buried alive by male historians. "The Dinner Party" opened our eyes to the silenced contributions of women scientists, artists, activists, philosophers. Not only is the content feminist, but her execution signals the dawn of a newfound respect for ancient techniques and styles. Technically, Chicago's use of needlework and china painting validates two old, traditionally female activities, often relegated to the category of "crafts." She transformed these crafts into art. The vehicle she chose to celebrate women, a dinner party, validates the familiar territory of feminine work: the kitchen, cooking, nurturing. Added to these, the female sexual imagery depicted in the thirty-nine china plates elevates the female body while challenging accepted notions of representation. It is no surprise, then, that conservative art institutions have not yet been able to offer "The Dinner Party" a permanent home.

The controversy that surrounds her most notable artwork raises questions about the nature of art and its place in society. Who decides what is "good" art, worthy of exhibition in museums and art institutes? Whom does art serve, and how? As Judy Chicago herself has said, a monumental work of art like "The Dinner Party" is perceived as a threat to conservative values because "art is a symbol system that gets passed into the future" (Meyer 1995, 138). In a recent interview she also expressed her hope that her life and artwork might function as "a testament to [the importance of] believing in yourself and finding the courage to risk being who you are" (Meyer 1995, 139). As for the future, Judy Chicago stresses the importance of including everyone's voice through making, viewing, and discussing art. This inclusivity is essential in defining human experience for any society to succeed and flourish.

WORKS BY JUDY CHICAGO

Through the Flower: My Struggle as a Woman Artist. New York: Doubleday, 1975; New York: Anchor, 1977; Japan: Parco, 1979; New York: Anchor (rev. ed.), 1982; England: Women's Press, 1982; Germany: Verlag (neue frau) Dirch die Blume, 1984; New York: Penguin, 1993; China: Yuan-Liou, 1996.
The Dinner Party: A Symbol of Our Heritage. New York: Doubleday/Anchor, 1979.
Embroidering Our Heritage: The Dinner Party Needlework. New York: Doubleday/Anchor, 1980.
The Birth Project. New York: Doubleday/Anchor, 1985.
The Dinner Party. Germany: Athenaeum, 1987.
Holocaust Project: From Darkness into Light. New York: Viking/Penguin, 1993.
Beyond the Flower: The Autobiography of a Feminist Artist. New York: Viking/Penguin, 1996.
The Dinner Party. New York: Viking/Penguin, 1996.

WRITING ON JUDY CHICAGO AND HER WORK

Meyer, Laura, with Judy Chicago. "Judy Chicago: Feminist Artist and Educator." *Feminist Foremothers in Women's Studies, Psychology, Mental Health.* Ed. Phyllis Chesler, Esther Rothblum, and Ellen Cole. New York: Haworth Press, 1995.

SHIRLEY CHISHOLM
(1924–)

Frederick J. Simonelli

Shirley Anita St. Hill Chisholm was born in the Bedford-Stuyvesant section of Brooklyn, New York, on November 30, 1924, to Charles Christopher and Ruby Seale St. Hill, immigrants from Barbados in the West Indies. At the age of four Chisholm was sent to live with her grandmother in rural Barbados, where she attended Vauxhall Coeducational School. Reunited with her parents in New York in 1933, Chisholm continued her education in the New York public school system, graduating from Girls' High School in 1942. Chisholm's academic promise brought offers of scholarships from Vassar College and Oberlin College, but family financial constraints compelled her to stay closer to home. That fall Chisholm enrolled at Brooklyn College, where she graduated cum laude with a bachelor's degree in sociology in 1946. While at Brooklyn College Chisholm's social, racial, political, and feminist consciousness developed as she became an active member in the National Association for the Advancement of Colored People (NAACP), the Urban League, the League of Women Voters, the Bedford-Stuyvesant Political League, and the Seventeenth Assembly District Democratic Club. While at Brooklyn College she also married Conrad Chisholm, a social service investigator, whom she divorced in 1977.

Following graduation from college, Chisholm's interest in child development and child welfare issues matured during the seven years she worked as a teacher's aide at the Mount Calvary Child Care Center in Harlem. During those years she also pursued graduate studies at Columbia University. In 1952, Chisholm received a master's degree in early childhood education from Columbia and took the position of nursery school director at the Friend in Need Nursery School in Brooklyn. Recognizing the value of bilingualism in a multicultural community, Chisholm worked to become fluent in Spanish. Within a year she accepted the directorship of the larger Hamilton-Madison Child Care Center. By 1959 Chisholm's expertise in her field was widely recognized, and she accepted an appointment as an educational consultant in New York City's Bureau of Child Welfare, Division of Day Care.

In 1960, Chisholm's activism on behalf of African American political candidates and feminist and social justice issues led her to spearhead the formation of the Unity Democratic Club, an organization that worked outside the regular party apparatus to elect blacks and women to political office. In 1964, Chisholm was elected to the New York State Assembly, the first African American woman elected to that body. Four years later Chisholm sought a wider forum and ran for the U.S. House of Representatives. Her fluency in Spanish was an enormous advantage in the Puerto Rican neighborhoods of her urban Brooklyn district. Votes from the Hispanic community propelled her to a narrow victory in the Democratic primary against a popular state senator. Her victory in the general election, a much easier race in her overwhelmingly Democratic district, recorded another historic precedent by making Shirley Chisholm the first African American woman elected to Congress.

When she took her seat in January 1969, Chisholm vowed to work for greater employment and educational opportunities for women and minorities, early education programs for disadvantaged children, federal assistance in the fight against hunger and poverty, and the dismantling of legal constraints against women. In Congress, Shirley Chisholm quickly established a reputation as a tenacious fighter for her deeply held beliefs. Her feminist convictions manifested themselves in practical issues that became the centerpiece of her legislative program: the inclusion of domestic workers under minimum wage protection, increased federal funding for child care facilities available to working mothers, and protection of women's reproductive rights. Several years before the issuance of the *Roe v. Wade* decision by the U.S. Supreme Court made abortion legal in all of the United States, Chisholm led the fight for the repeal of discriminatory antiabortion laws throughout the country. Chisholm helped organize the National Association for the Repeal of Abortion Laws and was named honorary president of that organization in 1969. As an outspoken opponent of the Vietnam War, Chisholm spoke often, on the floor of the House of Representatives and at meetings across the country, against the waste of human and material resources caused by America's obsession with that conflict.

Shirley Chisholm was also an active member of the National Organization for Women (NOW) and an early congressional supporter of the Equal Rights Amendment (ERA). Her impassioned testimony for the ERA before the U.S. Senate Judiciary Committee in 1970 helped galvanize support for the ratification campaign among minority women nationwide. Throughout her congressional career and beyond, Chisholm continued to work for the ratification of the ERA as a member of the Equal Rights Amendment Ratification Council.

An astute politician, Chisholm understood the necessity of increasing the number of women in elected office at all levels of government if feminist issues were to receive a sympathetic hearing. In 1971, she organized the National Women's Political Caucus (NWPC) to pursue this goal. The NWPC was designed to cut across party lines to organize women as political activists and to promote women candidates for local, state, and federal office. Believing that gender issues transcended race and class, Chisholm diligently worked to make the NWPC broad-based and inclusive.

On January 25, 1972, Congresswoman Shirley Chisholm again blazed a new path when she declared her candidacy for president of the United States, becoming the first African American woman to seek the presidential nomination of a major party. Her campaign enunciated feminist and peace issues, calling for racial and gender equality as well as for an end to the waste of resources in Vietnam and a redeployment of the money spent on that war to education, fighting poverty, and rebuilding America's cities. Chisholm's candidacy brought together activists from the feminist and antiwar movement, as well as notable, but disparate, African American leaders such as California congressman Ron Dellums, Rev. Jesse Jackson, and Black Panther Party leader Bobby Seale. Chisholm took her hard-fought campaign to primaries in twelve states, winning twenty-eight delegates and receiving 152 first-ballot votes at the 1972 Democratic National Convention. Many of the issues Chisholm promoted were embraced by the convention's eventual nominee, Senator George McGovern.

Chisholm's work in Congress after the 1972 election benefited from her raised visibility, but she found herself increasingly isolated from the center of power during the Republican administrations of Richard M. Nixon and Gerald R. Ford. She became the leading congressional critic of the Nixon administration's plan to eliminate the Office of Economic Opportunity and to dismantle all vestiges of the 1960s Great Society program. She worked to convince feminist and labor leaders that they had a common interest in social welfare legislation, particularly issues dealing with wages and working conditions for female workers. Chisholm led the effort in the House of Representatives to override President Ford's veto of federal assistance in meeting health and safety standards in day care centers, and she fought, usually unsuccessfully, against cuts in assistance programs for minority students.

Chisholm briefly regained a sympathetic ear in the White House when Jimmy Carter assumed the presidency in 1977. Chisholm's role in the Congress, with a strong Democratic majority, rose in recognition of her hard-earned status as a veteran legislator with a national reputation. She won a seat on the powerful House Rules Committee and was elected secretary of the Democratic Caucus in the House of Representatives. Ronald Reagan's election just four years later, however, ushered in a new era of conservative Republican dominance and once again consigned Chisholm to the margins of power.

Chisholm retired from Congress in 1982, citing the nation's increasing conservative political climate as an obstacle to achieving the legislative goals she held dear. In retirement, Shirley Chisholm has continued to work for feminist and racial equality issues. In 1985, she helped organize, and became the first president of, the National Political Caucus of Black Women. Issues such as gender equity, the rights of children, educational opportunities for all, and the preservation of affirmative action, as well as teaching and lecturing, continue to occupy her time and energy.

Throughout her career Shirley Chisholm advanced both a gender and a race agenda while trying to maintain her standing within the power structure of the Democratic Party. Conflicts were inevitable and not infrequent. When advancement of the issues she cared most about—gender equity, economic justice, and racial equality—conflicted with the interests of the Democratic Party, as in the 1969 New York City mayoral election, Chisholm invariably chose the path that served her beliefs. Her support of Republican John Lindsay in 1969 was a key factor in Lindsay's victory. While Chisholm won a city administration sympathetic to her concerns, she alienated the city's Democratic Party regulars, who repaid her perceived political disloyalty by refusing to support her 1972 presidential bid.

Chisholm's repudiation of status quo politics secured her position as a political outsider. Her 1972 campaign slogan, "Unbought and Unbossed," reflected her career-long challenge to entrenched political power, which Chisholm saw as overwhelmingly male and white. As a black feminist, Chisholm sought common ground between the civil rights and feminist movements. As a founding member of both NOW and the National Political Caucus of Black Women (NPCBW), Chisholm kept her attention focused on the issues of common concern to all women, especially those dealing with questions of political and economic empowerment. One of the major disappointments of her failed presidential bid, however, was the failure of black and feminist leaders to find common ground in her candidacy. Neither feminist organizations nor black civil rights groups rallied to her support, although she, more than any other candidate in that race, articulated their concerns. Both the black and feminist leaderships proved to be far more willing to accommodate the entrenched political powers than Chisholm had ever been in pursuit of feminist or civil rights objectives. That realization left Chisholm disillusioned and bitter.

Chisholm's legacy remains in the historic firsts she achieved: the first African American woman elected to the New York State Assembly, the first African American woman elected to the U.S. Congress, and the first African American woman to mount a serious campaign for president of the United States. Throughout her career she fought tirelessly for the interests of women, racial minorities, and the economically underprivileged. Ultimately, Shirley Chisholm's career of public service had its greatest impact in the people she introduced to the political process and the encouragement her example gave to women, especially black women, to seek power and change within the political system.

WORKS BY SHIRLEY CHISHOLM

Unbought and Unbossed. Boston: Houghton Mifflin, 1970.
"Race, Revolution, and Women." *Black Scholar* (1971).

"Sexism and Racism: One Battle to Fight." *Personnel and Guidance Journal* 51 (October 1972): 123–125.
The Good Fight. New York: Harper and Row, 1973.

WRITINGS ON SHIRLEY CHISHOLM AND HER WORK

Brownmiller, Susan. *Shirley Chisholm: A Biography.* New York: Doubleday, 1970.
Duffy, Susan. *Shirley Chisholm: A Bibliography of Writings by and about Her.* Metuchen, NJ: Scarecrow Press, 1988.
Haskins, James. *Fighting Shirley Chisholm.* New York: Dial Press, 1975.
Hicks, Nancy. *The Honorable Shirley Chisholm, Congresswoman from Brooklyn.* New York: Lion Books, 1971.
Jackson, Garnet. *Shirley Chisholm: Congresswoman.* Metuchen, NJ: Modern Curriculum, 1994.
Kuriansky, Joan, and Catherine Smith. *Shirley Chisholm, Democratic Representative from New York.* Washington, DC: Grossman, 1972.
Pollack, Jill S. *Shirley Chisholm.* New York: Chelsea House, 1994.
Ragsdale, Bruce A., and Joel D. Treese. "Shirley Anita Chisholm." *Black Americans in Congress, 1870–1989.* Washington, DC: U.S. Government Printing Office, 1990.
Scheader, Catherine. *Shirley Chisholm: Teacher and Congresswoman.* Springfield, NJ: Enslow, 1990.

ESTHER NGAN-LING CHOW
(1943–)

Linda Wong

My goal is for human liberation and empowerment regardless of race, class,
sexual orientation and gender. We have to transcend those kinds of boundaries when we do scholarship, teach, serve other people or by just being a
person.

—Esther Ngan-Ling Chow

To begin talking about Esther Ngan-Ling Chow, the words "multicultural feminist" and "Asian activist" come to mind. But what exactly is a multicultural
feminist? According to bell hooks and Elaine Showalter, a multicultural feminist
fights to end all oppression of a minority group while maintaining a self-conscious
effort in celebrating the values, beliefs, ideas, and behavior uniquely or traditionally characteristic of one's ethnic group. Politically, this means the desire to
end the domination of the majority group over the minority.

An activist is a person whose concern for these issues stems from the desire to
correct the wrongs that have been historically leveled against women and minority ethnic groups. As an Asian American activist, Chow sets out to correct
all the stereotypes, negative images, racism, and walls set up to prevent the
acceptance and integration of Asians into the United States. Historically, women
of color have suffered oppression because of their race, class, and gender. These
factors then shape the experiences and produce a reality for women of color
"different" from that of white women. Esther Chow is at the forefront of Asian
American women addressing the mitigating experiences of Asians in the United
States and outside in the global community. Her critical assessment on feminist
thought and dissemination of her findings have put her at the forefront of Asian
American activism.

Chow believes that people cannot approach an issue today without factoring
in the elements of race, class, gender, and sexuality. This uncompromising belief

has fueled her desire to fight for those who cannot fight, give voice to those who do not have one, and provide hope to those who see none. From the beginning she has not forgotten those who helped her, her culture, or her roots. This appreciation, learned from her mother, reveals itself through her name. In all her professional publications, Chow has always kept her full name, Esther Ngan-Ling Chow. For Esther, maintaining her full name allows her to assert her own personal identity as a Chinese American woman. In Chinese culture, to change a person's name, give him or her a nickname, or call people names is an insult, not a joke. People take offense to any name change. For Chow, keeping her maiden name throughout her professional life preserves a tradition carried on from her mother and mother-in-law and maintains the connection to her culture and ethnicity. Most importantly, it separates her identity from that of her husband. In China, keeping the maiden name was women's common practice. In Chinese character, the name is written with the husband's name on top and the maiden name on the bottom. This name ordering still reflects a patriarchal control over women's identity, but it allows women to keep their family name. In the United States, women commonly drop their maiden names and assume their husband's name. Esther thought that was different and unfortunate and used a hyphenated name in English.

Growing up in Hong Kong, she and her family struggled. As a youngster, she lost her older brother and father to the Japanese invasion of Hong Kong and a sister to the war. Her mother was the only one left to raise Esther. Esther's grandmother, mother, and father were all factory workers: realizing the lack of opportunities for women and the hopelessness in factory work, her mother decided to push Esther into education. She borrowed money from friends and relatives to send Esther to school and endured intense criticism, since a typical path for a girl her age at that time was factory work. Education was seen as a waste of time for women. Fortunately for Esther, school provided her an introduction to a world of opportunities. There she met her future role models, educators who left an indelible impression on her and encouraged her into a life in academe.

As a British colony, Hong Kong modeled its school system after the British, with admission to each level of schooling based on examination scores. Even at the end of four years of college, students received only a diploma. For a degree, another examination was required. Since a degree determined salary levels, however, it was essential for success. Esther not only passed but excelled.

In between studying, Esther actively participated in her community. In high school, she was the principal of the Sunday school. In college she worked for the student cabinet, focusing on projects that aided the poor. Although not politically involved in Hong Kong, because the Chinese were not allowed to participate in politics, she remained interested. She decided to continue school in the United States and seek out greater opportunities.

Arriving in the United States for graduate studies, Chow was swept up into the 1960s movements and protests in California. Here she discovered People's Park, site of major rallies and demonstrations, and the anti-Vietnam War, women's, civil rights, and elderly movements. She was automatically drawn into the midst of all this social turbulence: the questioning of authority, debates about the relevance of school, and questions of how public issues should seep into the classroom. Surrounded by social unrest, her desire to be active sprouted. Chow grew from an observer to an active participant and further solidified her interest in sociology.

During her years in graduate school, Chow began to reassess her education. Whose theories she was learning? Why study sociology if it had no meaning outside academe? Most importantly, she noticed the lack of presence women had in the canon. Here were our forefathers, but where were our foremothers? Why study social movements if half the population was not addressed or listened to in academe? Gradually, Chow discovered her role in academe, linking the outside world with the academic environment. She would talk and write about the people she grew up with, creating an interplay between academe and community.

As an Asian American woman, Chow was at a disadvantage for being a woman, nonwhite, and non-middle-class. Women of color were ignored by the feminist movement. Despite raising relevant issues, the movement failed to address the "whole" picture; in fact, most of the people in the picture remained ignored. This prompted Chow to become involved in the establishment of a women's organization specifically for Asian and Chinese women. This became a safe space for Asians to address issues around cultural differences, lack of inclusiveness, the double patriarchy that women of immigrant cultures experienced, and issues dealing with race and class within their community. Within this assessment, she found the desire to work with groups that advocated for the improved conditions of their own race and ethnicity in addition to gender, rather than those that focused solely on gender issues.

In academe, Chow encountered another culture with conflicting values. Laced with prescribed values and ascribed manners, this institution made particular demands. Perplexed by this game, where success meant tenure, she did not know if she could survive. Partly because of this, she accepted a position with the U.S. Commission on Civil Rights as a senior social science analyst, to try a career outside academe. Here she saw she could play an important role in shaping public policy. After one year, two prestigious grants came through, which resulted in her project on Asian American women in the workforce. Then, fresh from her stint on the Civil Rights Commission and keenly politicized, she wrote a series of papers analyzing the situation of Asian American women in the United States and their cultural integration into the workforce and society. This marked Chow's return to academe and the beginning point in her research on gender issues. Her landmark article "The Development of Feminist Consciousness among Asian American Women," published in Gender and Society in 1987 represents a revolutionary approach in sociology and social movements. She began with a simple question, Where were all the Asian American women during the women's movement? Her research since then has continued to grapple with that question.

Chow does not locate her inspiration in the feminist movement specifically:

her involvement with various organizations opened doors and opened her eyes to a multilayered and complicated society that views people in relation to specific groups rather than who they are deep down. A good academician who views research and teaching as the essential parts of her work, Chow feels the most important connection is to the lives she studies. If her research fails to touch the lives of the people she studies, its meaning is lost. As Chow once said, "How much I want to accomplish is not important, how much I am able to do things to make the lives better of those I study and try to understand and serve centers my work." Women remain at the center of her analysis, but gender is not the sole focus.

Historically, the women's movement in the United States has fielded criticism for lack of inclusiveness and a myopic vision. Chow has actively participated in these critiques: along with her colleagues Bonnie Dill and Maxine Baca Zinn she formulated a "talk back" to the system, which led to a critical examination of white feminism. This grew into an area of research that attempted to talk about the "whole woman" issue in women's studies and gender studies differently. They addressed issues within the communities of color, issues generally ignored by mainstream society. They began to look at how certain institutions like government, schools, and marriage embodied stratification of race, class, and sexual orientation. As Dill and Zinn state in the book that resulted from these talks, *Women of Color in U.S. Society*, feminists of color are going beyond the mere recognition and inclusion of differences to permit them to reshape the basic concepts and theories of the discipline.

The idea of a multicultural, pluralistic feminist movement has become a tangible concept. Yet it remains complicated. Chow's seminal work on Asian American women and gender consciousness reveals how community cultural traditions lie at the heart of the "differences" between Asian Americans and mainstream Americans. In Chinese culture, male domination and the family remain the center of interaction, thus preventing women from having relations with other women. For women to act out against male authority is to defy cultural traditions. This can lead to alienation, not only within families but also with communities.

The direction of Chow's research in the last few years moves away from a critical approach of gender in the United States to a more global critique of gender. One of her areas of interest is the introduction of women's studies programs in China and Asia. One example of her global focus is recent research on the one-child policy in China, which was enacted to help curb the growing population. Initial assumptions stated that the policy would change the gender imbalance in the family and that the heavy preference for a male child would dissipate. Chow noticed that the policy started out as a population policy and later became a family policy facilitating modernization, but not one that equalized gender relations. It was introduced as a panacea for the country's pressing problems: population growth, poverty, inflation, and unemployment. Ultimately, the one-child policy is geared toward economic development, not gender equality; in actuality it disadvantages women.

Today Chow continues her scholarly research in the field of Asia and women at American University. While her current research focuses abroad, Chow still participates in her local community, whether it is holding a class on adaptation for recent immigrants in D.C. or sending her children to Chinese-language classes and community events.

Rethinking gender as a relational concept along with race, class, and sexuality, Chow is a revolutionary feminist thinker whose life and work make a difference.

WORKS BY ESTHER NGAN-LING CHOW

Books

Acculturation of Asian American Professional Women. Washington, DC: National Institute of Mental Health, Department of Health and Human Services, 1982.

With Doris Y. Wilkinson and Maxine Baca Zinn, eds. *Race, Class, and Gender.* Special Issue of *Gender and Society* (September 1992). Also coauthor, the "Introduction."

And Catherine White Berheide, eds. *Women, the Family, and Policy: A Global Perspective.* Albany: State University of New York, 1994. Also chapter coauthor with Catherine White Berheide, "Studying Women, Families, and Policies Globally: An Introduction" and "Perpetuating Gender Inequality: The Role of Families, Economies, and States" and, with Kevin Chen, "The Impact of the One-Child Policy on Women and the Family in the People's Republic of China."

With Doris Wilkinson, and Maxine Baca Zinn, eds. *Common Bonds, Different Voices: Race, Class, and Gender.* Newbury Park, CA: Sage, 1996. Author of the introduction chapter, "Transforming Knowledge: Race, Class, and Gender," and of a reprinted chapter, "The Development of Gender Consciousness among Asian American Women."

Selected Articles in Books and Journals

"Acculturation Experience of the Asian American Woman." *Beyond Sex Roles.* Ed. Alice Sargent. St. Paul, MN: West, 1984.

"Teaching Sex and Gender in Sociology: Incorporating the Perspective of Women of Color." *Teaching of Sociology* 12 (April 1985): 23–36.

"Sex-Role Identity and Socioeconomic and Psychological Well-Being of Asian American Women." *Psychology of Women Quarterly* 11 (Winter 1987): 69–81.

With Catherine White Berheide. "The Interdependence of Family and Work: The Framework for Family Life Education, Policy, and Practice." Special issue on "Feminism and the Family," *Journal of Family Relations* 37 (January 1988): 23–28.

"The Feminist Movement: Where Are All the Asian American Women?" *Making Waves: Writings about Asian American Women.* Ed. Diane Yen Mei Wong and Judy Yung. Boston: Beacon Press, 1989.

"The Development of Gender Consciousness among Asian American Women." *Gender and Society* 1 (September 1987): 4–10; reprinted in *Social Construction of Gender.* Ed. Judith Lorber and Susan Farrell. Newbury, CA: Sage, 1990a.

"Rethinking Gender Studies in Chinese Societies: Future Directions." Abstract in the

Proceedings of the Conference on Gender Studies in Chinese Societies, sponsored by the Center for Hong Kong Studies, Chinese University of Hong Kong, 1990b.

"Sociology of Gender and Women's Studies," *China: Present State and the Future Direction.* Zhenzhou, China: Zhenzhou University, 1993.

"Asian American Women at Work." *Women of Color In U.S. Society.* Ed. Maxine Baca Zinn and Bonnie Dill. Philadelphia: Temple Press, 1994.

"Asian American Feminism." *International Encyclopedia of Women's Studies.* London: Harvester Wheatsheaf, Paramount Publishing International, 1996a.

"Family, Economy, and the State: A Legacy of Struggle for Chinese American Women." *Origins and Destinies: Immigration, Race, Ethnicity in America.* Ed. Silvia Pedraza and Ruben G. Rumbaut. Belmont, CA: Wadsworth Press, 1996b.

"Making Waves, Moving Mountains: Reflections on Beijing '95 and Beyond." *Signs: Journal of Women in Culture and Society* 22 (Autumn 1996c), 185–192.

With Michael Zhao. "The One-Child Policy and Parent–Child Relationships: A Comparison of One-Child with Multiple-Child Families in China." *International Journal of Sociology and Social Policy* (September 1996d): 35–62.

PEARL CLEAGE
(1948–)

Linda Rohrer Paige

Born in Springfield, Massachusetts, the daughter of Doris Graham Cleage, a teacher, and Rev. Albert B. Cleage, Jr., minister and founder of the Shrines of the Black Madonna of the Pan-African Orthodox Christian Church, Pearl Lomax Cleage experienced a childhood steeped in lively political debate, "strategy meetings," and "books, books, books" (Interview 1996). Indeed, the noted dramatist/poet and essayist considers her childhood home as "nothing less than a writer's paradise" (Interview 1996). Her earliest remembrances include a house strewn with writings, everything from works by Langston Hughes, to Simone de Beauvoir; from Richard Wright, to Margaret Sanger; and from Ossie Davis, to Arthur Miller. With parents passionate about the arts and politics, Cleage grew up in an atmosphere demanding intellectual excellence. At a time when many other young women of African American descent consumed their adolescence with boys, parties, sports, and sock hops, Cleage remembers excursions to the ballet and sights of Rudolf Nureyev, Margot Fonteyn, and the Ballets Africaines. Frequently visiting the theater and witnessing live performances of flamenco dancing, she delighted at the colorful dancers strutting metrically across polished floors (Interview 1996).

Influenced early by her mother, father, and older sister—and still later by her stepfather, lawyer Henry W. Cleage—the future award-winning playwright developed a personality as passionate as that of other family members. In Detroit, where she first met "our black and shining prince," Malcolm X (Cleage, *Deals* 1993, 147), the young student excelled in school. During this period, perhaps, the beginnings of a "feminist consciousness" evidenced itself, for at age six, Cleage became enamored of a seven-year-old transfer student from Alabama—a boy who made her "cheeks flush crimson" and her toes curl like fries in hot oil (Cleage, "In My Solitude" 1989, 57). Even then, however, she recognized that a disproportionate amount of her day had been spent thinking—either consciously or subconsciously—about this boy. By the time she reached thirty,

Cleage reflected on this earlier preoccupation and questioned why she had spent time wholly consumed with males at the expense of demanding time for her*self* (Interview 1996). After completing McMichael Junior High School, the future writer entered Northwestern High School, from which she graduated in 1966.

Inspired as a youth by the works of Langston Hughes, Cleage admired his propensity for "truth-telling," a quality, she felt, that spoke directly to her as an African American artist:

If I am forced to go to a desert island with only one book, it will have to be *The Big Sea*, the first volume of Hughes' autobiography. When he describes throwing his books off of the freighter which is pulling away . . . to Africa, I understood his desire to stop living in a book and start living his life. I continue to be in awe of his ability to so accurately describe the complexities of African Americans, *in all our terribleness*, without once sacrificing his absolute love for the group that loved and claimed him. (Interview 1996)

Cleage's penchant for literature, especially the study of African Americans' writings, extended into her college years. She attended Howard University between 1966 and 1969, Yale in 1969, and the University of the West Indies in 1971. Graduating with a B.A. from Spelman College in 1971, she did graduate study at Atlanta University in 1971.

Married to novelist Zaron W. Burnett, Cleage resides in Atlanta, Georgia, with her husband and daughter, Deignan Cleage Lomax, the child of her first marriage, to Michael L. Lomax. The author merges her writing interests with her hobbies and commiserates often with her husband about their individual and collective goals, about how to "satisfy" their artistic impulses, yet "still pay the rent" (Interview 1996). With other artist and activist friends, she remains politically and socially active.

Most recently, the writer's career has catapulted her into national prominence, with her new play *Blues for an Alabama Sky* performed as the United States' official theatrical presentation for Atlanta's 1996 Cultural Olympiad. Having earned her living as a columnist/contributor to the *Atlanta Tribune*, *Ms.*, and *Essence*, as the founding editor of *CATALYST* magazine, as a television host/interviewer, as a press secretary, and as an educator, Cleage has emerged as both a regional and national force. After teaching for several years at Spelman College, Cleage only recently has enjoyed being able to support herself wholly from her writing.

Despite educational and career success, Cleage admits to initial feelings of inadequacy in her early adult years. Judging herself harshly for not being able to "handle all of the roles [she] was expected to play—wife, new mother, director of communications for the first black mayor of Atlanta"—she became "frantic, exhausted and depressed": "Also like most women, I had no idea that what I was experiencing was not individual disorganization, but part of a much bigger problem called *sexism*" (Interview 1996).

Cleage was twenty-five when she first became involved in feminism. Introduced "to a womanfriend" of one of her husband's colleagues, she and her "kindred spirit"—also a writer—quickly bonded. Ordering books, attending meetings, exchanging poetry, and talking for interminable hours, Cleage and her "womanfriend" delved into feminist readings in an effort to fathom their mutual dilemma, their ultimate goal to "understand, analyze and change [their] *lives*" (Interview 1996). Before long, the pair received invitations to appear at feminist bookstores to read and to discuss their works. Cleage's black nationalist and activist roots—specifically, her knowledge of racial oppression—always informed her readings and discussions of feminism.

Cleage describes the discovery of feminism as "one of the defining moments" of her life, for it facilitated her growth as a person and as a writer (Interview 1996). Her feelings, however, about the feminist movement are circumscribed by her perceptions of the "white American feminist movement":

I know many black feminists, but I don't think I can truthfully call us a *movement*. Although I respect white American feminism, I know that the movement will never achieve what it might unless it can first honestly confront the racism and classism of the middle class, well educated white women who tend to be the face of American feminism. (Interview 1996)

Though she has attended many functions in which women appear to be of "one mind about sexism," Cleage believes that feminists accomplish little when issues of racism and classism remain unresolved. Without confronting feminism's problems honestly—even painfully—she conjectures, "successful coalitions" cannot be constructed:

At this point I am a feminist. I describe myself as a feminist. I live as a feminist. I write as a feminist and I support feminist causes with time, writing and money. I no longer attend white feminist gatherings, however, believing that to be an unproductive use of my own time. I'm not hostile, just realistic. (Interview 1996)

Though recognizing divisions among its ranks, Cleage credits the feminist movement, as a whole, with opening doors in the publishing and theater industries for females (Cleage 1996). She believes that the movement brought into public awareness the issues that are foremost in women's minds. The fire of the feminist movement, she submits, ignited a national dialogue about sexism, domestic violence, birth control, and safe and legal abortions. Further, she ascribes to the movement the advances that have become "the bedrock of economic parity for women."

Pearl Cleage explores these and many other issues in her writing. Intent upon her own truth-telling, she engages in serious introspection and with equal thoughtfulness examines character in others, including the controversial Supreme Court justice Clarence Thomas, whose appointment she deems a "travesty to the legacy of Thurgood Marshall" ("Clarity on Clarence," *Deals* 1993, 73).

But to the surprise of some, Anita Hill equally comes under Cleage's fire: "I can't understand how Anita Hill became an African American Shero [female hero]," she quips (Cleage, "Anti-Shero," *Deals* 1993, 75). When all the world applauded Magic Johnson for going public that he was HIV positive, Cleage pointed to his sexist behavior, his denigrating his lovers as "floozies" (Cleage, "Fatal Floozies," *Deals* 1993, 83). Cleage's admirers include President Clinton, about whom her relatives jocularly tease her, calling him "her boy" (French 1993, n.p.).

Cleage explores violence against women in the African American community in her essay collection *Mad at Miles: A Black Woman's Guide to Truth*. Forcing her audience to peer into the ugly, darkened basements of sexism—to view the battered Cicely Tysons crouched and trembling in small corners of rooms— Cleage seems like a "ferrywoman" transporting passengers over a modern-day River Styx, replete with floating corpses and a violent stench. In *Mad at Miles*, Cleage assumes a persona—one almost of naïveté—as if unbelieving of the sights her pages just traversed: "How can they [black men] hit us," she ponders, "and still be our heroes?" (Cleage 1990, 21).

Musician Miles Davis proves a major point of interest in Cleage's exploration of African American male and female relationships. Employing a series of rhetorical questions to punctuate the recurring theme of abuse, Cleage examines the incongruities implicit in love relationships peppered by violence. Indicting Davis for beating up his then-wife Cicely Tyson and for bragging about this behavior afterward, Cleage reiterates a call for boycotting the man and his music as she expresses fear that he had put a hex on her:

I thought somehow he had found out that I was writing a piece suggesting that *he is guilty of self-confessed violent crimes against women such that we should break his albums, burn his tapes and scratch up his CD's until he acknowledges and apologizes and agrees to rethink his position on The Woman Question.* (Cleage 1990, 13)

In "Last Day of the Year," Cleage recounts a scene in which she, her daughter, and her friend Zeke rescue an African American female who is chased on the freeway by her "significant other." Bolting ahead of the crazed man, the young woman jumps from her car screaming, "He's got a gun! He's gonna shoot me! Help me! Somebody call the police! He's trying to kill me!" (Cleage 1990, 23). Zeke exits the car, placing himself between the man and his object, while Cleage and her daughter entice the victim into the safety of their vehicle. Choking and exhausted, the escapee collapses into the seat, into living, perhaps, another day. After depositing the frightened woman at her apartment, Cleage innocently wonders:

And how can they prey on us and save us, all at the same time?
And how can they possess us and abandon us all at the same time?

And how can we tell the villains from the heroes and the beaters from the leaders and the good guys from the bad guys?

By what they *do*, not what they *say*. (Cleage 1990, 26)

In both *Mad at Miles* and *Deals with the Devil and Other Reasons to Riot*, Cleage calls for unity among her "black sisters" and harmony among all races and genders. In "Out Here on Our Own," she embraces the idea of "disagreeable black women" congregating, raising their voices, and demanding change: "I'm tired of being invisible," she complains, "except when the crimes against us or our children are so heinous they make the front page" (Cleage *Deals* 1993, 54). In an effort to give black women a voice, to render them "visible," Cleage provides in "Basic Training: The Beginnings of Wisdom" some definitions from which "blackwomen" may operate: "Racist is to black people," she explains, "what *Sexist* is to women; The Enemy" (Cleage 1990, 42). "Basic Training" further characterizes black women as doubly burdened: not only must they deal with race as a factor of sexism, but also they must find "strategies" for fighting against "black men's primarily unenlightened responses to, examinations of, the question, especially those that include discussion of their own sexist behavior": "Racism adds a layer of anger and stress in our lives as black people that makes it even more difficult for us to take on the responsibility of fighting yet another deadly 'ism' " (Cleage 1990, 43).

Cleage finds black women's struggle against sexism "as part of a group that is also racially oppressed" analogous to "walking to work with bad feet": "you know you have to do it, but those bunions make the journey just that much harder" (Cleage 1990, 43).

Recognizing in "Why I Write: An Introduction" that the horrors of sexism are relegated neither to the office nor to the home, Cleage recounts her despair at the news of the 1989 Montreal massacre of female students, fourteen women murdered and thirteen others wounded (Cleage 1990, 3). This incident, she maintains, reinforced her activist commitment. Employing understatement in her description of the lone gunman as one "who apparently had a grudge against women," Cleage tells how the killer raged before his terrified victims, "You're all feminists!" (Cleage 1990, 3). Puzzled by the implausibility of this attack against women who may or may not have been feminists, Cleage admits succumbing to feelings of shock and speechlessness; initially, she felt unable even to console her daughter, who reacted with equal disbelief. As if experiencing an epiphany, Cleage realized suddenly that this incident is exactly why she writes—that she must raise her voice in protest: "So I said a prayer for my fallen sisters and for the five women who are murdered in America every day by their husbands or ex-husbands or boyfriends and tried to answer the questions as honestly as I could so I wouldn't forget it when there were no headlines or front page horror stories to remind me" (Cleage 1990, 4).

With equal fierceness, Cleage greets uncomfortable issues in her plays and poetry. She categorizes *Chain* and *Late Bus to Mecca* as her "morality plays"

(Cleage, *Chain* 1993, 265), for both intimate the values needed if black women are to survive in society.

Similarly, Cleage emphasizes values in her collection of vignettes and poems *The Brass Bed and Other Stories*, which celebrates female community and black sisterhood. Her *Flyin' West*, a play about black homesteaders in Kansas in 1898, blends serious feminist concerns with melodrama, balancing motifs of sexism, rape, wife-battering, miscegenation and racism, betrayal and murder. This play, particularly, demonstrates Cleage's philosophy of writing:

I am writing to expose and explore the point where racism and sexism meet. I am writing to help myself understand the full effects of being black and female in a culture that is both racist and sexist. I am writing to try and communicate that information to my sisters first and then to any brothers of good will and honest intent who will take the time to listen. (Cleage 1990, 4–5)

The plot of *Flyin' West* pivots around a primarily female cast whose efforts to establish, protect, and defend each other and their property withstand attacks not only from outside (whites encroaching upon their territory) but also from inside (one of their own men betrays them). The issue of woman's right to ownership, including ownership of her own body, repeatedly surfaces, and ultimately, the women—fierce competitors and survivors in a precarious world—prevail. Woman's inheritance, the stories and secrets handed down from within the female community, proves to be the salvation of the family and of the African American community:

MINNIE. Why won't you let Fannie write down your stories?

MISS LEAH. Everything can't be wrote down. No matter what Fannie tell you, some things gotta be said out loud to keep the life in 'em. (Cleage 1995, 40–41)

Blues for an Alabama Sky, set during the 1930s Harlem Renaissance, offers theatergoers yet another vision of black resilience. Unabashedly, Cleage introduces a slate of difficult issues: birth control and abortion, black flight and civil rights, homophobia, right-wing reactionaries, and feminism. The playwright breathes life into such historical personages as Adam Clayton Powell, Jr., Langston Hughes, and Josephine Baker.

"Embrac[ing] a tradition of black writing that combines aesthetic excellence and social activism," Cleage vows to continue "to struggle in all phases of [her] work" (Interview 1996). Her newest play, *Bourbon at the Border*, commissioned by the Alliance Theater, retains many of her previous themes. Because of Cleage's persistent, in-your-face approach to uncovering truth in a world that repeatedly denies culpability or responsibility, she has emerged as a compelling feminist voice that must be heard.

WORKS BY PEARL CLEAGE

We Don't Need No Music. Detroit: Broadside Press, 1972.
Banana Bread. Videotaped and premiered as part of local PBS series *Playhouse 30*. Atlanta, GA, 1985.
Hospice. New Plays for the Black Theatre. Ed. Woodie King, Jr. Chicago: Third World Press, 1989.
"In My Solitude." *Essence* (February 1989): 58+.
Mad at Miles: A Black Woman's Guide to Truth. Southfield, MI: Cleage Group, 1990.
The Brass Bed and Other Stories. Chicago: Third World Press, 1991.
Chain. Playwriting Women: Seven Plays from the Women's Project. Ed. Julia Miles. Portsmouth, NH: Heinemann, 1993, 263–296.
Deals with the Devil and Other Reasons to Riot. New York: Ballantine, 1993.
Late Bus to Mecca. Playwriting Women: Seven Plays from the Women's Project. Ed. Julia Miles. Portsmouth, NH: Heinemann, 1993, 297–322.
Flyin' West. New York: Dramatists Play Service, 1995.
"Interview with Linda Rohrer Paige," 1996.

WRITINGS ON PEARL CLEAGE AND HER WORK

"Cleage, Pearl Michelle." *Contemporary Authors*. Online. Galileo. August 9, 1996.
French, Mary Ann. "In the Chasm of Racism and Sexism; Pearl Cleage, Fighting Back with Nationalism and Feminism." *Washington Post*, July 29, 1993, final ed.: Cl. Online. Lexis/Nexis, NEWS Library; WPost File. December 11, 1996.
Rush, Theressa Gunnels, et al., eds. "Lomax, Pearl Cleage." *Black American Writers Past and Present: A Biographical and Bibliographical Dictionary*. Metuchen, NJ: Scarecrow Press, 1975.
Stearns, David Patrick. "Breezy 'Alabama Sky' Gets Lost in the Clouds." *USA Today*, May 28, 1996, final ed.: 8D. Online. Lexis/Nexis, NEWS Library; CURNWS File. December 31, 1996.

KATE CLINTON
(1945–)

Annmarie Pinarski

Comedian Kate Clinton begins her performances by politely thanking everyone in the audience for "coming out," a double entendre that immediately affirms the political and social contexts of her humor. Clinton herself has always been "out" as a lesbian and a feminist since she started performing stand-up comedy in 1981 in church basements, in women's bars and coffeehouses, and at women's music festivals. Her routines seamlessly blend punchy one-liners or "whyscracks" with longer, rambling personal anecdotes and free associations that engage subjects ranging from Catholicism, to national politics, to abortion, to her first "tampon-insertion experience." While Clinton has achieved widespread recognition with gay and lesbian audiences for the past decade, most recently she has moved into more "mainstream" venues, for example, appearing with other women comics on HBO's "Women Aloud" and providing cultural commentary on *Good Morning America/Sunday*, a network television program. Cautious about her "crossover" success, Clinton nonetheless maintains a sharp political focus in her act, targeting current events as well as issues particular to lesbian communities, thus never allowing her mainstream audiences to overlook her lesbian identity.

Clinton believes that "comedy is a great medium for social change. When people are laughing, they can hear things they'd otherwise be closed to" (Vann 1994, 44). Accordingly, Clinton theorizes that "there's a window of opportunity that opens when people are laughing. They let their guard down and new ideas can come in" (Warren 1995, 54). In this regard, Clinton brings together "feminism" and "humor" in her performances, a conjoining that she perceives as natural because, as she told Roz Warren, "women *are* funny, and we have been laughing together for survival for years" (Warren 1995, 54). As a self-proclaimed feminist humorist or "fumerist," Clinton addresses subjects that are of particular concern for women, finding humor especially in historically taboo topics such as menstruation. On the album *Making Light*, for instance, she recounts her experiences as a teenager who "struggled with those mattress pads" and furiously concealed the "2×2×4 foot boxes of Modess" purchased from the drugstore. In other routines incorporating menstrual humor, Clinton describes "pre-menstrual stress syndrome, the fear that I won't stop getting my period." Because they are rich with experiences interpreted from a feminist standpoint, Clinton's stand-up routines distinguish her from many other women comedians, such as Joan Rivers, whose acts often use women as targets of their humor.

Much of Clinton's material for her comedy, especially early in her career, is intensely personal. She draws from her experiences and satirizes many of the difficult stages of her life. For example, she speaks candidly about her status as a "recovering Catholic" who survived schooling at "Our Lady of Psychological Warfare," an environment where she learned to "experience guilt without sex." Moreover, she recalls the problems she encountered from her family and the medical establishment because she was "heavy" as a teenager. She reveals the painful ironies of living in a household where her football player brothers "were always *trying* to make weight" when she "had no difficulties in that area." Her parents relentlessly tried to police her body size and even gave her a "doctor's supervised diet" as a high school graduation gift. Her first visit to this doctor provides the setting for one of the routines recorded on the album *Kate Clinton Live at the Great American Music Hall*:

The first time I went in the guy could hardly talk to me. He weighs me in, he's very quiet . . . he gets his calipers out to check my body density. He can't even talk to me. . . . He finishes up and he *finally* talks to me. He said to me "what do you want to be when you grow up?" And I said, "a teacher." Of course, I now know I should have said thin. And then he said to me "well, how do you expect to discipline your students when you can't even discipline yourself?"

As the audience hisses in disgust at the doctor's response, Clinton delivers her punch line: "I'll sit on them." This reply turns the tables on the oppressive social forces that attempt to regulate all women's bodies, transforming an otherwise hurtful, individual memory into a moment of collective empowerment. In this regard, Clinton's storytelling gives rise to sympathetic laughter from her primarily all-female audience.

While supportive of all women, Clinton's humor specifically affirms lesbian cultures and sexualities as her performances smoothly blend gender-specific and lesbian-focused materials. For instance, after admitting that she still holds "crazy ideas about food" because of her adolescent experiences with doctors and dieting, Clinton concludes, with much pleasure, that since "coming out, I noticed a real change in my attitude toward food and eating." Attributing this change to the supportive environment of the lesbian community, Clinton shares anecdotes about the role that food plays in her lesbian relationships, a focus that resonates clearly with her lesbian feminist audiences. She reveals: "I love to cook and I love women who love to cook. I love to talk about food with other women while we are eating." These confessions indicate a shift in her personal "attitude" toward food as well as a positive resignification of the meanings that women conventionally associate with food. In this particular routine, Clinton then follows these celebratory remarks with another shift in focus when she presents her "guaranteed weight loss program, the Kate Clinton non-monogamy and weight loss diet." This sardonic title makes reference to a specific and controversial subject within lesbian communities, the role of monogamy and commitment in relationships. The tentative laughter that this reference generates makes sense for an audience that understands the history of debates about "acceptable" lesbian sexual behaviors. While the connotations about monogamy in this context are stereotypical, suggesting a one-dimensional model of lesbian relationships, the humor that results is perhaps inaccessible to outsiders and thus instrumental in creating a feeling of camaraderie between Clinton and her audiences, encouraging what Linda Pershing calls "group cohesion" and a "means for socialization" (Pershing 1991, 219). In this way, Clinton's performances actively construct a sense of solidarity for her lesbian and feminist audience members based on shared ideological assumptions and common experiences.

The history of Clinton as a performer helps explain her widespread recognition and success with lesbian and feminist audiences. Clinton acknowledges that she "was very much in the lesbian community" when she first came out, supported by the women's alternative music scene and a network of feminist coffeehouses and performance spaces that emerged in conjunction with the contemporary women's movement, the ideology of consciousness-raising, and post-Stonewall gay and lesbian activism (Breslauer 1993, 76). Indeed, the 1970s witnessed a proliferation of lesbian culture that helped to crystallize modern lesbian identity by providing what Jeffrey Escoffier refers to as the "cultural reinforcements" upon which identity politics thrives (Escoffier 1996, 170). Urvashi Vaid attributes the consolidation of a politicized lesbian identity in the wake of Stonewall to the growth of specific lesbian cultural products, especially women's music, Olivia Records, and the national system of women's music festivals (Vaid 1995, 64–65). Other cultural reinforcements include such phenomena as the " 'coming out novel' as a genre, the use of gay and lesbian consumer goods, residence in gay and lesbian neighborhoods, [and] participation in gay and lesbian choirs," to name a few (Escoffier 1996, 170). These cultural productions in tandem with the development of gay and lesbian businesses in urban areas reflected and created a desire in audiences and consumers for positive lesbian images. The still-prevalent desire for lesbian visibility set the stage for new and additional cultural forms in the 1980s and thus contributed to the success of lesbian comics, including Clinton, Lea Delaria, and Suzanne Westenhoffer.

The content of Clinton's routines typifies the interests and desires of mainstream gay and lesbian communities as she mixes jokes about insider gay and lesbian matters with opinions and quips on popular culture and politics. In her one-woman off-Broadway show *Out Is In*, Clinton touches on current events such as President Clinton's ineffectual "don't ask, don't tell" stance on gays and lesbians in the military as well as a network television interview with Candace Gingrich, the lesbian sister of Newt Gingrich, speaker of the U.S. House of Representatives. On the 1991 album *Babes in Joyland,* recorded live in Boston, Clinton opens her performance by discussing "outing," first clarifying its definition for "the two of you who don't know" and then suggesting its futility for producing new knowledge for gay and lesbian audiences in particular: "The tabloids, they dragged Richard Chamberlain out of the closet—but how hard was that?" The joke here assumes that gay and lesbian audience members will recognize the irony of this last statement based on their "insider" status and, concurrently, their perceived ability to identify other gays and lesbians before this knowledge enters the public realm. This type of humor aims to naturalize gay and lesbian experiences and further strengthen the sense of shared identity that audience members may desire, especially when faced with antigay and lesbian propaganda and legislation in the dominant culture. So, when Clinton announces that her favorite sign at a Washington peace rally read "Read *these* lips," the meaning of this irreverent double entendre clarifies Clinton's goal—"to amuse lesbians" (Warren 1995, 53).

Clinton unapologetically celebrates gay and lesbian life, analyzing a spectrum of events in her routines like the Gay Games, the annual pride parades, and gay and lesbian participation in national peace marches. Another common topic for Clinton and other lesbian comedians is the process of coming out, an occasion ideal for Clinton to indulge in her trademark storytelling. Yet, she tempers her excitement for the joys of lesbian life, conceding that despite her mainstream breakthroughs, "it's hard to be a lesbian comedian these days." Perhaps because of highly visible local and national campaigns against gay and lesbian civil rights, most notably, those efforts spawned by the religious Right, Clinton deliberately shifted the focus of her performances in the late 1980s. She explains that "with Reagan and the atomization of the women's movement, my work changed so that it was not so much about the lesbian community but about being a lesbian in the world" (Breslauer 1993, 76). Indeed, her sarcasm surfaces when she points out that she "started to perform comedy the same year as the master of the one-liner, President Reagan." Lesbian-specific references remain integral to her work, but her performances in the 1990s indicate a melding of the personal and the political that purposefully situates her references to lesbian culture within a national context. In this regard, sharp political messages replace the succession of bawdy lesbian in-jokes—such as "she wouldn't know a lesbian if her mouth was full of one"—that constituted her early routines. Another excerpt from *Babes in Joyland* that comments on lesbian visibility in the media illustrates this new strategy: "The only way people know about lesbians is through talk shows. . . . Remember on the Oprah Winifrey show when they had the show about lesbian separatists? I can make fun of them because they're my people. . . . Now, when women go off by themselves they call it separatism, but when men go off by themselves they call it Congress." One of her most frequently cited jokes further exemplifies the conjoining of sexuality, identity politics, and governmental issues:

"People ask me all the time, 'Is [Attorney General] Janet Reno a lesbian? Well, I don't know, but her hair is.'"

Clinton confirms that "in every context, I do a lot more political material. I'm still very clear that I'm a lesbian, but I'm not talking about my softball team anymore" (Kuehl 1993, 75). The theme that Clinton consistently reiterates is the significance of gay and lesbian visibility as a vehicle for social change, a thesis that reinforces her status as a "political comic." She remarks in her shows: "I think the more we say gay and lesbian the more the rest of the world *has* to. Absolutely. They'll get over it." Her mainstream recognition seems to suggest that audiences have "gotten over it," even while segments of the broader public continue to voice homophobia and battle against gay and lesbian civil rights. To this extent, rather than signifying complete tolerance and acceptance for gays and lesbians, Clinton's mainstream breakthroughs, as well as the wave of popular culture attention to lesbianism exemplified in "lesbian chic," underscore the pervasive tensions that exist among competing ideologies and political communities within a national context. Despite these admonitions, critics from the mainstream press have enthusiastically received Clinton's brand of humor, an achievement that also signifies the changing character of stand-up comedy itself.

Breslauer writes that stand-up comedy "has long been considered a hotbed of homophobia and misogyny, symbolized by such figures as Andrew Dice Clay" (Breslauer 1993, 5). The exclusion of women from comedy in general has been supported by traditional female standards for behavior and an entrenched cultural resistance to women's laughter and agency. Furthermore, as Nancy Walker notes, feminists in particular have been portrayed as lacking a sense of humor, an image that spans history and includes "the temperance crusader taking an ax to the whiskey barrel, the thin-lipped women's rights speaker of the nineteenth century, and the bra-burners of the 1960s" (Walker 1988, 139). Within this context, feminist humor seems impossible to imagine, but Clinton describes the genre as emerging from the limitations of its own history: "Feminist humor is active, based as it is on the possibility of change. . . . Feminist humor is not escapist. It is transformational. It transforms painful expression, and in transforming, it transcends [pain]. . . . it is good practice, an antidote against absurdity" (quoted in Pershing 1991, 223).

For Clinton, her mainstream success as a lesbian feminist comedian perhaps marks a convergence of numerous changes in the attitudes of the dominant culture about gender expectations, gay and lesbian sexuality, and the nature of comedy itself.

The impulse for Clinton to continue her work is clear, for she has professed an unwavering belief in the "power of words" to provoke and delight. She sometimes concludes her performances with speculations on the function of laughter for women: "When women are laughing together, it's like women coming together. You make sounds you wouldn't ordinarily make. You gasp for air. You rock back and forth and there's soft moaning afterward. And, if you're lucky, your face hurts." The connection between sex and laughter moderates the controversial subject matter that Clinton addresses while not diminishing her indisputable feminist messages. Though mainstream critics are inclined to describe Clinton's performances as tame, palatable, and friendly to all (most notably, heterosexuals), her work maintains a political edge and an unwavering affiliation with feminist politics. To Richard Stayton of the *Los Angeles Times* Clinton may be "the lesbian you want to take home to meet your parents," but for a generation of lesbian and feminist women, she continues to challenge sexism and homophobia without compromise.

WORKS BY KATE CLINTON

Making Light. Whyscrack Records, 1982.
Kate Clinton Live at the Great American Music Hall. Whyscrack Records, 1985.
Babes in Joyland. Whyscrack Records, 1991.

WRITINGS ON KATE CLINTON AND HER WORK

Breslauer, Jan. "Heard the One about Lesbian Comics?" *Los Angeles Times/Calendar*, July 18, 1993, 5, 76–77.
Escoffier, Jeffrey. "Culture Wars and Identity Politics: The Religious Right and the Cultural Politics of Homosexuality." *Radical Democracy: Identity, Citizenship, and the State.* Ed. David Trend. New York: Routledge, 1996, 165–178.
Johnson, Allan. "Truth in Labeling: The Comic Aspects of Kate Clinton." *Chicago Tribune*, April 21, 1995, sec. 7, 23.
Kuehl, Sheila James. "A Clinton without Compromise." *Advocate: The National Gay and Lesbian Newsmagazine* (November 16, 1993): 73–79.
Obejas, Achy. "This Clinton Mines Humor from Politics." *Chicago Tribune*, April 24, 1995, sec. 1, 14.
Pershing, Linda. "There's a Joker in the Menstrual Hut: A Performance Analysis of Comedian Kate Clinton." *Women's Comic Visions.* Ed. June Sochen. Detroit: Wayne State University Press, 1991, 193–236.
Stayton, Richard. "Kate Clinton's Adult Ed Class on Gay Politics." *Los Angeles Times*, July 23, 1993, 30F.
Vaid, Urvashi. *Virtual Equality: The Mainstreaming of Gay and Lesbian Liberation.* New York: Doubleday, 1995.
Vann, Korky. "Funny Girl." *10 Percent* (July/August 1994): 42–45.
Walker, Nancy. *A Very Serious Thing: Women's Humor and American Culture.* Minneapolis: University of Minnesota Press, 1988.
Warren, Roz. "Kate Clinton." *Revolutionary Laughter: The World of Women Comics.* Ed. Roz Warren. Freedom, CA: Crossing Press, 1995, 51–59.

MARY DALY
(1928–)

Margaret R. LaWare

According to Mary Daly's autobiographical writings, the beginning of her journey toward becoming a radical feminist philosopher might well be traced to her pre-birth experiences of "choosing" to come into this world as a woman. An only child, Daly grew up in a Catholic, working-class environment in Schenectady, New York. Her parents, Frank and Anna, were both of Irish descent. Despite economic struggles—her father worked on commission as a traveling salesman selling ice cream freezers—Daly received significant validation and support at home. She credits her mother, who "passionately loved learning" but had to drop out of school to work, with "unfailingly" encouraging her to develop her intellectual interests.

Daly attended Catholic educational institutions from elementary grades through her three doctorates. As a young girl, she loved books and, in high school, wrote essays and poetry. Her educational aspirations emerged from a keen interest in Catholic philosophy. Daly refers to her determination to become a philosopher as her "Taboo-breaking Quest." After graduating from high school, Daly attended a Catholic women's college close to home, the College of St. Rose in Albany, New York.

Within the all-female environment of the College of St. Rose, Daly became aware of what she refers to as the "Hidden Broken Promise," the pervasive lack of encouragement for women to reach beyond traditionally prescribed roles. She soon discovered that while students had to minor in philosophy, they could not pursue philosophy as a major because it was considered an inappropriate area of study for young women.

Upon graduation, Daly applied to graduate school at Catholic University of America in Washington, D.C., which offered her a full-tuition scholarship. Daly was forced to matriculate into the literature master's program since the university would not allow graduate students to pursue a graduate degree in a subject outside their college major. She came as close as she could to philosophy by focusing on literary theory in her thesis and taking elective classes in philosophy. Daly received her master's degree in 1952.

Sometime before receiving her master's, while sitting in a class, Daly had a vision of herself in front of the class teaching theology. This vision surprised her, because at that time, in the early 1950s, it was "unheard of" for women to teach Catholic theology or even study it seriously. Shortly after her "vision," Daly stumbled upon an advertisement in a liberal Catholic magazine for the School of Sacred Theology, which offered a Ph.D. in religion for women at St. Mary's College in Notre Dame, Indiana. She wrote to the president of the college and was accepted into the program.

Daly received her doctorate in religion from St. Mary's College in 1954, at the age of twenty-five. After finishing her Ph.D., she applied to the University of Notre Dame to study for a second doctorate in philosophy but was turned down because of her gender. Disappointed, Daly applied for teaching jobs and found a job at a two-year college in Brookline, Massachusetts, teaching theology and philosophy. In Boston, Daly continued her study of philosophy at Boston College and in summer programs.

In the mid-1950s, when Daly started her teaching career in Boston, the women's movement had not yet begun. However, Daly discovered Simone de Beauvoir's *Second Sex*, which gave her an understanding of the oppressive social environment that she found undermined her self-esteem and eroded her determination to write a book.

Unhappy intellectually with her work at the two-year college, Daly sought a "better" doctorate. She applied to the Catholic University of America again, to study for "the highest of the higher degrees in theology" but, after a delayed reply, was turned down. Her alternatives were universities in Europe, in Germany and Switzerland in particular, where government regulations prevented discrimination against women applicants. In 1959, Daly was accepted into the Faculty of Theology at the University of Fribourg. At the end of her fourth year, in the summer of 1963, Daly became the first woman to receive her doctorate in sacred theology at Fribourg, passing the final exams summa cum laude.

Still determined to realize her dream of studying Catholic philosophy, Daly enrolled in the faculty of philosophy at Fribourg and wrote a dissertation in that field, completing her degree in 1965. During that time, she traveled to Greece, which she found to be a particularly powerful experience, especially her visit to Crete and the Palace of Knossos, which she says greatly influenced her writing of *Gyn/Ecology*.

Daly's feminist voice emerged in her response to an article that appeared in the Catholic publication *Commonweal* in December 1963. The article, written by Rosemary Lauer, a professor of philosophy at St. John's University in New York, argued for the equality of women in the Catholic Church. For Daly, the article "awakened in me the power to speak out and to Name women's oppression . . . it awakened my sleeping Powers of Be-speaking" (Daly 1992, 77). Daly wrote a response to Lauer's article in which she announced that she was "ashamed" that she had not published the article. In her response, she predicted a coming flood of future articles and books dealing with this issue. In 1965, Daly was contacted by a London publisher who invited Daly to write a book on women and the church.

In 1966, Daly reluctantly returned to the United States after accepting a position as an assistant professor in the Theology Department at the Jesuit-run Boston College. In 1968, her first book, *The Church and the Second Sex*, was published in the United States (after an initial printing in England) and received significant publicity. As one reviewer points out, "*The Church and the Second Sex* was a ground breaking event for American Catholic feminists" (Weaver 1985, 112). Shortly after the book's appearance, Boston College gave Daly a terminal contract. Students at the college protested the administration's decision. Consequently, the administration, embarrassed by the national and international publicity their move and the student protested received, granted Daly tenure and promotion. Daly continues to teach at Boston College, despite the college's lack of enthusiasm for, and recognition of, her feminist scholarship. She has put in her application for promotion to full professorship twice, in 1975 and during the 1988–1989 academic year. Boston College turned down her application both times despite her prodigious publication record and letters of support from colleagues around the world. In addition to teaching, Daly travels around the world to speak about her work. The working title of her next book is "Quintessence: Re-Calling the Outrageous, Contagious Courage of Women."

Not only have Daly's writings contributed a critical understanding of the distortions inherent in religious doctrines and other patriarchal discourses, but, most importantly, they have also provided a new vocabulary to imagine a world beyond patriarchy, a world made manifest by the realization of a radical feminist sisterhood. The importance of creating a new vocabulary to critique patriarchy becomes apparent in Daly's assertion that women (crones) "have inherited a contaminated language" (Daly 1978, 368). A reviewer of Daly's last theoretical work, *Pure Lust*, argued that "what Daly does with and to language stands as the boldest experiment yet in creating a new language of and for women" (Johnson 1986, 328). Daly's intellectual contributions to the feminist movement focus in particular on the use of language to generate a feminist consciousness that breaks away from the symbolic confines of patriarchal discourse. From an analytical perspective, Daly's writings have been used to create a more comprehensive theoretical framework for understanding the complexity and richness of women's private and public communication (Griffen 1993; Gill 1994).

After the publication of her first book, *The Church and the Second Sex*, which argued for women to be given an equal standing in the church, Daly's writings turned toward a rejection of patriarchal religions, of Catholicism. Yet, as Mary-Jo Weaver writes, Daly "cannot entirely relinquish her Catholic heritage" (Weaver 1985, 112). Even in her most recent theoretical book, *Pure Lust* (1984), Daly "undertakes to re-define some traditional Catholic doctrines—the Immaculate Conception, for example" (Weaver 1985, 112). As a scholar trained in theology,

Daly understands the writings of Catholic theology as "a treasure chest containing archaic gems" (Daly 1996, 78). Daly argues that patriarchal cultures and religions have systematically attempted to extinguish the divine spark within women. For Daly, this divine spark enables what she refers to as "Be-ing," the power of self-realization. To rekindle the divine spark, Daly turns to religious texts and archaic meanings of words to recover the occluded background of religious and intellectual discourse where she locates the "Elemental" powers of women. In the background she locates memories of the female divinity eclipsed by the masculine image of the divine.

In *Beyond God the Father*, Daly begins her journeying toward developing a feminist language that breaks free of the semantic bonds of patriarchy. Her quest begins with the declaration that "women have had the power of naming stolen from us" (Daly 1973, 8). She replaces the patriarchal church with "sisterhood as cosmic covenant," a concept that she explains involves a process of "beginning to rename the cosmos" (Daly 1973, 159). Realizing a space for "sisterhood as cosmic covenant" requires transforming the idea of the divine from a static noun into a verb, to Be-ing. She therefore reinterprets the "Second Coming" to mean the "new arrival of female presence" (Daly 1973, 97). As the notion of the divine becomes a verb, so, too, the space of the cosmic covenant of sisterhood cannot be fixed and reified but becomes a moving space that, as Daly explains, "will not be merely unorthodox or reformist, but will be on its way beyond unorthodoxy as well as orthodoxy, discovering and bringing forth the really new" (Daly 1973, 158). In this book, Daly also argues for "psychic androgyny" to overcome false dichotomies and hierarchies, but she rejects and moves beyond the idea of androgyny in her later writings as she concentrates on the recovery of women's unique powers of self-realization.

In *Gyn/Ecology* (1978) Daly continues to reconstitute the "Background," recovering the "stolen mythic power" held by women by exposing the "lies" of the patriarchal foreground. In exposing the lies of the foreground, her carefully honed critical and analytical powers sweep across cultural practices beyond the Judeo-Christian West. Daly writes, "Patriarchy is itself the religion of the entire planet, and its essential message is necrophilia" (Daly 1978, 39). Here she concentrates on describing the "sado-society" and the "sado-rituals" aimed at destroying women's spirits and stopping "the Journey of women finding our Selves—a Journey which is questing and be-ing" (Daly 1978, 131). As she explains, "sadomasochism is the style and basic content of patriarchy's structures, including those antecedent to and outside christianity" (Daly 1978, 96). The sado-rituals she exposes include Indian suttee, Chinese foot-binding, African genital mutilation, European witch burnings, and American gynecological practices (which she compares to Nazi medicine). She explains how these sado rituals respond to the patriarchal myth that all women are impure and must be purified.

In the second half of *Gyn/Ecology*, Daly stresses the necessity of a separate feminist space where women's powers might be allowed to grow. Daly's descriptions of the "sado-rituals" are intended to instill a "positive paranoia" in women. The feminist movement she seeks involves the burning away of "false selves" constructed by the "contaminated language" of patriarchy and the reweaving of true selves. She urges "Crone-ographers, Hags, Spinsters, Amazons" to participate in the spinning and weaving of a space beyond patriarchy, a female-identified space that allows women to explore "our otherness, our wildness, our strangeness" (Daly 1978, 383). This space celebrates, rather than obliterates women's diversity. Daly's journey toward the "promised land" of radical sisterhood involves, therefore, a twofold process. The first step involves unknotting the "mindbinds" by applying the labrys, the double-edged ax of a critical feminist consciousness, to cut through the misogynistic meanings of the foreground and sail through the "labyrinth of patriarchy" into the background like a spider carried backward by the wind. The second step requires the radical feminist act of reweaving and restoring the semantic connections that have been broken by the rigid structures of patriarchy, especially women's connections to each other.

While Daly suggests that the voyage into the background and the restoration of woman's power will enable women to reconnect their unique webs of Be-ing to each other, her willingness to expose the varied and destructive manifestations of patriarchy cross-culturally without also providing a cross-cultural discussion of the symbols of women's power hidden in the "background" of these cultures allows Daly's radical feminist space to be interpreted as an exclusionary space. Audre Lorde, in a letter written to Daly after reading *Gyn/Ecology*, suggests that Daly has fallen prey to the assumption that "the herstory and myth of white women is the legitimate and sole herstory and myth of all women to call upon for power and background, and that nonwhite women and our herstories are noteworthy only as decorations, or examples of female victimization" (Lorde 1984, 69). Lorde urges Daly to "re-member what is dark and ancient and divine within yourself that aids your speaking" (Lorde 1984, 69). Lorde makes it clear that in order for Daly to realize a radical sisterhood that truly celebrates and embraces difference and diversity, she and, by implication, the feminist movement must confront her own and the movement's racism.

Mary Daly did not immediately respond to Audre Lorde upon receiving her letter, and, consequently, Lorde made the letter an "Open Letter to Mary Daly," publishing it in collections of her work. In her autobiography, Daly explains that she did, in fact, speak to Lorde several months after receiving the letter. Daly believes her book is an "Open Book" that invites critical reading and reflection. Further, she writes, "I regret any pain that unintended omissions may have caused others, particularly women of color" (Daly 1992, 233).

In *Pure Lust* (1984), Daly continues this process of critically dismantling the distorted myths of patriarchy in order to reclaim an intellectual space where women can realize their true selves. Her initial discussion of the "double-sided" meaning of lust sets the process in motion. She begins by contrasting the "necrophilic" tendencies of patriarchy, which constructs lust as "the life-hating lechery that rapes and kills the objects of its obsession/aggression," with the biophilic powers of women who experience lust as "pure Passion: unadulterated, absolute, simple sheer striving for abundance of be-ing" (Daly 1984, 2–3).

Pure Lust is divided into three sections: "Archespheres," "Pyrospheres," and "Metamorphospheres." In each section Daly carries on the twofold process introduced in *Gyn-Ecology*, first discussing the patriarchal foreground, which must be understood and overcome in order to reach the realm where women can restore their connection to "our Original, Elemental Race" and revive "Elemental Wisdom." In "Archespheres," Daly inverts the archetypes of patriarchy. Thus, archetypes become "Arch-Images" that enable women to remember images of the goddess and engage in a process of "Realizing" their own inherent spiritual powers. In "Pyrospheres," Daly recognizes that the realization of a feminist philosophy is connected to the rekindling of the passions, the rediscovery of fire. For Daly, the intellectual and psychological separation from patriarchy requires "the force of righteous Fury, unleashed Rage," rather than the stultifying "potted passions" and "pseudovirtues" attributed to women. Finally, Daly seeks transcendence through a process of metamorphosis, as she discusses in the chapter "Metamorphospheres." The metamorphosis requires "metapatriarchal abstract thought," the creation of a new code that supports radical feminist consciousness, feminist sisterhood, and Be-ing.

In *Pure Lust*, Daly uses her feminist language to achieve her goal of recovering the background, the space of feminist consciousness and spirituality. Her challenging transformations of language can make this book a difficult journey for the uninitiated reader. But for Daly, language is clearly the key for unknotting and dismantling the "sado-society," since metapatriarchal thought requires a language free from patriarchal codes.

Daly provides a compilation of her feminist language in *Webster's First New Intergalactic Wickedary of the English Language*, written "in cahoots" with Jane Caputi. The feminist lexicon of the *Wickedary* consists of three "world-webs." The first world-web gathers together "Elemental Philosophical Words and Phrases and Other Key Words," such as Be-ing, biocide, female castration, Biophilic Bonding, sadospirituality, Sisterhood, and Weaving. The second world-web, titled "The Inhabitants of the Background, Their Activities and Characteristics," provides a semantic journey into the space of women's elemental powers through words such as Nag-Gnostic (as in, Mary Daly is a Nag-Gnostic philosopher), Dragon Eyes, Crone-Power, Moon-Wise, and Pro-Lifer ("one who puts her Life on the line in the struggle against necro-apocalyptic nobodies who are running/ruining the world"). The third world-web provides a lexicon of terms associated with "The Inhabitants of the Foreground, Their Activities and Characteristics," including abominable snowmen of androcratic academe, boreocracy, fembot, media potters/plotters, token torturers, and verbicide.

Daly emphasizes the importance of spelling, capitalization, and punctuation in the first part of *Webster's*. In order to break the spell of the patriarchal code, she argues, the spelling of words must be transformed along with their pronunciation, since spells must be pronounced to be potent. Further, she uses capitalization (e.g., Realizing) and hyphenation (e.g., be-ing) as a means to call attention to particular words, to indicate their transformation, their liberation from patriarchal contexts, and to enable women to hear the powers these words call forth.

Daly discusses her own sensitivity to hearing and seeing glimmers of the background in her autobiographical *Outercourse: The Be-Dazzling Voyage*. Daly's intimations of the background are accorded to feelings and experiences that came before her association with the feminist movement. She recounts sensing the presence of the goddess in her travels through Europe. She also recalls moments of self-realization through vision and intuition, such as her dream of "Elemental Be-Dazzling Green," the dream she associates with her desire to become a philosopher. The *Outercourse* conveys a sense of Mary Daly's resilience, determination, and her wickedly daring, elemental sense of humor that "Be-laughs" in the face of patriarchy and cements the bonds of radical sisterhood.

WORKS BY MARY DALY

Beyond God the Father: Toward a Philosophy of Women's Liberation. Boston: Beacon Press, 1973.
The Church and the Second Sex (With a New Feminist Postchristian Introduction by the Author). New York: Harper Colophon Books, (1968) 1975.
Gyn/Ecology: The Metaethics of Radical Feminism. Boston: Beacon Press, 1978.
Pure Lust: Elemental Feminist Philosophy. Boston: Beacon Press, 1984.
With Jane Caputi. *Webster's First New Intergalactic Wickedary of the English Language*. Boston: Beacon Press, 1987.
Outercourse: The Be-Dazzling Voyage. San Francisco: HarperSanFrancisco, 1992.
"Sin Big." *The New Yorker* (February 26, March 4, 1996): 76, 78, 80–81.
Quintessence: Realizing the Archaic Future. Boston: Beacon Press, 1998.

WRITINGS ON MARY DALY AND HER WORK

Gill, Ann. *Rhetoric and Human Understanding*. Prospect Heights, IL: Waveland Press, 1994.
Griffen, Cindy L. "Women as Communicators: Mary Daly's Hagiography as Rhetoric." *Communication Monographs* 60 (1993): 158–177.
Johnson, Fern L. "Coming to Terms with Women's Language." *The Quarterly Journal of Speech* 72 (1986): 318–329.
Lorde, Audre. "An Open Letter to Mary Daly." *Sister Outsider*. Trumansburg, NY: Crossing Press, 1984.
Weaver, Mary Jo. "Daly, Daly, Sing to Mary." Rev. of *Pure Lust: Elemental Feminist Philosophy* by Mary Daly. *Cross Currents* 35 (Spring 1985): 111–115.

ANGELA DAVIS
(1944-)

Jennifer Oldham

Considered one of the founders of black feminist theory, Angela Davis' call for inclusiveness in the modern woman's rights movement is akin to the great nineteenth-century orator Sojourner Truth's call to white feminists to take notice of the class and race bias that infested their burgeoning suffrage activities. In much of her groundbreaking work Davis discusses black women's experiences during slavery and the historical interrelationships between sexism, racism, and classism. Ironically, Davis often finds herself trying to escape the shadow of her own history. Perhaps best remembered as a 1970s revolutionary who was falsely accused of murder, Davis has spent decades trying to debunk myths surrounding black women and to raise the world's consciousness about oppressed peoples.

As a black woman who came of age in the pre-civil-rights-era South, Davis was no stranger to racism. Born in 1944 in Birmingham, Alabama, she moved at age four to a middle-class neighborhood nicknamed Dynamite Hill for explosions set by whites who disapproved of blacks' disrupting their segregated community. Her mother, Sallye, was an elementary school teacher, and her father, B. Frank, was a service station owner. Davis and her three siblings were restricted to "colored" movie theaters, restaurants, drinking fountains, and rest rooms.

A shy, bright child, Davis had strong female role models. Her mother studied for her master's degree in education at New York University during the summers and had been involved in antiracist activities and the campaign to free nine young men implicated in the Scottsboro rape case. Her grandmother, who died when she was twelve, was one of thirteen children. The daughter of slaves, she urged Davis not to forget how slavery affected blacks.

Eager to escape what was termed by some as the "Johannesburg of the South" (Davis 1989, 98), Davis traveled at fifteen to New York City to attend Elisabeth Irwin High School. There she discovered socialism, a theory that allowed her to see "the problems of Black people within the context of a large working class movement" (Davis 1974, 110). Oppressed groups would truly be free, Davis con-cluded, once they were released from the grip of a profit-mongering capitalist society.

Throughout her education, Davis struggled with her growing geographical iso-lation from the burgeoning civil rights movement in the South. In 1961 she entered Brandeis University on scholarship and majored in French literature. But even when she traveled overseas to study in France, Davis could not escape the racism that racked her hometown. In 1963, she learned four of her childhood friends had been killed when an explosion ripped through a Birmingham church.

Determined to avenge her friends, Davis returned to Brandeis in search of a political philosophy that could provide a framework for black liberation. In that search she met her mentor, philosopher Herbert Marcuse, in 1964. Marcuse's enthusiasm for philosophy infused Davis, who graduated from Brandeis magna cum laude in 1965 and flew to Germany to attend graduate school at the Uni-versity of Frankfurt.

Unable to stay overseas while Watts, Los Angeles, burned at home, Davis traveled in 1967 to San Diego to finish her master's degree in philosophy under Marcuse at the University of California. In search of a political connection, Davis joined the Student Nonviolent Coordinating Committee and the Black Pan-thers. In 1968 she joined the Communist Party. Davis writes in her autobiography of the pervasive sexism she encountered in these movements: "In organizing for this rally back in San Diego, I ran headlong into a situation which was to become a constant problem in my political life. I was criticized very heavily, especially by male members of [Ron] Karenga's organization, for doing a 'man's job.' Women should not play leadership roles, they insisted" (Davis 1974, 161).

Davis decided to split her time between finishing her doctorate and teaching when she accepted a position as an assistant professor of philosophy at the Uni-versity of California, Los Angeles, in 1969. When word leaked out that she was a communist, California governor Ronald Reagan and the Board of Regents fired her. Davis taught for a year while her dismissal was appealed. It was ultimately upheld by the U.S. Supreme Court. As she was fighting to retain her job, Davis spearheaded a nationwide effort to free three men, known as the Soledad Broth-ers, who had been falsely accused of killing a Soledad Prison guard. One of the men, George Jackson, and Davis struck up a long-distance relationship that pro-foundly influenced the course of her work.

In August 1970, Jackson's brother Jonathan Jackson, using guns registered in Davis' name, burst into a courtroom at the Marin County Courthouse and took the judge and several others hostage. As they entered a van in the parking lot, it was engulfed in a hail of gunfire, killing Jackson, the judge, and two prisoners and leaving a juror and the district attorney wounded. Police quickly traced the firearms to Davis, who went into hiding. During the time she was underground, Davis was placed on the Federal Bureau of Investigation's (FBI) Ten Most Wanted List, bringing her instant celebrity. She was arrested two months later in New York and charged with murder, kidnapping, and conspiracy. In the New York Women's House of Detention she began seventeen intellectually productive months in jail.

Davis corresponded with George Jackson from jail, and her efforts to challenge some of his theories about black women—that they were domineering matriarchs and castrating females—became the basis for her seminal research on the role of black women in slavery and how these experiences impact black women in the twentieth century. Although Davis did not consider herself a feminist until the mid-1980s, the theories she formulated in jail and later expanded upon in books and speeches are considered among the founding principles of contemporary black feminist studies.

Indeed, although the women's movement in the late 1960s was sparked, in part, by black women, Davis said that she and other women of color, many of whom were busy furthering the black liberation movement, didn't feel connected to white women, who dominated the early "women's circles." As a result, they chose not to participate in the women's movement or to identify as feminists.

In December 1970, Davis was extradited from New York to the Marin County Jail in San Rafael, California, where she set to work compiling and editing an anthology with Bettina Aptheker, a high school classmate. Published in 1971, *If They Come in the Morning: Voices of Resistance* documents several political prisoners' cases and discusses how they were victimized by a racist judicial system. Shortly thereafter, Davis, a concise writer with a powerful voice, published an article in the *Black Scholar* that became the bedrock for her future work. In the piece, titled "Reflections on the Black Women's Role in the Community of Slaves," Davis laments: "The paucity of literature on the Black woman is outrageous on its face" (Davis 1971, 3).

Paradoxically, this article's strengths are also considered its weaknesses. The piece presents "a model that can be expanded to other historical periods," but care must be taken not to "take the particular historical reality which she illuminated and read it into the present as if the experiences of Black women followed some sort of linear progression out of slavery" (Moses and Hartmann 1995, 28, 283). Davis sums up the piece with what became her lifelong quest: to draw attention to the relationship between women's oppression and the oppression of other peoples. She emphasized this relationship in speeches and writings, such as a 1975 Ms. article in which she wrote: "The oppression of women is a vital and integral component of a larger network of oppression which claims as its foremost victims Black people, Chicanos, Puerto Ricans, Asians, Indians and all poor and working class people" (Davis 1975, 107).

Meanwhile, a committee formed to free Davis had plastered its "Free Angela" slogan on billboards, in newspapers, and on posters all over the world. Soon most Americans could identify the six-foot-tall, light-skinned Davis with her trademark Afro. This image was to dog her over the coming decades, when many would simply refer to her as "the Afro." Her frustration with this trend peaked in 1994, when she wrote a piece for *Critical Inquiry* in which she detailed her reaction to calls from reporters for interviews "about the resurgence of the Afro." She writes: "It is humiliating because it reduces a politics of liberation to a politics of fashion" (Davis 1994, 37).

Rallies protesting her imprisonment as a political prisoner took place in Los Angeles, Paris, and Sri Lanka. Despite this wellspring of support, the women's movement—with some notable exceptions—failed to take up her cause. Author Kate Millett emphasized this as she prepared to attend Davis' trial, writing in Ms. that "we have done little enough for her" (Millett 1972, 54). Millett's first impression when she met Davis is telling: "She takes my breath away. Here perhaps at last is the Joan one hoped for, come in a day when no one will have a match and the fire will never fly about its target—a woman at length unwilling to be martyred" (Millett 1972, 108).

Davis was released on $102,000 bail five days before her trial in February 1972. She worked with a team of lawyers to defend herself, even giving her opening statement, in which she excoriated the prosecutor's plan to prove her passion for George Jackson drove her to murder. Davis was acquitted in June 1972. After her release, she transformed the movement created to free her into the National Alliance against Racist and Political Repression, of which she remains a member today.

In 1974 Davis published her autobiography, in which she takes a characteristically humble approach to her newfound celebrity, saying she decided to tell her story at a young age not to revel in her own glory but so others may understand what prompts oppressed peoples to undertake a revolution.

After lecturing at a number of California schools during the 1970s, Davis accepted a professorship at San Francisco State University in 1979, where she taught women's and ethnic studies. That year Davis was awarded the Lenin Peace Prize. During the 1970s she lectured at Moscow University and spent time in Cuba, where she lectured at Havana University.

In 1981, Davis published *Women, Race and Class*, a tome filled with insights that defined her work for the next decade. Davis was among the first to argue that rape of African American women was not simply an expression of lust but an instrument of control used to discipline the slave labor force as a whole. As one reviewer put it, the book "helped to establish the guidelines for critical analysis in current American feminist scholarship through its insistence on the investigation of the historically specific ways in which the inequalities of race, gender and class interact" (Clark 1990, 19). Among the book's most memorable discussions is a look at how racism infested the nineteenth-century women's movement and how women's confinement to the domestic sphere strips them of power. Davis urged inclusion in the feminist movement, saying: "Racism has always served as a provocation to rape, and white women in the United States have necessarily suffered the ricochet fire of these attacks. This is one of the many ways in which racism nourishes sexism, causing white women to be indirectly victimized by the special oppression aimed at their sisters of color" (Davis 1981, 177). Critics agree but argue further that Davis and other feminists must go beyond chronicling how sexuality has been used to oppress women by dictating steps to empower black women (Collins 1991, 160).

Davis continued her political involvement, running as the Communist Party's candidate for vice president in 1980 and 1984. In the mid-1980s she became a member of the executive board of the National Political Caucus of Black Women and the National Black Women's Health Project. In a speech to the Tenth National Women's Studies Association Conference in 1987, Davis called for the creation of a "revolutionary multiracial women's movement that seriously addresses the main issues affecting poor and working-class women" (Davis 1989, 7). In the tradition of Sojourner Truth's "Ain't I a Woman" speech, Davis repeatedly used a motto popularized by the black women's club movement in 1895: "We must lift as we climb" (Davis 1989, 11).

Women, Culture and Politics, published in 1989, contains this speech and others Davis gave throughout the 1980s, as well as articles that first appeared in periodicals, including the *Harvard Educational Review* and *Vogue*. In the book Davis expands on ideas in *Women, Race and Class* through discussions about women's health, nuclear warfare, South African apartheid, and Egyptian women's oppression. She also attempts to dispel myths surrounding black teens and pregnancy, black families headed by women on welfare, and women and rape.

Hailed as a fitting record of Davis' worldwide influence and her determination to reach people outside academe, the book was also criticized as being too repetitive of her earlier writings. One review remarked on the absence of speeches addressing the working class, in which she has ceaselessly tried to foment a revolution, and for not making "a single reference to the misogyny of black nationalists such as Eldridge Cleaver, [Amiri] Baraka and Ishmael Reed" (Stevens 1989, 279).

Davis became a professor in the History of Consciousness program at the University of California at Santa Cruz in 1991, the same year the U.S. Communist Party disintegrated. In 1994 her life came full circle when lawmakers protested her appointment to a prestigious presidential chair on African American and feminist studies at the university. Davis admitted the partisan attacks gave her a "very bizarre sense of deja vu" (Wallace 1995, 3).

Writing on reproductive policies in the 1990s, Davis links capitalism to the historical exploitation of women, remarking that "new developments in reproductive technology have encouraged the contemporary emergence of popular attitudes . . . that bear a remarkable resemblance to the 19th-century cult of motherhood" (Kauffman 1993, 355).

Davis' most recent book, *Blues Legacies and Black Feminism: Gertrude "Ma" Rainey, Bessie Smith, Billie Holiday*, was published in 1998. In this work Davis discusses how these three singers' work divulges an "unacknowledged tradition of feminist consciousness in the working class black community" (Davis 1998, xi). She argues that the lyrics they offered provided black women with both advice and a foundation for feminist awareness.

Today, Davis travels and lectures extensively for humane treatment of prisoners, a moratorium on prison construction, gay rights, and welfare reform. She often urges crowds to take action to rid the country of what she sees as ever-worsening racism and sexism. One of the black women who "broke the silence" (Collins 1996, 9) in the rebellious 1970s, Davis has witnessed the black women's movement develop its own voice. Despite a rising awareness of black women's issues, however, Davis' struggle is not taught extensively in schools, and relatively little attention has been given to her contributions to the women's movement. But the countercultural icon would certainly deny that her political struggles have been about her. "It's not so much me as an individual who made a difference," she told a *Los Angeles Times* reporter. "My case came at a particular moment in the evolution of the black movement in this country, when dedicated people learned how to organize" (Beyette 1989, 1).

SELECTED WORKS BY ANGELA DAVIS

Nonfiction

With Bettina Aptheker, eds. *If They Come in the Morning: Voices of Resistance.* New York: Third Press, 1971.
Angela Davis/An Autobiography. New York: Random House, 1974; reprinted 1988 and 1996, New York: International.
Women, Race and Class. New York: Random House, 1981; reprinted 1983, New York: Vintage Books.
Women, Culture, and Politics. New York: Vintage Books, 1989.
Blues Legacies and Black Feminism: Gertrude "Ma" Rainey, Bessie Smith, Billie Holiday. New York: Pantheon Books, 1998.

Articles

"Reflections on the Black Women's Role in the Community of Slaves." *Black Scholar* (December 1971): 2–15.
"Joanne Little: The Politics of Rage." Ms. (June 1975): 74–77+.
"Afro Images: Politics, Fashion and Nostalgia." *Critical Inquiry* (Autumn 1994): 37–45.

SELECTED WRITINGS ON ANGELA DAVIS

Books

Aptheker, Bettina. *The Morning Breaks: The Trial of Angela Davis.* New York: International, 1975.
Chow, Esther Ngan-Ling, Doris Wilkinson, and Maxine Baca Zinn, eds. *Race, Class and Gender: Common Bonds, Different Voices.* Thousand Oaks, CA: Sage, 1996.
Collins, Patricia Hill. *Knowledge, Consciousness and the Politics of Empowerment.* New York: Routledge, Chapman, and Hall, 1991.
Hull, Gloria, Patricia Bell Scott, and Barbara Smith, eds. *All the Women Are White, All*

the Blacks Are Men, but Some of Us Are Brave. Old Westbury, NY: Feminist Press, 1982.

Kauffman, Linda S., ed. *American Feminist Thought at Century's End: A Reader.* Cambridge, MA: Blackwell, 1993.

Kopp, Claire B., ed. *Becoming Female: Perspectives on Development.* New York: Plenum Press, 1979.

La Blanc, Michael, et al. *Contemporary Black Biography.* Vol. 5. Detroit: Gale Research, 1992–.

Moses, Claire Goldberg, and Heidi Hartmann, eds. *U.S. Women in Struggle: A Feminist Studies Anthology.* Chicago: University of Illinois Press, 1995.

Nadelson, Regina. *Who Is Angela Davis? The Biography of a Revolutionary.* New York: P. H. Wyden, 1972.

Parker, J. A. *Angela Davis: The Making of a Revolutionary.* New Rochelle, NY: Arlington House, 1973.

Tobias, Sheila. *Faces of Feminism: An Activist's Reflections on the Women's Movement.* Oxford: Westview Press, 1997.

Zinn, Maxine Baca, and Bonnie Thornton Dill, eds. *Women of Color in U.S. Society.* Philadelphia: Temple University Press, 1994.

Articles, Reviews, and Interviews

Beyette, Beverly. "Angela Davis Now: On a Quiet Street in Oakland, the Former Radical Activist Has Settled In but Not Settled Down." *Los Angeles Times,* March 8, 1989, sec. E, 1.

Bhavnani, Kum-Kum. "Complexity, Activism, Optimism: An Interview with Angela Y. Davis." *Feminist Review* (Spring 1989): 66–81.

Clark, Carolyn M. "Race, Class, Gender and Sexuality: On Angela Y. Davis' Women, Culture and Politics." *Social Justice* (Fall 1990): 195–202.

Collins, Patricia Hill. "What's in a Name? Womanism, Black Feminism, and Beyond." *Black Scholar* (Winter 1996): 9–17.

duCille, Ann. "The Occult of True Black Womanhood: Critical Demeanor and Black Feminist Studies." *Signs* (Spring 1994): 591–629.

Miles, Sara. "Angela at Our Table." *Out* (February 1998): 62–67.

Millett, Kate. "On Angela Davis." *Ms.* (August 1972): 55.

Rouse, Deborah L. "Rediscovering Angela Davis." *Emerge* (June 1997): 88.

Stevens, Jackie. "Women, Culture, and Politics—Book Reviews." *The Nation* (February 27, 1989): 279.

Wallace, Amy. "Angela Davis Again at Center of UC Storm." *Los Angeles Times,* February 20, 1995, sec. A, 3.

Weathers, Diane, and Tara Roberts. "Kathleen Cleaver and Angela Davis: Rekindling the Flame." *Essence* (May 1996): 82.

SUSAN FALUDI
(1959-)

Ann Mauger Colbert

Susan Faludi, born in 1959 to a photographer father and a writer/editor mother, became famous as the young woman who showed the relevance of the women's movement to a younger generation. In her book *Backlash*, sometimes derided as "journalism, not theory" (Olendorf 1993, 152), she has presented an astonishing number of examples of a media backlash against women and the progress made by the women's movement. Her evidence is staggering and current; her case against popular media and their continuing unwillingness to understand women's issues and willingness to perpetuate myths is overwhelming but extremely readable, even entertaining. Susan Faludi has been a Pulitzer Prize-winning reporter and staff member of several prestigious publications, including the *New York Times* (1981–1982), *Miami Herald* (1983), *Atlanta Journal-Constitution* (1984–1985), *West* magazine (1985–1989), and *Wall Street Journal* (San Francisco bureau, 1990–1992), and has written for *Mother Jones* and *Ms.* magazines.

As suggested, despite her impressive record of reporting, Susan Faludi's work has received criticism from various arenas as not "theoretical" enough. Like Gloria Steinem, she has been defined and derided for her work as a journalist. As a reporter, she has amassed facts that seem to offer theoretical framework enough, but while male writers receive kudos for amassing facts, female journalists are more frequently seen as narrow or parochial. (Similar compilations of facts about men and media/politics would be called "massive" or "hard-hitting.") While Faludi's work has provided the ammunition needed to rally general readers against media agenda-setters, she is apt to be seen as less of a theoretician than someone who has edited a collection of others' writings. Accordingly, she has frequently been described as not critical enough (Olendorf 1993, 152). This problem of seeing those who write for popular media as parochial or narrow is an important one for feminists who are themselves working journalists. Because their orientation is journalistic investigation, and because they are women writing about women's issues, they must be even more careful to walk a line of

objectivity. To be seen as "polemical" would make a piece of reportage unpro-
fessional; colleagues from the working press would see the work of polemicists as
more involved with public relations than with journalism. Support from would-be
peers in the feminist community is therefore essential to encourage reporting like
Faludi's.

Another aspect of concern for those like Faludi—those who have chosen the
journalistic genre—is the importance of making the evidence acceptable and
understandable to a popular media audience. At the same time that the words
of "common" women are seen as important to the record of women's lives,
women who have compiled evidence against institutional prejudice and harassment and who have used the popular media to report their findings are sometimes
discounted, and their work has not been defended as vigorously as others'. To
be described as one who produces work that is more like reportage than theory,
then, is both boon and bane for writers like Faludi. Indeed, this ability to uncover
and report the facts makes her book about women and the backlash in media so
important to women who have dismissed feminism and the women's movement
as "finished."

Faludi told the story of the book's origins to writer Kim Hubbard in *People* this
way: like others, she was surprised to read, initially in *Newsweek*, of a woman's
diminishing marriage prospects, but her original reaction to this highly published
story about age and diminishing marriage prospects was to question it. Indeed,
when she checked the facts behind the story, Faludi discovered that the research
itself was flawed; additionally, obvious flaws had been ignored or misinterpreted
by mainstream media. Her criticism focused on her own peers' widespread mis-
reporting of unsubstantiated facts—particularly those relating to women.

Accordingly, in *Backlash*, she was especially critical of media that have set
themselves up as "trend-watchers" (Faludi 1991, 79–111). This media invest-
ment in "trend-watching" and reporting has created what Faludi calls a "backlash" of reports critical of women and of the women's movement. As Faludi
continued her examination, she discovered that much information was more
than "trendy"; it was inaccurate and myth-building. Faludi's resulting compendium of evidence provides proof of a backlash from practically every sector, from
the rewriting of the script of *Fatal Attraction* to not believing—in fact, ignoring—
sales reports about underwear and the miniskirt (Faludi 1991, 112–123). As
Faludi tells the story in the book, one of the most important cultural myths to
be part of the backlash is the so-called infertility epidemic. Women over the age
of thirty who were having trouble getting pregnant were troubled not by career-
ism, as reported and assumed, but by chlamydia, a disease frequently spread by
men. Years later, in 1996, the Centers for Disease Control reported that chlamydia is the most prevalent of the sexually transmitted diseases (Faludi 1991,
28–32).

Faludi, born in New York City on April 18, 1959, says that her parents—
Steven Faludi, a photographer, and Marilyn Faludi, a writer and editor—encouraged her critical approach to media. They were divorced in 1976, and Susan

Faludi has been quoted as saying that her mother's frustrated existence and buried, ignored talents were key to her original understanding of women's circumscribed existence. Her talents for exposé came early. Attending Harvard University on an Elks Club scholarship, she wrote about sexual harassment for the *Harvard Crimson*. A dean and the professor accused of the crime both fought publication, but Faludi's story appeared anyway. As a result, the professor was asked to take a leave of absence. In 1980 Faludi was named Phi Beta Kappa; she graduated summa cum laude in literature and history in 1981 after receiving an Oliver Dabney History Award for her senior thesis.

Susan Faludi then joined the *New York Times* as a news and copy clerk, and, as has been reported elsewhere, when she tried to move up the ranks, her progress was halted. Indeed, a male reporter told her that because women were able to carry a baby for nine months, they were "biologically more patient" than men. Because of this biological patience, he explained, Faludi was better suited for an assistantship position than a male peer would be. Not surprisingly, she decided to leave the *Times* and soon accepted a job with the *Miami Herald* and then a general reporting position at the *Atlanta Journal-Constitution*. In 1985, she won a first prize for news reporting and feature writing from Georgia's Associated Press. After moving to the West Coast, she worked at the Sunday magazine of the *San Jose Mercury News*. At the same time, she began important freelance work for *Mother Jones*, *Ms.*, and *California Business*.

Before her general fame with the book, Susan Faludi's journalistic work had brought her into the center of those expected to rise in the field of journalism. She received honors and awards from a number of professional organizations, and in 1990, she became a staff writer for the San Francisco bureau of the *Wall Street Journal*. During this time she took her first lengthy look at a situation that was to make her nationally famous, and two years later, her investigative piece on the human costs of the $5.65 billion leveraged buyout of Safeway Stores won a Pulitzer Prize.

While working on the Safeway story, Faludi continued to be bothered about misreported information on women and the media's interpretation of women-related articles. She decided that she was one of the "voiceless" affected by the media's reports on women and that she would begin work on the media's role in perpetuating myths about women. One example was the "marriage crunch," mentioned earlier. No one had suggested, she noted, that women's marrying "late" was related to a lack of compelling reasons for marrying or that women's choices not to marry were quite threatening to men. After the *Newsweek* article had been published and much talked about, Faludi noticed a recurring theme: women who asked for equality met with punishment, in news media, popular novels, and popular movies.

Backlash was written during an eighteen-month leave from other work and uses Faludi's growing reputation as someone willing to immerse herself in statistics and facts to find the story behind the media's headlines. The resulting piece was a compendium of examples of the misinterpretations and misrepresentations of news about women that has been reviewed widely and, for the most part, favorably. Excerpts immediately appeared in *Mother Jones* and *Glamour*, a measure of Faludi's ability to speak to audiences of all types. While most reviews were positive, Faludi received some negative reviews in both the conservative and the feminist press. While some feminist reviewers praised Faludi for taking on the media, others complained that her focus on women in the mainstream ignored the realities of many women's lives. Despite these dissident voices, most reviewers agreed that the writing is readable and that the extensive evidence is clearly presented.

Faludi's sources for the book range from the work of literary scholars Sandra M. Gilbert and Susan Gubar, to Carol Gilligan; from interviews with disparate figures from Eleanor Smeal, to leaders of Operation Rescue; and from debates on issues ranging from politics, to miniskirts. Faludi examined advertising copy and images and quoted industry publications and fashion writers. She looked at legal language and the life of the woman who wrote the Family Protection Act. She examined the created images of women who ran for office, offering particularly poignant remarks about the so-called Year of the Woman. If a journalist wrote down a quote that was particularly offensive to women and to women's equality, Faludi was there to pluck it from the pages of various newspapers and use it in her book. For example, she cites Richard Cohen, *Washington Post* columnist, who complained that Walter Mondale had been "henpecked" and had succumbed to the "hectoring and—yes—threats of the organized woman's movement" (Faludi 1991, 269).

Faludi also looked at the nation's antifeminists, particularly George Gilder, whose personal life underscores his politics (Faludi 1991, 402–3). She examined the life and writings of Allan Bloom, Carol Gilligan, and Betty Friedan (Faludi 1991, 327–331, 318–325). With these short biographies, she asks pertinent— sometimes clearly antagonistic—questions. Her book, in fact, while a masterwork of "reporting," also serves as a watermark for future writers on the contemporary relationship between media and women.

In addition to the Pulitzer for her 1991 work on Safeway in the *Wall Street Journal*, Susan Faludi won an earlier Robert F. Kennedy Memorial Journalism Award citation, about 1987; a John Hancock Award, 1991; and a National Book Critics Circle Award, 1992, for *Backlash: The Undeclared War against American Women*.

WORKS BY SUSAN FALUDI

Backlash: The Undeclared War against American Women. New York: Crown, 1991; London: Chatto and Windus, 1992.

Backlash: The Undeclared War against American Women (audiocassette; read by Faludi), Publishing Mills, 1992.

WRITINGS ON SUSAN FALUDI AND HER WORK

Hubbard, Kim. "Lashing Back at the Backlash." *People* (November 11, 1991): 138–140.
Olendorf, Donna, ed. "Susan Faludi." *Contemporary Authors*. Vol. 138. Detroit: Gale Publishers, 138. 1993, 150–152.
Shapiro, Laura. "Why Women Are Angry." *Newsweek* (October 21, 1991): 41–44.

SHULAMITH FIRESTONE
(1945-)

Karen Garner

Born and raised in an Orthodox Jewish family in Ottawa, Canada, Shulamith Firestone became aware early in her life that both the family and wider society privileged the cultural, economic, political, and intellectual expressions of men. By the time she was a teenager Firestone had deliberately trained herself to erase the "phony," "simpering" smile that society's oppressed groups—women, children, nonwhite races, and the working class, as she identified them—were supposed to wear to please their oppressors. Therefore, Firestone recalled that she "smiled rarely" (Firestone 1970, 101).

In the mid-1960s, Firestone attended the Art Institute of Chicago, where she earned a fine arts degree and was active in socialist Zionist politics. She was also peripherally involved with the anti–Vietnam War and pro–civil rights politics of the New Left. In 1967, disillusioned with the New Left's disdain for women's issues, Firestone joined with Naomi Weisstein, Jo Freeman, and other women to form a pioneering women's liberation association. This association, the Chicago Westside Group, focused on theorizing and eliminating sexual oppression. In October 1967, Firestone moved to New York City and with Pam Allen organized New York Radical Women, the city's first women's liberation group.

Soon thereafter, Firestone began participating in public demonstrations that focused on women's concerns. In August 1968, at the Miss America Pageant in Atlantic City, Firestone joined the New York Radical Women in a public protest to denounce the concept of beauty contests and to destroy symbolically "beauty aids" that tortured and objectified women's bodies. In January 1969, together with 5,000 women, Firestone joined a counterinaugural and antiwar demonstration in Washington, D.C. Disappointed again by the New Left's expression of antiwomen attitudes at the demonstration, she later concluded that the New Left's actions had illustrated women's political invisibility (Firestone 1970, 32). The experience in Washington confirmed her commitment to women's autonomous organization to seize power. Firestone wrote to the left-wing *Guardian* in February 1969:

We say to the left: in this past decade you have failed to live up to your rhetoric of revolution. You have not reached the people. And we won't hitch ourselves to your poor donkey. There are millions of women out there desperate enough to rise. Women's liberation is dynamite. And we have more important things to do than to try to get you to come around. You will come around when you have to, because you need us more than we need you. . . . The message being: Fuck off, left. You can examine your own navel from now on. We're starting our own movement. (quoted in Echols 1989, 118–119)

In February 1969, with Ellen Willis, Firestone formed a new women's liberation group. They named it the Redstockings to mock the derogatory appellation "bluestocking" tagged onto learned, pedantic women and to take up the mantle of the "revolutionary red" tradition. Yet the Redstockings aimed to be an explicitly radical feminist group that clearly separated its feminist revolutionary goals from the sponsorship of the socialist-oriented Left. The Redstockings specifically excluded men. They issued a manifesto that defined all men as part of an integrated class of oppressors of women, pledged to raise women's consciousness, and urged all women to fight for liberation from their oppressors.

In the fall of 1969, Firestone and Anne Koedt founded another new association, the New York Radical Feminists. Intending to build up a mass women's liberation movement, Firestone and Koedt coedited a mimeographed journal, *Notes from the First Year* in 1969 and *Notes from the Second Year* in 1970. *Notes from the Second Year* included the New York Radical Feminists' manifesto. The manifesto asserted that the dominant and domineering male ego sought to subordinate and to dehumanize the female ego and argued that when women's egos were destroyed, they couldn't take action to protest against male power (Koedt 1973, 379–383).

Ironically, Firestone's fellow Radical Feminists often attacked her for the very things Firestone argued against: dominating group discussions and demonstrating elitism in group interactions (Echols 1989, 150–151, 192). Firestone had organized the New York Radical Feminists to act as an umbrella group encompassing small, leaderless cell groups, called brigades. These brigades were supposed to adopt the "sister system" of positive reinforcement to build group unity. However, when other Radical Feminists criticized Firestone's cell, the Stanton-Anthony brigade, for its overbearing domination of leadership positions, Firestone dissolved the brigade in anger and withdrew from the New York Radical Feminists organization.

Yet all these activities contributed to the development of Firestone's radical feminist political orientation and led to the 1970 publication of her path-breaking work, *The Dialectic of Sex: The Case for Feminist Revolution*. In this book Firestone indicted patriarchal oppression of women and developed a theory of feminist revolution. She analyzed the historical origins and cultural expressions of patriarchy and identified biological differences between men and women as the source of male dominance. Most importantly, Firestone claimed that technology could change the nature of reproductive labor and eliminate the source of male dominance: the sexual division of labor in the family.

Firestone argued that biological differences had led to an unequal distribution of the reproductive functions between the sexes and had erected the first division of labor in human society. This unequal distribution of reproductive functions and original sexual division of labor had, in turn, created an unequal distribution of power within the biological family. The female reproductive functions, which include menstruation, gestation, childbirth, nursing, and infant care, rendered women dependent on men for their physical survival. Men, in turn, exploited women's (and children's) dependency. This fundamental dependency had material, cultural, and psychological consequences for human society that were manifested in unequal power relations.

In Firestone's analysis, historic and contemporary sex class distinctions, dominant/subordinate identities, and psychosexual expressions all resulted from the independent/dependent reproductive relations between males and females. Thus, Firestone compared her radical feminist theory of human sexuality with Sigmund Freud's psychoanalytic theory and praised Freud's identification of sexuality as the primary force motivating human behavior. However, Firestone argued that Freud failed to recognize the political implications of his psychoanalytic theory. In particular, she faulted Freud for failing to interpret female "penis envy" as female desire for the power men monopolized. She also argued that the incest taboo, which Freud theorized was necessary for the differentiation and maturation of male and female sex roles, was a concept that had been used by the patriarchy to preserve the nuclear family and its inherently unequal power relations between men and women and between parents and their children. The patriarchy had co-opted the Freudian incest taboo, Firestone asserted, to socialize men and women to accept an "artificial sex-role system" (Firestone 1970, 79). Firestone therefore inverted Freudian theory and asserted that biology, or the reproductive functions of the female anatomy, did not consign women to a subordinate political destiny. If humanity chose to, it could, through feminist revolution, destroy the sexual imbalance of power that hitherto had been based on biological difference.

Firestone also compared her radical feminist theory of revolution to Marxist revolutionary theory. She rejected Karl Marx and Frederick Engels' doctrine of historical materialism, identifying sex-class distinctions as more fundamental than economic class distinctions in explaining human power relations. Firestone used the historical example of the Russian Marxist revolution to prove her point, asserting that the revolution failed because the revolutionary leaders failed to eliminate repressive sexual relations within the family. According to Firestone's analysis, attempts to "soften" the family's repressive power over women by including women in the productive workforce were "reformist" measures that left the power of the patriarchy intact (Firestone 1970, 240).

Yet Firestone also praised and adopted the philosophical foundation, dialectical materialism, that Marxists employed to explain the laws regulating the workings of the universe. Indeed, Firestone's theory of feminist revolution carefully incorporated the fundamental laws of dialectical materialism: that a series of gradual, quantitative changes laid the groundwork for revolutionary, qualitative change; that concrete reality was actually a unity of opposites or contradictions; and that these opposites, in constant conflict with one another, eventually negated each other and produced a new level of historical development.

According to Firestone, the necessary preconditions for a successful feminist revolution, which she identified as the "ultimate" revolution to eliminate the distinctions between sexes, had evolved over time and existed in advanced industrial societies in 1970 (Firestone 1970, 232). Firestone argued that developments in reproductive technology in the eighteenth and nineteenth centuries that had allowed women to exercise some control over the reproductive cycle had led to an "inevitable" response: the emergence of a feminist consciousness (Firestone 1970, 235). Firestone then argued that, by the mid-twentieth century, total control over biological reproduction would be made possible through technological developments that allowed for the artificial, ex-utero reproduction of human beings. Children could then be born to both sexes equally, and a small group of self-selected "parents" could raise the children. The mother–child interdependency, as well as women's and children's dependency on the adult males, that had been fostered by the exclusively female realm of reproductive labor, would thus be eliminated. In Firestone's view, the elimination of unequal power relations between men and women and their sources within the biological nuclear family would shake the foundations of unequal power relations outside the family. Eventually and inevitably, such power imbalances would completely dissolve as well.

Anticipating the objections of some of her critics, Firestone argued that "artificial reproduction is not inherently dehumanizing" (Firestone 1970, 226–227). Indeed, she asserted that pregnancy was "barbaric," deforming, and extremely painful and that through new technology, humanity could progress to a more human, less animalistic state. Yet Firestone's critics have argued that women's "power" is based in their biological reproductive capabilities. Stripping women of their inherent biological power and relegating that power to technologies that might likely fall under male control would further consolidate men's power over women. Firestone's critics have also asserted that women should strive to take more political and emotional control over biological reproduction and child raising in order to attain the unity of their physical and intellectual selves, rather than turn to technological reproduction as an all-encompassing solution to unequal sexual power relations.

Yet Firestone has expressed a strong faith in the benefits that technology could bring to human society. In *The Dialectic of Sex*, Firestone argued that further advances in technology and cybernetics were also in the process of changing the nature of productive work and were, in fact, eliminating the need for men to engage in productive labor. In Firestone's view, these advances would completely eliminate any remaining division of labor within the workplace that supported sexual and other inequalities. Firestone envisioned the outcome of the ultimate feminist revolution as the abandonment of capitalist production as well as biological reproduction. Although leftist radicals have criticized Firestone's utopian vision of feminist revolution for overestimating the ability of feminist revolution to undermine capitalism, she has asserted that "cybernation, by changing man's relationship to work and wages, by transforming activity from 'work' to 'play' (activity done for its own sake), would allow for a total redefinition of the economy, including the family unit in its economic capacity" (Firestone 1970, 230).

Firestone's universalist approach to the source of all social, economic, political, and cultural inequalities has been alternately praised as daring and brilliant and criticized as overambitious and naive. There is no doubt, however, that Firestone's organizational efforts and her tour de force, *The Dialectic of Sex*, have had an energizing and mobilizing impact on the second wave feminist movement.

WORKS BY SHULAMITH FIRESTONE

The Dialectic of Sex: The Case for Feminist Revolution. New York: William Morrow, 1970.
"Love in a Sexist Society." *Eros, Agape, and Philia: Readings in the Philosophy of Love.* Ed. Alan Soble. New York: Paragon House, 1989.
"Redstockings Manifesto." *Feminism in Our Time: The Essential Writings, World War II to the Present.* Ed. Miriam Schneir. New York: Vintage Books, 1994.

WRITINGS ON SHULAMITH FIRESTONE AND HER WORK

Castro, Ginette. *American Feminism: A Contemporary History.* Trans. Elizabeth Loverde-Bagwell. New York: New York University Press, 1990.
Echols, Ann. *Daring to Be Bad: Radical Feminism in America, 1967–1975.* Minneapolis: University of Minnesota Press, 1989.
Hoffmann, Frances Lee. "Foundations of Feminist Social Theory: Implications of Freudian and Existentialist Ontologies." Ph.D. diss., University of Oregon, 1976.
Humm, Maggie. *Modern Feminisms: Political, Literary, Cultural.* New York: Columbia University Press, 1992.
Jackson, Stevi, et al., eds. *Women's Studies: Essential Readings.* New York: New York University Press, 1993.
Koedt, Anne. "Politics of the Ego: A Manifesto for N.Y. Radical Feminists." *Radical Feminism.* Ed. Anne Koedt, Ellen Levine, and Anita Rapone. New York: Quadrangle Books, 1973, 379–383.
Schneir, Miriam, ed. *Feminism in Our Time: The Essential Writings, World War II to the Present.* New York: Vintage Books, 1994.

Snitow, Ann. "Returning to the Well." Review of *The Dialectic of Sex: The Case for Feminist Revolution*, by Shulamith Firestone. *Dissent* 41 (Fall 1994): 557–560.

Tong, Rosemarie. *Feminist Thought: A Comprehensive Introduction*. Boulder, CO: Westview Press, 1989.

JO FREEMAN
(1945–)

Jennifer Scanlon

Jo Freeman, activist, political scientist, writer, and lawyer, was born in Atlanta, Georgia, and raised in Los Angeles, California. Her mother, Helen Mitchell Freeman, hailed from Marion County, Alabama, where both of her parents had occasionally served as local elected officials. She moved to California shortly after Jo's birth and taught junior high school until her death in 1973.

Freeman attended Birmingham Junior and Senior High in the San Fernando Valley and graduated from Granada Hills High School in 1961. She felt her four years at the University of California at Berkeley, where she received her B.A. with honors in political science in 1965, were her "personal liberation" from the narrow constraints imposed on girls during her childhood. At Berkeley she could live on her own and make her own decisions.

One of those decisions was to become deeply involved in the student political groups and larger social movements that were prevalent at Berkeley in the 1960s. She was active in the Young Democrats and SLATE, a campus political party, lobbying to remove the campus ban on controversial speakers and to promote educational reform, writing for the *SLATE Supplement*, which evaluated teachers and courses from a student perspective, and working in local "fair housing" campaigns. In 1963–1964, Freeman immersed herself in the Bay Area civil rights movement, organizing and participating in demonstrations demanding that local employers hire more African Americans. She was arrested in two of those and spent six weeks on trial, garnering one acquittal and one conviction. The trials interfered with her plans to go to Mississippi for Freedom Summer but ended in time for her to hitchhike to the Democratic Convention in Atlantic City to join the vigil of the Mississippi Freedom Democratic Party. On her return, the student political groups were informed that they could no longer pass out literature on the edge of campus, at the traditional locale for political activity that was forbidden on the campus itself. This rule change prompted the Berkeley Free Speech Movement (FSM), whose massive sit-ins and student strikes shook the political establishment in California, led to the dismissal of the university president, opened the entire campus to political activity by student groups, and became a beacon for student protests all over the country for years to come.

Freeman was involved in the FSM for its entire existence, but often as a critic of the radicals in the leadership. Nonetheless, she was one of "the 800" arrested for occupying the administration building and was tried and convicted with the other students. These experiences profoundly affected her future scholarship. She found that she liked to merge thought with action, to critically analyze what she and the others were doing, and to do what her studies taught her was the right thing to do. She wrote her senior thesis on "Civil Disobedience" and years later drew on her experiences to publish several contributions to the literature on social movements. Reading about the abolitionist movement convinced her that the next major movement would be one of women, but when she told this to others, they only scoffed. Freeman did not enter graduate school until 1968, because she thought it was more important to do social change than social science. Instead, she worked in the civil rights movement, participated in antiwar protests, and was one of the founders of the women's liberation movement.

After graduation she went to Atlanta to work for the Southern Christian Leadership Conference (SCLC), headed by Dr. Martin Luther King, Jr. Beginning as a summer volunteer, she soon joined the SCLC field staff and for a year and a half worked in various southern counties, doing voter registration, political education, and community organizing. Most of her activity was in Alabama, though she also worked in South Carolina, Mississippi, and Chicago and spent a few days in two southern jails. Her work in the South ended when the *Jackson Daily News*, at the urging of the Mississippi State Sovereignty Commission, "exposed" her as a professional agitator, implying from her FSM activities that she was a communist sympathizer. The five photographs that accompanied the editorial made her an easy target, so after a few weeks in Atlanta working as an assistant to Coretta Scott King, SCLC sent her to Chicago.

Freeman credits the civil rights movement for the insights that made her a nascent feminist. Its demands for "equal rights" and objections to "separate but equal" provided the analytical framework from which to critique society's assumptions about women's natural inferiority to do anything except serve men and raise children. In addition, the black community provided an alternative model for woman that compared favorably to the limited roles women had in white society and in which strength was admired, and leadership by women was more accepted. From these observations Freeman realized that there was nothing natural or inevitable about woman's place, nor was there anything wrong with those women who refused to confine their interests to home and family.

After SCLC's Chicago project petered out, Freeman worked for the *West Side TORCH*, a quasi movement and community newspaper, where she developed her photographic and journalistic skills. However, when she applied for a job to the traditional newspapers and reporting services in Chicago, she was told that they hired very few women because "girls couldn't cover riots." This forced her to confront the limited employment options women had regardless of talent, training, or personal interests. Eventually, she found a position as a rewrite editor for a trade magazine, where she learned to edit and revise manuscripts for publication. This experience led her to edit five editions of *Women: A Feminist Perspective*. It quickly became a leading introductory textbook for women's studies courses because Freeman's editing gave the contributed chapters a consistent style that combined readability with incisive analysis of available data.

While trying to become a journalist, Freeman met the women with whom she would organize Chicago's first women's liberation group. Early in 1967 she read about the formation of the National Organization for Women (NOW), but no one answered her letters. In June she went to a course on women at a free school at the University of Chicago taught by Heather Booth and Naomi Weisstein. The women she met there would eventually become the nucleus of the first group. However, the immediate stimulus was the women's workshop that met at the National Conference of New Politics, held in Chicago over Labor Day weekend. Between 50 and 100 women spent days talking about women's situation and writing a resolution, but the chairman of the plenary denied them an opportunity to discuss it. Freeman and Shulamith Firestone, whom she met at the workshop, left in anger and called together the women Freeman had spoken with three months earlier. They met weekly at Freeman's apartment on the West Side of Chicago, from whence came the group's name, first talking and then writing letters, articles, and pamphlets. The women in the Westside group organized other discussion groups around Chicago and spread the word to women in other cities who founded still more. By the time the Westside group dissolved in the spring (when Freeman closed her apartment and left Chicago for two months), small groups of women were mushrooming everywhere.

The Westside group also started the first newsletter, the *voice of the women's liberation movement* (*vwlm*), and by so doing gave the movement its name. Freeman knew from working in the South that a newsletter created a sense that something important was happening. She edited the first issues, maintained the mailing list, mailed out pamphlets, and corresponded with emerging feminists from all over the country. Her work on the newsletter and role as an information hub continued into 1969, by which time she was enrolled in graduate school in political science at the University of Chicago (UC). *vwlm* ended with issue no. 7 in the spring of 1969.

Freeman turned to other endeavors, helping to start a woman's center in 1968, chairing the Student Subcommittee of the Committee on University Women (created to report on women's experiences at the university after a major sit-in in the winter of 1969), teaching an unpaid, noncredit course at UC on the legal and economic position of women, organizing a major conference in the fall of 1969, organizing the University Women's Association to bring feminist speakers to campus, and, beginning in 1970, speaking and organizing at other campuses, mostly in the Midwest. In the summers of 1970 and 1971 Freeman hitchhiked throughout Europe, distributing feminist pamphlets wherever she could find women organizing. Women in the Netherlands and Norway later credited her with making a contribution to the development of their movements.

As a graduate student, she wrote term papers on women and on feminism, most of which were published. In 1972 she ran for delegate to the Democratic Convention committed to presidential candidate Shirley Chisholm. As a result she attended the 1972 convention as an alternate with the Chicago Challenge that unseated Mayor Daley's machine delegation.

The excitement of starting a new movement was tempered by the usual rivalries, jealousies, manipulation, and undermining that are typical of social change organizations. Freeman sought to understand and analyze these in three papers she wrote under her movement name, Joreen. "The BITCH Manifesto" (1969), "The Tyranny of Structurelessness" (1970), and "Trashing: The Dark Side of Sisterhood" (1975) became minor classics that were frequently reprinted because they illuminated others' experiences in many movements. "Tyranny," the best known of all her work, argued that there was no such thing as a structureless group; pretending there was allowed responsibility to be shirked and power to be hidden. In fact, every group had a structure, usually based on friendship networks, and, in the absence of formal democracy, these networks would make the important decisions.

Freeman wrote many articles on women and women's liberation for popular magazines, scholarly journals, and anthologies, changing her style to fit the audience. Her most comprehensive work on the movement was her 1973 dissertation, "The Politics of Women's Liberation: A Case Study of an Emerging Social Movement and Its Relation to the Policy Process," which was published in 1975. Later that year it won a $1,000 prize given by the American Political Science Association (to commemorate International Women's Year) for the Best Scholarly Work on Women and Politics. It identified two origins of the women's movement, one in the larger "movement" of civil rights, youth, and antiwar activists and another in the network created by the President's and State Commissions on Women. From these came two branches, with different styles, structure, and orientations. The "younger branch" worked through small, autonomous "rap" groups, creating numerous projects and publications. It was the source of most of the movement's ideas. The "older branch" formed national organizations such as NOW and Women's Equity Action League (WEAL), which lobbied, mounted major demonstrations, and translated feminist ideas into laws and regulations. Freeman analyzed the actions and limitations of each branch, emphasizing how both impacted on, and were shaped by, public policy.

In addition to her pieces on the women's liberation movement, Freeman published contributions to social movement theory, critiques of how law and public policy treated women, and analyses of women's experiences in higher education. Her articles continue to be reprinted in numerous textbooks. Her only other book was an edited collection on *Social Movements of the Sixties and Seventies* (1983).

Freeman finally found NOW when she met Mary Eastwood on a trip to Washington, D.C., in 1968. She then helped Catherine Conroy start the Chicago chapter of NOW, worked on various committees, and participated in NOW demonstrations. She shifted her membership to New York City (NYC) NOW in 1974 and was also an active member of the Washington, D.C., chapter in 1977–1979. She chaired the NYC-NOW Committee on International Women's Year (IWY), helping coordinate NOW activities at the New York state preparatory meeting, where she was elected a delegate to the national IWY conference that met in Houston in November 1977. In 1974–1977, Freeman was an active member of the Women's Martial Arts Union, which gave self-defense demonstrations and classes for women in the NYC area.

In 1976, Freeman went to both the Democratic and Republican Conventions as a reporter for *Ms.* magazine. This started a continuing project of covering women's and feminist activities at both major party conventions every four years, usually for the feminist journal *off our backs*. This research finds its way into her more scholarly analyses of political parties and also led her to write a history of women and party politics (forthcoming). Hoping once again to merge thought and action, Freeman continued to work in practical politics, unsuccessfully running for delegate to the Democratic Convention in 1976, 1980, 1984, and 1988 and for the New York State Assembly in 1992.

After receiving her Ph.D. in political science from the University of Chicago in 1973, Freeman taught for four years at the State University of New York and spent two years in Washington, D.C., first as a Brookings Fellow and then as an American Political Science Association (APSA) Congressional Fellow. This stimulated her interest in public policy and led her to enter New York University Law School as a Root-Tilden scholar.

She received her J.D. in 1982 and was admitted to the New York state bar in 1983. Freeman currently is in private practice in New York City, where she has served as counsel to pro-choice demonstrators and to women running for elected office. She dabbles in local politics, writes, and lectures.

WORKS BY JO FREEMAN

Books

Ed. *Social Movements Since the Sixties.* Boulder, CO: Rowman and Littlefield, 1999.
Ed. *Social Movements of the Sixties and Seventies.* New York: Longman, 1983.
Ed. *Women: A Feminist Perspective.* Mountain View, CA: Mayfield Publishing Company, 1st ed., 1975.
The Politics of Women's Liberation. New York: McKay, 1975.

Articles

"The Tyranny of Structurelessness." *The Second Wave* 2, no. 1 (1972): p 20.
"The Legal Basis of the Sexual Caste System." *Valparaiso University Law Review* 5, no. 2 (Spring 1971): 203–236.

"The Social Construction of the Second Sex." *Roles Women Play: Readings towards Women's Liberation*. Ed. Michele Garskof. Belmont, CA: Brooks/Cole, 1971, 123–141.

"Women's Liberation and Its Impact on the Campus." *Liberal Education* 57, no. 4 (December 1971): 468–478.

"The BITCH Manifesto." *Notes from the Second Year*, ed. by Shulamith Firestone and Anne Koedt. Mimeograph, 1970.

"Structure and Strategy in the Women's Liberation Movement." *Urban and Social Change Review* 5, no. 2 (Spring 1972): 71–75.

"The Building of the Gilded Cage." *Radical Feminism*. Ed. Anne Koedt, Ellen Levine, and Anita Rapone. New York: Quadrangle, 1973, 127–151. ("BITCH" and "Tyranny" are also in this book.)

"The Origins of the Women's Liberation Movement." *American Journal of Sociology* 78, no. 4 (January 1973): 792–811.

"How to Discriminate against Women without Really Trying." *Women: A Feminist Perspective*. Ed. Jo Freeman. Palo Alto, CA: Mayfield, 1st ed. 1975, 194–208; 2d ed. 1979, 217–232.

"Political Organization in the Feminist Movement." *Acta Sociologica* 18, nos. 2–3, (1975): 222–224.

"Trashing: The Dark Side of Sisterhood." *Ms.*, April 1976, pp. 49–51, 92–98.

"Republican Politics—Let's Make a Deal." *Ms.* (November 1976): 19–20.

"Something DID Happen at the Democratic Convention." *Ms.* (October 1976): 113–115.

"Crises and Conflicts in Social Movement Organizations." *Chrysalis: A Magazine of Women's Culture*, no. 5 (1978): 43–51.

"The Feminist Scholar." *QUEST: A Feminist Quarterly* 5, no. 1 (Summer 1979): 26–36.

"Women and Urban Policy." *Signs* 5, no. 3, Supplement (Spring 1980): 4–21. Issue republished as *Women and the American City*. Ed. Catherine R. Stimpson, Elsa Dixler, Martha J. Nelson, and Kathryn B. Yatrakis. Chicago: University of Chicago Press, 1981, 1–18.

"Women and Public Policy: An Overview." *Women, Power and Policy*. Ed. Ellen Boneparth. New York: Pergamon Press, 1982, 47–67.

"The Women's Movement and the 1984 Democratic and Republican Conventions." *off our backs* (February 1985): 11–13, 20; reprinted in *Women Leaders in American Politics*. Ed. James David Barber and Barbara Kellerman. Englewood Cliffs, NJ: Prentice-Hall, 1986, 236–245.

"Whom You Know vs. Whom You Represent: Feminist Influence in the Democratic and Republican Parties." *The Women's Movements of the United States and Western Europe: Feminist Consciousness, Political Opportunity and Public Policy*. Ed. Mary Katzenstein and Carol Mueller. Philadelphia: Temple University Press, 1987, 215–244.

"From Protection to Equal Opportunity: The Revolution in Women's Legal Status." *Women, Politics and Change*. Ed. Louise Tilly and Patricia Gurin. New York: Russell Sage, 1990, 457–481.

"How 'Sex' Got into Title VII: Persistent Opportunism as a Maker of Public Policy." *Law and Inequality: A Journal of Theory and Practice* 9, no. 2 (March 1991): 163–184.

"Feminism vs. Family Values: Women at the 1992 Democratic and Republican Conventions." *off our backs* 23, no. 1 (January 1993): 2–3, 10–17; abridged version in

Different Roles, Different Voices: Women and Politics in the United States and Europe. Ed. Marianne Githens, Pippa Norris, and Joni Lovenduski. New York: Harper-Collins, 1995, 70–83.

"From Suffrage to Women's Liberation: Feminism in Twentieth Century America." *Women: A Feminist Perspective.* 5th ed. Ed. Jo Freeman. Mountain View, CA: Mayfield, 1995, 509–528.

"The Real Story of Beijing." *off our backs* 26, no. 3 (March 1996): 1, 8–11, 22–27.

"Change and Continuity for Women at the Republican and Democratic Conventions." *off our backs* 27, no. 1 (January 1997): 14–23.

WRITINGS ON JO FREEMAN

American Men and Women of Science. 13th ed. S 1978.

Who's Who of American Women. 12th ed. 1981–1982.

Biography Index. Vol. 8, 1971.

Contemporary Authors. Vol. 61 (1976), Vol. 8NR (1983).

Contemporary Issues Criticism (1982): 196–200.

Gatlin, Rochelle, ed. *American Women since 1945.* Jackson: University of Mississippi Press, 1987.

Golemba, Beverly E. *Lesser-Known Women: A Biographical Dictionary.* Boulder, CO, and London: Lynne Rienner, 1992, 276.

Jacquette, Jane. "Assessing the Women's Movement." Review of *Politics of Women's Liberation,* in *Signs* 2, no. 1 (Autumn 1976): 154–155.

International Authors and Writers Who's Who. 9th ed., 1982.

Newsweek (March 23, 1970): 73.

O'Neil, Lois Decker, ed. *The Women's Book of World Records and Achievements.* Garden City, NY: Doubleday, 1979, 704.

Thorne, Barrie. Review of *Politics of Women's Liberation,* in *Sex Roles* 2, no. 1 (1976): 98–101.

Who's Who in American Politics. 1973, 1975, 1977, 1979.

The Writer's Directory. 1981, 1983, 1986, 1988.

BETTY FRIEDAN
(1921–)

Susan Butler

> If anything were to be said about me when the history of the movement is
> written, I'd like it to read, "She was the one who said women were people,
> she organized them and taught them to spell their own names."
> —Betty Friedan, quoted in Wilkes 1970

Borrowing from James Baldwin's claim that until the black man could learn to
spell his own name, he would never be free, Betty Friedan believes that until
women learn to spell out their needs, they will never realize equal status in
society. Friedan conceives that her contribution to second wave feminism is that
she provided women with the necessary tools. By articulating the undefined grievances of suburban housewives in *The Feminine Mystique*, she provided an alphabet
that women used to spell out their needs. By spearheading the formation of the
National Organization of Women (NOW), she gave them the necessary paper
and pencil.

Bettye Naomi Goldstein discovered as a child and adolescent that geographic
location and parental influence laid the emotional and intellectual foundation
for public life. Until college, Friedan lived in Peoria, Illinois, the considered
epicenter of American values. Never weaned from the values of middle America,
she has consistently argued for employing pragmatic tactics to achieve change in
the economic, social, and political status of women. Of even greater influence
than geography were her parents. Harry Goldstein immigrated from Russia and
established one of the finest jewelry stores in Peoria. When his daughter was shut
out of high school cliques because she was Jewish, smart, and an "ugly duckling,"
Harry empathized, telling her that often people friendly to him during the business day refused to speak to him "after sundown." Learning from her father that
discrimination exists beyond the insecurity of teenage status-seeking, Friedan
gained a passionate concern for those pushed to the margins of society.

From her mother, Friedan learned to make this passionate concern specific to women. Miriam Goldstein found that her role as wife and mother provided little happiness. Following the dictates of society, she gave up her profession as a journalist when she married. She exhibited her pent-up anger by belittling her husband and pressuring Bettye to find "feminine fulfillment" in a career. Her mother's carping left an indelible mark on Betty Friedan: it both pushed her into journalism and offered a foundation for *The Feminine Mystique*. Friedan has stated that her desire to write about the "comfortable concentration camp" came, in part, because she did not want to be like her mother. The example of her mother's unhappiness heightened Friedan's awareness of the "problem that has no name."

High school represented painful years for Friedan. She was excluded from the school's sororities, had few dates, and feigned stupidity in physics to get help from the "jocks." To fill the unhappy abyss, she read voraciously, started a literary magazine, wrote poetry, and often watched the sun set from a lonesome perch by the town's weed-filled, abandoned cemetery. Looking back, she believes that her exclusion and loneliness created in her the "social consciousness of an outsider," a quality "vital for a writer."

After graduating valedictorian of her class in 1938, Bettye moved to the East Coast to attend Smith College. These four years demonstrated to her that "having brains" did not make her a "freak." She had a group of friends, studied gestalt psychology with Kurt Koffka, wrote and served for one year as editor in chief of the campus newspaper (SCAN), became a member of Phi Beta Kappa in her junior year, and graduated summa cum laude. Academic success at Smith earned Friedan a fellowship to study psychology at the University of California, Berkeley. The year she spent at Berkeley was a success: she studied under Erik Erickson and earned a renewal and expansion of the fellowship. Though the fellowship would have provided support through graduate school, Friedan turned it down. She moved to Greenwich Village and worked as a labor journalist for the Federated Press and the UE News, both of which had a left-wing, popular-front slant. Although Friedan herself downplayed the importance of these writings in her future feminist work, recent criticism "rediscovers" this aspect of Friedan's work and ideological life (Horowitz 1996).

In 1947 Friedan met Carl Friedan, and after a seven-month courtship, they married. At the time, Friedan believed that the "haunting loneliness" she had felt as an adolescent and young adult had ended; in reality, her marriage evolved into one punctuated by verbal and physical violence. The marriage lasted until 1969, when Friedan decided to act on her feminism and sued for divorce.

As Mrs. Carl Friedan, Bettye began to live the mystique that she would later make into a household word. During these years she gave birth to her three children, Jonathan, Daniel, and Emily, and moved from apartment living in New York City to suburban Long Island. Yet unlike those suburban housewives who so readily identified with the "comfortable concentration camp" of suburbia, Friedan found ways to escape. Retaining her maiden name as a byline, Friedan continued to publish as a labor journalist from 1947 to 1952. In 1955, she switched that byline to Betty Friedan and emerged as frequent contributor to women's magazines, a genre that has continued to be a comfortable home base. More importantly, though apparently pressured by editors to mute her message, Friedan managed to get into print several articles that, at least implicitly, challenged middle-class conformity and presented a dismal picture of white women's lives in suburbia in the latter years of the 1950s. In 1960, for example, she published an article in *Good Housekeeping* that stated the basic premise underlying *The Feminine Mystique*.

In 1963 Friedan merged her private and public lives. That year W. W. Norton published 3,000 copies of her five-year study of the status of women in suburban America. *The Feminine Mystique* was an immediate best-seller, causing the publisher to reprint. Eventually, the hardbound version sold over 60,000 copies; a decade later the book had sold 3 million copies, been read by millions more, and been translated into several languages. It remains a significant signpost of the second wave feminist movement.

In 1966, Friedan spearheaded the formation of the National Organization of Women (NOW). She wrote its Statement of Purpose and served as its first president. In 1970 Friedan resigned as the organization's president, reallocating time to writing, teaching, and lecturing. Nonetheless, she remained active in the feminist movement by serving in an advisory capacity in NOW and using her influence in the fight for passage of the Equal Rights Amendment (ERA). In 1976, Friedan published *It Changed My Life*, which defends her ideas, actions, and approach to the feminist movement as well as recounts her own motivations to write *The Feminine Mystique*. In 1981, she followed with another book, *The Second Stage*, which embraces traditional male–female relationships and admonishes both men and women to consider feminism as a humanizing force in society at large rather than one antagonistic to traditional female roles. In 1993 she completed *The Fountain of Age*, which argues that the aging process should represent a positive experience in individuals' lives. Betty Friedan continues to advance her ideas. She often appears in "Letters to the Editor" or the opinion sections of the *New York Times* and *Los Angeles Times* as well as coauthors analytical studies for *Behavioral Scientist*. She maintains a home and office in New York City.

By asking the rhetorical question, "Is this all?" in *The Feminine Mystique*, Betty Friedan challenged the existing ideology of the value and necessity of "domestic containment." In keeping with traditional attitudes of gender roles, this postwar ideology updated the nineteenth-century notion of the "cult of domesticity" to meet the perceived dangers of a nuclear age. Shaping and imposing this ideology, according to Friedan, were experts and educators, advertisers and women's magazines, Freudian psychologists and functionalist social scientists. Friedan warned that this ideology was the same trap of "living with . . . feet bound in glorified femininity." Now it was merely dressed up in "new shiny clothes."

Friedan skillfully and powerfully defrocks this myth, using a preponderance of data. She describes the complicated theories of Sigmund Freud and functionalist sociologists, includes anecdotes from a vast array of interviews she conducted with women in suburbia, and shares her own feelings of entrapment in the "comfortable concentration camp."

For thirteen chapters Friedan defines the "problem that has no name"; in the final chapter, she offers a solution. This "new life plan" recommends a revamped approach to educational policies that would be designed to steer women toward careers. To give women the means to mesh family roles and vocational goals would be the means by which each woman could "find herself, to know herself as a person by creative work of her own."

A close reading of this book reveals that Betty Friedan's five-year project does not contain any original ideas, nor does it contain the same intellectual rigor as works of cultural critics such as David Riesman and C. Wright Mills. Friedan makes exaggerated claims regarding the confinement of women in suburbia and leaves the impression that this "feminine mystique" is a phenomenon unique to postwar American society. Friedan suggests that this myth has been imposed on women by a conspiracy of advertisers, psychologists, and educators, a conspiracy theory devoid of any evidence. For the most part, Friedan ignores women who, because of skin color, sexual preference, educational attainment, or socioeconomic circumstances, fall outside her own experiences as a woman in American society. So why is *The Feminine Mystique* cited as a powerful tract that helped shape an aspect of second wave feminism?

Most obvious is that Betty Friedan articulated the unarticulated grievances of white women living in suburbia. After reading *The Feminine Mystique*, they realized that there was more to life than the creativity of homemaking and joys of motherhood. But undergirding this theme are more powerful reasons that give this book its lasting value.

First, the underlying power of *The Feminine Mystique* is the tone of its author. Friedan demystified the experts for the housewife. More significantly, once she assembled this information, she employed a coffee-klatch vernacular to transmit her message. She employed the friendly, empathic, take-me-into-your-confidence tone used by women when they took a break from the dailiness of their lives and had coffee with friends; it is written in a style women encountered in *McCall's*, *Good Housekeeping*, *Redbook*, and the like. Second, Friedan's solution to the "problem that has no name" is nonthreatening. A recommendation to revamp education so that women can be hired for jobs with higher status and pay is a solution that is well within the comfort zone of middle-class values. Third, *The Feminine Mystique*, though targeted for the middle-class homemaker, resonated with women outside that sphere. Though outsiders, many aspired to becoming part of middle-class America. In that way, Friedan's book became a primer of what they were supposed to feel and think.

Despite its shortcomings, *The Feminine Mystique* is a powerful, polemical treatise that energized women to break out of their confinement and demand equal status. By verbalizing the unarticulated grievances of homemakers living in suburbia, Friedan's work changed the lives not only of these women but also of their daughters and of the women who later gained access to the middle class because of civil rights legislation, affirmative action, and broader acceptance of women as professionals and politicians.

The popularity of this book thrust Friedan into the limelight, making her the natural leader of the mainstream contingent of second wave feminism. As this leader, Friedan spearheaded the formation of NOW in 1966. For the next fifteen years, she worked arduously in and for NOW, aided in the foundation of Women's Equity Action League (WEAL) and National Abortion Rights Action League (NARAL), advocated a change in the laws regarding the legality of abortion, and lobbied hard for passage of the Equal Rights Amendment.

In these capacities, Friedan assured that her point of view became very much a part of the feminist movement. However, though loud, articulate, and backed by supporters, Friedan's voice represented only one of many. Voices from women whose experiences and attitudes differed markedly from the mainstream began to speak as well, although Friedan and her colleagues tried to silence them. Though their grievances were diverse, collectively these voices came from women whose political and sexual orientations and agendas were more radical than Friedan's. From their perspective, the "problem that has no name" had deeper and more insidious roots than myths and laws, and to remove the problem required removing the roots. Friedan considered that reform of policies and laws would give women equal status, whereas more radical feminists believed that the entire male-dominated hierarchy of the "establishment" had to be destroyed. Friedan shaped the agenda of NOW around pragmatic political tactics, whereas the radicals created an agenda based on sexual politics.

These differences soon led to political infighting. The debate escalated to power-play tactics and gave antifeminists ample ammunition to attack feminists, defeat the Equal Rights Amendment, and, most importantly, gain momentum for a conservative backlash that has created an environment that puts at risk practical gains such as affirmative action and the right to an abortion. During these years, Friedan has used every available forum to warn that this infighting would destroy the second wave of the feminist movement; events seem to have proven her right.

Yet Betty Friedan must share the blame. Though she worked hard to build a strong coalition among diverse groups, she also contributed to the escalation of the movement's cold war. This is most apparent in her writing. During the 1970s in magazines articles, interviews, and her second book, It Changed My Life, Friedan frequently derided feminists with agendas different from her own. She often diminished the importance of radical feminists; the first and perhaps most offensive attack she waged came in a McCall's column, tellingly titled "Everything I Know Has Come from My Own Experience" and later reprinted in a book. Here Friedan labeled radical feminists "pseudo radicals," attacked their tactic of consciousness-raising by calling it "navel-gazing, rap sessions," and reduced their advocacy of sexual politics to a diatribe on the "meanness of male chauvinist pigs, the comparisons of orgasms, [and] talk about getting rid of love, sex, children, and men" (Friedan 1976, 191–192).

Clearly, Betty Friedan imparts a sincere and impassioned concern that those advocating sexual politics would destroy the feminist movement. However, she might have been less dogmatic about her own agenda, more thoughtful about differences among women, and less inflammatory in her public statements. Her rhetoric and the attitude that informed it have weakened the feminist movement, making it vulnerable to the conservative backlash that began with Richard Nixon's election in 1968, reached its highest point in the Reagan presidency, and still informs American political culture in the mid-1990s.

Such a critique of Friedan does not, however, diminish her extraordinary achievements. She defined a problem that motivated countless women to make significant and positive changes in their lives, organized a feminist organization dedicated to equality for women and to political action as a means of achieving it, and continues to work passionately to find the means to bring those individuals who are pushed to the margins into the mainstream of American society. Her tireless efforts contributed significantly to the fact that the feminist revolt of the 1960s and 1970s has become one of the most successful and vibrant efforts of the "rights revolution" of those two decades.

WORKS BY BETTY FRIEDAN

Books

The Feminine Mystique. New York: W. W. Norton, 1963; rev. ed., 1974; twentieth-anniversary ed., 1983.
It Changed My Life: Writings on the Women's Movement. New York: W. W. Norton, 1976.
The Second Stage. New York: Summit Books, 1981.
The Fountain of Age. New York: Simon and Schuster, 1993.
Personal Papers. Schlesinger Library, Radcliffe College, Cambridge.

Articles

"I Say: Woman Are People Too!" Good Housekeeping 151 (September 1960): 59–61, 161–162.
"Up from the Kitchen Floor." New York Times Magazine (March 4, 1973): 8.
"Feminism Takes a New Turn." New York Times Magazine (November 18, 1979): 40, 90+.
"20 Years after the Feminine Mystique." New York Times Magazine (February 27, 1983): 34.
"How to Get the Women's Movement Moving Again." New York Times Magazine (November 3, 1985): 26, 28, 66.

WRITINGS ON BETTY FRIEDAN AND HER WORK

Bowlby, Rachel. "The Problem with No Name: Rereading Friedan's The Feminist Mystique." Feminist Review 27 (September 1987): 61–75.

French, Marilyn. "The Emancipation of Betty Friedan." *Esquire* 100 (December 1983): 510+.

hooks, bell. *Feminist Theory from Margin to Center.* Boston: South End Press, 1984.

Horowitz, Daniel. "Rethinking Betty Friedan and *The Feminine Mystique*: Labor Union Radicalism and Feminism in Cold War America." *American Quarterly* 48 (March 1996): 1–42.

May, Elaine Tyler. *Homeward Bound: American Families in the Cold War Era.* New York: Basic Books, 1988.

Meyerowitz, Joanne. "Beyond the Feminine Mystique: A Reassessment of Postwar Mass Culture, 1946–1958." *Journal of American History* 79 (March 1993): 1455–1482.

Moses, Jennifer. "She's Changed Our Lives: A Profile of Betty Friedan." *Present Tense* (May/June 1988): 26–31.

Wilkes, Paul. "Mother Superior to Women's Lib." *New York Times Magazine* (November 29, 1970): sec. 6, 27–29+.

RUTH BADER GINSBURG
(1933–)

Gwenn Brown Nealis

A descendant of Central European and Russian Jewish immigrants, Joan Ruth or Ruth Joan Bader was born on March 15, 1933, in New York City. Her parents were Nathan Bader and Celia Amster Bader. Her older sister and only sibling, Marilyn, died of meningitis when Ruth was one year old.

Even as an adolescent Ruth Bader distinguished herself as a scholar. She graduated first in her class at P.S. 238 and there at age twelve or thirteen wrote an editorial, "Landmarks of Constitutional Freedom," for the student newspaper. She was also confirmed with honors at East Midwood Jewish Center and at James Madison High School in Brooklyn. During her childhood and adolescence, Ruth had been positively influenced by her mother, who encouraged her love of reading and language and who continually saved money for Ruth's college education. In 1950, on the day before Ruth's high school graduation, her mother died of cervical cancer. Ruth Bader won a scholarship to Cornell University and was able to give her mother's financial legacy to her father. In a 1993 interview Ginsburg stated, "My greatest inspiration was my own mother. She never had the opportunity to go to college, but she taught me to pursue learning. She gave me confidence in myself that is invaluable" (Hunt 1993, 117).

At Cornell Bader earned a B.A. in government in 1954. She also met and married fellow Cornell student Martin D. Ginsburg. Both Ginsburgs decided to pursue careers in law. Their law studies were interrupted when Martin was called away from enrollment at Harvard University Law School for military service. Subsequently, the couple moved to Fort Sill in Lawton, Oklahoma, where they lived for two years while Martin finished a tour of duty. During the time at Fort Sill, daughter Jane Ginsburg was born.

In 1956, following Martin Ginsburg's discharge, the family moved to Cambridge, Massachusetts, where Martin continued his degree work, and Ruth enrolled in the law program. She was one of nine women in a class of over 500 students. Martin and Ruth studied hard and shared child care. Of her husband Ginsburg has said that "some men are less confident about themselves than my husband. You have to have a lot of self-security in order to regard your life's partner as someone who is truly equal not somehow less important" (Hunt 1993, 117).

In law school, Ginsburg's hard work earned her election to the editorship of the *Harvard Law Review*. During her second year there, Martin was diagnosed with a rare form of testicular cancer. Ruth copied notes taken by fellow students and typed Martin's papers while he was recovering from surgery and undergoing radiation therapy. With her support, he graduated in 1958. When he accepted a job in Manhattan, Ruth Ginsburg transferred to Columbia Law School, where she was a Kent scholar, served on the *Columbia Law Review*, and tied for first in her 1959 graduating class.

Ginsburg faced many obstacles in finding employment. She finally found a clerkship with Edmund L. Palmieri, a federal district judge. She also spent two years working on a Columbia Law School project in Sweden. Following that, she taught at Rutgers University Law School as one of the first twenty women to teach in an American law school. She gave birth to her son James in 1965 and continued to work at Rutgers. In the 1960s she began to take sex discrimination cases for the American Civil Liberties Union (ACLU). In 1971 she was hired by Harvard University to teach a course on women and the law, then hired by Columbia Law School as its first tenured female faculty member.

In the 1970s Ginsburg acted as director of the Women's Rights Project for ACLU. Between 1973 and 1976 she argued six gender equality cases before the Supreme Court and won five of them. She exposed the gender biases of existing laws and established a legal framework for women's equality to men. In 1980 President Jimmy Carter nominated Ginsburg to be a judge on the Court of Appeals for the District of Columbia Circuit. She was sworn in on June 30, 1980. During her thirteen-year term in that position she wrote over 300 opinions that dealt with abortion rights, gay rights, and affirmative action. Ginsburg is viewed as a centrist; she voted more often with her Republican colleagues rather than the Democrat-appointed judges.

President Bill Clinton nominated Ruth Bader Ginsburg to the Supreme Court on June 15, 1993. The American Bar Association gave Ginsburg the highest rating, and on August 3, 1996, her nomination was approved by the U.S. Senate by a vote of 96 to 3. She took the oath of office on August 10, 1993, becoming the second woman to accede to the Supreme Court and the first Jewish justice since the resignation of Abe Fortas in 1969.

Ruth Bader Ginsburg experienced a great deal of gender discrimination in her own life. At Fort Sill, when she revealed she was pregnant while applying for a job in the local Social Security office at the GS-5 level, she was demoted to the GS-2 level. The higher-level job went to another pregnant woman who had concealed her condition. This experience no doubt prompted her to disguise her pregnancy in 1965 while she was working at Rutgers University. She wore over-sized clothes, gave birth to her son James during summer recess, and returned to work in September.

At Harvard, Ginsburg faced opposition as one of only nine women law students in her class of 500. She was asked by a Harvard dean to justify taking up the place where a man could be. Another time, she was denied access to a magazine from a Harvard library periodical room because she was a woman. When the attendant even refused to bring her the article, Ginsburg sent a male colleague to check the reference for her. Later at Columbia, although she tied for first in her class and had served on the *Harvard* and *Columbia Law Reviews*, she applied for a job with several law firms but was rejected by all of them. She said, "Not a single law firm in the entire city of New York bid for my employment" (Carlson 1993, 38). She later said, "To be a woman, a Jew and a mother to boot, that combination was a bit much" (Thomas 1993, 1876). In addition, Ginsburg com-mented:

I came from a world where women were protected out of everything. Protected out of being lawyers, out of being engineers, out of being bartenders. . . . The days of not hiring women are over. Of course, anyone who emerges as a spokesperson will have to put up with a certain amount of unpleasantness. I am thinking of the days (when lawyers met) in all-male clubs. I was considered a pest for even suggesting that it was inappropriate. . . . I don't know how many times I've had the experience of people laughing at me. You just don't give up. You keep trying. (Hunt 1993, 117)

Ruth Bader Ginsburg kept trying.

Even though Ginsburg experienced discrimination, she did not interpret it at the time as being the result of gender bias. She has commented that she was a latecomer to the fight for woman's rights. "I did not go into law with the purpose of becoming an advocate of equal rights. I became a lawyer for selfish reasons. I thought I could do a lawyer's job better than any other [job]" (Graham 1994, 214). In the late 1960s, two things seemed to compel Ginsburg into the feminist movement. She read Simone de Beauvoir's book *The Second Sex*, and at about the same time the American Civil Liberties Union began referring her sex dis-crimination cases. As she read the material dealing with these cases, she realized that gender biases distorted most of the laws in this country. "Once I became involved, I found the legal work fascinating and had high hopes for significant change in the next decade" (Graham 1994, 214).

As general counsel to the ACLU and project director of the Women's Rights Project of the ACLU, she argued six cases before the Supreme Court and won five of them. These cases exposed the gender biases of existing laws. In most cases the laws were established to protect women, but as Ginsburg argued, they "could often perversely, have the opposite effect" (Roberts 1993, 26), because they depicted women as weak and incompetent. In *Reed v. Reed*, a November 1971 unanimous Supreme Court decision supported Ginsburg's case against an

Idaho law giving precedence to men over women in naming the administrator of an estate. This law was founded on the idea that there was a "rational basis" for believing a man would be more capable in the role of estate administrator than a woman would be; the burden of proof was on the woman. Ginsburg sought to place the burden of proof on the state to prove that the man would be more competent by changing the standard from "rational basis" to "strict scrutiny." Even though the Supreme Court did decide its first sex-bias case in the woman's favor, they did not agree with Ginsburg's application of strict scrutiny. In her second case, *Frontiero v. Richardson* (1973), Ginsburg contended that the laws regarding dependent-housing allowances in the military should be applied equally to servicemen and servicewomen. The husband of Sharon Frontier, a U.S. Air Force lieutenant, was denied benefits unless his dependency on her could be proved. Wives of servicemen were assumed dependent. Here Ginsburg defended the principle of gender equality even when women had benefited from a law. The Supreme Court was convinced by Ginsburg to redefine its guidelines for gender-biased laws.

In her third and fourth Supreme Court cases, Ginsburg defended two widowers who wanted the same benefits that widows automatically received. Ginsburg lost her third case, but in the fourth case the Court voted to strike down the double standard concerning a spouse's Social Security benefits. This victory may have been due to the fact that the widower's wife died in childbirth, and the judges viewed the child as the victim in this case and not because they found the law unequal in the treatment of widows and widowers.

In the 1976 case, *Craig v. Boren*, Ginsburg attacked an Oklahoma law that allowed the sale of beer to eighteen-year-old women but denied it to males who were not at least twenty-one years old. It was assumed that young women were less likely to drive drunk than young men were. Ginsburg said that the Supreme Court, by overturning this law, acknowledged that the "familiar stereotype: the active boy, aggressive and assertive; the passive girl, docile and submissive" (Graham 1994, 215) should not be the basis for law.

In Ginsburg's final Supreme Court case, in 1978, *Duren v. Missouri*, she argued that the Missouri laws that made jury duty optional for women but not for men showed that the state placed a higher value on the citizenship of men over women. Ginsburg's determination provoked the Supreme Court and other political institutions to "rethink ancient positions" (Roberts 1993, 26) on woman's rights. Her stoic crusade has been to remove all of the "protective" laws that have, in fact, held women in check.

Ruth Bader Ginsburg's judicial record displays the restraint that has surprised the people who viewed her as a rebel taking on gender discrimination in the American legal system. What she has demonstrated again and again is her ability to use logic over emotion. She states that as a judge she was guided by the words of Chief Justice William H. Rehnquist in reference to a judge's obligation to act fairly "even when the decision is not . . . what the home crowd wants" (*Facts on File*, 1993, 444). In two cases in particular Ginsburg's rulings provoked surprise.

In 1984 she concurred in the navy's discharge of a gay sailor and the Central Intelligence Agency's (CIA) dismissal of a homosexual employee for no reason other than sexual orientation. In a 1986 opinion she wrote upholding Kawasaki Motors' clandestine use of antiunion consultants while Kawasaki was engaged in negotiations with the United Auto Workers.

The Ginsburg comments that have fired more publicity and controversy than any others are those dealing with *Roe v. Wade*, the 1973 ruling that legalized abortion. Ginsburg did not disagree with the outcome of the case. Instead, she criticized the grounds on which the decision was based. She felt that the rationale should have been equal protection rather than privacy. According to Ginsburg, *Roe v. Wade* "halted a political process that was moving in a reform direction and thereby . . . prolonged divisiveness and deferred stable settlement of the issue" (Graham 1994, 216). As she sees it, the Supreme Court should have invited the state legislatures to discuss the specifics of access. The sweeping decision on the part of the Supreme Court caused too much upheaval and damaged the stature of the Court. The Supreme Court, according to Ginsburg, "generally follows, it does not lead, changes taking place elsewhere in society." She also states that "without taking giant strides and thereby risking a backlash, the Court, through constitutional adjudication, can moderately accelerate the pace of change" (Graham 1994, 216). Here once more is the mixture of political liberalism and judicial conservatism that have put Ruth Bader Ginsburg into a position that *Vogue*'s Elaine Shannon claims "defies categorization" (Shannon 1993, 472).

Her Supreme Court post acceptance speech on June 14, 1993, reflected her feminist ideology when she said, "[I want to thank] my mother, Celia Amster Bader, the bravest and strongest person I have known, who was taken from me too soon. I pray that I may be all that she would have been had she lived in an age when women could aspire and achieve and daughters are cherished as much as sons" (Graham 1994, 216). Her congressional hearings reveal her commitment to woman's rights. She argued that "[abortion] is something central to a woman's life, to her dignity. It's a decision she must make for herself. And when government controls that decision for her, she's being treated as less than a fully adult human responsible for her own choices" (Graham 1994, 216). She also spoke about the Equal Rights Amendment: "I would like to see for the sake of my daughter and granddaughter and all the daughters who come after, that statement as part of our fundamental instrument of government" (Graham 1994, 216).

Since her appointment to the Supreme Court, according to Joan Biskupic of the *Washington Post*, "Ginsburg's frank and revealing personal accounts of the obstacles facing women have established her as one of the nation's most prominent feminist voices" (Biskupic 1995, A1). She has spoken to many women's groups and on college campuses. She often speaks of women's liberation in terms of men and women giving equal time to child care. At a Brooklyn appearance she said, "If I had an affirmative action program to design, it would be to give men every incentive to be concerned about rearing children." She has also commented: "Motherhood has been praised to the skies, but the greatest praise men can give to that role is for them to share in doing it. That's my dream for the next generation" (Hunt 1993, 117). But Ginsburg is not a woman of words and ideas only. She has put into practice her words by allowing male court clerks to have flexible work schedules so they can share equal child care with their spouses.

On the Supreme Court Ginsburg has exhibited the same judicial restraint that was established on the Court of Appeals, but the feminist crusader is still present. The Court has dealt with several important gender-based cases since Ginsburg was sworn into office. In *Harris v. Forklift Systems*, the full Court ruled that a worker who claims she was sexually harassed need not prove she was psychologically injured to win money damages. Ginsburg's concurring opinion said that "the critical issue is whether members of one sex are exposed to disadvantageous terms or conditions of employment to which members of the other sex are not exposed" (Biskupic 1995, A4). In *J. E. B. v. T. B.*, the Supreme Court on April 19, 1994, prohibited sex bias in jury selection. Ginsburg argued that the stereotypes that have long led to the exclusion of prospective jurors because of their sex are "evil" (Biskupic 1993, A3). For the June 26, 1996, decision in the case of the *United States v. Virginia*, Ginsburg delivered the majority opinion, which ended a 157-year tradition of state-supported, all-male education at the Virginia Military Institute (VMI). As she put it, while Virginia "serves the state's sons, it makes no provision whatever for her daughters. That is not equal protection" (Biskupic 1996, A1). A 1995 U.S. Court of Appeals for the Fourth Circuit in Richmond had ruled that most women would not fit in, or benefit from, attendance at VMI. Ginsburg pointed out that was beside the point and stated, "Generalizations about 'the way women are,' estimates of what is appropriate for most women, no longer justify denying opportunity to women whose talent and capacity place them outside the average description" (Greenhouse 1996, A1).

With all of her triumphs and accomplishments for the rights of women one must not forget Ruth Bader Ginsburg the wife, mother, friend, reader, athlete, opera fan. Martin and Ruth's children, Jane and James, are now adults, and the Ginsburgs are grandparents. James has said of his family life: "The family was always home for dinner. And a night did not go by when my mother did not check to see that I was doing my schoolwork. She was always there when I wanted her to be—and even when I didn't" (Hewitt 1993, 50). Ginsburg reads mysteries, plays the piano, watches classic movies, horseback rides, and plays golf. She has also been described by some as schoolmarmish, shy, and reserved. She is as she has always been, a complex, intellectual person.

In her professional career and personal life, Ruth Bader Ginsburg is a testimony to her background, her intelligence, her use of strategy, her determination, and her diligence. She said, "I do think that being the second woman (on the Supreme Court) is wonderful, because it is a sign that being a woman in a place of importance is no longer extraordinary. It will become more and more natural" (Goldberg 1993, 43). When asked in 1996 to recall a memory of artwork from her school days, Ginsburg recalled "the knobs of brass once found on the doors of every City of New York public school because they were fine in design and never slipped from one's grasp" (Pollak 1996, 28). Ruth Bader Ginsburg shares these qualities. She possesses a fine life's design and has not let her goals and principles slip from her grasp.

WORKS BY RUTH BADER GINSBURG

For a list of all publications, including Supreme Court Cases in which Justice Ginsburg argued or submitted a brief, see Rubin, Alvin B. *Selected Bibliography of the Writings of Justice Ruth Bader Ginsburg* (Baton Rouge: Louisiana State University Law Center, 1996).

WRITINGS ON RUTH BADER GINSBURG AND HER WORK

Biskupic, Joan. "Justices Consider Banning Sex-Based Exclusion of Jurors." *Washington Post*, November 3, 1993, sec. A, 3.
———. "High Court's Justice with a Cause." *Washington Post*, April 17, 1995, sec. A, 1+.
———. "Supreme Court Invalidates Exclusion of Women by VMI." *Washington Post*, June 27, 1996, sec. A, 1+.
Carlson, Margaret. "The Law according to Ruth." *Time* 141 (June 28, 1993): 38.
Gilbert, Lynn, and Gaylen Moore. *Particular Passions: Talks with Women Who Have Shaped Our Times*. New York: Clarkson N. Potter, 1981.
Goldberg, Stephanie B. "The Second Woman Justice: Ruth Bader Ginsburg Talks Candidly about a Changing Society." *ABA Journal* (October 1993): 40–43.
Graham, Judith, et al., eds. "Ruth Bader Ginsburg." *Current Biography Yearbook 1994.* New York: H. W. Wilson, 1994.
Greenhouse, Linda. "Military College Can't Bar Women, High Court Rules." *New York Times*, June 27, 1996, sec. A, 1+.
Hewitt, Bill. "Feeling Supreme: Tireless Ruth Ginsburg Heads for the High Court." *People* (June 28, 1993): 49–50.
Hunt, Angela. "Women Right Now: Meet Our New Supreme Court Justice." *Glamour* (October 1993): 116–117.
"Judge Ginsburg Nominated to Replace White on Supreme Court; Ex-Rights Lawyer Would Become Court's Second Woman." *Facts on File* 53 (June 17, 1993): 443–444.
Pollak, Michael. "A Gallery of Memories." *New York Times*, January 7, 1996, sec. 4A, 28.
Roberts, Steven V. "Two Lives of Ruth Bader Ginsburg." *U.S. News and World Report* 114 (June 28, 1993): 26.
Rubin, Alvin B. *Selected Bibliography of the Writings of Justice Ruth Bader Ginsburg*. Baton Rouge, LA: Paul M. Hebert Law Center Library, 1996.
Shannon, Elaine. "Justice for Women." *Vogue* (October 1993): 392+.
Thomas, Jennifer S. "Ruth Ginsburg: Carving a Career Path Through Male Dominated Legal World." *Congressional Quarterly Weekly Report*, July 17, 1993.

BELL HOOKS
(1952–)

Lara E. Dieckmann

bell hooks is an African American writer, poet, teacher, and cultural critic who, in an attempt to depersonalize identity politics, considers herself an advocate of feminist politics, rather than a feminist intellectual or activist. Born Gloria Jean Watkins on September 25, 1952, in Hopkinsville, Kentucky, she is the daughter of Rosa Bell Watkins and Veodis Watkins. Her mother worked in the home, raising the children, and her father was the janitor at the local post office. She has one brother and five sisters.

The Watkins family shared an interest in poetry. Inspired by poetry readings at home, Gloria performed for her church community. In addition to reciting the works of Gwendolyn Brooks, William Wordsworth, Elizabeth Barrett Browning, and Langston Hughes, Watkins wrote original verse, which was published in her Sunday school magazine. However, these early experiences of performing and writing were not exclusively positive; the punishment for "talking back" or speaking equally with an adult was severe. Watkins remembers many occasions when her dissenting opinions and her proclivity for drama were condemned as crazy, serving as an impetus for the development of her critical consciousness and creative intellectualism.

In addition to her immediate family, Gloria was heavily influenced by her maternal grandfather, Gus, who offered her an alternative, nonpatriarchal model of black masculinity, and her great-grandmother, Bell Hooks, legendary for her sharp-tongued opinions. It is this ancestral, maternal history that Watkins self-consciously evokes in her pseudonym. According to Watkins, the writing persona of bell hooks—written in lowercase letters to deflect the emphasis on personality over ideas—was a way to embrace her emerging, independent voice.

Growing up, the female presence of her mother, sisters, grandmothers, and aunts was powerful. However, the Watkins household was strictly patriarchal. Significantly, the experience of sexism and male domination, not racism, seemed most salient to her in her childhood. Hopkinsville was segregated in her youth, and although she was aware of the severity of white racism, African Americans in the community formed a tightly knit kinship structure, regardless of social status or economic class. Within the black half of this segregated town, however, there was another kind of segregation based on gender. Although the older women in her family spoke intensely and passionately, the final, authoritative statement on any subject was always her father's. She attributes her feminist consciousness to an early awareness of sexual inequity and paternal domination in her home; her younger brother had privileges none of the sisters enjoyed, and her father's censure was fearfully avoided.

While sexism and racism decisively conditioned her daily life, Watkins found refuge in the segregated educational system. In this context she learned the power of oppositional thinking. In particular, Watkins notes that early exposure to black female teachers provided her with a model of education as the "practice of freedom," to quote Paulo Freire, the Brazilian teacher and activist. Without the empowering presence of black women in her youth, she doubts she would have survived the many struggles she confronted in her higher education at primarily white institutions.

Watkins began her undergraduate studies at a small, southern liberal arts school. After one year, she transferred to Stanford University, where she majored in English literature. At Stanford, Watkins experienced for the first time class differences among blacks and, for the first time, the exclusionary, institutional violence of the academy. Though Watkins sought refuge in the women's studies and African American studies departments, she felt that her interests were ignored in the former and dismissed in the latter. Frustrated by the lack of interest in race issues by white women scholars and gender issues by black male scholars, Watkins began her first book, Ain't I a Woman? at the age of nineteen. Ain't I a Woman? centralized the radical, inseparable intersection of race, sex, and class at the core of black women's lives, a topic to which she would repeatedly return.

After she received her undergraduate degree, Watkins attended the University of Wisconsin at Madison, earning her master's degree in English literature. She returned to the West Coast, where she taught courses in English and ethnic studies at the University of Southern California and creative writing, composition, and African American literature at the University of California at Santa Cruz and San Francisco State University. During this period, Watkins began her doctoral studies, eventually completing her degree at the University of California-Santa Cruz. She earned her Ph.D. in 1983; her dissertation focused on the novels of Toni Morrison.

Watkins accepted a joint appointment in the English and African American studies departments at Yale University in 1985. She has spoken very pointedly about the devaluation of race, politics, and identity on that campus, among many others. Noting that the ideal of "academic freedom" is often used to deflect attention away from educational policies that foster various inequalities, Watkins challenges the concept that any educational system is politically neutral. Watkins began her tenure at Oberlin College in 1988. In 1994, she accepted the prestigious Distinguished Lecturer of English Literature post at the City College of New York, where she currently lives and works.

hooks has stated that she considers teaching a job but writing her true calling. Under her pseudonym, hooks published a volume of poetry entitled *And There We Wept* in 1978. In 1981, she published *Ain't I a Woman? Black Women and Feminism*, which she had begun ten years earlier. The title echoes Sojourner Truth's succinct summary of gender and racial prejudice uttered nearly a century before. In addition to Truth, hooks draws upon the work of nineteenth-century black women educators, activists, writers, and community leaders, including Mary Church Terrell, Anna Julia Cooper, and Frances Ellen Watkins, in her analysis. She traces the contemporary devaluation of black women to the atrocious legacy of slavery. Arguing that black women are "rarely recognized as a group separate and distinct from black men, or as a present part of the larger group, 'women' in this culture" (hooks 1981, 7), she suggests that this double bind constitutes a major force of domination, precluding the possibility of liberation. Wide-ranging and polemical, hooks' discussion ranges from the impact of imperialist patriarchy on black women to racism within the women's movement, concluding with her vision of the future relationship between black women and feminism.

While largely well received, this text garnered harsh criticism from some feminists for its omission of lesbians and lesbianism. Charging homophobia, critics like Michele Wallace, Adrienne Rich, and Barbara Smith questioned the validity and depth of hooks' conclusions. Although hooks has answered many of the particular criticisms leveled against her by other feminists, she maintains her belief that homophobia is a logical extension of sexism, thereby privileging gender over sexuality in her analyses, a common, albeit controversial, view. While the critical reception of *Ain't I a Woman?* was mixed, it contributed significantly to the burgeoning articulation of black women's studies. Along with the edited collection *All the Women Are White, All the Blacks Are Men, But Some of Us Are Brave*, published in 1980, hooks' early work helped forge the emergence of black feminist scholarship in the academy.

hooks published *Feminist Theory: From Margin to Center* in 1984. While in many ways a continuation of the conversation she began in *Ain't I a Woman?*, *Feminist Theory* demonstrates a shift in focus. While *Ain't I a Woman?* emphasizes the experience of sexism in the lives of black women, *Feminist Theory* foregrounds the concerns of race and class. In this book, hooks explicitly calls for a more inclusive analytical scope within feminist theory. She argues persuasively that race and class impinge significantly and in interlocking ways with gender identity. Recognizing and including the voices of nonwhite and working-class women would work to expand and deepen critiques of patriarchy developed by white, middle-class women, foundational to the second wave of the women's movement.

Talking Back: Thinking Feminist, Thinking Black, published in 1989, marks another shift in hooks' writing. In this series of personal essays, hooks focuses on the impact of white, imperialist, patriarchal domination in daily life. Offering anecdotes and recollections from her childhood, hooks delineates the psychological and spiritual injuries induced by racism and sexism in particular. She speaks throughout these pieces about the importance of "de-colonizing" one's mind, of expunging deeply internalized self-hatred and prejudice promoted by every aspect of culture and society. In addition to documenting the particularities of personal experience—now considered a hallmark of hooks' style—these essays centralize the importance of popular culture and representation vis-à-vis identity, community, and politics.

The publication of *Yearning: Race, Gender, and Cultural Politics* in 1990 firmly situated hooks as a cultural critic. In these essays, hooks analyzes rap music, advertising trends, and popular films as sources of racist, sexist representation. In working toward a flexible, politicized notion of a black postmodernist sensibility, hooks locates the potential for resistance in the reception of dominant representations by oppositional cultural "readers." As she states in the Introduction, recognizing and intervening within the politics of culture are "crucial for colonized groups globally in the struggle for self-determination" (hooks 1990, 3–5). hooks invokes the powerful concept of a "homeplace" as a "site of resistance" to oppression, directly acknowledging the importance of home, memory, and community to the efficacy of progressive politics.

Wildly various and often paradoxical, hooks seems to construct her text through methodological contradiction, deliberately confounding any singular reading of this work. This is due, in part, to her adoption of multiple writing strategies, including self-referential interviews of bell hooks by Gloria Watkins. Playing with the tensions of identity and personae, Watkins questions herself regarding her own assumptions and assertions. According to Natalie Alexander in her review of *Yearning*, the collection as a whole functions metaphorically to represent the quilted piecings of hooks' own history: "hooks stitches together the old words she takes up like scraps for a crazy quilt, transforming this quilted space, this complex landscape, this site of erotic, spiritual, political, aesthetic yearning" (Alexander 1992, 187). This yearning to which hooks and Alexander refer signifies the larger search for, and articulation of, a critical voice, integral to transformation and liberation.

In 1991, hooks collaborated with Cornel West on a book entitled *Breaking Bread: Insurgent Black Intellectual Life*. Structured in the call-and-response format evocative of African American religious practices, West and hooks alternate essays on the role of intellectualism in the lives of black people. The text also includes interviews and dialogues between the two authors, particularly focusing on the relationship between social activism and intellectual work. While timely and often candid, *Breaking Bread* also exposes the limits of a text-based approach to dialogism; though a trace remains, much of the spirit, humor, and complexity of human interaction is lost in the translation from speech to writing.

Black Looks: Race and Representation, a collection of essays, was published in 1992. hooks takes as her primary subject the image of blackness in popular culture, arguing that what is seen and what cannot be seen determine, in large measure, our sociopolitical consciousness. She returns to the idea of an oppositional gaze in her essay of the same title. Critiquing Laura Mulvey's groundbreaking work on narrative cinema, in particular, her analysis of its construction of (white) passive female spectators, hooks suggests that an oppositional gaze, born of necessity, allows black women to "choose not to identify with either the victim or the perpetrator" (hooks 1992, 122). For hooks, this is the key to transforming the politics of domination operative within the representational strategies of mainstream cinema, television, and music. She is especially effective in her analyses of the ways that blackness is commodified, bought, and sold as a symbol of "Otherness." "Eating the Other" and "Selling Hot Pussy," for example, offer a critical treatment of race, gender, and capitalism through a discussion of the ways black women's bodies are packaged and consumed for whites hungry for "difference." As a whole, however, the essays are somewhat uneven; at times, hooks privileges didacticism over demonstration. While not entirely problematic, this approach is belied by her claim that she (along with other black intellectuals and artists) is attempting to create new paradigms with which to conceptualize race and representation.

In her 1993 publication *Sisters of the Yam: Black Women and Self-Recovery*, hooks articulated the need for black women to address internalized racism and colonization through psychological healing. The product of several related projects, including a regular column in the alternative Z *Magazine* and a self-help group she founded, *Sisters of the Yam* sets out to dismantle the stereotype of the strong black woman. Distinguishing the ability to endure from the potential to flourish, hooks argues that this pervasive myth works to obscure the need black women have for viable, healthy support systems. In *Sisters of the Yam*, hooks' concern for spirituality and psychology merges in an explicit analysis of the personal toll that racism, sexism, and poverty take on the daily lives of black women in this country, while simultaneously pointing to the diasporic connections between black women of many different cultures. She also published her second volume of poetry in 1993, entitled *A Woman's Mourning Song*.

Teaching to Transgress: Education as the Practice of Freedom centralizes an important undercurrent that runs throughout hooks' oeuvre: critical pedagogy. Simultaneously invoking and challenging the work of Paulo Freire, hooks attempts to apply his theory of progressive pedagogy to the American educational system. For Freire, students must become connected to, and accountable for, their own intellectual development. In order to accomplish this conceptual shift, Freire and hooks advocate for the active participation of students in their own learning processes.

Outlaw Culture: Resisting Representations, her second major publication of 1994, features a series of essays covering a wide range of topics, including standards of beauty, reactionary feminism, and contemporary films. hooks followed this collection in 1995 with another volume of essays, *Art on My Mind: Visual Politics*. In this text, hooks explicitly articulates the relationship between political domination and visual art in culture. Primarily comparative, hooks describes the aesthetic divergences from a conventional, white, Western tradition by black

artists. Published in the same year, *Killing Rage: Ending Racism* addresses a pre-
dominant theme of hooks'—the intersection of class, race, and gender—through
a favored method, a series of essays that mix personal experience, pedagogical
observation, and theoretical claims. Though often provocative and insightful,
the articles do not attempt to organize a comprehensive vision of antiracism,
contrary to the text's subtitle.

Recently, hooks published another volume of essays that deal with contemporary films: *Reel to Real: Race, Sex and Class at the Movies.* While this collection
continues her discussion of the relationship between representation and politics,
she has included several interviews of film directors and producers. In addition
to continuing her vast publication record in journals and magazines, hooks is
currently working on a two-volume set of memoirs, titled *Bone Black: Memories
of Childhood* and *Cat Island Woman.*

hooks' writing has been a notable source of celebration and controversy within
the feminist movement as well as academic and intellectual circles. Many critics
take exception to her lack of traditional, scholarly documentation, for example;
hooks has explained that while she wants to provide a model for black women
interested in pursuing an intellectual life, she wishes to remain accessible to the
widest audience possible. For her, then, the use of footnotes is a mark of privilege
and elitism, rather than a helpful guide to related texts and ideas. This assumption
remains uninterrogated in her writing but has not gone unnoticed in the criticism
of her work. In her review of *Art on My Mind* for *The Village Voice*, Michele
Wallace suggests that rather than empowering the uneducated, hooks is ultimately serving herself by avoiding painstaking historical research and comprehensive literature reviews. Furthermore, Wallace notes that hooks frequently
overlooks the scholarship of other black feminist critics, often with dissenting
views from hers, in the pursuit of "ahistorical, essentialist fantasies" marked by
self-indulgence and political correctness. Defenders of hooks claim that criticisms
such as these amount to little more than professional jealousy, ignoring the methodological problems and philosophical contradictions to which they point.

Critics and apologists alike miss the crucial questions her unconventional style
raises, namely, To what degree should standards of scholarship shift in light of
recent political challenges? What are the relative advantages and disadvantages
of constructing theory in the form of a polemic? What are the benefits and
limitations of writing about oppression in a personal voice? To what extent can
the paradigm of identity politics address concerns obscured, ignored, and erased
in traditional scholarship? Rather than unequivocally dismissing or uncritically
celebrating her as a feminist theorist, hooks' work could offer a place from which
to begin these important, difficult discussions.

Certainly one of the most visible feminist intellectuals writing on gender, class,
and race today, hooks insists on the validity of personal experience, the insepar-
ability of theory and practice, and the importance of deploying multiple strategies
in the struggle for social transformation and political liberation. Whether advocating the development of an oppositional consciousness to popular culture or

critiquing the limitations of an exclusively gender-based approach to feminist theory and activism, hooks is often incisive and rarely predictable. Prolific, polemical and ambitious in scope, bell hooks' contribution to contemporary feminism has been profound.

WRITINGS BY BELL HOOKS

And There We Wept: Poems. Los Angeles: Golemics, 1978.
Ain't I a Woman? Black Women and Feminism. Boston: South End Press, 1981.
Feminist Theory from Margin to Center. Boston: South End Press, 1984.
Talking Back: Thinking Feminist, Thinking Black. Boston: South End Press, 1989.
Yearning: Race, Gender, and Cultural Politics. Boston: South End Press, 1990.
And Cornel West. *Breaking Bread: Insurgent Black Intellectual Life.* Boston: South End Press, 1991.
Black Looks: Race and Representation. Boston: South End Press, 1992.
Sisters of the Yam: Black Women and Self-Recovery. Boston: South End Press, 1993a.
A Woman's Mourning Song. New York: Harlem River Press., 1993b.
Outlaw Culture: Resisting Representations. New York: Routledge, 1994a.
Teaching to Transgress: Education as the Practice of Freedom. New York: Routledge, 1994b.
Art on My Mind: Visual Politics. New York: New Press, 1995a.
Killing Rage: Ending Racism. New York: Henry Holt, 1995b.
Bone Black: Memories of Girlhood. New York: Henry Holt, 1996a.
Reel to Real: Race, Sex and Class at the Movies. New York: Routledge, 1996b.

WRITINGS ON BELL HOOKS AND HER WORK

Berube, Michael. "Public Academy: African American Intellectuals." *The New Yorker* 70, no. 43 (1995): 73–81.
Fox, Tom. "Literacy and Activism: A Response to bell hooks." *Jac: Journal of Composition Theory* 14, no. 2 (1994): 564–570.
Guy-Sheftall, Beverly, ed. *Words of Fire: An Anthology of African-American Feminist Thought.* New York: New Press, 1995.
Martin, Joan M. "The Notion of Difference for Emerging Womanist Ethics: The Writings of Audre Lorde and bell hooks." *Journal of Feminist Studies in Literature* 9, nos. 1–2 (1993): 39–52.
McKinnon, Tanya. "Sisterhood: Beyond Public and Private—Interview with bell hooks." *Signs* 21, no. 4 (1996): 814–830.
Mullings, Leith. *On Our Own Terms: Race, Class, and Gender in the Lives of African American Women.* New York: Routledge, 1997.
Olson, Gary A., and Elizabeth Hirsh, eds. *Women Writing Culture.* Albany: State University of New York Press, 1995.

REFERENCES

Alexander, Natalie. "Piecings from a Second Reader: Review Essay of *Yearning.*" *Hypatia* 7, no. 2 (1992): 177–188.

Freire, Paulo. *Pedagogy of the Oppressed*. New York: Herder and Herder, 1970.
Hull, Gloria T., Patricia Bell Scott, and Barbara Smith, eds. *All the Women Are White, All the Men Are Black, But Some of Us Are Brave*. Old Westbury, NY: Feminist Press, 1982.
Wallace, Michele. "For whom the bell tolls." *The Village Voice* 40, no. 45 (1995):SS19–24.

DOLORES HUERTA
(1930–)

Nerea A. LLamas

La causa, the cause, has been the focal point of Dolores Huerta's life for more than forty years. She has remained undeterred from her goal of obtaining better working conditions for farmworkers throughout the United States. As César Chavez once said of her, "Dolores is absolutely fearless, physically and emotionally" (Coburn 1976, 12–13). From humble beginnings, Dolores Huerta has risen to be one of the most respected and admired women labor leaders of the twentieth century.

Dolores Huerta's story begins in the small mining town of Dawson, New Mexico, where she was born to Juan and Alicia Fernández on April 10, 1930. After her parents' divorce, Dolores moved with her mother and two brothers to Stockton, California. In Stockton, Dolores' upbringing was in many ways nontraditional. She enjoyed life in an unusually multicultural community. Alicia Fernández worked as a cannery worker and managed to save enough money to buy a business, first a restaurant and then a 70-room hotel, which housed poor farmworkers. Unlike traditional families, Dolores later recalled in *Intercambios Femeniles* that her mother never showed favoritism toward her brothers. "I never had to cook for my brothers or do their clothes like many traditional Mexican families" (Carranza 1989, 12). She encouraged Dolores to join Girl Scouts and church groups and take violin, piano, and dance lessons.

Sheltered from prejudice in her early years, Dolores soon faced the realities of racism in high school. In a 1972 article originally in *La Voz del Pueblo* and later reprinted in *An Awakened Minority: The Mexican Americans*, she related one incident that illustrated her struggle: "When I was in high school I got straight A's in all of my compositions. But the teacher told me at the end of the year that she couldn't give me an A because she knew that somebody was writing my papers for me" (Huerta 1974, 284–285).

After high school, Dolores married Ralph Head, had two daughters (Celeste and Lori), and divorced by the early 1950s. With her mother's help, she attended

Stockton College, now known as Delta Community College, and earned a teaching certificate. An English teacher for one year, Huerta left the profession when, she related in La Voz del Pueblo, "I realized one day as a teacher I couldn't do anything for the kids who came to school barefoot and hungry" (Huerta 1974, 20). About this time she met Fred Ross, the founder of the Community Service Organization (CSO) and the one person she would repeatedly credit as her greatest professional influence. Ross founded the CSO in an effort to organize the Chicano community. Although skeptical at first, Huerta soon threw herself into the cause, devoting all of her time and energy to the CSO. As a CSO worker, she began by organizing voter registration drives. After one particularly successful registration drive in 1960, César Chavez, then executive director of CSO, decided that Huerta should continue her work with the organization as a lobbyist. So, armed with nothing but sheer determination and an unfailing belief in the cause, she went to the California State Capitol in Sacramento. With no previous lobbying experience, she successfully lobbied for numerous rights not previously granted to noncitizens. These included old age pensions, the right to register voters door-to-door, and the right to take driver's license exams in Spanish. Most significantly, through the efforts of Dolores and César and the CSO the U.S. Department of Labor ended its bracero program, which had imported farm laborers from Mexico since its inception in 1942.

Despite Dolores Huerta's success with the CSO, she couldn't come to terms with her personal life. Shortly before going to Sacramento, she divorced her second husband, Ventura Huerta, whose name she continues to use. César, in fact, encouraged her to continue to use the name "Huerta," which means "sorrow in the orchards." With Huerta she had had five more children: Fidel, Emilio, Vincent, Alicia, and Angela. Huerta later attributed her unsuccessful marriages to her priority of helping others: "I cared more about helping other people than cleaning our house and doing my hair" (Baer 1975, 39).

Not one to dwell on her misfortunes, Huerta continued her organizing efforts. In 1962, she and César Chavez formed the National Farm Workers Association (this NFWA later became the United Farm Workers [UFW] of America) and continued the work they had done earlier of organizing workers. Their efforts paid off in 1965, when NFWA joined the Filipino workers in the Agricultural Workers Organizing Committee in the Delano grape strike. Growers responded with violence and legal injunctions, so the union devised a new plan, boycotts. Ultimately, the boycott proved successful in winning the first-ever collective bargaining agreements for farmworkers.

But the fight for farmworkers' rights never ends. In response to presidential candidate George Bush's declaration in 1988 that he would never boycott grapes, Huerta joined a protest. Outside the St. Francis Hotel, where Bush was attending a fund-raiser, she was beaten by police. She was then forced to undergo emergency surgery for a ruptured spleen and two broken ribs. She later sued the city and was victorious. Huerta has also reported to Congress on farmworkers and served on the Congressional Commission on Agricultural Workers.

Dolores Huerta attributes contact with Gloria Steinem in 1968–1969 as her first entry into the feminist movement. From that point on, she would consciously incorporate feminist themes in all aspects of her work. However, Dolores had always been a feminist. While working in the fields herself, she witnessed the unique problems faced by female farmworkers. "Women in the fields get treated very badly . . . with additional humiliation and indignities," she stated in 1971; "When you get propositioned by a foreman, all you can do is quit" (Murphy 1971, 20). This treatment prompted her to focus on the issues faced by the women in her own organization. But more importantly, Huerta knew the power of these women. Women who worked in the fields, tended to their husbands, and kept the family together would also fight to improve their families' working conditions. She intuitively knew that these women would be the union's driving force, so she set out to recruit female farmworkers for the union.

With Dolores Huerta as an inspiration, women who had never worked outside the home or fields ran UFW programs. César's wife, Helen, managed the credit union, while Gloria Soto was in charge of services, and Ester Uranday managed membership. They became the backbone of the UFW's organizational structure. The women's contributions did not end there, however. Under Dolores Huerta's leadership, they often took a more active role, standing as a buffer between striking farmworkers on the picket lines and the growers. Huerta told Caminos that "women provided an awful lot of leadership in keeping the strikes nonviolent" ("Los Ganadores" 1982, 15).

From the beginning, her role in the union was unconventional: she was a cofounder, the UFW's first vice president, and its most vocal member. While César Chavez felt more comfortable in the fields with the workers, Dolores Huerta spent most of her time in the role of negotiator, a role that would make her the first female and Chicano negotiator in labor history. She not only was instrumental to negotiations during the Delano Grape Strike, but later organized the lettuce, table grape, and Gallo wine boycotts and the international table grape boycott. She organized workers on the East and West Coasts. Not one to compromise, Dolores Huerta quickly gained a reputation for her emotional negotiating style. So unnerved were the growers' representatives that one commented in *The Progressive*, "Dolores Huerta is crazy. She's a violent woman, where women, especially Mexican women, are usually peaceful and pleasant" (Baer 1975, 40). Such racist and sexist comments, Huerta notes, have had little effect on her character. Like her mother, she is a determined woman who lets nothing stand in the way of *la causa*.

Over the years Dolores Huerta managed to clothe, feed, and educate eleven children (the last four, Juanita, María Elena, Ricky, and Camilla, with Richard Chavez, César's brother). With a five-dollar per week salary and no permanent residence, the family depended largely on donations. The children often stayed with family, friends, or supporters. While many of her critics have reprimanded her for not providing a traditional home, Huerta herself has no regrets. As she related in *La Voz del Pueblo* in 1972, "Giving kids clothes and food is one thing, you know, but it's much more important to teach them that other people besides themselves are important, and that the best thing they can do with their lives is to use them in the service of other people" (Huerta 1974, 288).

Along with her continuing duties as secretary-treasurer of the United Farm Workers, Dolores Huerta travels the country speaking at colleges and universities and other gatherings. Recognizing the needs of her community, she speaks regularly to Chicana groups. Chicanas have always struggled with discrimination. Mirta Vidal explains in *Women: New Voice of La Raza*: "Raza women suffer a triple form of oppression: as members of an oppressed nationality, as workers, and as women" (Vidal 1971, 6). Huerta has spent most of her life fighting against oppression. Now she serves as a role model for Chicanas. She broke new ground, proving that she could be both a mother and an organizer without forgetting her roots. In a traditionally male-dominated culture, she provides the community with much-needed female leadership.

Dolores Huerta also continues to work for woman's rights in both the social and political arenas. In California, she works regularly to get female candidates elected to office. Nationally, she served on the National Organization for Women's Commission for Responsive Democracy, which voted to create a third political party. Most recently, she participated in Feminist Expo '96, sponsored by the Feminist Majority Organization, and sits on the board of that same organization. She was the first Latina inducted into the National Women's Hall of Fame and was one of the founders of the Coalition of Labor Union Women (CLUW). In turn, the community has honored Dolores Huerta numerous times with civic and humanitarian awards. Among them are the National Organization of Women's "Woman of Courage" award and the ACLU's Bill of Rights Award. She is even the subject of *La Ofrenda*, a mural in Los Angeles by artist Yreina Cervantez. "She was one of the first strong role models we Chicanas and Latinas had," Cervantez told the *Los Angeles Times* in 1991. "She defied stereotypes and remained a positive force in our community" (Vaughn 1991, E5).

WORKS BY DOLORES HUERTA

"Dolores Huerta Talks about Republicans, César, Children, and Her Home Town." *La Voz del Pueblo*, November–December 1972. Reprinted in Manuel P. Servin, *An Awakened Minority: The Mexican Americans*. Beverly Hills, CA: Glencoe Press, 1974.

WRITINGS ON DOLORES HUERTA AND HER WORK

Books

Bonilla-Gonzales, Sonia. *Women Developing Effective Leadership*. San Diego: Marin, 1992.
Day, Mark. *Forty Acres: César Chavez and the Farm Workers*. New York: Praeger, 1971.

Dunne, John Gregory. *Delano: The Story of the California Grape Strike.* New York: Farrar, 1967.
Levy, Jacques. *César Chavez: Autobiography of La Causa.* New York: Norton, 1975.
London, Joan, and Henry Anderson. *So Shall Ye Reap.* New York: Thomas Crowell, 1970.
Majka, Linda C., and Theo J. Majka. *Farm Workers, Agribusiness, and the State.* Philadelphia: Temple University Press, 1982.
Matthiessen, Peter. *Sal Si Puedes: César Chavez and the New American Revolution.* New York: Random House, 1969.
Meister, Dick, and Anne Loftis. *A Long Time Coming, the Struggle to Unionize America's Farm Workers.* New York: Macmillan, 1977.
Taylor, Ronald B. *Chavez and the Farm Workers.* Boston: Beacon Press, 1975.
Telgen, Diane, and Jim Kamp, eds. *Notable Hispanic American Women.* Detroit: Gale Research, 1993.
Vidal, Mirta. *Women: New Voice of La Raza.* New York: Pathfinder Press, 1971.

Articles

"ACLU Celebrates the Bill of Rights." *Los Angeles Times*, December 4, 1989, Home Ed.
Baer, Barbara. "Stopping Traffic: One Woman's Cause." *The Progressive*, September 1975, 38–40.
Baer, Barbara L., and Glenna Matthews. "The Women of the Boycott." *Nation* 240 (1974): 232–238.
Carranza, Ruth. "From the Fields: Into the History Books." *Intercambios Femeniles* (Winter 1989): 11–12.
Coburn, Judith. "Dolores Huerta: La Pasionaria of the Farmworkers." *Ms.* (November 1976): 11–16.
"$825,000 Proposed for Union Activist Injured by Police." *Los Angeles Times*, January 25, 1991, Home Ed.
"Expo '96 Speakers Include over 160 Leaders, Thinkers, Activists," http://www.feminist.org/action/speakers.html, September 27, 1996.
Genasci, Lisa. "UFW Co-Founder Comes Out of Shadow." *Los Angeles Times*, May 11, 1995, Orange County Ed.
Hancock, Michael. "The Fox Takes Charge of the Chickens." *Los Angeles Times*, August 22, 1990, Home Ed.
Kriper, Beth Ann. "Power: They Want It Now." *Los Angeles Times*, July 2, 1990, Home Ed.
Lopez, Lalo. "Si, se puede: United Farm Workers Co-Founder Dolores Huerta Looks to the Future." *Hispanic*, August 1996, 41–44.
"Los Ganadores." *Caminos*, February 1982, 15.
Murphy, Jean. "Unsung Heroine of La Causa." *Regeneración* 1, no. 10 (1971): 20.
Oates, Mary Louise. "Hayman: He Says Thanks with a Party." *Los Angeles Times*, November 30, 1988, Home Ed.
Rose, Margaret. "From the Fields to the Picket Line: Huelga Women and the Boycott: 1965–1975." *Labor History* 31 (1990a): 271–293.
———. "Traditional and Nontraditional Patterns of Female Activism in the United Farm Workers of America, 1962–1980." *Frontiers* 11, no. 1 (1990b): 29–32.
Vaughn, Susan. "Back to the Wall: Four Hour Bus Tour Will Visit Some of L.A.'s 1500 Murals." *Los Angeles Times*, February 14, 1991, Home Ed.

JUNE JORDAN
(1936–)

Nikki Senecal

June Jordan believes a women's movement should be as large and as complicated as she believes the world is. "I don't see feminism as a narrow preoccupation. It seems to me to have absolutely to do with the full realization of freedom, the full realization of whoever you happen to be" (Jordan 1985b, 16). Her poetry, essays, novels, plays, and librettos express and explore her concern for diversity and the interconnectedness of all oppression. Her interest in internationalism has often been misunderstood as an adherence to political correctness. A *New York Times* critic called her libretto *I Was Looking at the Ceiling and Then I Saw the Sky* politically correct because of its multiethnic characters. She dismisses this misunderstanding, explaining that "what you call politically correct is my life" (Schwarz 1995, H25). Jordan's life comes complete with black, white, Asian, Hispanic, and Native American, male and female, straight and gay characters. Her remedy for the oppression faced by people everywhere lies in self-determination. She writes in "Where Is the Love?" that "if the acquirement of my self-determination is part of a worldwide, an inevitable, and a righteous movement then I should become willing and able to embrace more and more of the whole world, without fear and also without self-sacrifice" (Jordan 1981a, 143–144). Jordan's self-determination doesn't abide oppression of others. She identifies herself as part of a majority (the racially oppressed Third World female majority); as a result, the self-determination of women, people of color, and the poor everywhere is intrinsic to her own.

Jordan recalls understanding the power of words even at a young age. As a result of her mother's taking her to the Universal Truth Center, she learned "the scriptural concept that 'in the beginning was the Word and the Word was with God and the Word was God'—the idea that the word could represent and then deliver into reality what the word symbolized—this possibility of language, of writing, seemed to me magical and basic and irresistible . . . by declaring the truth, you create the truth" (Jordan 1981a, x). At school, she wrote poetry to sell to her friends. She understands this experience as leading her to believe that making a living through poetry was not only possible but also not out of the ordinary. Although a career in poetry seemed natural to Jordan, her father wanted her to be a doctor, while her mother wanted her to marry one. They were disappointed in her career choice.

Her parents, Granville Ivanhoe and Mildred Jordan, were Jamaican immigrants. Born in Harlem, Jordan grew up in the Bedford-Stuyvesant section of Brooklyn. Her father worked as a postal clerk, and her mother as a nurse. Jordan describes her home life as a "relentlessly frightening situation." She reports that her father "was the first regular bully in [her] life" who inflicted "corporeal violence" upon her (DeVeaux 1981, 140). However, his love of literature was a gift to her; he had her read the Bible and Shakespeare as well as Paul Lawrence Dunbar. Poetry was a part of her life as well as her education.

Despite her family's modest means, Jordan was sent to school at Northfield (now part of Northfield-Mount Hermon), where she was the only black student. After graduating in 1953 Jordan attended Barnard College. There, she met her future husband, Michael Meyer, a white student at Columbia. They married in 1955, a marriage that was then a felony in forty-three states. She left Barnard to attend the University of Chicago with her husband when he continued his studies there. She explains that she felt obliged to support her husband while he was in graduate school. "I thought I was going to concentrate on my writing but there were pressures on me as Michael's wife to defer anything about myself because he was still a grad student and somebody was going to have to support this couple, this marriage" (DeVeaux 1981, 143). In 1958 Jordan and Meyer had a son, Christopher David. Jordan describes her life after her son was born: "I had uppermost in my mind being a good wife, being the best housekeeper ever and being the best mother that ever existed. Those were my top priorities. After Christopher went to sleep at night and I had interacted with my husband, then— very calmly and with no resentment—I sat down to do my reading and writing" (DeVeaux 1981, 143). At this time Jordan was writing freelance articles concerning current social issues.

But in Chicago, Jordan explains, she was subject to racist verbal assaults as she and her husband walked the streets. She left the city twelve months later and reentered Barnard, while her husband remained in Chicago. She dropped out of Barnard altogether finally to support her family taking a job as assistant to the producer on the film *Cool World*. A year later, Jordan and Meyer divorced. Having supported her son and herself in New York while her husband continued his studies, she was already, for all intents and purposes, a single mother. In the fall of 1967, she took a teaching position at City College in New York. She has since taught at Connecticut College, Sarah Lawrence College, the State University of New York, Stony Brook, Yale University, and the University of Wisconsin. Since 1989 she has been professor of African American studies and women's studies at the University of California at Berkeley.

Jordan compares her poetry to "women's work" in the sense that she hopes others find it nurturing and nourishing.

What's been called "women's work" traditionally includes the nurturing of young people, maintaining a house, providing the wherewithal so that people can keep going. My work is closely related in purpose to the traditional work; it just takes a different form. I would be very proud if people found in my poetry things that were as useful to them as a decent breakfast before they go to work. (DeVeaux 1981, 82)

This concern for "women's work" is part of what disturbed her about the women's movement. Not only did the early movement not seem to address all of the oppressions women faced, but it also seemed that liberation might leave children without caregivers. "Will we liberate ourselves so that the caring for children, the teaching, the loving, healing, person-oriented values . . . will be revered and honored . . . ? Or will we liberate ourselves so that we can militantly abandon those attributes and functions, so that we can despise our own warmth and generosity even as men have done, for ages?" (Jordan 1981a, 120). Nonetheless, Jordan dedicated herself to the early women's liberation movement and to its expansion.

Her concern for children is evident in her creation of the Voice of the Children Poetry Project with Terri Bush and the resulting anthology by the same name that resulted. Additionally, Jordan has written several novels for young people: *His Own Where*, *Dry Victories*, *Fannie Lou Hamer* (biography), *New Life, New Room*, and *Kimako's Story*. *His Own Where* prompted controversy, as it was written in black English. Jordan feels this language is important: "[S]incere recognition of Black language as legitimate will mean formal instruction and encouragement in its use, within the regular curriculum. It will mean the respectful approaching of Black children, in the language of Black children" (Jordan 1981a, 67). While some black parents felt the book encouraged the wrong sort of learning and attempted to have the book banned from schools, it was, nonetheless, nominated for a National Book Award in 1972.

Jordan's feelings for children notwithstanding, she does understand the self-negation that can occur in motherhood. Written for the Black Women's Conference, "Getting Down to Get Over" is a poem not only for mothers—especially her mother, to whom it is dedicated—but for all black women. The poem begins: "MOMMA MOMMA MOMMA/momma momma/mammy/nanny/granny/ woman/mistress/sista/ . . . luv/blackgirl/slavegirl" listing the history of relationships of black women (Jordan 1977b, 27). Although Jordan deplores the position of black women generally in this poem, she also feels proud of her sisters; she asks the reader over and again to "Consider the Queen" (32) and outlines difficulties that the queen is able to overcome. The poem ends with her asking her mother for help in writing the black woman back into history: "momma/teach me how to hold a new life/momma /help me/turn the face of history/to your face" (37). Her mother's face, her mother's history, is one that Jordan explores in her poetry.

Another poem, "Ah Momma" originally printed in *Things That I Do in the Dark*, enlarges her mother's position by voicing her secret desires. The poet tells of her mother's " 'little room' of your secrets, your costumery, perfumes and photographs of an old boyfriend you did not marry" (Jordan 1977b, 38). This little room is contrasted with the kitchen, a woman's space, but one where "you . . . never dreamed about what you were doing or what you might do instead, and where you taught me to set down plates and silverware, and even fresh-cut flowers from the garden, without appetite, without excitement, without expectation" (38). That woman's space—the kitchen—is public and still regulated by social norms; the poet must show the reader the possibility of her mother—the one who existed in the "little room." By making her mother's secret self public, she writes her mother back into life, into history. This move is especially important, since, as Jordan explains in *On Call*, her father could not tell whether his wife was dead or alive after she committed suicide. Jordan sees this as a metaphor for the self-abnegation of her mother's position both in society and in relation to her husband. She shows that her mother died "many, many times" (Jordan 1985d, 26). When Jordan writes against this kind of death in women, the move is certainly feminist.

Many of Jordan's poems begin with the black woman's oppression and connect with other oppressions the world over. For instance, "Poem about My Rights" begins with a woman who needs to go out on the streets at night but cannot because of the threat of rape. She must change herself to do so because she is "the wrong/ sex the wrong age the wrong skin" (Jordan 1980, 86). The poem explores the issue of rape not only for the individual but also through other countries' legal views on rape, spinning out to other violations, "which is exactly like South Africa/ penetrating into Namibia penetrating into/ Angola" (86)— figurative and collective rape. The connection of oppressions in her poetry illustrates her belief about political organizing: we cannot protect ourselves unless we are willing to change the oppression of others.

This theme is also explored in the context of sexuality. Jordan is bisexual, an identity that some find confusing, as her poem "A Short Note to My Very Critical and Well-Beloved Friends and Comrades" suggests. "Then they said I was too confusing altogether:/ Make up your mind! They said. Are you militant/ or sweet? Are you vegetarian or meat? Are you straight/ or are you gay?/ And I said, Hey! It's not about my mind" (Jordan 1980, 78). The poem implies that her "friends and comrades" feel her identity must fit into an either/or category. But Jordan rejects that pigeonholing; this question—where does she fit in?—is not hers to solve. Jordan rejects the terms of the question: it's not about her mind. Instead, in "A New Politics of Sexuality," she outlines the bisexual politics of sexuality, which "invalidates either/or formulations, either/or analysis" (Jordan 1992, 190) and leads to freedom for all. Jordan discusses sexual oppression—of women by men, of homosexuals by heterosexuals, and of bisexuals by both homosexuals and heterosexuals—and its connection with other types of oppression. Although some liberals have, according to Jordan, found it "blasphemous" to compare the oppression of gays, lesbians, or bisexuals to the oppression of racial minorities, she believes "freedom is indivisible; the Politics of Sexuality is not some optional 'special-interest' concern" (Jordan 1992, 190). She compares bisexuality to multiracial identity; members of these "groups" must "falter and anguish and choose and then falter again and then anguish and then choose yet again how they will honor the irreducible complexity of their God-given human being" (Jordan 1992, 192).

Jordan has occasionally been argued with for insisting on the complexity of the world beyond categorical labels. Although she understands the need to organize based on gender, race, or class, she feels "there is something deficient in the thinking on the part of anybody who proposes either gender identity politics or race identity politics as sufficient, because every single one of us is more than whatever race we represent or embody and more than whatever gender category we fall into. We have other kinds of allegiances" (Parmar 1989, 61). She is careful, however, not to dismiss "issue oriented unity"—she thinks that "it may be enough to get started on something," but she doubts whether identity politics is "enough to get anything finished" (Parmar 1989, 62).

In an interview with Joy Harjo, Jordan wishes that someone would "take my work seriously enough to give serious critical attention to the craft elements," claiming to be "weary of a sociological approach to my and other political poets' various work" (Jordan 1988, 75). In a dissertation written in 1985, Doris Davenport does just that. Her work seeks to locate a black feminist poetics. Although her analysis begins by examining Jordan's works that are driven by a black, female culture, it goes on to focus on satire, irony, and tonal semantics; she finds these elements of the poetry to be feminist. "By focusing on the system's absurdity, her humor challenges and negates America's racist and sexist practices" (Davenport 1985, 129). We see this humor operating in " 'The Rationale' or 'She Drove Me Crazy' "; Jordan relates one-half of a dialogue between a criminal and a judge: "Well, your Honor,/ it was late. Three A.M. Nobody on the streets./ And I was movin along, mindin my business when/ suddenly there she was/ alone/ by herself/ gleamin under the street lamp. . . . Then I lost my control; I couldn't resist./ What did she expect?" (Jordan 1980, 11). The reader expects that the speaker is a rapist; he sees a "she" alone at night on the street, and he loses control—a euphemism. The line "What did she expect?" further confirms the identity of the speaker; women out alone at night can "expect" to be violated. The final couplet, however, reveals a twist: the suspect is "third time apprehended/ for the theft of a Porsche" (Jordan 1980, 12). The implied juxtaposition of the Porsche and a woman shows the absurdity of the position of women in a sexist culture; both are or could be "protected" by an "owner" or "the man in her life." But the absurdity comes from the feeling that the Porsche is blameless, whereas a woman alone in the street at night has agency in her violation.

Jordan is an important feminist poet not only for the political positions she explores. As poet Marylin Hacker reveals, she uses Jordan's work to "illustrate that North American Feminist poetry could not be segregated from a tradition of politically engaged writing" (Hacker 1990, 139). So, while some critics have struggled to justify the politics of Jordan's poetry or to separate the politics from the poetry, others hold Jordan as exemplary. Readers can continue to expect this politically driven work from Jordan; "My life has been about the de-ghettoization of my opinion and my experience. I am a Black woman, and as far as I am concerned every issue is a Black issue and every issue is a woman's issue" (Jordan 1985b, 17).

WORKS BY JUNE JORDAN

Who Look at Me. New York: Crowell, 1969.
Ed. *Soulscript: Afro-American Poetry.* Garden City, NY: Doubleday, 1970.
And Terri Bush, eds. *The Voice of the Children.* New York: Holt, Rinehart, and Winston, 1970.
His Own Where. New York: Dell, 1971.
Some Changes. New York: Dutton, 1971.
Dry Victories. New York: Holt, 1972.
Fannie Lou Hamer. New York: Crowell, 1972.
New Days: Poems of Exile and Return 1970–1972. New York: Emerson Hall, 1974.
New Life, New Room. New York: Crowell, 1975.
Okay Now. New York: Simon and Schuster, 1977a.
Things That I Do in the Dark: Selected Poetry. New York: Random House, 1977b.
Passion: New Poems 1977–1980. Boston: Beacon, 1980.
Civil Wars. Boston: Beacon, 1981a.
Kimako's Story. Boston: Houghton, 1981b.
Bobo Goetz a Gun. Willimantic, CT: Curbstone Press, 1985a.
"Feminism Is Not a Narrow Preoccupation." *Sojourner* (June 1985b): 16–17.
Living Room: New Poems. New York: Thunder's Mouth Press, 1985c.
On Call: Political Essays. Boston: South End Press, 1985d.
Lyrical Campaigns: Selected Poems. London: Virago Press, 1989a.
Moving Towards Home: Political Essays. London: Virago Press, 1989b.
Naming Our Destiny: New and Selected Poems. New York: Thunder's Mouth Press, 1989c.
Technical Difficulties: African American Notes on the State of the Union. New York: Pantheon, 1992.
Haruko/Love Poetry: New and Selected Poems. New York: High Risk Books, 1993.
Libretto. *I Was Looking at the Ceiling and Then I Saw the Sky: earthquake/romance.* Music by John Adams. New York: Scribner, 1995.

WRITINGS ON JUNE JORDAN AND HER WORK

Davenport, Doris. "Four Contemporary Black Women Poets: Lucille Clifton, June Jordan, Audre Lorde, and Sherley Anne Williams (A Feminist Study of a Culturally Derived Poetics)." Ph.D. diss., University of Southern California, 1985.
DeVeaux, Alexis. "Creating Soul Food: June Jordan." *Essence* 11 (April 1981): 82.

Hacker, Marylin. "Provoking Engagement." Review of *Naming Our Destiny: New and Selected Poems*, by June Jordan. *The Nation* 250, no. 4 (January 29, 1990): 135–139.

Harjo, Joy. "An Interview with June Jordan." *High Plains Literary Review* 3, no. 2 (1988): 60–76.

Parmar, Pratibha. "Other Kinds of Dreams." *Feminist Review* 31 (1989): 55–65.

Pollon, Zélie. "Naming Her Destiny! June Jordan Speaks on Bisexuality." *Denueve* (January/February 1994): 26.

Schwarz, K. Robert. "In a Tough Neighborhood on the Border of Opera." *New York Times*, July 9, 1995, H25.

EVELYN FOX KELLER
(1936–)

Anne F. Eisenberg

Evelyn Fox Keller was born on March 20, 1936, in New York, one of three children of Albert and Rachel Fox. Educated in New York City's public school system, she was strongly influenced by her older siblings, Frances, who is a professor of political science, and Maurice, a professor of biology. Frances introduced Keller to the idea of the unconscious, which led to her lifetime fascination with psychoanalysis. Maurice stimulated Keller's interest in science by introducing her to popular science fiction writers. He also encouraged her to transfer to Brandeis University after completing a freshman year at Queens College, where she had started studying physics at the advice of a math instructor.

Keller's goal was to continue studying physics at Brandeis as a way of gaining entrance to medical school to study psychoanalysis. However, theoretical physics captured Keller's imagination in her senior year at Brandeis. A combination of her interest in theoretical physics and the attention paid to her by graduate school recruiters convinced Keller to pursue a doctorate in physics. Keller's decision to attend graduate school in physics at Harvard was an important juncture in her life. Accustomed to receiving accolades for her achievements and expecting to be treated as a scholar joining an elite intellectual community, Keller was surprised to feel isolated and treated as a novice. Although she passed her oral examination at Harvard, Keller found she did not want to stay in physics and decided to find a field of study that would satisfy her intellectually while providing a welcoming and inclusive environment for a woman scientist.

After spending a summer at Cold Spring Harbor with her brother, Keller returned to Harvard having decided to do her thesis work in the area of molecular biology. At the same time Walter Gilbert was switching his research interests from physics to molecular biology and served as official adviser for her work in biology. After completing the Ph.D. in 1963, she conducted research with mathematician Joseph Bishop Keller and married him a year later. Over the next fifteen years Keller built her career in mathematical biology while having two children, Jeffrey and Sarah, and eventually divorcing her husband.

Keller's first involvement with feminism happened during the women's movement of the late 1960s and early 1970s. During this time Keller first experienced the feeling of "sisterhood" that, she has stated in several articles, was missing during her tenure in graduate school at Harvard. In defining "sisterhood," Keller refers to the idea of women's supporting one another to accomplish their goals. Over the years Keller's concerns became more philosophical, but a combination of participating in the women's movement and undergoing psychoanalysis encouraged her to critique the implicit assumptions that seemed to guide science, scientists, and science education. In fact, Keller claims that her work in gender and science is actually an extension of her continuing interest in psychoanalysis.

Keller is currently professor of history and philosophy of science in the Program in Science, Technology, and Society at Massachusetts Institute of Technology. She considers herself a historian and philosopher and no longer considers herself a practicing scientist. In her roles as scientist and observer of science, however, Evelyn Fox Keller has had a significant impact on both the critical analysis of science and the feminist movement. She helped create a feminist movement in science with far-reaching effects on the academy.

In autobiographical pieces and interviews, Keller acknowledges that her tenure as a graduate student at Harvard was lonely and discouraging. She taught her first women's studies course in 1974 at the State University of New York at Purchase, which seemed to be an epiphanal year for Keller, after having spent the past eleven years teaching and researching in mathematical biology. During that same year Keller gave a series of talks at the University of Maryland on mathematical aspects of biology and concluded the series with a talk discussing the disturbing absence of women in science. Finally, that year she wrote "The Anomaly of a Women in Physics," which was published in 1977, along with other pieces on women and their work in *Working It Out*. In this piece she detailed the loneliness and hardships faced during her career as one of relatively few women in science.

Over the next few years Keller wrote about women, gender, and science, but the publication of two books propelled her into the scientific imagination. In 1983, *A Feeling for the Organism: The Life and Work of Barbara McClintock* was published. In this book Keller charts McClintock's determined efforts in uncovering the secrets of science. Keller later recalled that she had been fascinated by McClintock when they first met at Cold Spring Harbor while still in graduate school. Keller's first impression of McClintock focused on the eccentric loneliness that seemed to surround her. The biography demonstrated how McClintock had been treated like a freak and ignored by most of her peers for the majority of her career. More importantly, the biography argued that the reason McClintock was treated in this fashion was her gender and the way in which she conducted research. Only relatively recently are the contributions made by McClintock being fully realized.

In 1995, Keller published *Gender and Science*, in which the proverbial can of worms was opened. In this text Keller challenged the ideology of "objectivity" that surrounds science and posited that it reflected a male bias that has often ignored other avenues of inquiry. With this book Keller initiated a feminist critique of science by positing that science does, indeed, reflect the priorities, biases, and gender-based interpretations of society. In other words, science is seen as objective and neutral, and alternative approaches to scientific work are considered nonscientific, weak, and not legitimate. Prior to publication of *Reflections on Gender and Science*, issues related to gender and science had been studied, but in a very different way. Sociologists and historians examined the roles occupied by women in science and described the ways in which science seemed to be stratified in terms of gender. However, no other writer had challenged the underlying ideology driving all of science.

Keller had anticipated that there would be criticisms of the book but was surprised at the vehemence of the attacks. She was accused of trying to tear down the entire enterprise of science as well as characterized as being an ignorant feminist who simply did not understand science. Yet, the *Reflections* book was the beginning of both a feminist and postmodern examination of science. Keller's work encouraged the work of other feminist critiques of science by authors such as Sandra Harding, Donna Haraway, Helen Longino, and Nancy Tuana. Keller's work has continued to focus on the issues originally raised in *Reflections* and to challenge commonly held assumptions concerning the conduct of science.

The work of Keller and other feminist scholars also encouraged similar endeavors in such diverse fields as rhetoric, sociology of science, history, philosophy, and medicine. As importantly, the work of feminist and postmodern scholars has begun to force the academy to consider the consequences of a gendered science. Specifically, graduate programs are now beginning to encourage interdisciplinary training for its students so that students of "hard" sciences are taking history and philosophy courses. Additionally, the sciences are beginning to acknowledge that more qualitative modes of thinking and research (usually characterized as female and not legitimate) help their students think more creatively about research issues.

It is obvious from Keller's career that her work has been groundbreaking for feminist and postmodern critiques of science and that it is already having a potentially profound effect on the academy. A fundamental component of her critique comes from her involvement with feminism. When Keller first encountered the women's movement in the late 1960s and early 1970s she found the sisterhood that she had craved earlier in life. During those years the women's movement was driven by several overarching goals, including the support and encouragement of women's efforts to improve their lives in society. This translated into creating opportunities for women in business, government and politics, and science. The women's movement has evolved into today's feminist movement, and Keller believes that her work has played a role. Her overarching goal is to improve science by creating opportunities for it to be expressed in many diverse ways, including from a feminist view. Keller's work is as vital to the feminist movement today as it was in initiating the feminist critique of science in the 1970s.

WORKS BY EVELYN FOX KELLER

"Women in Science: An Analysis of a Social Problem." *Harvard Magazine* (October 1974): 14–19.

"The Anomaly of a Woman in Physics." *Working It Out: 23 Women Writers, Artists, Scientists, and Scholars Talk about Their Lives and Work.* Ed. Sara Ruddick and Pamela Daniels. New York: Pantheon Books, 1977, 77–91.

"Gender and Science." *Psychoanalysis and Contemporary Thought* 1 (1978): 409–433.

"Cognitive Repression in Contemporary Physics." *American Journal of Physics* 47, no. 8 (1979): 718–772.

"Baconian Science: A Hermaphroditic Birth." *Philosophical Forum* 11, no. 3 (1980a).

"Feminist Critique of Science: A Forward or Backward Move?" *Fundamenta Scientiae* 1 (Summer 1980b): 341–349.

"Lewis Carroll: A Study of Mathematical Inhibition." *Journal of the American Psychoanalytic Association* 28, no. 1 (1980c): 133–160.

"Ahead of Her Time." *Science* 81 (October 1981a).

"Women and Science: Two Cultures or One? Commentary on Hein, Lowe, Fee, and Goodman and Goodman." *International Journal of Women's Studies* 4 (1981b): 414–419.

"Feminism and Science." *Signs* 7, no. 3 (1982): 589–602.

"Feminism as an Analytic Tool for the Study of Science." *Academe* (September/October 1983a): 15–21.

With C. Grontowski. "The Mind's Eye." *Discovering Reality: Feminist Perspectives on Epistemology, Metaphysics, Methodology and Philosophy of Science.* Ed. S. Harding and M. Hintikka. New York: Reidel, 207–224.

"Women, Science, and Popular Mythology." *Machine Ex Dea.* Ed. Joan Rothschild. New York: Pergamon, 1983b, 130–150.

"Contending with a Masculine Bias in the Ideals and Values of Science." *The Chronicle of Higher Education* (October 2, 1985): 96.

"The Bounds of Biology." *New Republic* 194, no. 5 (1986a): 37–39.

"Make Gender Visible in the Pursuit of Nature's Secrets." *Feminist Studies/Critical Studies.* Ed. T. de Lauretis. Bloomington: University of Indiana Press, 1986b 67–77.

"One Woman and Her Theory." *New Scientist* 111 (July 3, 1986c): 46–50.

"Competition and Feminism: Conflicts for Academic Women." *Signs* 12 (Spring 1987a): 493–511.

"Is Sex to Gender as Nature Is to Science?" *Hypatia* 2, no. 3 (1987b): 37–51.

"Sexual Reproduction and the Central Project of Evolutionary Theory." *Biology and Philosophy* 2 (1987c): 383–396.

"Women and Basic Research: Respecting the Unexpected." *Technology Review* 87 (November/December 1987d): 44–47.

"Working Scientists and Feminist Critics of Science." *Daedalus* 116, no. 4 (1987e): 77–91.

"Feminist Perspectives on Science Studies." *Science, Technology and Human Values* 13, nos. 3/4 (1988): 235–249.

"Holding the Center of Feminist Theory." *Women's Studies International Forum* 12, no. 3 (1989): 313–318.

With Mary Jacobus and Sally Shuttleworth. "Body/Politics: Women and the Discourses of Science." *Conflicts in Feminism*. Co-ed. Marianne Hirsch. New York: Routledge, 1990.

"The Wo/Man Scientist: The Outer Circle: Women in the Scientific Community. Issues of Sex and Gender in the Pursuit of Science." Ed. H. Zuckerman et al. New York: W. W. Norton, 1991.

With Elisabeth Lloyd, eds. *Keywords in Evolutionary Discourse*. Cambridge: Harvard University Press, 1992a.

Secrets of Life, Secrets of Death. New York: Routledge, 1992b.

A Feeling for the Organism: The Life and Work of Barbara McClintock. New York: W. H. Freeman, 1993 [1983].

"The Body of a New Machine." *Perspectives on Science* 2, no. 3 (1994): 302–322.

Refiguring Life: Metaphors of Twentieth-Century Biology. New York: Columbia University Press, 1995a.

Reflections on Gender and Science. New Haven, CT: Yale University Press, 1995b.

With Helen Longino, eds. *Feminism and Science*. New York: Oxford University Press, 1996.

WRITINGS ON EVELYN FOX KELLER AND HER WORK

Barinaga, Marcia. "Feminists Find Gender Everywhere in Science." *Science* 260 (April 16, 1993): 392–393.

Casalino, Larry. "Decoding the Human Genome Project: An Interview with Evelyn Fox Keller." *Socialist Review* 21 (April 1991): 111–128.

Hirsch, Marianne, and Evelyn Fox Keller, eds. *Conflicts in Feminism*. New York: Routledge, 1990.

Horning, Beth. "The Controversial Career of Evelyn Fox Keller." *Technology Review* 96 (June 1993): 58–68.

May, Hal, and Susan M. Trosky, eds. "Evelyn Fox Keller." *Contemporary Authors*, vol. 125. Detroit: Gale Research, 1993, 250–251.

Soble, Alan. "Gender, Objectivity, and Realism." *The Monist* 77, no. 4 (1994): 509–530.

Worley, Sara. "Feminism, Objectivity, and Analytic Philosophy." *Hypatia* 10 (Summer 1995): 138–156.

FLORYNCE KENNEDY
(1916–)

Cheryl Rodriguez

With complex and diverse perspectives on race, social class, abortion, and sexuality, black women presented unique challenges and new dimensions to feminist politics in the 1970s. Some black women joined predominantly white feminist organizations, demanding inclusion and visibility on these agendas. Some black women, in coalition with other women of color, created separate feminist organizations through which they addressed the interconnectedness of gender, race, class, and sexuality. Marching to her own offbeat tune, Florynce Kennedy pursued both of these political paths and became one of the most audacious and unrelenting feminist activists of the twentieth century. Her work as an attorney, writer, public speaker, black feminist, activist for human rights, and self-proclaimed outside agitator spans several decades and is a testament to the power of commitment.

Florynce Rae "Flo" Kennedy was born on February 11, 1916, in Kansas City, Missouri. The second of five daughters born to Wiley and Zella Kennedy, she spent her childhood years in Missouri and California. Kennedy's unabashed sense of self, her activist spirit, and sense of commitment to oppressed people were inspired by her parents, who struggled to raise their daughters during the Jim Crow era, a time of vicious and socially sanctioned racism. From her mother, who was formally educated at a time when few blacks had educational opportunities, Flo Kennedy learned to demand the extraordinary from life. From her father, who had stared down Ku Klux Klan members at his own front door, she learned to take outrageous risks in the name of human rights. In her autobiography, *Color Me Flo: My Hard Life and Good Times*, Kennedy describes her parents as gentle people who were never extremely authoritative and did not impose harsh restrictions on their daughters. Rather, the Kennedys instilled confidence in Flo and her sisters and convinced them that they were special. Kennedy said that "my parents gave us a fantastic sense of security and worth. By the time the bigots got around to telling us we were nobody, we already knew we were some-body" (Kennedy 1976, 140).

Because she knew she was somebody, a very young Florynce Kennedy decided, even before entering high school, that she would become a lawyer. She indicates in her autobiography, "My theory has always been that whatever the people who have all the money don't want you to do, that's what you ought to do" (Kennedy 1976, 33). After high school, she remained in Kansas City for a few years, running a hat shop and performing with her sisters on a radio show. In a 1974 interview with Charlotte Reed, Kennedy explained that her first experiences with activism and agitation occurred in Kansas City. Through her involvement with the Negro Chamber of Commerce and the local National Association for the Advancement of Colored People (NAACP), Kennedy helped to organize a boycott against the Coca Cola Bottling Company to force them to hire African American truck drivers. Of this action and others that occurred during the early civil rights movement, Kennedy argues, "I have never sought out revolution, but I was cer-tainly always prepared to move in that direction" (Reed 1974, n.p.).

In 1942, Flo Kennedy moved to New York City, and in 1944, at the age of twenty-eight, she entered Columbia University. After receiving her bachelor's degree, Kennedy applied to Columbia Law School but was denied admission. She was informed by the law school that the quota for women students had already been filled. Kennedy remarked to the Law School dean, "Some of my more cynical friends think I'm being discriminated against because I'm black" (Ken-nedy 1976, 39). After Kennedy threatened to file a discrimination lawsuit against Columbia, the university found a place for her. She received her law degree in 1951 and passed the New York bar examination in 1952.

By 1954 Kennedy had established her own law practice. She represented the estates of such performers as Billie Holiday and Charlie Parker, recognizing that record companies had discriminated against both the singer and the musician because they were black. She also defended black activist H. Rap Brown, who experienced enormous difficulties with the court system. However, Kennedy's most notable roles as an attorney are strongly connected to her work as a black feminist. In this capacity, she devoted many years to work on abortion rights and women's political empowerment. Yet by the mid-1970s, Kennedy had reeval-uated the effectiveness of seeking justice through the legal system. After expe-riencing some of the realities of the justice system, Kennedy began to question the effectiveness of practicing law as a means of changing society (Kennedy 1976, 52). She gradually released herself from her duties as a lawyer and became a full-time activist, speaking on behalf of diverse groups, including people of color, lesbians and gay men, prostitutes, the poor, and women. In a 1974 interview, Kennedy explained that she spent most of her time traveling across the United States speaking to university students and other socially active groups.

In a 1996 interview, Flo Kennedy, at the age of 80, indicated that her life as an activist continues despite health problems. From her home in New York City, she continues to attend political functions and encourages voters to help the Democrats gain control of the U.S. Congress. Kennedy also feels that access to the media for disfranchised groups is important. Transforming her beliefs into action, she hosts *The Flo Kennedy Show* on New York City's public access television. The television show is her most recent activist strategy in a life dedicated to struggle.

Kennedy's experiences with Columbia University Law School were very personal reminders of her status as a black woman of working-class parents in American society. However, her early writings reflect that even before being denied admission to the law school, Kennedy had developed a very keen awareness and understanding of the insidious and embedded nature of institutionalized racism and sexism in America. For example, in 1946, Kennedy wrote an essay for a sociology class entitled, "A Comparative Study: Accentuating the Similarities of the Societal Position of Women and Negroes" (Kennedy 1995, 102–106). In this essay Kennedy argued that an interaction of historical, cultural, psychological, and even physiological factors determines the social, economic, and political positions of women and black people. Kennedy supported her thesis by analyzing various tools of oppression inherent in America's capitalist hierarchy. Identifying the economic realm as strongly determining "cultural development and direction" (Kennedy 1995, 102), Kennedy illustrated the ways in which businesses and industry marginalize, manipulate, exploit, and subordinate women as a group and blacks as a group. The essay is anthropological as well as sociological in that Kennedy identified the ways in which laws, sexual behaviors, literature, films, clothing, religion, marriage, and other common, acceptable practices oppress women and black people. Kennedy also contended that the problems persist because many oppressed people unwittingly participate in the perpetuation of their own oppression. Calling for radical changes in the most sacred strongholds of American society, Kennedy argued that "the longer the history of an inferior position, the greater the necessity for a break with tradition" (Kennedy 1995, 105).

Kennedy broke with tradition quite often and took radical actions that called attention to the emotional, intellectual, and physical wrongs that stifled women in all aspects of life. For example, she was one of the founders of the National Organization for Women (NOW) but quickly grew disillusioned with their mild approach to social change. As one of the few African American women in the radical wing of the emerging women's movement, Flo Kennedy organized the Feminist Party in 1971 and protested with radical women at the Miss America pageant in 1968. In 1972 she filed a complaint against the Catholic Church for its monetary support of antiabortion groups. Also in the 1970s, Kennedy organized a "pee-in" at Harvard when "the previously all-male bastion was slow to install women's bathrooms" (Johnson 1995, 140).

In 1969 Flo Kennedy was a member of a legal team that filed a class-action suit to test the constitutionality of the New York state abortion laws. The rationale for the lawsuit and the official transcripts of depositions, as well as discussions on various dimensions of the issue, are all documented in the book *Abortion Rap*, coauthored by Diane Schulder. With its Foreword by Congresswoman Shirley Chisholm, *Abortion Rap* was one of the first books on this issue. The idea for the book came from an action organized in 1969 by the women's liberation group Redstockings. This group held the first gathering in which women publicly "rapped" about abortion. Schulder and Kennedy credited Redstockings with opening up "taboo subjects and [transforming] them into topics for public debate" (Kennedy and Schulder 1971, 3–5).

Inspired by the Redstockings action, Kennedy and Schulder decided to make public the testimonies of women who, at some point in their lives, were faced with unwanted or unplanned pregnancies. These testimonies revealed American society's oppressive attitudes toward pregnant women regardless of the marital status of the woman. *Abortion Rap* also revealed the ways in which the very personal issue of pregnancy becomes a public issue used to advance the sociopolitical agendas of others. For example, the most controversial chapter of this book is Kennedy's analysis of the black genocide theory of abortion. That is, in the 1960s and 1970s, a number of black nationalist groups argued that abortion and birth control were strategies for eliminating the African American population. As such, black women were encouraged to have babies, especially sons, for the revolution. Kennedy's work on the repeal of antiabortion laws placed her in direct opposition to members of the radical black community, whom she had supported on many other issues. While she understood the underlying historical reasons for this position, Kennedy opposed the black genocide theory, citing some of the racist as well as sexist implications of denying reproductive choice in any community. Kennedy pointed out that unwanted pregnancies and illegal abortions posed many physical and psychological difficulties for African American women. Yet, she also cautioned white women not to use black women's plight to further the cause for abortion. She argued, "White women must let the Black movement formulate its own ideas and strategies in its own time and way" (Kennedy and Schulder 1971, 161).

Flo Kennedy, like Shirley Chisholm and other black feminists, refused to examine only the racial dimension of social oppression. Instead, Kennedy addressed the interlocking hierarchies that characterized oppression. While she felt that racism was the most blatant and prevalent type of oppression, Kennedy also knew that sexist beliefs and practices were pervasive in communities of color. Realizing that the feminist movement had the potential to combat issues that were relevant to all women, Kennedy joined the National Organization for Women and attended its first organizational meeting in 1966. Although she quickly became disgruntled with NOW's establishment orientation as well as its lack of radical activity, Kennedy continued her involvement in feminist politics. On November 3, 1971, Kennedy founded the Feminist Party on the campus of Queens College. One of the strongest positions taken by the Feminist Party was its support of Shirley Chisholm's candidacy for president in 1972. By 1974, the Feminist Party had 175 chapters on college campuses across the country (Kennedy 1974).

Flo Kennedy's support of Shirley Chisholm's presidential bid was a bold stance, since Chisholm received lukewarm support from other feminist leaders and almost no support from black male leaders. Kennedy's unequivocal support of black women's leadership was also evident in her participation in the founding of the National Black Feminist Organization (NBFO). In 1973, Kennedy and Margaret Sloan (one of the founding editors of Ms. magazine), explored the idea of black women's coming together to discuss their experiences as feminists. From this idea emerged NBFO, which was "the first national Black women's organization that was explicitly feminist and dedicated to eliminating the dual oppression of racism and sexism" (Davis 1988, 43). Described as the "most heterogeneous group of any feminist organization" (Davis 1988, 45), NBFO held its first regional conference in November 1973 and featured several black women leaders as keynote speakers, including Eleanor Holmes Norton, Shirley Chisholm, Margaret Sloan, and Florynce Kennedy. NBFO was short-lived due to financial difficulties. However, the most damaging factor in the organization's demise was black women's skepticism about feminism. As Davis explains, in 1972 "there were comparatively few Black women who were actively and visibly participating in the feminist movement" (Davis 1988, 45).

During an activist career that spanned five decades, Flo Kennedy courageously remained among those few black feminists. Nevertheless, she never ceased challenging feminists to become more radical in the struggle for women's equality. In 1974, Kennedy questioned the existence of a feminist movement in America. She argued that some women were aware of the need for change, but no "takeover of the establishment" had occurred. In order to have a movement, one must "occupy unoffered territory within the establishment" (Kennedy 1974). Kennedy has maintained this position, and in 1996, while refusing to denigrate mainstream feminist organizations, she suggested that she would not adopt their strategies as her model for activism.

Kennedy's most significant contribution to the feminist movement has been her identification of what she terms "the pathology of oppression" (Kennedy 1974). Thus, her activism has involved an intense analysis of societal oppressors, the institutionalization of oppression, and the interrelatedness of all forms of oppression. Her strategy has always been to confront oppression rather than construct ways to comfort the oppressed. While Kennedy's innumerable attacks on oppression have made her appear outrageous, profane, and "crazy," her response to such criticism is, "I never stop to wonder why I'm not like other people. The mystery to me is why more people aren't like me" (Kennedy 1976, 79). Yet, as Alice Walker suggests, criticism will always be forthcoming for those who dare to assume radical positions in the name of human rights. Walker asks, "but what can one do about that? Nothing, but continue to work" (Walker 1983, 276). Well into the later years of her life, Flo Kennedy has continued the work of an undeterred feminist.

SELECTED WORKS BY FLORYNCE KENNEDY

With Diane Schulder. *Abortion Rap*. New York: McGraw-Hill, 1971.

Color Me Flo: My Hard Life and Good Times. Englewood Cliffs, NJ: Prentice-Hall, 1976.

With William Pepper. *Sex Discrimination in Employment*. Charlottesville, VA: Michie, 1981.

"A Comparative Study: Accentuating the Similarities of the Societal Position of Women and Negroes." *Words of Fire: An Anthology of African-American Feminist Thought*. Ed. Beverly Guy-Sheftall. New York: New Press, 1995.

WRITINGS ON FLORYNCE KENNEDY AND HER WORK

Davis, Beverly. "To Seize the Moment: A Retrospective on the National Black Feminist Organization." *Sage* 5, no. 2 (1988): 43–47.

Johnson, Pamela. "Wonder Women." *Essence* (May 1995): 112–148.

Nelson-Rick, Jill. "What the Future Holds." *Essence* (October 1984): 20–22.

Reed, Charlotte. Interview. *Flo Kennedy: The Self-Proclaimed "Outside Agitator" Tells It Like It Is*. Center for Cassette Studies, Inc, 1974.

Rodriguez, Cheryl. Interview, September 28, 1996.

Rudolph, Marva. "Flo Kennedy." *Epic Lives: One Hundred Black Women Who Made a Difference*. Ed. Jessie C. Smith. Detroit: Visible Ink Press, 1993.

Walker, Alice. "A Letter to the Editor of Ms." *In Search of Our Mothers' Gardens*. By Alice Walker. San Diego: Harcourt Brace Jovanovich, 1983.

AUDRE LORDE
(1934–1992)

Lara E. Dieckmann

On November 17, 1992, Audre Lorde died of cancer. At the time of her death, she was living on the Caribbean island of St. Croix, U.S. Virgin Islands. International in scope, the collective, public mourning that ensued was a testament to the profound impact that Lorde had and continues to have posthumously; hundreds of women's groups, socialist collectives, bookstores, colleges, and universities organized events to grieve her passing and to celebrate her life.

Primarily through black and Third World women's networks, many of the memorials were interconnected. Statements delivered by friends, colleagues, readers, and students at various gatherings were collected, reprinted in programs, and eventually published. The following excerpt from a speech given in London on February 18, 1993, Lorde's birthday, epitomizes the collective response to her death:

It was a strange but not uncharacteristic irony that upon hearing the news of Audre Lorde's passing, each of us turned to that poem, phrase, sentence, or essay from her writings which spoke most personally and powerfully to us. In our individual solitude, we remembered that Audre had shown us how to use the pain and terror of a loss that strikes deep at the heart of our sense of who we are. Her struggle against and with cancer became the metaphor through which we all might learn to share the development of a commitment to breaking the silences which cost nothing less than our lives. ("Audre Lorde" 1993, 7)

Also representative were the many creative projects that were produced in her honor: stage performances, dance pieces, original poetry, and visual art. In 1993, for example, the National Organization for Women dedicated its annual conference to her memory, organizing poetry readings and presentations. A documentary, *A Litany for Survival*, premiered in January 1995 at the Sundance Film Festival. Ada Gay Griffin and Michelle Parkerson's film—an eight-year project on which Lorde collaborated—focused on Lorde's writing, the difficult decisions she made throughout her life, and her bouts with breast cancer. In her death, as in her life, Lorde inspired others to survive and flourish through artistic expression.

In her influential essay "Age, Race, Class, and Sex: Women Redefining Difference," Lorde described herself "as a forty-nine-year-old Black lesbian feminist socialist mother of two, including one boy, and a member of an interracial couple" (Lorde 1984, 114). Following this laundry list of identity markers indicative of "difference," Lorde wryly, perhaps unnecessarily, remarks, "I usually find myself part of some group defined as other, deviant, inferior or just plain wrong" (Lorde 1984, 114). It was her lifelong project to embrace these multiple identities, refusing to prioritize one over another. Importantly, Lorde attempted to connect with others across these social boundaries, while simultaneously redefining them in empowering terms. Lorde undertook this daunting task through her writing and her activism.

A poet, public speaker, teacher, essayist, editor, critic, and feminist agitator, Lorde was born in New York City, grew up in Harlem, and lived much of her adult life in Manhattan. She attended Hunter College and Columbia University School of Library Science. She was a professor of English literature at Hunter College for fifteen years. During the span of her shortened career, Lorde produced five works of prose and ten volumes of poetry. Some of the most famous titles include *The Black Unicorn, Cables to Rage, From a Land Where Other People Live, Between Ourselves, The Cancer Journals, Zami: A New Spelling of My Name, A Burst of Light,* and *Sister Outsider.* In addition to her important literary contributions, she founded with Barbara Smith the Kitchen Table Press, the only publishing firm in the United States at the time that was exclusively devoted to the production of works by nonwhite women.

Lorde is perhaps best known and admired for her ability to create sophisticated, challenging feminist theory in her poetry, stories, and speeches, combining the strengths of her imagination and intellect. While much of her prose was composed of essays and public addresses, she also produced what she called "biomythography." Lorde defined biomythography as a form of revisionist mythmaking in which identity is performatively re-created through a model of interactional self-naming.

The process of creating a biomythography is detailed in Lorde's autobiographical work *Zami: A New Spelling of My Name;* Lorde translates "Zami" as "women who work together as friends and lovers" (Lorde, *Zami* 1982, 255). In this text, Lorde constructs her multiple subject positions through the metaphor of "homes" she variously occupies. Significantly, these homes are determined as much by others as by the character of the individual self. Inhabiting "the very house of difference" allows Lorde to create a new kind of writing: interactive, dialogic, confessional, playful, nonlinear, paradoxical (Lorde, *Zami* 1982, 48). This writing simultaneously invokes tropes from European and West African traditions, creating a hybrid form.

The politics of tradition and location play a decisive, if paradoxical, role in

Lorde's work. In many short stories and poems, such as "Tar Beach" and the collection *New York Head Shop and Museum*, Lorde evokes memories of her child-hood and her burgeoning sexual identity as a lesbian in New York City. However, even as she invokes the geography of New York, she complicates it by repre-senting the complexities of American social life. Her texts are peopled with exiles, refugees, and travelers, all of whom cross physical as well as social, sexual, and political boundaries. "Tar Beach," for example, depicts a love affair between two women set against the backdrop of Harlem and Greenwich Village during the summer of 1957. In this famous story, anthologized in Barbara Smith's col-lection *Home Girls*, Lorde introduces an elusive character named Afrekete. In the lexicon of Yoruba orisha, a religious belief of West African origin, Afrekete is a divine trickster who plays with, and subverts, language. Lorde returns to the Afrekete figure throughout her oeuvre.

The child of working-class, Grenadian immigrants, Lorde imagined her move from New York to the Virgin Islands late in her life as a kind of mythic home-coming. Heavily influenced by West African oral tradition, religion, and values, Lorde sought to enact and embody the sensibilities of an African diaspora in her writing and in her living. Just as she rejected the poor freedom of choosing a singular identity, she also refused to settle in one particular geographic location. In *Women Reading Women Writing*, AnaLouise Keating remarks that Lorde moved "within, between, and among the specialized worlds of academia and publishing; the private spaces of family and friends; the politicized communities of African Americans; and the overlapping yet distinct worlds of feminist, lesbian and gay, and U.S. women of color" (Keating 1996, 1–2). The hybrid world of Harlem and St. Croix, of New York and the Caribbean gave her not only a "double consciousness" but also the means by which she could communicate and collab-orate with black, poor, and Third World women all over the world.

A powerful feminist visionary, Lorde was instrumental in pointing out the limitations of a liberal approach to the struggle for woman's rights. She wrote and spoke frequently about the racism, classism, and heterosexism that blinded (and continues to blind) the feminist movement. Without truly acknowledging and grappling with the very real, material, often definitive differences between women, Lorde reasoned, the ideal of "sisterhood" would remain an empty fantasy. Lorde explained that while difference was nothing to be afraid of, it would pro-mote change, and change, while ultimately beneficial, often results in pain. Rather than avoiding this necessary pain, Lorde believed that dealing with dif-ference would not only sustain connections between women of different nation-alities, classes, religions, races, ages, and sexualities but eventually enrich them individually and collectively.

Perhaps the title of her essay "The Master's Tools Will Never Dismantle the Master's House," which appears in *Sister Outsider*, best expresses Lorde's philos-ophy. Originally penned for presentation at the Second Sex conference in New York City, this speech challenges the assumptions of white feminism, particularly within an academic context. "The failure of academic feminists to recognize difference as a crucial strength is a failure to reach beyond the first patriarchal lesson. In our world, divide and conquer must become define and empower" (Lorde 1984, 112). Lorde asserts that sociopolitical marginality affords its members a critical perspective on hegemony, often much more radical than the theory produced by women who are dependent on white, patriarchal value systems. While Lorde suggests that working within the system may provide opportunities to "beat him [patriarchal male] at his own game," it will never facilitate meaningful transformation (Lorde 1984, 112).

"Uses of the Erotic: The Erotic as Power" is another essay featured in the collection *Sister Outsider*. In this piece, Lorde outlines the damages incurred by disavowing particularly "feminine" forms of knowledge, especially those generated by eroticism, passion, and desire. Arguing for the reclamation of instinct and intuition, Lorde claims that feelings often guide energy toward healthy, creative expression. Furthermore, she suggests that the Cartesian split between the external, or rational, and the internal, or emotional, has led women to devalue their own inner voices, potentially a source of great power and inspiration. Summarizing her position, Lorde asserts that "recognizing the power of the erotic within our lives can give us the energy to pursue genuine change within our world, rather than merely settling for a shift of characters in the same weary drama" (Lorde 1984, 59). In order to take this courageous leap of faith, Lorde believed, along with her close friend and colleague Adrienne Rich, that women must become "woman-identified."

"The Transformation of Silence into Language and Action" was another important speech, published in *Sister Outsider*. Originally delivered at the Modern Language Association's annual conference in 1977, this address begins with Lorde's description of her first experience with cancer. During the period between the first visit to the doctor and the initial, positive diagnosis, Lorde stated that she underwent an intense, urgent reevaluation of her entire life. She concluded that speaking out profits one beyond any other effect, even given the risks of misunderstanding, ridicule, and violence. "I was going to die, if not sooner then later, whether or not I had ever spoken myself. My silences had not protected me" (Lorde 1984, 41). Creating an opposition between silence and speech is a common feminist rhetorical strategy; many feminists have equated liberation and autonomy with voice. However, this privileged metaphor may have its drawbacks, as bell hooks and others have noted. For hooks (1989), the issue is not "coming to voice" but rather being heard, often a significantly different relationship. Lester C. Olson (1997) is a noted rhetorician who has studied Lorde's speeches and essays extensively. In his analysis of "The Transformation of Silence into Language and Action," Olson questions the assumption that silence is always negative, suggesting that the relationship between silence and power is nuanced, complex, and shifting. Olson commends Lorde's powerful, effective rhetoric, noting that she prefigured the response to the AIDS crisis in her equation of silence and death. However, he insists that silence signifies a range of meanings and uses, some of which may be empowering, even crucial for survival, an argument that runs throughout Peggy Phelan's *Unmarked: The Politics of Performance* (1993).

Lorde's advocacy for alternative women's culture, personal expression, and working outside patriarchal systems of power positions her as a radical feminist. However, Lorde has been challenged by her peers for "naive essentialism," a critique of radical, or cultural, feminism in general. Some critics have questioned Lorde's dependence on the Cartesian split that she faults throughout her own analyses, demonstrating that an inversion of value, privileging "deep feeling" over "external thought," for example, does not alter the binary system that erroneously separates them in the first place. Kathy Ferguson (1993), for example, suspects Lorde's valorization of eroticism and instinct because of the close associations they share with a biological notion of "women's nature." Unwittingly fulfilling the Freudian prophecy "anatomy is destiny," Ferguson fears that uncritical ideals of "deep feeling" and "inner force" participate in the ideology of timeless, universal "femininity," ignoring the ways that instinct and reason are intertwined and, ironically, the ways women's experiences of their own biology may differ. Ferguson, along with many materialist feminists, prefers a model of the subject in which there is no clear division between an authentic inner self and an externally imposed social role, arguing that subjectivity is inherently a complex social construction.

In addition to the critique of essentialism, some feminists have articulated concerns about Lorde's advocacy of separatism. Through her utopian vision of woman-identified communities, Lorde often seems to preclude the possibility that some men may be willing participants in the struggle to transform gender, race, and class relations and that some women have little interest in upsetting hierarchical orders of oppression and domination. Assuming that all men are potentially propagators of patriarchal domination and that all women are potentially victims of that oppression assigns to power a biological condition that naturalizes ideology, collapsing the distinction between Man and men, Woman and women.

Certainly, Lorde's goal is to empower women. In "The Master's Tools" particularly, she encourages women to seek out alternative forms of support and validation. However, Lorde inadvertently attributes a monolithic power to patriarchy that it does not necessarily have by suggesting that transformation can never originate from within the system. Lorde represents "the system" as infallible, uniform, omnipotent, and therefore unchangeable. In reality, hegemonic institutions are constructions made and remade on a daily basis by individuals who are, among other things, contradictory, predictable, and ineffectual. Working within the logic of patriarchy may not achieve many of Lorde's stated objectives, but it can, at the very least, revise the terms of the debate, complicating dangerous essentialism.

Throughout her career, Lorde was honored with many distinguished awards and citations. From Hunter College and Oberlin College, she received honorary doctorates of literature in 1991 and 1990, respectively. Haverford College conferred on Lorde the Honorary Doctorate of Humane Letters in 1989. She was given the Walt Whitman Citation of Merit in 1991 and the Manhattan Borough President's Award for Excellence in the Arts in 1988. Recognized for her lifetime contribution, Lorde was named the New York State Poet from 1991 to 1993. However, the greatest measure of her success may be the testimonies of black women and lesbians for whom she encouraged self-love, women of privilege in whom she sparked difficult soul-searching, older women in whom she instilled a sense of worth and value beyond reproductivity, young poets she inspired by example, and members of the international feminist movement whom she challenged; all of these will continue to mourn her loss.

REFERENCES

"Audre Lorde: Reflections." *Feminist Review* (1993) 45: 4–8.

Ferguson, Kathy. *The Man Question: Visions of Subjectivity in Feminist Theory.* Berkeley: University of California Press, 1993.

hooks, bell. *Talking Back: Thinking Feminist, Thinking Black.* Boston: South End Press, 1989.

Keating, AnaLouise. *Women Reading Women Writing: Self-Invention in Paula Gunn Allen, Gloria Anzaldúa and Audre Lorde.* Philadelphia: Temple University Press, 1996.

Olson, Lester C. "On the Margins of Rhetoric: Audre Lorde Transforming Silence into Language and Action." *Quarterly Journal of Speech* 83 (1997): 49–70.

Phelan, Peggy. *Unmarked.* New York: Routledge, 1993.

Smith, Barbara, ed. *Home Girls: A Black Feminist Anthology.* New York: Kitchen Table: Women of Color Press, 1983.

WORKS BY AUDRE LORDE

The First Cities. New York: Poets Press, 1968.

Cables to Rage. London: Breman, 1970.

From a Land Where Other People Live. Detroit: Broadside Press, 1973.

The New York Head Shop and Museum. Detroit: Broadside Press, 1974.

Between Our Selves. Point Reyes, CA: Eidolon, 1976a.

Coal. New York: Norton, 1976b.

The Black Unicorn. New York: Norton, 1978.

The Cancer Journals. San Francisco: Spinsters/Aunt Lute Press, 1980.

Litany for Survival. Watsonville, CA: Blackwells, 1981.

Chosen Poems: Old and New. New York: Norton, 1982a.

Zami: A New Spelling of My Name. Freedom, CA: Crossing Press, 1982b.

Sister Outsider. Freedom, CA: Crossing Press, 1984.

Our Dead behind Us. London: Sheba Feminist, 1986.

A Burst of Light. Ithaca, NY: Firebrand Press, 1988.

Undersong: Chosen Poems Old and New Revised. New York: Norton, 1992.

The Marvelous Distance of Arithmetic. New York: Norton, 1993.

WRITINGS ON AUDRE LORDE AND HER WORK

Carillo, Karen. "A Litany for Survival: Race in Contemporary American Cinema." *Cineaste* 22, no. 2 (1996): 37.

Christian, Barbara. "Remembering Audre Lorde." *The Women's Review of Books* 10, no. 6 (1993): 5–7.

Collins, Patricia Hill. "What's in a Name?: Womanism, Black Feminism, and Beyond." *The Black Scholar* 26, no. 1 (1996): 9–18.

Dhairyam, Sagri. "Artifacts for Survival: Remapping the Contours of Poetry with Audre Lorde." *Feminist Studies* 18, no. 2 (1992): 229–257.

Gates, Henry Louis, ed. *Reading Black, Reading Feminist: A Critical Anthology.* New York: Meridian, 1990.

Ginzberg, Ruth. "Audre Lorde's (Nonessentialist) Lesbian Eros." *Hypatia* 7, no. 4 (1992): 73–91.

Guy-Sheftall, Beverly, ed. *Words of Fire: An Anthology of African-American Feminist Thought.* New York: New Press, 1995.

Holland, Sharon. "Which Me Will Survive?: Audre Lorde and the Development of a Black Feminist Ideology." *Critical Matrix* 1 (1988): 1–30.

Kader, Cheryl. "The Very House of Difference: *Zami*, Audre Lorde's Lesbian-Centered Text." *Journal of Homosexuality* 26, nos. 2–3 (1993): 181–195.

Martin, Joan M. "The Notion of Difference for Emerging Womanist Ethics: The Writings of Audre Lorde and bell hooks." *Journal of Feminist Studies in Religion* 9, nos. 1–2 (1993): 39–52.

Neff, Heather. "Now That I Am Forever with Child: The Construction of Womanself in the Works of Audre Lorde." *SAGE: A Scholarly Journal for Black Women* 10, no. 1 (1995): 104–107.

Oldfield, Sybil. "The News from the Confessional." *Critical Survey* 8, no. 3 (1996): 296–306.

Perrault, Jeanne. *Writing Selves: Contemporary Feminist Autobiography.* Minneapolis: University of Minnesota Press, 1995.

Piercy, Marge. "Elegy in Rock, for Audre Lorde." *Women's Review of Books* 10, no. 6 (1993): 5.

Provost, Kara. "Becoming Afrekete: The Trickster in the Work of Audre Lorde." *MELUS* 20, no. 4 (1995): 45–60.

Rich, Adrienne. "Need: A Chorale for Black Women's Voices." *Ms.* 2, no. 2 (1991): 75.

Tate, Claudia, ed. *Black Women Writers at Work.* New York: Continuum, 1983.

CATHARINE MacKINNON (1946-)

Eileen Bresnahan

Little has been reported about Catharine Alice MacKinnon's personal life, though it is known that she was named Catharine for her maternal grandmother Alice Davis' best friend, Radcliffe College fine arts professor Catharine Pierce (from whom MacKinnon also acquired her nickname, "Kitty"). Like her mother, Elizabeth Davis MacKinnon, she attended her grandmother's alma mater, Smith College, from which she received a B.A. magna cum laude with distinction in government in 1969. Then she was on to Yale, earning a J.D. in 1977 (she was admitted to the Connecticut bar in 1978) and a Ph.D. in political science in 1987. She presently lives in Ann Arbor with Jeffrey Moussaieff Masson, a former psychoanalyst well known for his own legal battles with writer Janet Malcolm.

Because, while she was growing up, MacKinnon's father was an activist in the Republican Party, it might be assumed that the roots of her political activism lie at least partly in his example. George E. MacKinnon not only advised the presidential campaigns of Dwight D. Eisenhower and Richard M. Nixon but also served one term as a U.S. Congressman from Minnesota and made a run for the governorship as Republican standard-bearer. The reward for his loyalty (and ultimate lack of electoral success) was presidential appointment to the lifetime employment of a federal appellate judgeship for the District of Columbia circuit, a plum prize indicative of influence in high places. MacKinnon herself, however, discounts her father's contribution to her particular brand of activism, marked as it is by a commitment to using the law as an instrument of social change. She said, "[T]hat politics is about change is—to put it mildly—not what I was brought up with" (Strebeigh 1991, 1044).

MacKinnon attributes the origins of her intellectual and political commitments to her days in New Haven (where she spent most of the 1970s) and especially to the women's movement, from which, she says, "I learned everything I know" (Strebeigh 1991, 1042). In New Haven, MacKinnon became a radical, working against the Vietnam War and becoming involved with the Black Panther Party. She also cofounded a law collective and created the first course offered by the Yale women's studies program, which employed her as a lecturer from 1977 to 1980.

While a law student, MacKinnon—as a way to address what she saw as the law's indifference to sexual inequality as it is experienced by women—pioneered the "dominance" approach to sex discrimination. This approach, pivotal to the development of feminist legal theory, argues that a practice is invidious sexual discrimination if it "participates in the systematic social deprivation of one sex because of sex." It was designed to supplant the traditional view of discrimination as illegal only in those circumstances where two *equivalent* groups were treated differently. This created the problem for women that because they were seen as sexually and thereby fundamentally *different* from men, it followed that their different treatment would not necessarily be seen as legally impermissible discrimination but might instead be excused as a response to "real" difference. So, should men pursue women sexually in ways that women found offensive and harmful, the courts traditionally saw this as a natural result of fundamental biological difference: in other words, "boys will be boys," and if this harmed women, it was not a legal matter. But MacKinnon argued that sexual harassment is, instead, part of the systematic social deprivation of women because they are women and therefore is sex discrimination prohibited by federal law.

MacKinnon in 1977 offered this argument in a case that for the first time sought to hold a university responsible under federal sex discrimination law for the sexual harassment of a student by a teacher (*Alexander v. Yale*). The argument that sexual harassment in the workplace is sex discrimination also formed the basis of her first book, *Sexual Harassment of Working Women* (1979), still considered definitive. In this book, MacKinnon distinguished two types of sexual harassment, one of which—the less ambiguous quid pro quo form of sexual harassment that describes a tit-for-tat situation in which a supervisor links specific rewards or punishments to an employee's sexual receptivity (as in "sleep with me or be fired")—had begun to be recognized by the courts (*Barnes v. Costle*). In convincing the Supreme Court to accept the second, "hostile environment" form as sex discrimination, however, MacKinnon would make her first major contribution to U.S. law. This came in 1986, when, as cocounsel in *Meritor Savings Bank, FSB v. Vinson*, MacKinnon argued that Mechelle Vinson had been a victim of sex discrimination prohibited by Title VII of the Civil Rights Act of 1964 when she left her job in order to escape two and a half years of alleged sexual advances, molestation, and rape by her male supervisor. Because the man had never threatened to fire Vinson, the bank's attorneys contended that Title VII—which they argued should be construed as limited only to tangible economic losses, rather than as also embracing "purely psychological aspects of the workplace environment"—did not apply. MacKinnon countered, however, that the two seemingly distinct forms of sexual harassment were merely different points on the same "timeline": a woman fired due to sexual harassment is clearly a victim of a quid pro quo, but why must she be forced to bring such "intensified injury upon herself in order to demonstrate that she is injured at all"? If hostile environment alone were not enough to establish discrimination, then the clever harasser, able to make a woman's work life miserable because of her sex while leaving her job "formally undisturbed," would in effect enjoy the Court's sanction. The Court unanimously agreed, establishing hostile environment sexual harassment as a form of illegal sex discrimination, a ruling it subsequently strengthened in *Harris v. Forklift Systems, Inc.* (1993), which reversed several lower courts' readings of *Meritor* to require the proof of severe psychological harm. Only that a harasser's behavior had "detract[ed] from [other] employees' job performance" need be shown in order to require redress under Title VII, the Court ruled.

By the time of *Meritor*, the central focus of MacKinnon's work had shifted to the issue with which she is popularly most readily associated, pornography. She had left New Haven to take a visiting position at Stanford Law School in 1981, beginning a series of temporary appointments that over the next decade would take her to numerous prestigious institutions, all without the offer of a permanent job. During this period—which she recalls as a "10-year job interview" (Strebeigh 1994, 1044)—she found herself at the University of Minnesota Law School (1982–1985), where she collaborated with an old friend, Andrea Dworkin, to design the first law school course on pornography. This brought them to the attention of some Minneapolis residents who wanted to enlist their support of a zoning ordinance to restrict sex businesses to commercial districts. But rather than offering support, MacKinnon and Dworkin declared their opposition to the entire logic of the ordinance, instead siding with the poorer residents of the commercial districts who did not want to see their neighborhoods saturated with pornography. What was really needed, they argued, was a new basis on which to attack pornography, which they developed into an antipornography ordinance for the Minneapolis City Council.

Andrea Dworkin had, since the publication of *Woman Hating* in 1974, been building a body of work that argues that women's subordination originates in the construction of heterosexuality, to which pornography is central. She charged that the zoning ordinance's failing was in focusing on the harm that pornography does to property values, instead of the harm that it does to women. Instead, the law should be changed to recognize pornography as itself a form of sex discrimination, integral to defining women as second-class citizens, fit only to be subordinated to men.

In MacKinnon and Dworkin's view, the more men see pornography, the more they progressively come to enjoy it and also to lose sight of its actual content, until finally violence stops being seen as violence, and women cease to be viewed as human beings. They proposed to recast the terms of the argument over pornography, abandoning attempts to define the "obscene" and, instead, focusing on harm. This would allow pornography prosecution to be taken out of the criminal courts (which judge obscenity) and instead pursued in civil court, where money is the remedy, and the burden of proof is less difficult to prove. It would address pornography's harm in terms of not tort law but civil rights law, allowing women (or those used "in place of women") to sue anyone who "coerced" them to appear in pornography, who "forced" pornography on them, or who produced a piece of pornography that "caused" them to be assaulted. Further, any woman might sue pornography traffickers on behalf of all women, on the logic that every woman is damaged by any pornography's depiction of women as lesser beings.

The City Council of Minneapolis was so excited by this new approach that it hired MacKinnon and Dworkin as consultants and had them organize two evenings of hearings at which women testified that they had been abused and exploited in the production of pornography and that pornographic materials had been used during sexual assaults against them. These hearings convinced the council, in late 1983 and again in 1984 (revised), to adopt the ordinance as an amendment to Minneapolis' antidiscrimination laws. Both times, however, the mayor—citing traditional civil rights concerns, and especially free speech concerns—vetoed it.

Meanwhile, MacKinnon and Dworkin were contacted by forces who wanted to try something similar in Indianapolis, limited only to violent materials. This time the ordinance both passed the City Council and was signed into law by the mayor, only to be challenged by the American Civil Liberties Union (ACLU). Litigation led to the Supreme Court, which in 1986 summarily affirmed lower court rulings that the ordinance violated the First Amendment (*Hudnut v. American Booksellers*).

In the ensuing years, resurrected versions of MacKinnon and Dworkin's ordinance have appeared in U.S. cities and states as well as in Western Europe, in Australia and New Zealand, in Tasmania, and in the Philippines. Their most notable success has come in Canada, whose Supreme Court in 1992 accepted the redefinition of obscenity to include materials that degrade, dehumanize, or subordinate women, saying that such materials pose a threat to women's equality by portraying women "as a class as objects for sexual exploitation and abuse" and by damaging individual women's "sense of self-worth and acceptance" (*R. v. Butler*). The Court also ruled permissible government suppression of materials deemed harmful to women, leading to a wave of government seizures of publications judged obscene.

Charges, though, that these seizures have disproportionately targeted lesbian and gay materials have provided ammunition to critics who have long argued that laws like MacKinnon and Dworkin's are more likely to be used by the government to crush sexual minorities than to protect women. This has fueled conflict in progressive circles over the wisdom of MacKinnon's campaign against pornography; some of her most vociferous opponents have been feminists and liberals, among them the Feminist Anti-Censorship Task Force (FACT), the ACLU, and the American Booksellers Association, while many political and religious conservatives have offered support. FACT, which includes Betty Friedan and Adrienne Rich among its members, prepared a legal brief, signed by more than fifty prominent feminists, attacking the Indianapolis ordinance as "vague" and an exercise in censorship, besides arguing that it tends to reinforce society's "central sexist stereotypes" (MacKinnon responded by calling FACT members feminist "Uncle Toms" who were "fronting for male supremacists"). These criticisms that MacKinnon's theory reinforces sexist stereotypes and that it opens the door to potentially repressive government policies strike to its very heart.

MacKinnon explains women's subordination using a modified Marxist framework in which reproduction (viewed as the material determinant of women's existence) takes the central place that Marx gave to production. In brief, MacKinnon argues that women's social subordination is rooted in their role in the reproduction of the species—which means that it is fundamentally sexual. Following Marx, she (like most feminists) believes that human beings are constructions of culture, not nature. Gender, therefore, is created—as well as continually re-created—in social life. In this process, consciousness itself, including the consciousness of maleness and femaleness and of what those things mean in a given culture, is formed. Because men desire to control women's reproductive power—which requires controlling women—they work to construct femaleness as subordinate to maleness. This construction is accomplished in the institution of heterosexuality, which creates femaleness as passive and dependent and maleness as aggressive and independent.

Thus far, MacKinnon's analysis might be thought of as "orthodox" radical feminism—and, indeed, MacKinnon does embrace that description. But she parts company with many other feminists in her argument that *pornography* is primary in creating "the social reality of gender" by causing "what a woman is" in society to be defined "in pornographic terms" "as what men want from sex." In MacKinnon's view, pornography is not speech or ideas but "a form of action, requiring the submission of women," itself a practice of sex discrimination through which the construction of gender, as dominance and subordination, is accomplished. Pornography thereby does harm to women that the law cannot see as harm, because it seems to be "just the way things are": in society, "men treat women as who they see women as being," and pornography "constructs who that is." Therefore, if society continues to define men's freedom as including the freedom "to make or consume pornography," it does so at the cost of women's equality, because "men's freedom to use [women] in this way creates women's second-class civil status."

In pornography can be found "in one place, all of the abuses women suffer." These abuses pornography "sexualizes," "eroticiz[ing] the dominance and submission that is the dynamic common to them," making this "dominance and submission into sex." By this process, it "legitimizes" the abuses, "sexualiz[ing] inequality" and making "hierarchy sexy." In pornography's "harmonious" world, acts of sexual violence "become acts of sexual equality," because women want them as much as men do. In this world, the most "liberated" woman is the one who most wants to provide what men want from her sexually. But though she must look free, this supposed freedom always coexists with a communication of "forcing," making pornography itself "a form of forced sex, a practice of sexual politics, and an institution of gender inequality" that "institutionalizes the sexuality of male supremacy, fusing the eroticization of dominance and submission with the social construction of male and female" (MacKinnon 1987, 163–166, 171–172).

Pornography comes together with sexual harassment in that they both work in the same way because in both of them words function as acts. The "sexual words and pictures" of sexual harassment "work the way pornography works," "not merely describ[ing] sexuality or represent[ing] it," but "in a sense . . . hav[ing] sex." MacKinnon argues that in determining whether speech is merely expressive or is, in fact, an act, "the distinction that matters . . . is . . . between speech that is sex and speech that is not. Harassment that is sexual is a sex act, like pornography," while "harassment that is not sexual works more through its content" (MacKinnon 1993, 56–58).

However, although sexual harassment always exists as "words, pictures, meaningful acts and gestures" that appear superficially as expression, this has not usually "been imagined to raise expressive concerns" or to prevent seeing sexual harassment itself "legally . . . in terms of what it does: discriminate on the basis of sex." The same, however, has not been true of pornography, whose regulation is almost always seen to raise First Amendment expressive issues. But because "language shapes social reality," to say that sexual language, whatever its context, does not do things that harm women "is to say that [these harmed women's] social reality does not exist" (MacKinnon 1993, 45–46, 57–58). MacKinnon's campaign against pornography is one with her campaign against sexual harassment in that both are motivated by a desire to force the law to address sexual inequality *as it is experienced by women*. In terms of the "dominance" approach to sex discrimination, pornography is every bit as much a practice that "participates in the systematic social deprivation of one sex because of sex" as is sexual harassment.

In this brief description, we can find the sources of both of the leading criticisms raised against MacKinnon. The first is that she reinforces sexist stereotypes. Because she wants to make her case against pornography as strong as possible, MacKinnon is essentially forced into the position that real women *are* the women we find in pornography: submissive, dependent, and masochistic. Her view of social human construction must be strongly deterministic, or she loses the force of her case against pornography as a primary factor in the creation of gender. If she is read as saying only that men *believe* real women are like the women in pornography, but real women may, in fact, not be that, her case for the way pornography constructs gender, by "eroticizing" dominance and submission, is undermined. This eroticization cannot be seen as proceeding only for men and not for women if pornography is to be seen as the central force in the creation of the genders.

MacKinnon's clear belief that women need special protection from sexually explicit materials is sometimes characterized as "maternalism" because it depends on the notion that women are passive, sexually pure "little flowers," damaged in some special way by sexuality, needing to be shielded from strong language and the lustful men who might "get dirty ideas" from pornography. MacKinnon sees no distinction between the use of women and the use of children in pornography, holding by definition that because it can never be in women's interest to appear in pornography, if they do so, they are coerced. Because she cannot allow that women might meaningfully choose to appear in, or to consume, pornography, MacKinnon effectively argues that women are without autonomy, a view not apparently compatible with establishing women as fully competent adult human beings and citizens. Many women who experience their own choices as autonomous and meaningful find such "infantilization" of themselves offensive and worry that, were MacKinnon's ideas put into practice, they would limit women's freedom and self-determination in service to a theory with very little hard evidence to back it up. (Indeed, some scholars who empirically study pornography have taken pains to distance themselves from MacKinnon's causal claims.)

The second common criticism of MacKinnon's position—that it potentially opens a door to governmental repression—responds to MacKinnon's view of pornography not as speech but as a form of action. This view attacks the public-private distinction that undergirds the liberal concept of the relationship between state and society, integral to central liberal ideals such as freedom, autonomy, and rights. Classically, liberals believe that conflict is inherent between the claims of collective bodies and the freedom of individuals. Because they believe that majorities in power naturally incline to tyranny, coercively imposing their preferences on minorities, liberals conceive of a social sphere of private freedom and immunity from collective interference. In this sphere, whose boundaries are determined by clearly secured rights, the individual may pursue her own self-interest, as she pleases, subject only to the provision that she not prevent others from doing likewise. Of the immunities of this private sphere, among the most closely guarded have been the freedoms of thought and expression, which in the United States are guaranteed by the First Amendment.

MacKinnon's war on pornography has raised two concerns among those who worry about freedom. The first is that she is heading down a "slippery slope": if the courts are to be used to attack pornography on the grounds that it is act and not words, what is to stop attacks on other speech on the same grounds? MacKinnon's answer is to distinguish between speech that "is sex" and speech that is not; for her, both sexual harassment and pornography are "sex acts." MacKinnon writes that sex is "different," hostile, sexual language operating not through content—not expressively—but as action against targeted individuals or groups.

But what about hostile, sexual language makes it different from any other hostile language? Would it not be possible to argue that a wide range of hostile, political speech, some of it sexual, some of it not, also operates as action? A legal distinction is usually made between speech that is an incitement to violence and speech that may be identical in content but because of context is not incitement, the former being proscribed and the latter protected. Though there is often, in practice, some difficulty in distinguishing between the two, MacKinnon's arguments obliterate this distinction entirely, always defining pornography as an act in social life as a whole, without further respect to context.

MacKinnon finds it inconsistent that the courts are able to recognize the harm in sexual harassment but not the harm in pornography, asking why speech involved in sexual harassment is not seen as expressive, while speech as pornography is. Boiled down to its essential logic, her argument is that pornography creates a hostile environment for women in the world, just as sexual harassment creates a hostile environment for women in the workplace. But although it is usually clear what and who are causing a hostile environment in a workplace, this is less readily apparent in terms of the hostility women face in social life. A woman alleging sexual harassment must demonstrate that she has been harmed by *that harassment*. MacKinnon believes that the same sort of thing can be proved about pornography—that it has harmed specific women in specific ways—but this contention is more problem-ridden. Though in sexual harassment, the connection between the harasser and the harassed is clear, this is much less obvious for pornography, not only because pornography is aimed—at least overtly—at men, not women. How would the effect of specific pornography be isolated in order to fix blame? If a man with pornography in his pocket raped someone, should this be blamed on the pornography in his pocket, on all the pornography he had ever read, or on all the pornography in the world? What is to be made of the fact that many people who have never raped anyone also have read pornography like that in his pocket? In hostile-environment sexual harassment, it is clearly behavior that is targeted, and this can be done without reference to the reasons for the behavior. But with pornography, MacKinnon moves from behavior to its alleged causes and therefore steps into the liberal sphere of private freedom of thought and expression, exciting fears that her ordinance would have a "chilling effect" on all sexual speech. Even though proof of harm is required for a suit's success, some might be financially ruined though ultimately legally vindicated, leading others to self-censor to avoid even the possibility of such a fate. Furthermore, it becomes clear in *Only Words* that MacKinnon's analysis can allow no distinction by medium, defining any sexually explicit material, as long as it can be seen to "harm" women in MacKinnon's extremely expansive definition of the term, as pornography. This would seem, at least potentially, to put at risk much material that is not presently thought of as pornographic. Indeed, it is arguable that the more literary, attractive, and fully explicated the sexual expression, the more dangerous it might be seen.

MacKinnon's policy prescriptions allow the courts ultimately to determine what is pornography and what is not, and this trust she practically puts in the government is the second cause civil libertarians have found to worry about MacKinnon's campaigning. She herself has defined the "regime" as a systematic embodiment of male power; this makes it more than a bit strange that she believes the government capable of distinguishing between sexually explicit expression that harms women and sexually explicit expression that tends toward their liberation. Clearly, to such a government, the expressions of sexual minorities are always going to look a lot more dangerous than heterosexual pornography, whatever its additional content.

Despite the defeat of her antipornography ordinances, MacKinnon has continued her campaign, and some legal scholars predict that she might eventually convince American courts that pornography no more deserves First Amendment protection than does sexual harassment. Recently, however, she has focused on the international arena, seeking recognition of woman's rights as human rights. In 1993, she filed suit in U.S. court, under the Alien Tort Claims Act and Torture Victim Protection Act (*K. v. Karadzic*), on behalf of Bosnian women who charged that they are victims of Serbian war crimes, including torture and genocidal rape and murder. Her 1996 victory on appeal marked the first time rape and forced pregnancy have been legally recognized as acts of genocide and also established that the right to be free of these is a human right that aliens may assert in U.S. courts under international law.

MacKinnon's conviction, even single-mindedness; her propensity to engage in passionate rhetoric that arguably generates heat more effectively than light; and her designs on changing laws in ways that must fundamentally alter American society combine to leave few observers neutral on her ideas or on herself. She has been called "elitist," "reductionistic," "undemocratic, perhaps even antidemocratic," and even "demented," besides being accused of alienating people from feminism and of writing arguments that rely "on slogans, false premises, half-information, sinister innuendo, and ad hoc reasoning" (quoted in *Current Biography Yearbook 1994*, 366, 367). Given the success she has achieved in the area of sexual harassment—where she, in effect, convinced the courts to shift from a man's to a woman's point of view, creating "one of the more dramatic and rapid changes in legal and social understanding in recent years" (Sunstein 1988, 829)—many people are frankly afraid of what she might accomplish with pornography. It is unarguable that she has already fundamentally altered the terms of the pornography debate from an obscenity analysis (concerned with public morality) to a pornography analysis (which emphasizes harm to women). But although there may be a woman's point of view on sexual harassment, it is clear that no such consensus exists on pornography. Nevertheless, students at schools that MacKinnon visited over the years tried to convince their institutions to retain her, and she is a renowned teacher and speaker. In 1990 she ended her decade of academic wanderings with a tenured appointment at the University of Michigan Law School, whose dean, Lee Bollinger, commended "the force of her scholarship and the quality of her mind" and the head of whose appointment committee, Joseph Weiler, called her "a major scholar" and a "major social theorist" (Sunstein 1988, 366).

WORKS BY CATHARINE MacKINNON

Books

Sexual Harassment of Working Women: A Case of Sex Discrimination. New Haven, CT: Yale
  University Press, 1979.
Feminism Unmodified: Discourses on Life and Law. Cambridge: Harvard University Press,
  1987.
And Andrea Dworkin. Pornography and Civil Rights: A New Day for Women's Equality.
  Minneapolis: Organizing against Pornography, 1988.
Toward a Feminist Theory of the State. Cambridge: Harvard University Press, 1989.
Only Words. Cambridge: Harvard University Press, 1993.
And Andrea Dworkin. In Harm's Way: The Pornography Civil Rights Hearings. Cambridge,
  MA: Harvard University Press, 1997.

Selected Essays

"Feminism, Marxism, Method, and the State: An Agenda for Theory." Signs 7 (Winter
  1982): 514–544.
"Feminism, Marxism, Method, and the State: Toward Feminist Jurisprudence." Signs 8
  (Summer 1983): 635–658.
"A Feminist/Political Approach, 'Pleasure under Patriarchy.' " Theories and Paradigms of
  Human Sexuality. Ed. William P. O'Donohue and James Greer. New York: Plenum
  Press, 1987, 65–90. [Later published as "Sexuality, Pornography, and Method:
  'Pleasure under Patriarchy.' " Ethics 99 (January 1989): 314–346.]
"From Practice to Theory, or What Is a White Woman Anyway?" Yale Journal of Law and
  Feminism 4 (1991a).
"Reflections on Sex Equality under Law." Yale Law Journal 100 (March 1991b).
"Crimes of War, Crimes of Peace." On Human Rights: The Oxford Amnesty Lectures 1983.
  Ed. Stephen Shute and Susan Hurley. New York: Basic Books, 1993, 83–109.

WRITINGS ON CATHARINE MacKINNON AND HER WORK

Bresnahan, Eileen. "MacKinnon, Catharine A." Feminist Writers. Ed. Pamela Kester-
  Shelton. New York: St. James Press, 1996, 299–301.
Contemporary Authors. Vol. 132. Detroit: Gale Research, 1991, 260–261.
Current Biography Yearbook 1994. New York: H. W. Wilson, 1994, 364–367.
Palczewski, Catherine Helen. "Catharine A. MacKinnon." Women Public Speakers in the
  United States, 1925–1993: A Bio-Critical Sourcebook. Ed. Karlyn Khors Campbell.
  Westport, CT: Greenwood Press, 1994, 287–305.
Strebeigh, Fred. "Defining Law on the Feminist Frontier." New York Times Biographical
  Service, vol. 22. Ann Arbor, MI: University Microfilms International, 1991, 1040–
  1045.

Sunstein, Cass R. "Book Review: Feminism and Legal Theory." *Harvard Law Review* 101 (February 1988): 826–848.

Tong, Rosemarie. *Feminist Thought: A Comprehensive Introduction*. Boulder, CO: Westview Press, 1989.

OLGA MADAR
(1915–1996)

Amy Beth Aronson

At the 1974 founding convention of the Coalition of Labor Union Women (CLUW), president-elect Olga Madar said that "one result of this meeting is that fewer and fewer union women will be saying 'we are not women's libbers.' By coming here, they have proved that they are" (Gabin 1990, 226). Madar's statement reflects—and hopes to resolve—the historical class antagonisms that have infected organized feminism in America almost since its origins in 1848. Through all of Madar's public activities—a life of activism that included being the first woman member of the International Executive Board of the United Auto Workers (UAW), a founder or organizer of several influential feminist organizations, a reformer of racial discrimination in sports, a champion of environmental protection, a proponent of consumer protection laws, and an advocate for the aging—she negotiated the sometimes-competing claims of unionism and feminism, all in the name of "democracy." In doing so, her perspective and political work helped redefine the agendas of both movements, pressing them toward a fuller recognition of equality.

Madar is best known for her leadership role in the founding of CLUW. Originally conceived as a lobbying organization comprising women labor union officials—an institutional structure criticized by some as elitist (Withorn 1976; Field 1975), careerist (Withorn 1976), or too much an insider's game to fulfill the need for a broad-based workingwoman's organization (Milkman 1985)—CLUW today consists of well over 20,000 members, with more than 60 local chapters across the United States. At the founding conference held in 1973, 3,200 women and some men—many more than were anticipated—crowded into the Pick-Congress Hotel in Chicago and adopted the four goals that remain at the core of CLUW: to strengthen the role and participation of women within their unions and the trade union movement; to seek affirmative action in the workplace; to organize the millions of unorganized women workers; and to encourage union women to play an active role in the democratic process.

Madar's election as president of the new organization surprised no one, since her initiative and consensus-building skills during the previous eighteen months had brought differently situated union women to the bargaining table, eventually resulting in the formation of a collective of high-powered union women. Under Madar, CLUW drew on the legacy of women's agitation in the labor movement, within the UAW in particular, and also the renascent feminist movement of the 1970s. In a 1974 interview with the *New York Times*, Madar commented that "the women's movement gave an impetus to our [union women's] moving ahead" (Gabin 1990, 225).

The need for an organization to increase the clout of union women arose from a range of factors affecting women's work. Economic pressures in the early 1970s, for example, had propelled more women into the workforce, even while a climate of scarcity disproportionately affected women's employment and advancement opportunities. Women faced unique barriers to workplace equity, even in the unionized trades. So-called protective labor laws prevented women from getting physically demanding and higher-wage jobs on the factory floor. Many states also "protected" women workers by restricting overtime hours—thus, the amount of pay—simply on the basis of sex. Sex segregation in employment classifications, long accepted everywhere, from factories, to classrooms, to airlines, to clerical and secretarial pools, also erected barriers to women's mobility and earning power in both unionized and nonunionized jobs. Although unions were limited in what they could do to combat this widespread discrimination against women workers— after all, they had to abide by laws and statutes—Madar felt that unions were either cooperating with, or inattentive to, workplace inequality. She and others believed one reason for such lapses was the male chauvinism that continued to shape union identity, issues, and goals, distorting the democratic principles on which, Madar held, unionism was based.

Madar had become an activist and union leader because she had always believed fervently in the collective ideal embodied in trade unionism, in the fundamental fairness and equality it implied. When she joined the UAW in 1944, she was proud to become a part of the union's long tradition of social activism. Madar joined at an auspicious moment for women's activism; 1944 was also the year the UAW formed its influential Women's Bureau, which would supply Madar with professional and political support throughout her life and work. (The bureau attained full departmental status in 1955.) Indeed, after the establishment of the bureau, the UAW gained heightened visibility as an agent of equality. The union lobbied for laws against sex discrimination and passed woman's rights resolutions at all its national conventions (Freeman 1975, 165).

But Madar built new bridges between unionist and feminist goals. Madar led the UAW in its unprecedented support of the Equal Rights Amendment (ERA), testifying in its favor before the Senate Judiciary Committee as a UAW official in 1970—a time when most unions staunchly opposed its passage, arguing that the amendment would undermine collective bargaining powers, among other things. Madar countered by testifying that federal legislation was needed to strengthen and support the spirit of fairness, equality, and unity for which such powers had been sought and won (Madar testimony 1970). Madar and other future CLUW women, including many from the UAW Women's Bureau, were key figures in securing the American Federation of Labor–Congress of Industrial Organizations' (AFL-CIO) support of ERA in 1973. The following year, CLUW, under Madar, also pioneered one tactic quickly picked up by NOW and other feminist organizations to press for ERA passage: the organization moved its 1975 convention from an unratified state (Illinois) to a ratified state (Michigan), putting both political and economic pressure on the institutional powers of those states to support the amendment.

For Madar, like many feminist women, the political stemmed from the personal. Madar had confronted the need for socially conscious and feminist unionism years before when, as a high school graduate, she was hired by the Chrysler Corporation largely because she had a regional reputation as a star softball player. She later remarked that "there was no union at the plant then. And the fact that they would hire me when other workers were being laid off—just because I could play softball—was incredible. It was my first indication that a union was badly needed," she said. Also during this time she first became aware of gender discrimination on the plant floor. At Chrysler, she observed that women were the last hired and the first fired and that promotion opportunities were almost nonexistent. By "protective" law, women were permitted to work only two or three days a week in the Michigan plant. Madar continued to work at Chrysler and at the Bower Roller Bearing plant for the next four years in order to work her way through college at Eastern Michigan University. The first in her family of thirteen children to attend college, she graduated with a B.S. in physical education in 1938.

Soon after graduation, Madar began teaching school in Flat Rock. There she again confronted what she saw as the need for a union. Teaching contracts contained only a thirty-day notice clause, and she opposed its use by school systems to downsize teaching staffs abruptly, often leaving employees, many of them women, desperate and adrift. Madar noted wryly that it gave her "great satisfaction to use the clause in reverse" when, after three years, she left teaching to take a job at the nearby Ford Willow Run bomber plant.

At the plant, she met several other activist-minded women with whom she would work in the years to come, and she also became involved in organizing recreation programs for employees. Madar's love of sport originated in her talent as an athlete and her tenacious spirit, but when she came to run recreation programs for others, these interests took on a distinctly "democratic" spin. As one union compatriot describes it, Madar acted from the belief that the "quality of public recreation should be excellent, and for everyone, the poor as well as the rich" (Mildred Jeffries interview, August 1996).

Madar would apply this "politics of recreation" at the UAW, and it would soon carry her into some leading activist issues of the day. In 1947, Madar became director of the UAW Recreation Department. Her first assignment was to eliminate race discrimination in professional bowling. Five years of politicking and persuasion finally resulted in the integration of the American Bowling Conference and the Women's International Bowling Congress, both in 1952 (Gabin 1990, 2). Madar would continue in this pursuit of race equality throughout her career. As head of the Detroit Parks and Recreation Commission from 1958 to 1966, Madar insisted that written job postings for promotion be issued and that the department hold competitive exams in connection with promotions. The first exams resulted in six African Americans among the top eight test takers, and all were promoted—something that had never occurred before.

As Madar moved up in the union hierarchy, she became increasingly visible and vocal as a proponent of the UAW's leftist, egalitarian politics. These developments helped sharpen her interest and involvement with feminism and also propelled her into more important roles as an advocate for a host of other social and political causes. In 1966 (after a failed effort in 1964), Madar became the first woman ever elected to the International Executive Board (IEB) of the UAW. She was reelected easily in 1968. She then became the first-ever woman vice president of an American union in 1970 and was reelected to that position in 1972.

Madar's prominence enabled her to become a respected voice for political change, despite her gender and uncertain status as an unmarried woman. She served simultaneously as head of several UAW departments, and in each job she pushed hard for equity and reform. As director of the Department of Recreation and Leisure-Time Activities, she continued to pursue racial integration in sports, including golf, a game she adored. As director of the Department of Conservation and Resource Development, Madar helped make the UAW a world leader in the struggle for a clean and healthy planet. Through her testimony and organizing efforts, she helped preserve the south Florida everglades, Redwood National Forest, Sleeping Bear Dunes Parks, Porcupine Mountains, and other places of natural beauty; she also fought to secure state and federal funds to clean up toxic sediments in the Great Lakes and participated in the successful national drive to ban the insecticide DDT.

In 1968, Madar took on a visible position as director of the union's newly formed Department of Consumer Affairs. There she devised an extensive advocacy program on consumer rights, ranging from local union complaint handling, to federal legislation. Madar pushed for educational programs and consumer affairs institutes in summer schools, and she initiated a broad-based information program in UAW publications. Her congressional testimony and organizational advocacy were instrumental in securing the Consumer Protection Act. The first labor official to testify in support of federal "Truth in Housing" legislation, she also vigorously supported a range of other legislative measures, including no-fault auto insurance, generic drug substitution, and protections against a host of consumer rip-offs. She spoke out for public ownership of cable television and urged the Federal Communications Commission (FCC) to reduce commercials during children's programming and to eliminate discrimination against women and minorities for both radio and television. A self-supporting woman who would twice share her own home with a fellow union woman, Madar also became a leader in the fight to eliminate discrimination against women in credit.

Madar retired from the UAW in 1974. During the years of her activism there, modern feminism flowered. In the same year that Madar was elected to the IEB, 1966, the National Organization for Women (NOW) was formed—and some say Madar was present in Betty Friedan's Washington, D.C., hotel room where the idea of "an NAACP for women" emerged. A range of other women's groups also arose at this time, including many explicitly dedicated to women's equality in the workplace. Madar was definitely present as a founding member of several of these groups, including the Women's Equity Action League (WEAL) in 1968, a small, but national, legislative organization designed to pursue equality by more moderate means than NOW, and the National Women's Political Caucus (NWPC) in 1971.

Madar's involvement with these women's organizations put her in contact with the issues that would divide feminists and unionists against themselves and each other at the time: protective labor legislation and, later, the comparable worth movement. Madar, essentially an equality feminist, was against special protections for women; she opposed any legislation or policy that would restrict women's freedom of choice in employment and earning power. While some activist women believed that special attention must be paid to women's needs to ensure their continued participation in the workforce, especially on dangerous and physically demanding plant floors, Madar, like prominent liberal feminists of the day, reasoned from the premise that American democracy guaranteed equal opportunity for women to live and work to their fullest potential. She backed letting democracy work for women, fair and square.

Comparable worth would have been a more complicated question for Madar. Since the comparable worth movement aimed to establish legal mechanisms to guarantee equal pay for work deemed of equivalent skill and/or responsibility, some union bargaining agreements would be superseded if the movement prevailed. Some unionists feared that union bargaining powers in general would be threatened amid a more legislated and standardized work climate. Madar believed that individual unions should retain the right as well as the responsibility to create fair and equitable job classifications and corresponding wage levels; she wanted to push unions to guarantee equal opportunity for women within their existing policies and powers.

Madar stepped down from the CLUW presidency in 1976 after two terms, remaining an active emeritus for the rest of her life. But her activism extended well beyond even these uncommon achievements by the ninth child and youngest daughter of Czechoslovakian immigrants from the coal-mining town of Sykesville, Pennsylvania. Dedicated to the proposition that democracy was the means to equality and social justice, Madar chose a "retirement career," as she once called it, that included involvement with a host of reform and civic organizations. She helped organize women's caucuses in the Democratic Party and worked with the National Committee on Pay Equity in Michigan into her final days (see Figart 1995). She continued to work with the environmental movement and served on the boards of dozens of civic groups, including United Community Services of Detroit, Michigan United Conservation Clubs, the Michigan Council for the Humanities, the U.S. Department of Labor's Advisory Council on Women, and the Girl Scouts of America.

Madar also stepped up her work with the aging, one of her deepest and, ultimately, most "democratic" commitments. Having served as codirector of the Older and Retired Workers Department at the UAW, Madar intensified her involvement with seniors after her own retirement, organizing action coalitions aimed at getting older Americans more involved in the legislative and political process. In an interview with the *Detroit Free Press* in 1972, Madar's comments suggest why her work with older American remained so central to her politics. "When the UAW was establishing its senior citizens centers," she recalled, the elderly reported "that [their] biggest problem was that they had too much time on their hands." Articulating her philosophy of "democratic leisure" that first appeared in connection with sports and recreation, Madar explained that "the question becomes, 'how do we use leisure in terms of the community? How does it get to be a plus factor in the development of the country and individuals in it?' " (April 7, 1972).

Answering these questions, Madar helped establish several multipurpose centers for senior citizens in the Detroit area, some of which now bear her name in tribute. Among her many other distinctions, Madar has been honored by the city of Detroit, the Coalition of Black Trade Unionists, and *Redbook* magazine. In 1989, she was inducted into the Michigan Women's Hall of Fame.

Madar's unionism, feminism, and community service all emanated from her lifelong belief in human dignity and equal opportunity for all. Allies describe her as "a visionary with guts," a "tenacious fighter," a "strong-minded woman"— probably without realizing that the latter phrase was the chosen moniker of the first organized feminists in the United States. Just before she died of heart failure, Madar, confined to a wheelchair, vowed that she "would get arrested even if it killed her" during a union newspaper strike in Detroit. But upon her death just days later, Madar made a final feminist mark on U.S. history. In her will, she had arranged for her small estate to become the endowment for the Madar Association for Participatory Democracy, an organization dedicated to furthering women's presence and empowerment in work, community, and nation.

WRITINGS ON OLGA MADAR AND/OR FEMINIST AND LABOR ORGANIZING

Blum, Linda. *Between Feminism and Labor: The Significance of the Comparable Worth Movement.* Berkeley: University of California Press, 1991.

Carabillo, Toni, Judith Meuli, and June Bundy Csida. *The Feminist Chronicles 1953–1993.* Los Angeles: Women's Graphics, 1993.

Cummings, Bernice, and Victoria Schuck. *Women Organizing: An Anthology.* Metuchen, NJ: Scarecrow Press, 1979.

Field, Jana. "The Coalition of Labor Union Women." *Political Affairs* 54, no. 3 (March 1975): 3–12.

Figart, Deborah M. "Evaluating Pay Equity in Michigan: A Strategic Choice Perspective." *Industrial Relations* 34, no. 2 (April 1995): 263–281.

Flick, Rachel. "The New Feminism and the World of Work." *The Public Interest*, no. 70 (Winter 1983), 33–44.

Freeman, Jo. *The Politics of Women's Liberation: A Case Study of an Emerging Social Movement and Its Relation to the Policy Process.* New York: Longman Press, 1975.

Gabin, Nancy F. *Feminism in the Labor Movement: Women and the United Auto Workers, 1935–1975.* Ithaca, NY: Cornell University Press, 1990.

Johansen, Elaine. *Comparable Worth: The Myth and the Movement.* London: Westview Press, 1984.

Milkman, Ruth. *Women, Work and Protest: A Century of U.S. Women's Labor History.* Boston: Routledge and Kegan Paul, 1985.

Newman, Winn, and Carole W. Wilson. "The Union Role in Affirmative Action." *Labor Law Journal* 32, no. 6 (June 1981): 323–342.

Troger, Annemarie. "The Coalition of Labor-Union Women: Strategic Hope, Tactical Despair." *America's Working Women.* Ed. Rosalyn Baxandall, Linda Gordon, and Susan Reverby. New York: Vintage, 1976.

Withorn, Ann. "The Death of CLUW." *Radical America* 10, no. 2 (March–April 1976): 47–51.

WILMA MANKILLER
(1945–)

Michaela Crawford Reaves

A-ji-luhsgi Asgaya-dihi, which means "flower" and "protector of the village," entered the world on November 18, 1945. Born in Tahlequah, Oklahoma, Wilma Mankiller, as she is better known to students of modern Cherokee history, was the sixth child of the eleven offspring of Charley Mankiller and Clara Irene Sitton Mankiller. Charley Mankiller was a full-blooded Cherokee from Oklahoma living on the family farm allotment of 160 acres at Mankiller Flats, land that Wilma Mankiller still inhabits. Clara Irene Sitton was of Dutch-Irish lineage from an agricultural family in Oklahoma. Despite the differences in their mutual heritages, Charley and Clara Irene married in 1937 and raised their children as traditional Cherokee.

Living in northeastern Oklahoma, Mankiller spent her early years outdoors, running and playing with her brothers and sisters. Her parents eked out a meager living from growing strawberries, peanuts, berries, and green beans, as well as cutting timber and picking crops as seasonal work became available. Food for the family grew in the vegetable garden, and wild game supplemented the family diet. The children all had chores, with the girls carrying the seemingly unending water supply back to the tiny house.

Wilma Mankiller remembers her youth as a "rich feast" of "little people" from the stories told her by her paternal aunt, Maggie Gourd (Mankiller 1993, 38). The stories of her heritage were rich and varied and filled her imagination. This thirst for stories translated into a love of literature later in her life. Skipping through the woods, Mankiller enjoyed her Cherokee heritage. Some of the best times were celebrations that often included the ceremonial dances of the Cherokee. Every day, Mankiller and her siblings walked three miles each way to Rocky Mountain School. Generally, Mankiller remembers her childhood as protected and carefree, though periodically she felt different from the non-Indian children. Her first awareness of this came at school when she realized that her flour-sack clothing set her apart from her contemporaries.

When Wilma was ten, the Mankiller family joined a government program sponsored by the Bureau of Indian Affairs that relocated Indian families from their traditional lands to urban centers. The program was part of the Eisenhower administration's "termination policy," designed to remove Indians from their status as wards of the U.S. government. Dubious at first but devastated by a two-year drought, Charley Mankiller hoped to provide his family with a better standard of living. In 1955 he opted to accept the offer. After a long train ride, the family established itself in San Francisco. The transition from rural Oklahoma to urban San Francisco was abrupt. For the children, the sound of sirens replaced the song of birds. Wilma Mankiller entered the fifth grade, where she felt herself to be different from her peers. The resultant culture shock left her feeling sad and lonely. She attended seventh grade in Daly City, but for eighth grade lived with her grandmother on the Sitton family dairy ranch in Escalon. She returned for high school to San Francisco, living in an area called Hunter's Point. The neighborhood was so crime-ridden that no ambulance would go there after dark. Despite the neighborhood this period became fundamental to the developing Mankiller. She learned to draw strength from the experiences of her ancestors, adopting what she terms a "Cherokee approach to life," which means being of good mind (Craig, *Sacramento Bee Final*, December 7, 1993, E5). She began to go the Indian Center for sanctuary and to meet friends.

The 1960s had begun with a new president, new music, and new conflicts in civil rights and around the globe. Nationally and in Wilma Mankiller's own life, 1963 was a harbinger of change. She finished high school, moved in with her sister, took a job in a finance company, and met Hector Hugo Olaya de Bardi, or simply Hugo Olaya, a native of Ecuador. On November 13, 1963, Hugo and the seventeen-year-old Wilma eloped to Reno, Nevada. On their honeymoon in Chicago, the news came of the assassination of John F. Kennedy. When the young couple returned to San Francisco, they found a place to live and settled into married life. Their first child, Felicia, was born on August 11, 1964, and Gina followed two years later.

During the early years of her marriage to Hugo, Wilma Mankiller suffered from a kidney infection, the first signs of her battle with polycystic kidney disease. She enjoyed caring for her babies, but she felt increasingly restricted by her marriage and looked for other outlets. She found them attending Skyline Junior College and then San Francisco State College, where she studied sociology. In 1969 the Indian occupation of Alcatraz island in San Francisco Bay became the biggest influence in her life. According to Mankiller, the occupation "changed me forever" (Mankiller 1993, 159). Not only did she become aware of the issues of Indian activism, since several of her siblings participated in the occupation, but it gave her life the focus she was seeking. The occupation lasted nineteen months. During that period, her father became very ill and died of polycystic kidney disease.

More and more often, Wilma Mankiller turned to Native American issues as her focus, and increasingly her husband objected to her activities. Mankiller became the director of the Native American Youth Center in Oakland and a volunteer for the Pit River people in their litigation for tribal land. In 1973 her heart turned to Wounded Knee, where her brother and others held off the Federal Bureau of Investigation (FBI) for 72 days. By the time the conflict was resolved in South Dakota, the resolution of Mankiller's own dilemmas also became apparent. Divorce from Hugo seemed imminent and became official in 1975, but not before he took her daughter from her in 1974 for nine months of international travel without telling Mankiller of his plans. Realizing she could not protect her daughters twenty-four hours a day, Mankiller decided to return to Oklahoma, where they would be safer. The following year she followed her heart and her heritage back to Oklahoma and the family at Mankiller Flats.

Once in Oklahoma, Mankiller went to work for the Cherokee nation in October 1977 for $11,000 a year. The job was a low-level management position as an economic stimulus coordinator. The primary focus was to encourage Cherokees to train in environmental health and science and return to their communities with the much-needed training. Working under the chief, Ross Swimmer, the Cherokee ratified a new constitution for tribal government in 1976. Mankiller's daughters were content in school, and in 1979 she finished her degree work and received a bachelor of science in sociology. She then entered the University of Arkansas at Fayetteville for her graduate degree. With an informal leave of absence from her post with the Cherokee nation, Mankiller devoted herself to her classes until tragedy struck on November 8, 1979. Traveling down a rural road that morning, she crashed head-on into another car that was trying to pass in the oncoming lane. Seriously injured with massive facial injuries, two broken legs, and fractured ribs, Wilma Mankiller was not aware for several days that the driver of the oncoming car killed in the accident was her best friend. Months of rehabilitation followed: months of mourning, thinking, reading, and writing. As her injuries began to heal, she noticed muscle weakness and an inability to perform normal activities like brushing her hair. During the 1980 Labor Day telethon for muscular dystrophy, she realized that she had the same symptoms as the television described. Shortly thereafter doctors diagnosed her ailment as myasthenia gravis, for which she underwent surgery in November. In January 1981, she returned to her post with the Cherokee nation.

Eager to embrace her new work, Wilma Mankiller accepted the position of director of the Cherokee Nation Community Development Department. Her job was putting together grants and volunteers for the project to revitalize the small community of Bell, Oklahoma. The project was massive, and community involvement validated Mankiller's belief in the interdependence of the Cherokee people and their willingness to work together. Her work on this project was the linchpin of the two most pivotal occurrences of her life for the next decade. First, she met a Cherokee named Charlie Soap on the Bell community project. After finding that they worked well together, the relationship grew, and they married in October 1986. The second important change also involved the work Mankiller contributed to the Bell project. She attracted the attention of Chief Ross Swimmer, who asked her to run as his deputy chief in 1983. Unexpectedly, the race became one based on gender, as opponents slashed her tires and harassed her with threatening phone calls and death threats. Despite these odds the ticket of Swimmer and Mankiller won the election on August 14, 1983.

In her new position as deputy chief, Mankiller oversaw the daily tribal oper-ations of an Indian nation in fourteen counties. Projects ranged from supervising health clinics and child care, to water projects, housing construction, and Head Start. Abruptly, in September 1985, President Ronald Reagan nominated Swim-mer to become head of the Bureau of Indian Affairs. The Cherokee constitution stated that the deputy chief would assume the position of primary chief if that chief did not finish the term. With Swimmer's departure, Mankiller assumed the mantle of primary chief of the Cherokee on December 5, 1985. At the end of that term Mankiller decided to seek her own full term in 1987. Three males ran against her in the race, and the issues sometimes focused on Mankiller's hospi-talization for kidney disease during the campaign. The election resulted in a runoff, which Mankiller won. That same year Ms. magazine selected her as Woman of the Year.

By 1990, however, Mankiller's health deteriorated to the point that she re-quired a kidney transplant from her brother, Don. The operation was successful, and Mankiller finished her term of office and decided to run again in 1991. She won reelection by an overwhelming 83 percent of the vote. She had already signed the self-governance agreement with the United States in 1990. This meant that the Cherokee nation would administer funds formally administered by the Bureau of Indian Affairs. Mankiller served as principal chief of a 150,000-person nation in fourteen counties and oversaw a budget of $78 million. So complex was the organization that Mankiller termed it "more of a republic than a reservation" (Koenenn, *Los Angeles Times*, November 1, 1993, E3). She revi-talized tribal courts and tribal police functions and established a Cherokee tax commission. She filled her tenure in office with many ambitious projects, in-cluding a new education plan, Cherokee language and literacy institutes, a com-prehensive health care system, housing initiatives, and child and youth projects, college scholarships, as well as environmental and economic development.

In 1992 President-Elect Bill Clinton chose her to represent Native Americans at a national summit on economics in Arkansas. With all these projects Wilma Mankiller still found time in 1993 to publish her autobiography, written with Michael Wallis, *Mankiller: A Chief and Her People*, and to be elected to the National Women's Hall of Fame. In April 1994, she told her nation that her "season here is coming to an end" as she decided to step down as principal chief of the Cherokee after the next election (*Time*, April 18, 1994).

Her tenure as principal chief successfully completed, Wilma Mankiller planned to return to her ancestral home in 1995, to what she termed "my books, my art, my grandchildren and the natural world" (Mankiller 1993, 256). Felicia married in 1995 and presented Mankiller with three grandchildren, Aaron, Jaron, and Breanna Swake. Gina also married and had one son, Kellan Quinton. Mankiller's retreat to a private life did not last. In 1996 she became a Montgomery Fellow at Dartmouth College, teaching and lecturing. She also battled lymphoma with chemotherapy while maintaining her speaking schedule and editing *The Reader's Companion to the History of American Women*. In 1998 President Clinton recognized her commitment and contributions by awarding her the Presidential Medal of Freedom.

Wilma Mankiller stands out as a symbol of contemporary feminism, but she also is a banner carrier for cultural feminism that reaches back into the history of the Cherokee nation. In her autobiography, as the title suggests, Mankiller is careful to explain that her story is also the story of her people. When she evaluates her contribution, it is within the framework of the twentieth century, but it is also tangibly the restoration of her gender to its rightful historic place within the Cherokee nation.

In a speech at Harvard University in 1987, Wilma Mankiller pointed this out: "True tribal tradition recognizes the importance of women. Contrary to what you've probably read in history books, not all tribes were controlled by men." History tends to portray all Indian women as either drudges or princesses without recognizing the fact that many tribes, including the Cherokee, were matrifocal and matrilineal. In Cherokee history the Women's Council played an important role. Cherokee are linguistically tied to the Iroquois, who had a female clan head called the *ohwachira*, whose descendants chose the male representative to the council. The Cherokee title was *ghigau*. Cherokee women traditionally owned the property and maintained the home to such a degree that European reporters commented on the "petticoat" government of the tribe since women even went to war. Mankiller, therefore, felt that her election "was a step forward and a step backward at the same time" (Wallace 1988, 68).

Despite this history, Mankiller found that her campaign for principal chief resulted in one of the "first times I experienced overt sexism" (Mankiller 1993, 246). That is not to say that Mankiller was unaware of the issues of feminism from the 1960s, both as a movement and as a very personal issue. By the time she was twenty-one she had a very real urge to stretch her wings and not become a "Stepford wife" (Mankiller 1993, 157). College contributed to that sense of independence. By 1968 she was aware of small bands of daring women's liberationists in San Francisco. She discovered that many of these women were wives, mothers, and students who met to discuss sexuality, employment experiences, and male tyranny. In her private life Mankiller actually once slugged her boss at a Christmas party in San Francisco when he tried to kiss her. Mankiller understood what it meant to be her own person. Yet when asked, she chooses the Alcatraz island occupation as the pivotal event in her life, an incident in which women played a vital role. "Alcatraz was a benchmark. After that I became involved" (Mankiller 1993, xxi). She further commented, "The growth of the women's movement ushered in a new era—greatly influencing my life" (Mankiller 1993, 159).

The role Wilma Mankiller played in the Cherokee nation demonstrates the power of that influence. Despite death threats she ran for the office of principal chief. In her own words she stated that she was "returning the balance to the role of women in our tribe. Prior to my becoming chief, young Cherokee girls never thought they might be able to grow up and become chief themselves" (Mankiller 1993, 246, xviii). She feels that her impact from the start was noticeable on the younger women of the Cherokee tribe and that more women would pursue tribal leadership roles. This has been the case. The fifteen-member Cherokee tribal council now includes six women.

Wilma Mankiller's contribution to contemporary feminism is an abiding one. Two legacies stand out. The first is her gift to future generations in her willingness to lead by example. "I like to encourage young women to be willing to take risks, to stand up for the things they believe in, and to step up and accept the challenge of serving in leadership roles." She feels "kids" increasingly view feminism as something "older people" do (Ms., July 1994, 59).

Her second legacy reaches back into her culture and brings down through the generations a knowledge of the role women can play. Traditionally, Native American tribes have some degree of harmony and balance in the roles of men and women. A Lakota saying that Mankiller quotes states, "A nation is not defeated until the hearts of the women are on the ground" (Mankiller 1993, 246). In this spirit she applauds the nomination of Judge Ruth Bader Ginsburg to the Supreme Court, as well as the role of First Lady Hillary Rodham Clinton and Nobel Peace Prize-winner Rigoberta Menchu, a Native American woman from Guatemala. Mankiller explained it this way in 1984, "Women can help turn the world right side up. We bring a more collaborative approach to government. And if we do not participate the decision will be made without us" (Mankiller 1993, 242). Mankiller's role as a bridge from traditional Native American matrifocality to contemporary feminism is poignantly drawn out in her own summation that ties her heritage to her modern feminist ideals. As she told Ms. magazine, "I represent a different kind of Cherokee feminism. What I consider to be women's work—by that I mean work that promotes the role of women in society—is done within the context of the community. . . . If I bring women and men together, that is just as much a part of my role as to educate sexist men" (Wallace 1988, 69).

Wilma Mankiller wants to be remembered not just because she is a woman and a chief but because of what she has accomplished for her people. She does not want to be seen as a "poster child for female Indian chiefs." Instead, Wilma Mankiller would like to be remembered as a woman who focused on the attributes women bring to leadership as she moved her people beyond the Trail of Tears to the position of a responsive and progressive nation in the twenty-first century.

WORKS BY WILMA MANKILLER

With Michael Wallis. A Chief and Her People. New York: St. Martin's Press, 1993.
With Gwendolyn Mark, Marysa Navarro, Barbara Smith, and Gloria Steinem, eds. The Reader's Companion to the History of American Women. Boston: Houghton Mifflin, 1998.

Speech

Speech at Harvard University. Cambridge, MA: University Archives, 1987.

WRITINGS ON WILMA MANKILLER AND HER WORK

Craig, Paul. "A Cherokee Woman's Rocky Rise to Power." *Sacramento Bee Final*, December 7, 1993, E5.

Devlin, Jeanne. "Wilma Mankiller." *Oklahoma Today* (January/February 1990): 32–37.

Koenenn, Connie. "Heart of a Nation." *Los Angeles Times*, November 1, 1993, E3.

"The Many Faces of Feminism." *Ms.* 5 (July/August 1994): 33–64.

Merina, Anita. "Interview with Wilma Mankiller." *NEA.* (October 1994).

"Milestones." *Time* 143 (April 18, 1994): 16.

Schwarz, Melissa. *Wilma Mankiller: Principal Chief of the Cherokees.* New York: Chelsea House, 1994.

Verhovek, Sam Howe. "One Woman's Trail of Tears." *New York Times*, November 4, 1993, April 6, 1994.

Wallace, Michele. "Wilma Mankiller." *Ms.* (January 1988): 68–69.

DEL MARTIN
(1921-)

Danielle DeMuth

Dorothy (Del) Martin, cofounder of the Daughters of Bilitis, coauthor of *Lesbian/Woman* and author of *Battered Wives*, has been an early and constant activist in the feminist and lesbian movements in the United States. The controversial nature of her early research and writing on domestic violence served as a catalyst for feminist activism for battered women, and she is considered by many to be the founder of the battered women's movement in the United States. In her search for the cause of domestic violence, her analysis of the treatment of battered women by police and social agencies, and her proposals to prevent such violence, Del Martin identified the role of the patriarchal family structure as integral to the issue. Her early and constant activism in the gay and lesbian liberation movement has educated many on necessary social reform, created greater visibility for gays and lesbians, and opened up communication between gays and lesbians nationally.

Martin became involved early in the women's movement as a result of the discrimination she faced as a single, divorced, workingwoman. She found that as a lesbian in the homophile movement she experienced much the same sexism. As a result, Martin was eager to join or help found organizations for lesbians and women. She has helped to cofound several organizations both in California and nationally, and she speaks frequently on human rights issues and political issues for women and lesbians. Martin received a commendation in 1983 from the California State Assembly, an Award of Merit from the city and county of San Francisco in 1985, and the Earl Warren Civil Liberties Award in 1990 from the northern California chapter of the American Civil Liberties Union.

Del Martin was inspired as an activist very early in life. Growing up during the Great Depression, she remembers vividly the fireside chats of Franklin D. Roosevelt. His words, "There is nothing to fear but fear itself," were words she has never forgotten and that echo in the fearless manner in which she has carried on the bold work of activism on extremely controversial issues in her lifetime.

She was inspired not only by the words of Franklin Roosevelt but also by the role model of Eleanor Roosevelt, who was also outspoken and unflinching as a public figure.

Martin was born in San Francisco on May 5, 1921, to parents Richard and Mary Ristow. She grew up with her mother, who worked as an apartment house manager, and her stepfather, who worked as an auditor for the San Francisco Hotel. As a young student she was very active in extracurricular activities. Although her parents did not belong to a church, they required that their children attend some kind of religious service every Sunday, so Martin grew up seeing religion through many different perspectives. The variety of possibilities for religious practice was important to her years later when she cofounded and worked with the Council on Religion and the Homosexual.

Del Martin attended the University of California at Berkeley from 1938 to 1939 and San Francisco State College from 1939 to 1941. She received her doctor of arts in 1987 from the Institute for Advanced Study of Human Sexuality, San Francisco. She began her career in journalism as a reporter for the *Pacific Builder* in San Francisco in 1948 and 1949, then served as editor of the *Daily Construction Reports* in Seattle from 1949 to 1951, and has since been a freelance writer.

Although her parents opposed it, she married Jon Martin in her third year of college. She and Jon had one daughter, Kendra Martin Mon. Del Martin was unhappy in the marriage, and they eventually divorced. She realized, however, that she was in love with the woman next door and came out to herself as a lesbian. Eventually, she met her partner, Phyllis Lyon, who is also a writer, and they have been together since February 14, 1953.

As a couple they quickly recognized that, although they had heterosexual friends, it was difficult to find other lesbians and lesbian couples with whom to talk and socialize. Gay bars were the only obvious place to go and meet other lesbians, but in the years before the Stonewall rebellion the bars were in constant danger of being raided and did not offer the kind of open and positive environment many seek in a social life. Martin and Lyon were not alone in their disappointment with the situation for lesbians.

In 1955, with six other women, they cofounded the Daughters of Bilitis. It began mostly with the mission of being a social club to help fill the gap that the gay bars left. They started small with parties and regular discussion groups. Unfortunately, the group grew slowly. Although they chose the name of the organization for its respectable sound, akin to organizations such as the Daughters of the American Revolution, and the encoded sapphic reference to the *Songs of Bilitis*, many lesbians were too afraid to be associated with an organization of that nature. Ironically, many lesbians who stood out like sore thumbs on the street and frequented gay bars often raided by the police were among those who refused to be associated with an organization that could out them.

Del Martin was the first president of the Daughters of Bilitis, and, although the group started as a social club, she and Phyllis Lyon also knew that there was a need for the organization to grow to work for social reform. That was not an altogether popular notion, particularly for those who required anonymity. At the end of the first year the group grew to fifteen members, and the mission grew to include the promotion of changes in the legal system. Before long, chapters of the organization were launched around the country. Martin was the president of the national organization of the Daughters of Bilitis from 1957 to 1960.

The Ladder, which was the first nationally distributed lesbian magazine, began as a publication of the Daughters of Bilitis. It began publication in San Francisco in October 1956 and was published continuously until 1972. Phyllis Lyon was the first editor, under the pseudonym Ann Ferguson. Del Martin was the editor of the magazine from 1960 to 1962. Eventually, the magazine moved out from the Daughters of Bilitis, and it remains one of the most important primary sources of information about the lesbian liberation movement in America.

Martin's involvement with the feminist movement also includes cofounding the Lesbian Mothers Union in 1971 and working as a member of the national Board of Directors of National Organization for Women (NOW) from 1973 to 1974. The early years in the feminist movement and NOW were very exciting for Martin. The emerging and outspoken leaders of the women's movement, working together to create positive change for women, helped her to continue her work.

In 1976, when Del Martin's book *Battered Wives* came out, it was a revolutionary investigation of the problems experienced by battered wives as well as a discussion of potential solutions. The book was then and still remains revolutionary because it locates the origin of wife battering in the patriarchal structure of the family. The large problem of wife battering in the United States required investigation and solution. Although violence against women in the form of rape had become an issue for discussion, many people, surprisingly, avoided the topic of domestic violence. Martin found this particularly disturbing, as a solution to such a problem could not come about without open discussion. As she says in *Battered Wives*, "Any lasting solution to this complex problem should come from the collective thinking of researchers in government and private social agencies, the institutional religions, and political action groups" (Martin 1976, 8). Such wide-scale cooperation is necessary, in her opinion, because all violence indicates a larger flaw in our culture, the refusal to acknowledge that "violence in the home is not a private affair but a grave social problem" (Martin 1976, 8).

Martin's work encouraged the development of this collective vision because she thoughtfully analyzed the system that created and sustains such violence. She was surprised, but not deterred, by the silence surrounding domestic violence. In her unafraid manner she continued her research and came to realize, despite the silence, that many women were suffering in isolation at the hands of their batterers and that violence and silence were rooted in the patriarchal marriage contract that makes a wife property to the husband and therefore subject to his will. In her book and in her subsequent work on battered women she surveys the history of the marriage contract that has created this situation, which not only permits violence but also prohibits third-party intervention in the violent house-hold.

Martin's initial research on battered wives helped to create a movement with which she is still involved. In 1975 she helped to cofound the Coalition for Justice for Battered Women. She is also a cofounder of the San Francisco refuge for battered women and their children, La Casa de las Madres. Through her involvement with the Coalition for Justice for Battered Women, she helped to write the protocol for the San Francisco criminal justice system upon which the 1984 California bill mandating domestic violence training for police was based. Her 1980 appointment to the California Commission on Crime Control and Violence Prevention lasted three years and led to her interest in prevention of domestic violence. Her belief that the roots of violence are a basic unit of the patriarchal family structure is a radical charge, particularly in light of the family values rhetoric of this decade.

In the midst of ever-present homophobic rhetoric reinforced by the work of the early sexologists and of Freud, Martin and her longtime partner, Phyllis Lyon, found themselves enraged, amused, and discouraged by the books written about female homosexuals. Once again, they set out to fill a gap in the lives of lesbians, and together they wrote *Lesbian/Woman*. It is very candid, timeless, and inclusive in its audience and coverage of a wide range of relevant subject matter. In it they survey existing publications on homosexuality and address coming out, family issues, U.S. history, relevant legislation, and psychology. They tell their story and the stories of countless lesbians in a way that is accessible to a wide audience, including lesbians and the families and friends of lesbians as well. The book addresses the common problems lesbians face as well as the issues common to family and friends who seek to combat their own homophobia and understand some of the joys and the hardships lesbians face.

Although the book has been criticized for not being well documented, it does not pretend to be an objective or scientific book. It is subjective and told from the point of view of two lesbians who want to record the everyday experiences of lesbians in the world, and for that it is an important and necessary book. The book's popularity and acclaim have remained steady. It received the Second Annual Gay Book Award from Task Force on Gay Liberation, Social Respon-sibilities Roundtable, American Library Association in 1972. An excerpt from *Lesbian/Woman* appeared in Ms. magazine July 1972; it has been and is still used as a textbook in women's studies and gay studies classes throughout the country and the world; and *Publishers Weekly* named it as one of the top twenty women's books of the 1970s and 1980s.

For their outstanding achievement with regard to public awareness of homo-sexuality, Del Martin and Phyllis Lyon received the Public Service Award from the Society for the Scientific Study of Sexuality in 1996. Del Martin's lifetime achievement as an advocate for feminist issues and as an educator through her research and her provocative writing on homophobia, misogyny, the patriarchal family, wife battering, and lesbianism has improved the lives of women through-

out the United States and the world. Most inspiring are her unquestioning outspokenness on issues of great personal importance to her and the way in which
she reaches out to others for whom these issues are equally important.

SELECTED WORKS BY DEL MARTIN

"The Conspiracy Revealed." *Challenge: A Theological Arts Journal* (1965).
"I Am a Lesbian"; "By Whose Authority?" "History of the Homophile Movement"; "The
     Council on Religion and the Homosexual Movement"; "Homosexual Identifica-
     tion—Society and Church Responsibility." *Essays on Religion and the Homosexual.*
     San Francisco: Council on Religion and the Homosexual, 1966.
And Phyllis Lyon. "What Is a Lesbian?" *Les Gals* (February/March 1968).
"If That's All There Is." *Lesbians Speak Out.* San Francisco: Free Women's Press, 1972.
     45–46.
And Phyllis Lyon. *Lesbian Love and Liberation.* San Francisco: Multi Media Resource Cen-
     ter, 1973.
————. "The Reality of Lesbianism." *Motive* 32 (1974): 233–241.
"Beating Her, Slamming Her, Making Her Cry." *New York Times*, October 6, 1975, op-
     ed. p. 29.
"Battered Wives." *The Osteopathic Physician* (November 1977a).
"A Feminist Analysis of Wife Beating." Paper presented at American Psychiatric Asso-
     ciation annual meeting, Toronto, May 1977b.
"Society's Vindication of the Wife Batterer." *The Bulletin of the American Academy of
     Psychiatry and the Law* 5, no. 4 (1977c).
"Battered Women: Society's Problem." *The Victimization of Women*, Ed. Jane Roberts
     Chapman and Margaret Gates. Beverly Hills, CA: Sage Yearbooks in Women's
     Policy Studies. 111–142.
"Psychological Implications in Lesbian Mother Custody Cases." Paper presented at the
     American Psychiatric Association annual meeting, San Francisco, May 17, 1979a.
"What Keeps a Woman Captive in a Violent Relationship? The Social Context of Bat-
     tering." *Battered Women.* Ed. Donna M. Moore. Beverly Hills, CA: Sage, 1979b,
     33–57.
Battered Wives. San Francisco: Glide Productions, 1976; Volcano, CA: Volcano Press,
     1981.
"Wife Beating: A Product of Sociosexual Development." *Women's Sexual Experience: Ex-
     plorations of the Dark Continent.* Ed. Martha Kirkpatrick. New York: Plenum Press,
     1982, 239–246.
With Daniel Jay Sonkin and Lenore E. A. Walker. *The Male Batterer: A Treatment Ap-
     proach.* New York: Springer, 1985.
"The Historical Roots of Domestic Violence." *Domestic Violence on Trial.* Ed. Daniel Jay
     Sonkin. New York: Springer, 1987.
"About Censorship." *On Our Backs* (September–October 1990).
And Phyllis Lyon. *Lesbian/Woman.* Rev. ed. Volcano, CA: Volcano Press, 1975, 1995.
"The Many Shades of Gray." *The Advocate*, March 5, 1996.

WRITINGS ON DEL MARTIN AND HER WORK

Brandt, Kate. "Del Martin (1921–) and Phyllis Lyon (1924–)." *Leaders from the 1960s: A Biographical Sourcebook of American Activism*. Ed. David DeLeon. Westport, CT: Greenwood Press, 1994, 260–266.

Martin, Murray S. "Del Martin." *Gay and Lesbian Literature*. Ed. Sharon Malinowski. Detroit: St. James Press, 1994, 249–251.

Penn, Patricia E. "Del Martin." *American Women Writers: A Critical Reference Guide from Colonial Times to the Present* Vol. 3. Ed. Lina Mainiero. New York: Frederick Ungar, 1981, 128–129.

KATE MILLETT
(1934-)

Nancy McCampbell Grace

Considered by many to be one of the most important founding members of the contemporary feminist movement, Kate Millett has had a profound impact on the development of feminism internationally and in the United States. Her career as a teacher and literary scholar, beginning with the publication of *Sexual Politics* in 1970, paved the way for an enormous proliferation of feminist scholarship in the United States and advanced the restructuring of the academy itself. Since then, as political activist, artist, and writer, Millett has continued to play a major role in advocating for victims' rights, the end of political terrorism, and the advancement of all women.

Katherine Murray Millet was born into an Irish-Catholic family in St. Paul, Minnesota, on September 14, 1934. She and her two sisters, Mallory and Sally, attended parochial schools. Their father, James Albert Millett, was an engineer who deserted his wife, Helen Feely Millett, in 1945. To support her family, Helen Millett began to search for employment, but despite the fact that she had a college degree and had been a teacher before her marriage, she had difficulty finding work and finally had to take a job selling insurance. But even this did not ease the family's burden, since unlike her male coworkers, Helen Millett was not paid weekly wages but had to work on a commission basis. Her perseverance paid off, however, and she was able to send her seventeen-year-old daughter Kate to the University of Minnesota, where Kate graduated magna cum laude and was elected into Phi Beta Kappa in 1956. Following Kate's commencement, Dorothy Millett Hill, the wealthy sister of Kate's father (and affectionately called A. D. for "Anno Domina" by the three Millett sisters), offered to fund Millett's graduate education at Oxford—but only if Millett agreed to sever her relationship with a woman whom her aunt considered a bad influence. Millett was in awe of her aunt, who was a leading figure in St. Paul and knew F. Scott Fitzgerald, but this reverence did not stop Millett from lying to A. D. As she wrote years later, "Being twenty-one and good at school I thought I was entitled both to a lover and an education" (Millett 1995, 44). Pretending to have ended the relationship, she worked in a factory over the summer to earn her friend's passage money before she sailed for England. Only after Millett returned from Oxford did her aunt learn of the subterfuge. A. D. never forgave her niece for the lie, and the two remained somewhat estranged until A. D.'s death in 1984. While at Oxford, Millett studied at St. Hilda's College, specializing in the Victorians and earning first-class honors in English literature in 1958. After returning to the United States that year, she taught kindergarten in Harlem, New York, and briefly taught at the Women's College of the University of North Carolina. During this time, she fell in love with sculpting and resigned her teaching post to return to New York "to spend a year in a freezing studio on the Bowery" (Millett 1970, ix), a place that was to become a critical source of artistic and spiritual renewal for her throughout her life.

Pursuing the study of sculpting, Millett traveled to Tokyo in 1961. Here, as she stated several years later, she "liv[ed] on nothing and sculpt[ed] a lot" (Millett 1970, ix). Also in Japan she met the sculptor Fumio Yoshimura, who became her companion for many years. While living in Japan, Millett briefly taught English at Waseda University, and her first art show was held at Mirami Gallery that same year. Two years later, Millett and Yoshimura returned to the states, and she worked in New York City as a file clerk because she didn't have the doctorate necessary to teach English. In 1965, she and Yoshimura married to avoid his deportation.

Millett was active as an artist during this period, exhibiting whimsical "pop furniture" such as chairs, tables, beds, and piano benches with human legs, some wearing shoes. She exhibited a suite of furniture at Judson Gallery in Greenwich Village in March 1967, and photographs of two of her pieces appeared in *Life* magazine in June that same year.

Also during this time Millett become involved in the women's movement and other efforts for social reform. In the winter of 1964–1965, she attended a lecture series on women's issues, and after hearing a lecture titled "Are Women Emancipated?" she was hooked on women's liberation. Her interest in feminism had initially been sparked years earlier when she was at Oxford and read Simone de Beauvoir's *The Second Sex*, which "changed her life" and opened her eyes to many of the issues relevant to being female in Western culture (Millett and Hinden 1995, 353). As a committed feminist, protester against the war in Vietnam, and pacifist, Millett also joined the National Organization of Women (NOW) and the Congress of Racial Equality in 1966.

She balanced these activities with her studies in the doctoral program in English and comparative literature at Columbia University and supported herself by teaching English for $308 a month at Barnard College, a division of Columbia University. However, her career as a Barnard faculty member was cut short when she was fired two days before Christmas in 1968, an action prompted by her involvement in the student strike at Columbia in April of the same year.

The Columbia strike, instigated by Students for a Democratic Society, centered on several student demands, including the end of construction of a gym to be placed in the midst of a Harlem recreation area and the severing of Columbia University ties with the Institute for Defense Analysis. Millett supported the students, asking for amnesty for the strikers so they wouldn't be expelled. She remembers this period of her life as terribly vibrant: "The academy asserted itself, drew away from government and business, existed for a while on its own terms. Intellectual values became as real as I remembered them at Oxford" (Millett 1970, x).

Prior to being fired by Barnard, Millett had constructed a plan for her doctoral thesis, and when she found herself without work, she decided to forge ahead on the project. After drafting the first chapter, she contacted Betty Prashker at Doubleday, who had politely refused to publish a NOW pamphlet that Millett had written some years earlier, and asked her to read the rough draft. Prashker agreed and after reading the manuscript offered Millett an advance of $4,000.

Under the direction of Steven Marcus at Columbia, Millett finished the dissertation. She credits him with providing the guidance necessary to produce a rigorous academic argument. She has also acknowledged that the text could not have been produced without the contributions of the Downtown Radical Women, "a long-vanished. . . . debating society where each detail of the theory of patriarchy was hatched, rehearsed, and refined upon again" (Millett 1970, xi). Feminist scholars Robin Morgan and Shulamith Firestone, longtime friends, also helped Millett to conceptualize the text.

The dissertation was awarded distinction, and in 1970 it hit the bookstores as *Sexual Politics*. Drawing praise as well as condemnation, *Sexual Politics* became a national phenomenon, selling 80,000 copies within six months of publication. Since then, it has become a required text in many women's studies courses. It was reissued in 1990 with a new introduction by Millett, and excerpts from the book have been published in numerous collections of feminist criticism and philosophy.

Often described as the first major piece of literary criticism written from a feminist perspective, *Sexual Politics* explores gender and sexuality in the literature of Henry Miller, Jean Genet, Norman Mailer, and D. H. Lawrence. Millett's feminist critiques are accompanied by an astute history of the sexual revolution from 1830 to 1960, featuring an investigation of the impact of Freudian thought as well as discussions of reactionary political movements in Nazi Germany and the Soviet Union. As Millett later explained to her aunt Dorothy, "I was trying for a combination of English critical writing. . . . and then threw in a bit of direct American plain talk too. Outside the academy but not quite the Bowery" (Millett 1995, 228). Despite Millett's stylistic intentions, *Sexual Politics* reads very much like a hard-hitting scholarly treatise. This is its strength, and the book stands as one of our most perceptive philosophical discussions of the integral connections between sociohistorical belief, sexuality, and literature.

Sexual Politics propelled Millett into the national spotlight. In the wake of the book's success, she was extremely busy on the talk show circuit. She also filmed

Three Lives, a feminist film shot entirely by a female crew, in which three women (including her sister Mallory) talk about what it's like being a woman in America. Also during this period Millett openly acknowledged her lesbianism during a speech that she gave at Columbia University in 1970. However, Millett later claimed in a 1974 *Ms.* magazine article that she had been quite open about her sexual orientation months before the Columbia episode.

In 1973, Millett edited *The Prostitution Papers*, which consisted of oral narratives from prostitutes and a feminist lawyer. It also included an essay of her own positing that prostitution exemplifies the reduction of the female to a commodity.

Riding high on the success of *Sexual Politics*, Millett was soon to face one of the most difficult periods of her life. In 1973, she was institutionalized, diagnosed as a manic-depressive, and put on lithium. For the next seven years, she lived as what she calls a "lithium patient," suffering disturbing side effects including a hand tremor, diarrhea, and the possibility of kidney damage (Millett, *Loony-Bin Trip* 1991a, 11).

The experience did not stop her from writing, however, and in 1974, Millett published what she has since publicly described as "the most fun [she] ever had as a writer" (Millett, *Flying* 1974, ix). *Flying* marked her abandonment of the academic structure of *Sexual Politics* and the beginning of her lifelong enchantment with female autobiography, a form that allowed her to write for the first time with what she called her "own voice." In a 1991 article about Anais Nin, Millet described with self-revelatory clarity the importance of this genre: "To make your life a book. Rather than to write books for a living, books that you peel off in disassociated little segments, sell and publish and be done with, each one rounded off like a bead, as separate as a tree. To make your life into a book, to take that chance—with self and ego and friends and events—to take it straight off the bone" (Millett 1991b, 5).

Flying began as a text about her experience with sexual molestation when she was a young girl. At the time, she did not realize that this diary-like writing would become "the germ of autobiography, the transcendence of shame" (Millett, *I Never Told Anyone*, 1983, 215). But the honest and spiraling voice that emerges in this text set the standard for some of Millet's most important books and established her as a leading proponent of the genre of autobiography.

Her departure from the more conventional, scholarly form of *Sexual Politics* was not altogether well received. Elinor Langer, in a "Forum" article for *Ms.* in 1975, questioned the viability of Millet's "confessional" book, stating "solicitousness overwhelms objectivity. . . . *Flying* should not have to bear the weight of the entire confessional genre. But I think it can remind us of the absence of a genuinely critical tradition in the Women's Movement" (Langer 1975, 71). The next month, Millett responded to Langer, denying the confessional character of *Flying* and declaring,

We have come to a turning point; the establishment has come to accept and perhaps therefore to have become immune to as well, feminist theory, argument, ideology—things we have hammered out already and so go on to the next—expression. In beginning to express . . . we go forward from that starting line where we stood and argued our humanity. Now we live it and create it. (Millett 1975, Ms. 27)

Refusing to cave into negative reviews of the autobiography, Millett began to work on *Sita*, a continuation of her efforts to explore her own life through literary form. Based on a journal she kept during 1975 recording a three-year affair that she had with Sita, a university administrator and mother, the book is a brutally frank expression of Millett's intense love for Sita as well as her equally intense despair when she realizes that Sita has lost interest in her. Much like *Flying*, it is heavily repetitious and perhaps a bit too pitiful in tone for many readers, but it is an honest rendering of subjects rarely broached in public through the female voice. While it generally received highly negative reviews, *Sita* remains an important testimony to Millett's belief in the power of love and the centrality of one's life as the substance of literary expression.

Millett's development as a writer reached a new level with the publication of *The Basement: Meditations on a Human Sacrifice* in 1979. The book is a response to the death of sixteen-year-old Sylvia Likens, who was tortured and murdered in 1965 by a woman with whom her parents had boarded her. The story of Sylvia's death haunted Millett for years, and she even constructed a series of sculptures to express her feelings about the murder. In *The Basement*, Millett moves into the realm of fictobiography, creating the minds of both Sylvia and her killers in order to understand human cruelty.

During this time, Millett was also involved with an organization called the Committee for Artistic and Intellectual Freedom in Iran (CAIFI), which used university and college lectures to reveal the injustices practiced by the shah of Iran against his people. The plight of the Iranians touched Millett deeply, creating an anger similar to what she had felt over Sylvia Likens' death (Millett 1982, 12). In March 1979, Millett and Canadian journalist Sophie Keir were invited by Iranian feminists to visit Iran to celebrate International Women's Day. Millett did so and found herself in the midst of the overthrow of the shah and the installment of the Ayatollah Khomeini. *Going to Iran*, published in 1982, details her experiences with hundreds of Iranian women struggling for freedom, under both the shah and the Ayatollah. It also bravely reveals her own naïveté— her belief that freedom for Iranian women would come with the overthrow of the shah. Unfortunately, it did not, and, as *Going to Iran* clearly and poignantly reports, Millett's own notoriety as a feminist activist resulted in her arrest and expulsion from the country.

After her return from Iran, Millett began an experiment that was to have severe consequences for her but would produce a book that has since been compared to Ken Kesey's *One Flew over the Cuckoo's Nest*. In 1980, while living in Poughkeepsie, New York, on a Christmas tree farm that she had turned into a women's art colony, she decided to stop taking lithium. Feeling much freer than she had in years, Millett at first believed her experiment to be a success, but manic symptoms returned, and her family attempted to have her institutionalized. She then left for Ireland, where she was institutionalized in a Roman Catholic "rest home" after exhibiting strange behavior at the airport. She was force-fed lithium and thorazine but eventually won her freedom and returned to the United States, where she became suicidal and began once more to take lithium. From 1982 through 1985, she wrote *The Loony-Bin Trip*, her return to memoir, to chronicle her battle with mental illness and psychiatric authorities. The book, published in 1990, received generally favorable reviews.

In 1985, Millett and Yoshimura divorced. Since then she has continued to pursue her art, live in the Bowery, and foster the women's art colony on her New York farm, an endeavor that she has called "one of the great things in my life" (Millett and Hinden 1995, 360). Millett's art, like her writing, reflects her deeply held commitment to political and social criticism and reform. For example, four of her sculptures, displayed at Noho in 1995 and improvisational in form, critique U.S. foreign policy, bureaucracy, and psychiatry. An exhibition entitled *Kate Millett, Sculptor: The First 38 Years*, the first major retrospective of her work, opened at the University of Maryland Baltimore County Fine Arts Gallery in the spring of 1997. The exhibit was accompanied by lectures by Millett, Arlene Raven, and Angela Davis. Each of the speakers addressed the issues of art, politics, and feminism, which have surrounded Millett's work.

While focusing on her art, Millett has not abandoned her writing or social activism. In 1994, she published *The Politics of Cruelty*, an investigation and critique of the use of political torture worldwide. She returned to autobiographical writing with her most recent book, *A. D.*, published in 1995. *A. D.* is a moving story of Millett's slow and painful process of acknowledging her great love for her aunt and coming to terms with their separation. The memoir addresses not only her personal battle to achieve resolution but also her great love of, and need for, the community of women represented by her attachment to A. D. As she was finally able to declare:

"We are one then in being women, in being wise and intelligent women, . . . two women, neither aunt nor niece but that as well, and the green eyes do not turn from me nor do they grow cool and treacherous as in life. . . . And I am trust itself for at last all that I had cherished is given me" (Millett 1995, 171).

WORKS BY KATE MILLETT

Books

Sexual Politics. New York: Simon and Schuster, 1970.
The Prostitution Papers: A Candid Dialogue. New York: Avon Books, 1973.
Sita. New York: Farrar, Straus, and Giroux, 1976.
"From Flying." *I Never Told Anyone: Writings by Women Survivors of Child Sexual Abuse*.
        Eds. Ellen Bass and Louise Thornton. New York: Harper Perennial, 1983.
Going to Iran. New York: Coward, McCann, and Geoghegan, 1982.

Flying. New York: Simon and Schuster, 1974; revised 1990.
The Basement: Meditations on a Human Sacrifice. New York: Simon and Schuster, 1979, 1991.
The Loony-Bin Trip. New York: Simon and Schuster, 1991a.
The Politics of Cruelty: An Essay on the Literature of Political Imprisonment. New York: W. W. Norton, 1994.
A. D., a Memoir. New York: W. W. Norton, 1995.

Selected Journal and Book Articles

"The Balance of Power." *Partisan Review* 37 (1970): 199–218.
"The Shame Is Over." *Ms.* 3, no. 7 (1975): 26–29.
"Sexual Politics." *Issues in Feminism: An Introduction to Women's Studies.* Ed. Sheila Ruth. Mountain View, CA: Mayfield, 1990, 496–502.
"Anais—A Mother to Us All: The Birth of the Artist as a Woman." *Anais: An International Journal* 9 (1991b): 3–8.
"Henry Miller." *Critical Essays on Henry Miller.* Ed. Ronald Gottesman. New York: G. K. Hall, 1992, 145–64.
With Betsy Hinden. "Adventures of a Feminist." *Women and Therapy* 17, nos. 3/4 (1995): 347–360.

WRITINGS ON KATE MILLETT AND HER WORK

"Eye-Fooling Furniture." *Life* 62, no. 23 (June 1967) 111, 117.
Langer, Elinor. "Confessing." *Ms.* (December 1974): 69–71, 108.
O'Dell, Kathy, Curator. "Kate Millett, Sculptor: The First 38 Years." Catonsville: University of Maryland, Baltimore County, 1992.
Wei, Lily. "Kate Millett at Noho." *Art in America* 83 (December 1995): 92.
Wrenn, Marie-Claude. "The Furious Young Philosopher Who Got It Down on Paper." *Life* 69, no. 10 (September 1970): 16–17.

CHERRÍE MORAGA
(1952–)

Grace Sikorski

Cherríe Moraga is a Chicana lesbian poet, playwright, essayist, editor, and teacher. She has edited several anthologies of Chicana literature and has written three collections of her own poetry and prose, several plays, and one musical. She is perhaps best known as coeditor of *This Bridge Called My Back: Writings by Radical Women of Color* and cofounder of Kitchen Table: Women of Color Press in New York. In addition to her many writing awards, Moraga was presented the National Endowment for the Arts Theatre Playwright's Fellowship in 1993. Her most recent book, *Waiting in the Wings: Portrait of a Queer Motherhood*, published in 1997, explores the experience of being a lesbian mother. Moraga's work is marked by her critique of homophobia, racism, and classism within the feminist movement and of heterosexism and cultural assimilation within the Chicano community.

Moraga was born on September 25, 1952, in California to a "U.S.-born Mexican mother" and a "San-Francisco-born French and British-Canadian father" (Moraga 1993, 114). Although she was surrounded by siblings, cousins, aunts, uncles, and grandparents, Moraga felt distanced from her Mexican heritage. Early in her life, she felt that she had been "anglocized" (Moraga 1983, 28). She writes that "everything about my upbringing . . . attempted to bleach me of what color I did have . . . the more effectively we could pass in the white world, the better guaranteed our future" (Moraga 1983, 28). Moraga recalls, "At the height of the Chicano Movement in 1968, I was a closeted, light-skinned, mixed blood Mexican-American, disguised in my father's English last name" (Moraga 1993, 145).

While she was completing her B.A. at a small private college in Hollywood, then teaching at a Los Angeles high school from 1974 to 1977, and later earning her M.A. from San Francisco State, Moraga's early attempts at writing were frustrating for several reasons. She was discouraged first by her college teachers from pursuing a career in writing, because she was a Chicana and did not have the vocabulary they expected of a writer, and by other women writers, not only because she was not well read but also because she was a lesbian. There did not seem to be a place within contemporary literature for a writer who attempted to capture the language of Chicanos (what Moraga calls Spanglish) or who described lesbian desire. She recalls, "I didn't have enough words, which was the class thing; and two, I couldn't write a poem to a woman" (Umpierre 1986, 61).

Such classism, sexism, and homophobia within feminism, academe, and literature motivated Moraga to write against the grain of popular expectations, to resist assimilation into the hegemonic culture, and to bridge the gaps between women who have been separated by differences in race, class, and sexual orientation. Moraga's writing, then, is marked by its bilingualism, its defiance of genre boundaries, its treatment of taboo subjects, and its deconstruction of negatively gendered, racial, and sexual images. In many ways, Moraga's writing redefines "woman," "literature," and "feminism" by breaking boundaries, upsetting conventions, and questioning the exclusivity of categories. Moraga explains, "I am a woman with a foot in both worlds; and I refuse the split. I feel the necessity for dialogue" (Moraga with Anzaldúa 1983, 34).

This attempt to create dialogue between identities, cultures, and languages is thematized in Moraga's work. Specifically, when Moraga and Barbara Smith founded Kitchen Table: Women of Color Press in New York in 1983, a press dedicated to publishing the writings of women of color, their first project, *This Bridge Called My Back*, challenged the privileged term "woman" of the feminist movement by offering testimonies, poetry, and fiction written by women of color, emphasizing the multiplicity of experience within feminism. Moraga explains, "What began as a reaction to the racism of white feminists soon became a positive affirmation of the commitment of women of color to our own feminism" (Moraga with Anzaldúa 1983c, xxiii–xxiv), not separate from other women, but in dialogue with them (Moraga with Anzaldúa 1983, 34).

In 1983, Moraga also edited another anthology, *Cuentos: Short Stories by Latinas*, with Alma Gómez and Mariana Romo-Carmona. The motivation for this collection was to "connect U.S. Latinas with Latin American women and cover all the classes too that a lot of bourgeois Latin American women had ignored" (Brady 1993, 152). The stories in *Cuentos* retell stories inherited from mothers, transcribe stories out of oral tradition, and break the silences around taboo subjects. These first two anthologies were the first of their kind, providing a venue for the writings of women of color that granted them more control over the production of their work with little editorial censorship and emendation.

In the same year, Moraga's first collection of mixed genres, original poetry, and essays, *Loving in the War Years: Lo Que Nunca Pasó Por Sus Labios*, was published. As the subtitle indicates, this book attempts to give voice to what has been silent in the past; specifically, Moraga explains, "*Loving in the War Years* is very much . . . about being specifically Chicana and a lesbian" (Umpierre 1986, 56).

Moraga calls *Loving* "a love letter to my mother" (Brady 1993, 156), because it explores the private aspects of family and, more specifically, the relationship between mother and daughter. For example, the last essay in this collection, "A Long Line of Vendidas," revises the Mexican myth of Malinche, in which the tensions between mother and daughter are dramatized. Several scholars have analyzed how Moraga uses the Malinche myth to explore her relationship with her own mother and the tenuous loyalty she feels to a woman whose mother tongue and "brown" body simultaneously represent the land and culture of Moraga's Mexican heritage and her object of lesbian desire (Adams 1994; Sternbach 1989). In paralleling her love for mother with her love for heritage and her love for women, Moraga emphasizes how feminism, Chicano culture, and lesbianism are not incompatible and how various modes of oppression—against women, against Chicanos, against lesbians—are interconnected.

Moraga's next collection of essays and poems, *The Last Generation: Prose and Poetry*, which appeared in 1993, continues this theme. It is a lengthy meditation on the state of Chicano activism and the potential for coalitions built on a utopian vision of Chicano nationalism and queer nationalism.

Moraga's plays also explore the connections between women across differences and forms of oppressions within and without the Chicano communities. Her first play, *Giving Up the Ghost: Teatro in Two Acts* (1986), creates a dialogue between Gorki, a young girl growing up in East Los Angeles and coming to terms with her homosexuality; Marissa, the adult version of Gorki; and Amalia, a heterosexual woman. This play, perhaps more than the others, brings to light how the term "woman" does not adequately name the multiple subject positions women can and do assume.

Moraga's plays also explore issues within families and between Chicano culture and "la tierra." For example, *The Shadow of a Man* (Moraga 1994), Moraga's next play, and *La extranjera*, her first musical (unpublished), dramatize the relationships between women and men within Chicano families. *Heroes and Saints* (Moraga 1994) is about a Chicano community confronted with pesticide-drenched crops, deformed offspring, and the corruption of the land. *Circle in the Dirt* (unpublished, performed in 1994), Moraga's next play, dramatizes the commercialization and corruption of east Palo Alto. Moraga's most recent play, *Watsonville* (unpublished, performed in 1996), dramatizes a cannery workers' strike and their escape from a major earthquake. The earthquake destroys their town but spares their lives as they pray to Our Lady of Guadeloupe, who appears in the trunk of an oak tree.

As a writer, Moraga does not count herself among the many American writers of this century. Instead, she consistently identifies herself as a writer within the first generation of a Chicana literary tradition that preserves "a cultural sensibility" and "indigenous influences" that are "puro latino" (Umpierre 1986, 60) and that draws from a "racial memory" (Umpierre 1986, 59) of Aztlan, ancient Mexican North American territory. Within this Chicana literary tradition she includes Sandra Cisneros, Ana Castillo, Gloria Anzaldúa, Lorna Dee Cervantes, Denise Chávez, and Helena María Viramontes. She explains, "To be a Chicana is not merely to name one's racial/cultural identity, but also to name a politic, a politic that refuses assimilation into the U.S. mainstream" (Moraga 1993, 56). This tradition, Moraga says, is "passionately committed to an art of 'resistance,' resistance to domination by Anglo-America, resistance to assimilation, resistance to economic and sexual exploitation" (Moraga 1993, 60–61).

Moraga also identifies herself as a feminist, but as such, she is "not front-line" (Brady 1993, 153); that is, although she does work around issues of rape and incest, she does not consider herself an activist. Rather, she considers her writing and her teaching to be "a way to raise consciousness, to advocate, to agitate, to cultivate a new generation of people who will be challenging agendas" (Brady 1993, 153).

Cherríe Moraga practices a feminism that makes visible all oppressions, and she posits a feminism that "is almost so integrated into other struggles that it almost threatens to become invisible again, but it can't" (Umpierre 1986, 65). Moraga's contribution to feminism, as a poet, playwright, essayist, editor, and teacher, is her constant attention to the intersections among oppressions and her critique of racism, classism, and heterosexism within feminism communities. Moraga's future work will undoubtedly continue in this vein.

WORKS BY CHERRÍE MORAGA

With A. Gómez and M. Romo-Carmona, eds. *Cuentos: Stories by Latinas*. New York: Kitchen Table: Women of Color Press, 1983a.

Loving in the War Years: Lo Que Nunca Pasó Por Sus Labios. Boston: South End Press, 1983.

With G. Anzaldúa, eds. *This Bridge Called My Back: Writings by Radical Women of Color*. New York: Kitchen Table: Women of Color Press, 1983.

With N. Alarcón and A. Castillo, A., eds. *The Sexuality of Latinas*. Berkeley, CA: Third Woman Press, 1988.

The Last Generation: Prose and Poetry. Boston: South End Press, 1993.

Heroes and Saints and Other Plays: Giving Up the Ghost, Shadow of a Man, Heroes and Saints. Albuquerque, NM: West End Press, 1994.

Waiting in the Wings: Portrait of a Queer Motherhood. Ithaca, NY: Firebrand Books, 1997.

WRITINGS ON CHERRÍE MORAGA AND HER WORK

Adams, K. "Northamerican Silences: History, Identity, and Witness in the Poetry of Gloria Anzaldúa, Cherríe Moraga, and Leslie Marmon Silko." (Eds.). *Listening to Silences: New Essays in Feminist Criticism* Ed. E. Hedges and S. F. Fishkin. New York: Oxford University Press, 1994, 130–45.

Alarcón, N. "Interview with Cherríe Moraga." *Third Woman* 3, nos. 1–2 (1986): 126–134.

———. "Making Familia from Scratch: Split Subjectivities in the Work of Helena Maria Viramontes and Cherríe Moraga." *Chicana Creativity and Criticism: New Frontiers in American Literature* Ed. M. Herrera-Sobek and H. M. Viramontes. Albuquerque: University of New Mexico Press, 1996, 220–232.

Bow, L. "Hole to Whole: Feminine Subversion and Subversion of the Feminine in Cherríe Moraga's *Loving in the War Years.*" *Dispositio: Revista americana do estadios comparados y culturales/American journal of comparative and cultural studies* 16, no. 41 (1991): 1–12.

Brady, M. P. "Coming Home: Interview with Cherríe Moraga." *Mester*, 22, no. 2 (Fall 1993): 149–164.

DeRose, D. "Cherríe Moraga: Mapping Aztlan." *American Theatre* 13 (October 1996): 76–78.

Jay, J. "(Re)claiming the Race of the Mother: Cherríe Moraga's Shadow of a Man, Giving up the Ghost, and Heroes and Saints." *Women of Color: Mother–Daughter Relationships in 20th Century Literature.* Ed. E. Brown-Guillory. Austin: University of Texas Press, 1996, 95–116.

Sternbach, N. S. " 'A Deep Racial Memory of Love': The Chicana Feminism of Cherríe Moraga." *Breaking Boundaries: Latina Writing and Critical Readings.* Ed. A. Homo-Delgado et al. Amherst: University of Massachusetts Press, 1989, 48–61.

Umpierre, L. M. "Interview with Cherríe Moraga." *The Americas Review: A Review of Hispanic Literature and Art of the USA* 14, no. 2 (Summer 1986): 54–67.

Ward, S. "Cherríe Moraga." *Contemporary Lesbian Writers of the United States: A Bio-Bibliographical Critical Sourcebook.* Ed. S. Pollack and D. D. Knight. Westport, CT: Greenwood Press, 1993, 379–83.

Yarbo-Benjarno, Y. "Cherríe Moraga's Giving up the Ghost: The Representation of Female Desire." *Third Woman*, 3, nos. 1–2 (1986): 113–120.

ROBIN MORGAN
(1941–)

Stacey Donohue

Robin Morgan is a poet, novelist, political theorist, feminist activist, and journalist. She is one of the leaders of the contemporary U.S. feminist movement as well as the founder of the Sisterhood Is Global Institute, the first international feminist policy group. In 1970, she edited what is still considered a pivotal text of the women's liberation movement, *Sisterhood Is Powerful.*

Morgan was born in 1941 in Lake Worth, Florida. From ages two to sixteen, Morgan was a child actress in theater, radio, and television, starring as Dagmar in the popular television series *Mama.* Morgan graduated from the Wetter School, in Mount Vernon, New York, at age fifteen and was privately tutored in the United States and in Europe from 1956 to 1959; she then attended classes in literature and classics at Columbia University. In 1992, Morgan received an honorary doctorate in humane letters from the University of Connecticut at Storrs.

In 1962, Robin Morgan married Kenneth Pitchford, a poet and self-identified homosexual. According to Morgan, her mother had wanted a boy, to be named Robin Kenneth, and Robin found it highly amusing that she married a Kenneth. Their marriage was alternately celebrated as a truly feminist union and criticized as being an impossibly traditional relationship for a radical feminist like Morgan. Pitchford read and edited many of Morgan's published works. Her 1984 essay, "Blood Types: An Anatomy of Kin," a dissection of marriage and family relationships, is the first essay she published, in a publishing career that had already spanned over twenty years, without benefit of her husband's editorial contributions (Morgan 1984, 185–210). In 1969, they had a son named Blake Ariel Pitchford (he later changed his last name to Morgan), who was raised as a feminist. In a 1993 essay published in *Ms.*, "Raising Sons," Morgan writes, "He is the only man I truly love." Morgan and Pitchford divorced in 1983.

A prolific writer of over fourteen published works of fiction, poetry, and essays, Robin Morgan often juxtaposes her personal experiences with her political and feminist theorizing. In 1992, she identified her evolution as a feminist as seen in her writings: in the 1960s she explained the "basics of" feminism, with a defensive, reactive, and jargoned tone; in the 1970s she reexplained the basics but with a clear and refreshingly angry tone; in the 1980s she reexamined those basics, with a stronger, more philosophical, and more lyrical personal voice; and in the 1990s she has become less concerned with the basics and writes with a more impassioned tone and less rhetorical approach (Morgan 1994, 16).

Morgan's involvement in feminism began with her dissatisfaction with the New Left's sexism. In 1965–1966 she became a member of the first Women's Liberation Caucus of both Congress on Racial Equality (CORE) and Student Nonviolent Coordinating Committee (SNCC). Morgan became publicly identified as a radical feminist during her involvement in the 1968 protest of the Miss America pageant in Atlantic City—seen by many as the birth of the second feminist wave. In 1969 she founded the first New York Women's Center, and in 1970 she edited the groundbreaking feminist text *Sisterhood Is Powerful*. Morgan also started the Women's International Terrorist Conspiracy from Hell, or WITCH, a more radical, activist offshoot of New York Radical Women and an early indication of Morgan's interest in international women's issues. In 1989 Morgan became editor in chief of the floundering feminist publication *Ms*. Morgan says that she took over *Ms*. "to reconceive and relaunch it as an international, editorially free, hundred-page bimonthly that accepted no advertising whatsoever" (Morgan 1994, 21). The July 1990 issue was sold out within a few days. After she resigned her post as editor of *Ms*. in 1993, Morgan became the magazine's international consulting editor. Today, Robin Morgan lives in New York City and continues writing on international women's issues. She is also at work on a novel and a memoir.

Robin Morgan made a name for herself as a major figure in the contemporary U.S. feminist movement by editing one of the most influential texts on feminism, *Sisterhood Is Powerful*. Morgan writes in her Introduction that the process of editing the book radically changed her position on the women's movement. She had believed the women's liberation movement to be an important "wing" of the Left; she did not believe that she herself was oppressed, and she was hostile toward those women who depended on the movement for emotional support. However, in working with other women in composing the text, impressed by the level of cooperation unseen in the male Left, Morgan changed. In 1970, when women writers for the left-wing journal *Rat* seized the paper and renamed it *Women's Rat*, Morgan wrote "Goodbye to All That" for the first issue, an essay "saying farewell to working with men on the Left" (Morgan 1977, 116).

Despite her disavowal of the male-controlled Left movements, much of the book is clearly centered on issues of the Left: class, ethnicity, race, protest, and revolt. According to Rochelle Gatlin, one of the few historians of the women's movement to recognize Morgan's contribution, the women's liberation movement was a "logical continuation of 1960s political principles and experiences" (Gatlin 1987, 95), embracing the best of the New Left and civil rights movement and trying to rectify their inability to recognize the oppression of women. In *Sisterhood Is Powerful*, Morgan defines herself as a radical feminist or "revolutionary" feminist, distancing herself from such groups as the National Organization for Women (NOW), fearing that they create a "bourgeois feminist movement that never quite dared enough, never questioned enough, never really reached out beyond its own class and race" (Morgan 1984, xxii). The Introduction ends with a call to the woman reader: "I hope this book means something to you, makes some real change in your heart and head . . . because you are women's liberation. This is not a movement one 'joins.' There are no rigid structures or membership cards. . . . It exists in your mind, and in the political and personal insights that you can contribute to change and shape and help its growth" (Morgan 1984, xxvi).

Seven years later in *Going Too Far: The Personal Chronicles of a Feminist* (1977), Morgan looks back at the early feminist movement and recognizes that it had adopted the tendencies of the "boys' movement" of the Left: "abstract rhetoric but ejaculatory tactics," as well as the inability for long-range planning (Morgan 1977, 5). The text is a collection of her essays (which she calls "documentary papers") from 1965 to 1977. It is a midstream retrospection, an examination of what worked, what did not, in preparation for a continuing activism. Each essay begins with an italicized analysis from her 1977 perspective. Looking back at the 1968 Miss America demonstration, Morgan, who proudly cherished that feminist milestone for years, now admits that their tactics perhaps were not the most effective because it appeared that they were attacking the contestants rather than the pageant itself. They mock-auctioned a dummy Miss America and threw dishcloths, steno pads, and other paraphernalia associated with women's oppression, including bras, into a trash can (despite media reports, they did not burn the bras). Later, WITCH protested against a New York Bridal Fair. Such actions, Morgan realizes, alienated women rather than educated them. In addition, she apologizes for a 1970 *New York Times* op-ed piece in which she attacked the Equal Rights Amendment (ERA), "willfully" misrepresenting its goals (Morgan 1970, 90). In 1977 she supported the ERA, though she wished it were stronger.

However, Robin Morgan's reflections are not all self-evaluations. Morgan argues that the early 1960s women's liberation movement was much more diverse than history says it was. She claims that the media contributed to the problem by focusing only on white, middle-class feminists, ignoring the Chicano and black women who were also part of the early movement. But she does not hesitate to admit that the tensions within the movement alienated some women. "I have watched some of the best minds of my feminist generation go mad with impatience and despair" (Morgan 1977, 12). Morgan reveals that most women activists were hostile to housewives, that many were antimotherhood, and that there was a major split between lesbians and heterosexuals. She fears that the movement's divisiveness in the early days hurt its effectiveness, echoing the first feminist wave: the reformists ("feminist but not radical"), the social crusaders ("radical but not feminist"), and the radical feminists "like Elizabeth Cady Stanton—whose challenging thought was finally ignored, ground down in the friction between the other two groups" (Morgan 1977, 156). Morgan sees herself in the latter group (though formerly in the crusader group). Her 1974 essay "On Women as a Colonized People" was seen as "going too far" by other feminists (Morgan 1977, 3).

In 1984, Robin Morgan published *The Anatomy of Freedom*, a text that combines metaphysics, philosophy, and self-reflection on freedom in her life and in the lives of all women and men. The book ends with a dialogue between Morgan and other public and historical figures concerning her fears about the combination of styles in the book, though it ultimately concludes with a call for men and women to choose freedom over absolution. Quantum physics is the metaphor for feminism and freedom in this: "The themes of relativity and interrelationship, and the holographic [multidimensional] character of modern physics itself, best demonstrate . . . what I mean in my metaphrasing of feminism. Besides, quantum physics already is acknowledged to have drastically altered our perceptions of reality [like feminism]" (Morgan, *Anatomy* 1984, xv). The metaphor is expressed more concretely in the 1984 text she edited, *Sisterhood Is Global: The International Women's Movement Anthology*, which celebrates the interconnectedness of "gender, race, global politics, family structures, economics, the environment, childhood, aging" (Morgan, *Sisterhood* 1984, xiv).

Although *Anatomy* was published after her divorce from Pitchford, Morgan admits that he wrote some of the book with her, and a large chunk is devoted to her ruminations on raising a feminist son and creating a feminist marriage. "The Bead of Sensation" chapter is on the ebbs and flows of the unmapped territory of a "liberated" marriage. Despite the ebbs, the essay is a beautiful ode to marriage, an institution that Morgan defends as an active and public commitment.

The most impressive chapter, reminiscent of Susan Brownmiller's work on the restrictions of femininity (*Femininity*, also published in 1984), is "The Two-Way Mirror," in which Morgan describes her own body: what she's learned to love and what she has not yet come to terms with (her nose, a birthmark). Here she alludes to her days as a child actress, forced to color her hair blond, and she expresses reluctant compassion for those women who "cling" to defenses such as long nails, body hair, makeup (though she herself admits that a skirt does feel cooler on a humid New York City day). She concludes: "The woman who wishes to understand her body image in this culture attempts a task as paradoxical as that of a child who longs to see how its face looks when asleep. Neither task can be accomplished except through dreaming" (Morgan, *Anatomy* 1984, 80).

In 1970, Morgan organized the first feminist antipornography demonstrations in New York City, and in a 1974 essay "Pornography and Rape" (reprinted in *Going*), Morgan gives voice to the antipornography sector of the feminist movement: "Pornography is the theory, and rape the practice" (1974, reprinted in Morgan 1977, 169). Susan Brownmiller, author of *Against Our Will*, a landmark study of rape, based her work on this phrase, as did Andrea Dworkin and Catharine MacKinnon. The issue of pornography remains one of the most divisive issues among feminists today. Morgan's concern about rape and violence against women comes up again in a 1979 essay cowritten with Gloria Steinem, "The International Crime of Genital Mutilation," which calls for education programs and legislation in all countries against female circumcision.

In 1989, Robin Morgan published one of the first feminist analyses of terrorism, including a review of cross-cultural attitudes toward violence, *The Demon Lover: On the Sexuality of Terrorism*. The terrorist is like the demon lover: women are often involved with violent terrorist movements because they succumb to the demon lover myth. She argues that the terrorist figure is glamorized by religion, philosophy, the state, and Hollywood. "I do think that national liberation movements—however just, and however many women are involved in them—have been demonstrably male-led for male purposes with male tactics and male definitions of power. Incidentally, they've all betrayed women after 'liberation'" (Morgan 1989, 155). Environmental movements and the civil rights movement were female-founded; they did not resort to violent actions until men controlled them; later, these same men left to be respectable and well-paid national spokesmen for their organizations. *Demon Lover* includes an interview with Patricia Hearst, an essay that begins with Morgan's obvious hostility toward the woman and ends with understanding. Although she is not a biological determinist, calling this philosophical position a "failure of intellectual nerve," Morgan concludes that historically, women have tended to act peaceably, men belligerently, and that this persistence over time has resulted in the disbelief that men are violent while women are conciliatory. The work concludes with a call for women to replace terror with action.

Although much of her writing, particularly since the late 1970s, is quite personal, including love letters to her husband, it is interesting to note that Morgan has written little about her childhood as an actress, her parents, or her life before marriage (although she is currently working on a memoir). However, Morgan's 1987 novel, *Dry Your Smile*, is a self-consciously autobiographical work about a forty-five-year-old woman who, as a child, was on a television series called *Family*; who marries at age eighteen to escape a suffocating mother; who at age twenty-five embraces the feminist movement; and who, after her twenty-five-year marriage to a feminist husband ends, falls in love with a possessive woman in a subconscious attempt to exorcise her mother's hold on her. The protagonist, Julian Travis, quotes Mary McCarthy: "Only in fiction can I tell the truth." Despite being the autobiographical first novel of a feminist activist, the novel is surprisingly satisfying rather than polemical. It is a brutally honest portrayal of relationships with family, friends, and lovers.

In 1991, the Feminist Press published Morgan's first book for children, *The Mer-Child: A Legend for Children and Other Adults*. Unlike *Dry Your Smile*, it is an overtly didactic and politically correct story about a boy who is half-mermaid, half-human and a paralyzed girl whose father is black and whose mother is white; they become friends because both are outsiders in their own worlds. The heavy-handedness of the story (the girl's disability, though, is necessary for the plot—without it, she never would have met the boy) might be too much for adults and some children: nuclear testing eroding the coastline and the Exxon Valdez oil spill are part of the scenery. However, the work does give hope to those who are victims of bigotry and isolation. The girl grows up to be an activist oceanographer, continuing to visit the boy each summer as she has done since childhood. When both are elderly, she joins him in the ocean, two mermaid/ humans together.

Robin Morgan's most recent work is her second collection of essays, *The Word of a Woman: Feminist Dispatches* (1994), which includes essays from 1979 to 1993, plus several editorials she wrote for *Ms*. The essays cover the global feminist issues that Morgan is now focusing her attention on: "Genital Mutilation"; "A Paler Shade of Racism"; "A Massacre in Montreal"; "Women in the Intifada."

Morgan once admitted that when she meets nonactivists of her generation, "I wonder about their lack of moral vitality" (Morgan 1989, 219). This is a rather alienating comment; most women of her generation were still informed, shaped, and restricted by 1950s attitudes. Critics have complained that Morgan's feminism is overly harsh. Camille Paglia, for example, argued in 1994 that Morgan is bitter and the reason "85% of young women in this country don't identify with the word 'feminist'" (quoted in Mark Abernethy, 1984, 509), in response to a comment by Morgan that dismissed Paglia as a "burp on the surface," "invented" "by the boys, the patriarchs").

Paglia's hostility might be just one indication of why Morgan's name is not as well known or well received as that of her colleague Gloria Steinem. Robin Morgan is rarely mentioned in books that profess to be histories of the second wave of the feminist movement, and this absence is peculiar. Yes, she was an outspoken radical activist and a publicly acknowledged bisexual married to a man, and she may have isolated herself from the mainstream movement. But then, she was editor in chief of *Ms*. in the 1980s, and *Ms*. has not been known for its radicalism. In the 1980s and 1990s, Morgan moved to international feminist and woman's rights, perhaps again just a few steps ahead of the mainstream movement, keeping her out of its history except as a footnote. Her antipornography stance could also contribute to her marginalization, as it has with her friend Andrea Dworkin.

Robin Morgan has always remained either ahead of the mainstream feminist movement or slightly outside it. This is unfortunate since she is an excellent and prolific writer, able to combine concise and precise analysis with personal experience to create essays that are extremely powerful and that just might be able to help sustain the feminist movement as it moves into the twenty-first century.

SELECTED WORKS BY ROBIN MORGAN

Ed. *Sisterhood Is Powerful: An Anthology of Writings from the Women's Liberation Movement.* New York: Random House, 1970.

"The Media and Male Chauvinism." *New York Times*, December 22, 1970, 33.
With Joanne Cooke and Charlotte Bunch-Weeks. *The New Woman*. New York: Fawcett, 1970.
Monster: Poems. New York: Random House, 1972.
Lady of the Beasts: Poems. New York: Random House, 1976.
Going Too Far: The Personal Chronicles of a Feminist. New York: Random House, 1977.
With Gloria Steinem. "The International Crime of Genital Mutilation." *Ms.* (March 1979): 65.
Death Benefits. Port Townsend, WA: Copper Canyon Press, 1981.
Depth Perception: New Poems and a Masque. Garden City, NY: Doubleday/Anchor, 1982.
"The Marriage Map." *Ms.*, July/August 1982, 112–115, 198, 202, 204.
The Anatomy of Freedom. New York: Doubleday/Anchor, 1984.
Ed. *Sisterhood Is Global: The International Women's Movement Anthology*. New York: Doubleday/Anchor, 1984; New York: Feminist Press, 1996.
Dry Your Smile: A Novel. Garden City, NY: Doubleday, 1987.
The Demon Lover: On the Sexuality of Terrorism. New York: W. W. Norton, 1989.
Upstairs in the Garden: Selected and New Poems. New York: W. W. Norton, 1990.
The Mer-Child: A Legend for Children and Other Adults. New York: Feminist Press, 1991.
"Raising Sons." *Ms.* (November/December 1993): 36–41.
The Word of a Woman: Feminist Dispatches. 2d ed. New York: W. W. Norton, 1994.

Works in Progress

Ideal American Girl: A Memoir.
The Tenth Power: A Novel.

WRITINGS ON ROBIN MORGAN AND HER WORK

Abernethy, Mark. "Feminist Fatale." *Penthouse* (Australian) (February 1984): 509.
Cook, Blanche Wiesen. "Robin Morgan." *Contemporary Lesbian Writers of the United States: A Bio-Bibliographical Critical Sourcebook*. ed. Sandra Pollack and Denise D. Knight. Westport, CT: Greenwood Press, 1993, 384–389.
Denworth, L. "Sisterhood Is Profitable." *Newsweek* (August 26, 1991): 60.
Gatlin, Rochelle. *American Women since 1945*. Jackson: University Press of Mississippi, 1987.
Kaveney, Roz. Review of *The Demon Lover*. *New Statesman*. (June 23, 1989): 40.
Newton, David. "Robin Morgan." *Gay and Lesbian Rights: A Reference Handbook*. San Francisco: Instructional Horizons, 1994.
Orenstein, Peggy. "Ms. Fights for Its Life." *Mother Jones* (November/December 1990): 32–36+.
Raven, A. "Uneasy Understanding." *Women's Review of Books* (October 1990): 14.
Walt, Vivienne. Review of *Sisterhood Is Global*. *Nation* (March 2, 1985): 248.
Weinberg, Joanna K. Review of *The Demon Lover*. *New York Times Book Review* (April 30, 1989): 17.

PAULI MURRAY
(1910–1985)

Uche Egemonye

Born on November 20, 1910, in Baltimore, Pauli Anna Pauline Murray's physical appearance evinced her multiracial—African American, Caucasian, and Native American—heritage. When she lost both her parents at an early age, Pauli moved in with her mother's sister Aunt Pauline and maternal grandparents, who lived in Durham, North Carolina. Aunt Pauline worked as a Durham schoolteacher until her retirement at age 75. She instilled a great reverence for education in her namesake and godchild, the young Pauli. In 1927, Murray graduated as valedictorian of her high school. Unable to tolerate the humiliating Jim Crow laws, she fled the segregated South for New York. A year after her arrival in New York, Murray started attending the all-women's Hunter College. During her college years, she secretly married a man whom she identified only as "Billy." The marriage lasted for only several months until they had it annulled.

At Hunter, Murray was one of a handful of African American women among 4,000 students. She paid for college by working at several jobs. Having spent the first two decades of her life nurtured and nourished by well-educated, sophisticated, and ambitious women, Murray was largely impervious to the limitations society placed on women. She grew up believing she could pursue any and every vocation that piqued her interest, and during her lifetime, she did.

Following her graduation from Hunter in 1933, during the Great Depression, Pauli Murray began working for the Works Progress Administration (WPA). During her stint at the WPA, she took classes at Brookwood Labor College, where she learned about Marxism and the economic exploitation of workers. She spent the next six years holding a variety of positions and writing poetry, until 1938, when she decided to attend graduate school.

Angered by the continued persistence of segregation in the South, Murray applied to the University of North Carolina at Chapel Hill (UNC). The university's decision to deny Murray admittance because of her race was ironic. Murray's white relatives had donated substantial sums to the university for the education of students. Her attempt to gain admittance to UNC marked the first step in her long fight against social injustice. In 1939, she and a female friend went to jail for refusing to comply with Virginia's segregated public transportation laws. The next year, as an employee of the Worker's Defense League, Murray worked on the defense committee of Odell Waller, a black sharecropper from Virginia who had murdered his white landlord in self-defense. The league took the case after the trial court sentenced Walker to death. Murray worked assiduously, touring the country with Waller's mother to raise funds for an appeal. When the appeal failed, and Waller was resentenced to death, Murray appealed to the governor of Virginia to commute Waller's sentence to life imprisonment. Notwithstanding her efforts, the state executed Waller in 1942. Her inability to save Waller devastated Murray, but it also sparked a nascent interest in the law. During the appeal process, Murray worked closely with two trailblazing civil rights attorneys from Howard University in Washington, D.C.—Leon A. Ransom and Thurgood Marshall. Impressed with her tenacity during the Waller case, Dr. Ransom invited Murray to attend Howard Law School. In 1940, at the age of thirty, Murray enrolled in Howard Law School.

Her experience as the lone female law student in her class prompted her to become a strong advocate for woman's rights. "She entered law school preoccupied with the racial struggle and single-mindedly bent upon becoming a civil rights lawyer but graduated an unabashed feminist as well. Murray earned the respect of her male classmates, who elected her to the highest student position, chief justice on the Court of Peers. While she was at Howard, Murray began her lifelong friendship with Eleanor Roosevelt. Her crowning achievement at Howard was to author a paper on the unconstitutionality of *Plessy v. Ferguson*. She eviscerated the doctrine of "separate but equal," arguing that it wreaked psychological havoc upon minorities. Thurgood Marshall and other civil rights attorneys employed her argument successfully in the *Brown v. Board of Education of Topeka* case, in which the U.S. Supreme Court overturned the doctrine of "separate but equal." During her law school years, Murray was involved in several sit-ins to desegregate D.C. restaurants. In 1944, she graduated at the top of her class at Howard.

Desiring a master's degree in law, Murray applied to Harvard University. Initially, Harvard awarded her one of its most prestigious fellowships to attend graduate school but later revoked the scholarship and rejected her with this curt dismissal: "Your picture and the salutation of your college transcript indicate that you are not of the sex entitled to be admitted to Harvard Law School" (Pauli Murray Papers). Subsequently, Murray attended the Boalt School of Law at the University of California at Berkeley, where she earned her L.L.M. degree in 1945. Her master's thesis, "The Right to Equal Opportunity in Employment," was the first published article on the topic. Four years later, she ran for the New York City Council, finishing second to the Democratic incumbent despite her paltry campaign budget. At this time, Murray was caring for her two aging and infirm aunts, Pauline and Sallie. Two years later in 1951, she published her first book, *States'*

Laws on Race and Color, which Thurgood Marshall pronounced his "bible" for the *Brown* case. In 1956, Murray published her second book, *Proud Shoes: A Story of an American Family*, a history of her family. She then went to work as the only black female attorney in a prestigious New York law firm, where she met Renee Barlow, one of her best friends, whose later death inspired Murray to renew her religious faith. After the Ghana School of Law offered her a professorship in 1960, Murray left to teach in Ghana. In 1961, she coauthored her third book, with Leslie Rubin, *The Constitution and Government of Ghana*, a trenchant analysis of Ghana's Constitution. After bringing a case against Ghana's president Kwame Nkrumah for human rights violations, Murray left the country abruptly.

When she returned to the United States, Murray earned her doctor of juridical science degree from Yale University in 1965. At Yale, Murray increased her involvement in the modern woman's rights movement. She was appointed to the President's Commission on the Status of Women. As a member, she authored a legal brief, "A Proposal to Reexamine the Applicability of the Fourteenth Amendment to State Laws and Practices Which Discriminate on the Basis of Sex Per Se," which called for the Supreme Court to review its position on woman's rights and sex discrimination. Her paper influenced the drafters of Title VII of the 1964 Civil Rights Act to include the clause on sex discrimination. During this time, she also wrote "Jane Crow and the Law—Sex Discrimination and Title VII," which called for the joint use of race and gender laws to give women equal rights. In February 1966, Murray's call was heeded when the Court, in *White v. Crook*, used the Fourteenth Amendment to declare all-white, all-male juries unconstitutional.

During this period, Murray was also elected to the American Civil Liberties Union's National Board of Directors. From this post, she fought for the Equal Rights Amendment. One of the most momentous events in her life occurred when she met Betty Friedan and suggested that women needed an organization devoted to securing their rights modeled on the National Association for the Advancement of Colored People (NAACP). On October 29, 1966, Pauli Murray, along with thirty-one other women, founded the National Organization for Women (NOW) She spent the following year working on a monograph, *Human Rights 1948–1966*, commissioned by the Women's Division of the Methodist Church. In this book she surveyed human rights struggles in the United States. She returned to academe in 1968 as a tenured professor at Brandeis University, where she established two new programs, legal studies and Afro-American studies. Her years at Brandeis were not entirely satisfactory ones, however, as she felt torn between her mostly black male students, who were espousing racial separatism, and her white female students, whose interests lay elsewhere. Murray rejected the black power movement because she felt integration and not segregation was the objective of black people. Further, she detected blatant sexism in many leaders of the black power movement, a defect she could not accept.

When Murray was 63, her trusted friend and confidante Renee Barlow was diagnosed with breast cancer. Barlow died two years later. Murray's need for

religious succor in the face of this calamity, coupled with her distaste for the
Episcopalian Church's refusal to admit women to its ministry, compelled Murray
to obtain her master's of divinity degree. In 1973, she enrolled at the New York
General Theological Seminary, the only black woman and the oldest student.
Three years later, the General Convention of the Episcopal Church approved
women for ordination as ministers. On January 7, 1977, Murray became the first
black woman ordained an Episcopal priest. She spent the next eight years serving
as the minister of Holy Nativity Church in Baltimore. She retired and moved to
Pittsburgh in January 1984. On July 1, 1985, at the age of 84, Murray died of
cancer.

Murray's life and accomplishments were as rich and varied as her multiracial
background. Her pioneering actions, although unacknowledged, paved the way
for men and women to dismantle Jim and Jane Crow laws. She anticipated many
of the concerns that confront minorities and women today. Always ahead of her
time, she proudly proclaimed her multiracialism, bravely confronted sexism, and
maturely called for an alliance between black and white women. Never one to
deny or to belittle any part of her complex character, she rejected efforts to place
her in race or gender camps. As she cogently stated:

I . . . must be involved with and necessarily concerned with racial liberation. But I must
also personally be concerned with sexual liberation because, as I often say, the two meet
in me, the two meet in any individual who is both woman and a member of an oppressed
group. . . . So that a woman of minority status shares the problems of the oppressed group,
of which she is a part, but she also shares the problems of all women. And the depressed
status of women is universal. (Murray 1977, 9)

Pauli Murray refused to allow oppression in any form either to stunt her growth
or to stymie her efforts to make American society better for all.

WORKS BY PAULI MURRAY

With Murray Kempton. "All for Mr. Davis: The Story of Sharecropper Odell Waller."
    New York: Workers Defense League, c. 1942.
States' Laws on Race and Color. Cincinnati, OH: Women's Division of Christian Service,
    Methodist Church, 1951.
Proud Shoes: The Story of an American Family. New York: Harper and Row, 1956; reprinted,
    1978, 1984.
With Leslie Rubin. The Constitution and Government of Ghana. London: Sweet and Max-
    well, 1961.
Dark Testament and Other Poems. Norwalk, CT: Silvermine, 1970.
"The Liberation of Black Women." Voices of the New Feminism. Ed. Mary Lou Thompson.
    Boston: Beacon Press, 1970, 87–102.
"The Fourth Generation of Proud Shoes." Southern Exposure 4, no. 4 (1977): 4–9.
Song in a Weary Throat: An American Pilgrimage. New York: Harper, 1987.

Manuscript Sources

Correspondence between Pauli Murray and the Roosevelts, 1939–1962. Franklin D. Roosevelt Library, Hyde Park, NY.

Pauli Murray Papers, 1941–1973. Schlesinger Library, Radcliffe College, Cambridge.

Marie T. Monahan Collection of Pauli Murray Papers, 1971–1972. Schlesinger Library, Radcliffe College, Cambridge.

Lillian H. Nelson Collection of Pauli Murray Papers, 1977–1981. Schlesinger Library, Radcliffe College, Cambridge.

Photographs of Pauli Murray. Schomburg Center for Research in Black Culture, Prints, and Photo Collection, New York City.

WRITINGS ON PAULI MURRAY AND HER WORK

Beckham, Sue Bridwell. Review of *Song in a Weary Throat: An American Pilgrimage. Journal of Southern History* 55 (May 1989): 353–354.

Blackett, Richard. Review of *Song in a Weary Throat: An American Pilgrimage. Georgia Historical Quarterly* 71 (Winter 1987): 753–754.

Bryant, Flora Renda. "An Examination of the Social Activism of Pauli Murray." Ph.D. diss., University of South Carolina, 1991.

Diamonstein, Barbaralee. *Open Secrets: Ninety-Four Women in Touch with Our Time.* New York: Viking, 1972, 289–294.

Humez, Jean M. "Pauli Murray's Histories of Loyalty and Revolt." *Black American Literature Forum* 24, no. 2 (Summer 1990): 315–335.

Jacobs, Sylvia M. "Pauli Murray." *Black Women in America: An Historical Encyclopedia.* Ed. Darlene Clark Hine, Brooklyn: Carlson, 1993, 825–826.

Leland, Elizabeth. "Pauli Murray Returns to Fulfill a Prophecy." *The Chapel Hill Newspaper,* February 14, 1977.

McKay, Nellie. "Pauli Murray." *Dictionary of Literary Biography.* Vol. 41, *Afro-American Poets since 1955.* Detroit: Gale Research, 1985, 248–251.

McNeil, Genna Rae. Interview with Pauli Murray, Alexandria, VA, February 12, 1976. Southern Historical Collection and Manuscripts, Wilson Library, University of North Carolina, Chapel Hill.

Metzger, Linda, ed. *Black Writers: A Selection of Sketches from Contemporary Authors.* Detroit: Gale Research, 1989, 352–354.

Ryon, Roderick N. Review of *Song in a Weary Throat: An American Pilgrimage. Maryland Historical Magazine* 83 (Summer 1988): 186–186.

Thomas, Gwendolyn. "Pauli Murray." *American Women Writers.* Vol. 125. New York: Frederick Ungar, 1981, 241–243.

Vick, Marsha C. "Pauli Murray." *Notable Black American Women.* Ed. Jessie Carney Smith. Detroit: Gale Research, 1996, 783–788.

ELEANOR HOLMES NORTON
(1937–)

Tracy Wahl

Legislator Eleanor Holmes Norton has a varied and rich history dealing with the major issues facing feminists at the end of the twentieth century. Whether it be welfare reform, sex discrimination and harassment legislation, citizen participation in government, or affirmative action, she has had practical experience in policy making. She also has a great deal of academic and theoretical knowledge about contemporary subjects, tempered by a long and distinguished history of grassroots activism. Norton is truly a unique contemporary legislator.

Eleanor Holmes Norton has a long and illustrious career as a policymaker, teacher, and scholar and is one of the few African American women to hold such a diverse range of influential positions in political advocacy, policy making, and the elected arena. Born in 1937 in the District of Columbia, she received an undergraduate degree from Antioch College and both a master's degree in American history and a law degree from Yale University. Now the Democratic congressional delegate to the U.S. House of Representatives from the District of Columbia, Norton has held that position since 1990.

From 1970 to 1977 Eleanor Holmes Norton chaired the New York City Commission on Human Rights; she was the first woman to lead this antidiscrimination agency. From 1972 to 1974 she served as the executive assistant to the New York City mayor's office and in that capacity oversaw the Office of Neighborhood Government. She then served as the director of the Equal Employment Opportunity Commission (EEOC) under President Jimmy Carter. According to one biographer, Norton revitalized the ailing agency: "When she took the post, she inherited a backlog of 130,000 cases, and the commission had the reputation of being a swamp of bureaucratic mismanagement. After only two years in office, she had transformed the EEOC into a highly productive and efficient agency (Nelson 1993, 886). She also taught law at Georgetown University until the late 1980s.

Norton came to politics after years of active involvement in the civil rights movement of the 1960s, when she was an activist and organizer for the Student Nonviolent Coordinating Committee (SNCC) in Mississippi. She later worked at the American Civil Liberties Union on the team of lawyers who drew up a brief in defense of Julian Bond when the Georgia House of Representatives voted to deny him his seat because of his opposition to war.

Eleanor Holmes Norton has served on the boards of the Martin Luther King, Jr., Center for Social Change, the Rockefeller Foundation, and the Southern Christian Leadership Conference. She has also served on the boards of the Pitney Bowes, Metropolitan Life, and Stanley Works Corporations. Finally, she serves on the advisory boards for the Carter Center in Atlanta, Georgia, and the National Women's Political Caucus and is a member of the Ford Foundation Study on the Future of the Welfare State.

Since serving in the House of Representatives, Eleanor Holmes Norton has distinguished herself as someone with a strong voice, if not a vote (because the District of Columbia is not a state, the D.C. delegate position has nonvoting status). Nevertheless, in 1992, Norton joined women Congress members in protesting Clarence Thomas' appointment to the U.S. Supreme Court, and she subsequently wrote the foreword to an edited volume on that issue (Hill and Jordan 1995). In 1994, she proposed the Fair Pay Act, which, had it passed, would have amended the Fair Labor Standards Act of 1938, effectively implementing a comparable worth standard (Isbell 1996, 369). Norton has also served on the Congressional Women's Caucus and serves as its cochair, with Republican Nancy Johnson, in the 105th Congress.

As an elected official, Eleanor Holmes Norton is well known for her introduction of the Nuclear Disarmament and Economic Conversion Act (HR-1647, 1995), which commits the United States to the elimination of all nuclear weapons if other nations also agree to disarmament; the act would earmark the billions saved to health care, housing, and environmental restoration. The House resolution was introduced after it won approval in a local initiative in the District of Columbia. She is also well known for her role in creating a financial oversight board for the District of Columbia in the midst of its budget crisis.

While Eleanor Holmes Norton does not publicly position herself as a feminist, her policy goals and accomplishments in Congress have been geared toward equality for two sets of persons: women and people of color. She stands in contrast to someone like Patricia Schroeder, the outspoken feminist from Colorado who served in the House of Representatives until 1996. Schroeder distinguished herself and, in fact, made a name for herself as a feminist member of Congress. Norton is known for her diplomatic skills, her negotiating skills, and her persona, not directly for her feminist stance. She is able to negotiate across differences. In so positioning herself, Norton has avoided alienating those for whom feminist politics are not a top priority and has achieved a diverse group of political allies. She has taken an approach that is collaborative and nonpartisan, establishing working relationships with Newt Gingrich and other Republican leaders.

However, family finances put Eleanor Holmes Norton in a negative media spotlight briefly when, after her first election to Congress in 1990, the media exposed her household's failure to pay taxes in the District of Columbia from 1982 to 1989.

In her career as activist, policymaker, and law professor, Eleanor Holmes Norton has worked in the midst of, and focused on, the welfare bureaucracy, poverty, and civil rights. She argues that lawyers are in a unique place to work as activists. In 1983, she wrote that lawyers and "legalism" have always played a major role in the evolution of the welfare system. "It remains to be seen," she argues, "whether the profession can play a role in meeting the crisis in governmental bureaucracy and regulation today" (Norton 1983, 1287). In 1988, in a retrospective on equal employment law, she says, "In most other areas of American social and economic life, lawyers are aides-de-camp attending to the needs of the lead actors—the business executives who make the deals, the senators who need the memos. But in the quest for equal rights, lawyers have been central characters, and the law has scripted an expansive liberty" (Norton 1988, 684).

Both from an academic perspective and from practical experience, Norton has wide-ranging knowledge of sex discrimination law, welfare reform, and bureaucracies and the use of law in advocating and achieving social change. In a March 1988 *Tulane Law Review* article, she gives a complete summary of the history of equal employment law and discusses the pitfalls and hurdles that Title VII of the 1964 Civil Rights Act has faced (Norton 1988). In a 1983 *Yale Law Journal*, Norton summarizes the crises the welfare bureaucracy faces in the latter part of the twentieth century (Norton 1983). Unique among discussants about the issue, she discusses it both from her experiences in New York City with the Office of Neighborhood Government and from her efforts to reform bureaucracy with public participation in mind (Norton 1983). In 1983, Norton was unequivocally in favor of major welfare reform, underscoring the limits of the system as it is set up: "AFDC [Aid to Families with Dependent Children] in anything resembling its present form is an anachronism that cannot adequately serve most of its present clientele. . . . the program was never designed to support large numbers of victims of other problems, such as structural and cyclical unemployment, racial discrimination, and generational poverty and disadvantage" (Norton 1983, 1298).

In 1996, when major welfare reform occurred, Norton served on the Democratic Task Force on Welfare Reform. She stated in an interview that the current system of welfare "has long been obsolete, particularly in inner cities," and that her main goal was to put work at the center of reform: "Work is where people get their identity." However, the version of welfare reform that passed through the Congress did not do what she or the task force had intended. Tragically, she laments, after a long history of helping the poor, "we're now going in the reverse direction" (Isbell, 1996, 369).

If anyone on Capitol Hill has the credentials to assess the welfare reform situation currently under way, it is Eleanor Holmes Norton. She has established an impressive record on the hill. She ranks among the top 25 of the House's 440 legislators in terms of bills sponsored, cosponsored, and enacted. Even without a formal vote, she has accomplished more than most elected officials, and she has done this as a woman and as an African American, two decidedly underrepresented groups in U.S. political life. After winning her 1996 race with more than 90 percent of the vote, Eleanor Holmes Norton is one of the most popular elected officials of the day. She has vision, expertise, and compassion about the issues that confront her constituents and all Americans most directly. Eleanor Holmes Norton is a political leader.

WORKS BY ELEANOR HOLMES NORTON

Selected Articles

"Affirmative Action, Have We Gone Too Far? Face Off!" (debate between Eleanor Holmes Norton and Orrin Hatch). *Common Cause* (December 1981): 18–21.

"Public Assistance, Post-New Deal Bureaucracy, and the Law: Learning from Negative Models." *Yale Law Journal* 92 (June 1983): 1287.

"The Private Bar and Public Confusion: A New Civil Rights Challenge." *Howard Law Review* 27 (Fall 1984): 1225–1230.

"Women's Right. An End, a Beginning." *Human Rights* 13 (Summer 1986): 44.

"Equal Employment Law: Crisis in Interpretation—Survival against the Odds." *Tulane Law Review* 63 (March 1988): 681.

"Affirmative Action: A Place in the Economy." *New Jersey Law Journal* 123 (May 1989): 11.

"Bargaining and the Ethic of Process." *New York Law Review* 64 (June 1989) 493–577.

"The End of the Griggs Economy. Doctrinal Adjustments for the New American Workplace." *Yale Law and Policy Review* 8 (Fall 1990): 199.

"Twenty-Five Years of the Civil Rights Act, History and Promise." *Wake Forest Law Review* 25 (Summer 1990): 150–195.

". . . and the Language Is Race." *Ms.* (January–February 1992): 4.

"Black Legacy and Responsibility" (from a 1992 speech at the Association of American Law Schools, Minority Teachers Luncheon). *New England Law Review* 27 (Spring 1993): 689–692.

"Law, Politics and Voting by Delegates; Bringing Democracy to the House." *Legal Times*, January 4, 1993, 22.

"Yes: A Denial of Human Rights (The District of Columbia: Should It Be Admitted to Statehood?)" *ABA Journal* 79 (August 1993): 46.

"Federalizing Protection." *Legal Times*, August 8, 1994, 24.

Forewords to Works by Others

Heineman, Ben W., Jr., et al. *Work and Welfare: The Case for New Directions in National Policy.* Washington, DC: Center for National Policy, 1987.

Shields, Cydney, and Leslie C. Shields. *Work Sister Work: How Black Women Can Get Ahead in Today's Work Environment.* New York: Friesdie Books, Simon and Schuster, 1993.

Hill, Anita Faye, and Emma Coleman Jordan. eds. *Race, Gender and Power in America: The Legacy of the Hill-Thomas Hearings.* New York: Oxford University Press, 1995.

WRITINGS ON ELEANOR HOLMES NORTON AND HER WORK

Nelson, Mecca. "Eleanor Holmes Norton." In *Black Women in America: An Historical Encyclopedia.* Ed. Darlene C. Hine et al. Vol. 2. Bloomington: Indiana University Press, 1993, 886–887.
Isbell, B. Tobias. "Gender Inequality and Wage Differentials between the Sexes. Is It Inevitable or Is There an Answer?" *Washington University Journal of Urban and Contemporary Life* 50 (1996): 369.
Lanker, Brian. *I Dream a World: Portraits of Black Women Who Changed America.* New York: Stewart, Tabori, and Chang, 1989.
London, Paul. "A Conversation with Eleanor Holmes Norton." *Employee Relations Law Journal* 3 (Winter 1978): 313–335.
Smith, Jessie Carney. *Epic Lives: One Hundred Black Women Who Made a Difference.* Detroit: Visible Ink Press, 1993.

WORLD WIDE WEB SOURCES

http://www.house.gov./norton   Eleanor Holmes Norton's homepage as a member of the House of Representatives. Includes press releases and copies of her monthly column to constituents.
http://www.propl.org/propl   A description of Proposition One, an initiative for economic conversion through nuclear disarmament. Congresswoman Norton sponsored a version of this proposition in the U.S. House of Representatives.

ALICE PAUL
(1885–1977)

Amy Butler

When Alice Stokes Paul introduced the Equal Rights Amendment (ERA) in 1921, she embarked on a controversial legislative campaign to eliminate discrimination against women in state and federal laws. Her organization, the National Woman's Party (NWP), founded originally as a radical segment of the American women's movement, almost single-handedly led the fight to ratify the ERA until 1937. For over fifty years, Paul and her supporters denied the validity of anti-ERA arguments, playing an important role in keeping the issue of equal rights on the national agenda (Rupp and Taylor 1987).

Most studies of Paul's career celebrate her leadership without analyzing the conflict she engendered between 1921 and 1972, the year Congress ratified the ERA. For over fifty years, she earned and maintained a reputation as an uncompromising and disputatious figure whose charismatic leadership, cunningness, and financial connections enabled her to build and maintain a minority, but nonetheless prominent, position in the American women's movement. To do so, Paul built a devoted and homogeneous following. NWP members were overwhelmingly white, middle-class, well-educated women who focused on equal rights legislation to benefit their professional interests.

Paul's leadership generated controversy because she premised her definition of equal rights on a narrow construction of womanhood. That construction ignored the diversity of women's lives and ignored expanding social and legal conceptions of equal rights in the late twentieth century (Cott 1987; Sklar 1984). When referring to women, she used the term "equal rights" to articulate the interests of her constituents, largely business and professional women. As a suffrage movement leader, she combated cultural and political constructions that all women are weak and dependent. Through magnificent publicity campaigns and militant acts of government defiance, she and her supporters distinguished themselves in the public eye as a new group of women who were self-motivated, well-educated, politically informed, and determined to force the government to support woman suffrage.

Paul described passage of the suffrage amendment as an important step in the movement for equal rights because it eliminated recognition of sex differences in politics.[1] To complete the movement for full legal equality for women, she reorganized the NWP to pursue the ERA with the aim "to get as much power in the hands of women as men, and . . . to do whatever will bring this about."[2] The ERA, she contended, would challenge existing common-law notions of women as dependent and weak and thereby eliminate all legal obstacles preventing her constituents from achieving professional mobility. The establishment of full legal equality between men and women as a constitutional provision, she argued, would create "a woman's and man's world with each sex participating equally in control of government, of family and of industry" (O'Leary-Archer 1988, 390).

Her definition of equal rights hinged on the acceptance of laissez-faire individualism, which protected the right of individuals to freely pursue their self-interest without governmental interference. She believed that workingwomen should be legally recognized as individual economic units competing equally regardless of their sex. She opposed laws that interfered with women's ability to compete in the workplace, preferring to leave "the matter to natural selection."[3]

Paul's definition of equal rights challenged the legislative agendas of organizations that worked to protect workingwomen's economic rights through the implementation of gender-specific laws. Her noninterventionist approach to equal rights instead pursued a program to reform industrial relations by making the state a third party to the labor contract (Kirkby 1991). Its agenda emphasized that workingwomen in industry were easily exploited and denied membership by male-dominated labor unions (Sklar 1984).

Paul believed that women's laws separated women as a special class and thus denied them equality of opportunity in all aspects of life. She proclaimed that "there is a sex struggle which has been going on as long as there have been two sexes, and which is quite apart from the economic struggle."[4] To this end, she constructed a category of womanhood that solely focused on sex discrimination, thus excluding other issues shaping women's equality, notably, racial and economic exploitation. Throughout her career, she refused to compromise her position in any way.

Alice Paul's commitment to equal rights and her construction of womanhood were directly linked to her race, class, and educational background. She was raised by one of the wealthiest and most influential families in the isolated, white, mid-to-upper-class, Quaker community of Moorestown, New Jersey, where she lived a comfortable life and never worked out of economic necessity. With her mother's financial support, Paul profited from the finest education available in the early twentieth century, for a man or a woman (Fry 1973). In 1905, she completed her B.A. at Swarthmore, a Quaker school that her grandfather William Parry had cofounded with Lucretia Mott. After receiving a social work degree in 1906, she enrolled at the University of Pennsylvania, where she received an M.A. degree in 1908. Paul then spent two years in England studying at the Quaker's Woodbrooke Institute of Social Work, the University of Birmingham, and London School of Economics before returning to the United States in 1910. She completed her Ph.D. two years later at the University of Pennsylvania.

To prepare for an academic career, Paul studied urban poverty and unemployment from both academic and fieldwork perspectives. The increasingly cumbersome responsibilities of direct interaction with the poor, however, fueled her impatience with social work so much that she did not "want to spend any more time on it."[5] When looking back on this period of her life, she remembered that "social workers were not doing much good in the world." Her "main impression was the hopelessness of it all, that there seemed nothing to do but to sweep all that poverty away" (Irwin 1921, 8; Lunardini 1986, 13). Paul's frustration with social work was so great that she searched for more challenging pursuits that would dramatically reform social and economic conditions.

Paul abandoned academic study in 1908, devoting all of her time to militant acts as a member of the Women's Social and Political Union (WSPU). Founded in 1903, the WSPU organized mass protests to generate public support for woman suffrage. When abiding by the law failed to achieve their goal, the militant suffragettes resorted to actions that defied state authority and challenged gendered conventions governing the lives of white, affluent women (Rosen 1991; Strachey 1928). WSPU tactics included destroying private property and heckling ministers to demonstrate behavior that was anathema to the culturally inscribed proprieties of respectable womanhood. That the militant suffragettes not only directly challenged government authority but also produced a new and sensational form of women's political activism starkly contrasted to Paul's social work responsibilities and launched the beginning of her devotion to woman's rights (Rosen 1991; Strachey 1928).

Using her WSPU experience and dedication to woman suffrage as a base, Paul began to articulate her conception of a new race of women that had evolved from a position of dependence to one of strength. As a Ph.D. student under the tutelage of Simon Patten, an outspoken defender of industrial expansion as the means to eliminate poverty, she expressed an optimistic belief that economic expansion improved women's social and economic status in society (Leach 1993; Patten 1968). For example, she described the WSPU as exemplars of a new womanhood, galvanized by their collective strength and rejection of male domination. She explained that women's lives in England had been revolutionized by the economic development within the country, but the revolution that she envisioned primarily applied to women of the moneyed classes (Paul 1910). The lives of the impoverished women that she once worked with had not been revolutionized. By linking economic status with political rights, Paul's limited construction of womanhood overlooked the social and economic reality of the vast majority of women in England at the time.

To further develop her views of womanhood, Paul became an expert on women's legal status, especially focusing on common-law traditions that restricted women's property rights, freedom of contract, and exclusion from full participation in the workplace. She argued that women's status had evolved from complete subordination resulting from strict domestic responsibilities, to increasing freedom created by industrial expansion and urbanization. Paul explained that the change in women's status "has been one uninterrupted movement in the line of giving woman greater and greater freedom from restrictions placed upon her by the common law."[6]

Between 1921 and 1947, Paul worked to continue the progressive improvement in women's legal status. She obsessed over the ERA and attempted to maintain autocratic control over the NWP. Though she held the title of honorary president, except for the years 1941–1943, she was never too far from the reins of power, directing all NWP policy and overseeing all publicity. Her leadership precipitated an embarrassing lawsuit initiated by an insurgent group seeking to remove her from power. Though Paul successfully quelled internal power struggles, she could not defeat the movement to expand the meaning of equal rights. As conceptions of civil rights began to change, her definition of women's equality was co-opted by the resurgence of the woman's rights movement (O'Leary-Archer 1988).

Throughout the 1950s–1960s, Paul and her supporters defended the ERA by maintaining their long-held interest of ensuring that the rights of white, Protestant, professional women were not superseded by the rights of different racial, ethnic, or religious groups.[7] She heavily relied on the NWP's Research Committee to substantiate her construction of womanhood. Under the chairmanship of Helena Hill Weed, sister of former NWP president Elsie M. Hill and staunch supporter of Alice Paul's leadership, the committee analyzed important government policies, notably, the President's Commission on the Status of Women and Title VII of the 1964 Civil Rights Act, that revealed the NWP's concern that racial minority interests would supplant elite, white women's rights. Overall, Paul used the committee to argue that race, color, national origin, and religion were all issues separate from sex equality.

Many considered the appointment of the president's commission an important step in government recognition of women's equality. Paul, however, was suspicious of commission members, arguing, "A favorite method of defeating a measure before Congress, or delaying it . . . is to create a Commission to study the subject."[8] Her suspicions were confirmed by the fact that all members appointed opposed the ERA. Despite her protestations, the commission's report claimed the Constitution embodied equal rights for men and women, therefore rendering a federal amendment unnecessary. Members expressed faith in the ability of the courts to remove remaining ambiguities regarding woman's rights and particularly emphasized the Fifth and Fourteenth Amendments as a key method to constitutionalize equal rights between men and women.

Paul refuted the commission's assertions, arguing that "there is no guarantee in the Constitution of any right to women other than the right to vote. Under federal and state laws there are many and varied discriminations against women." She contended that only a constitutional amendment can give women protection against discrimination under the laws of the United States. "We are against the proposal of the Commission . . . which would force women to wait for some far off day when the Supreme Court may possibly reinterpret the Constitution to give equal rights to women," Paul declared. She urged President John F. Kennedy to stop "any further studies made of discrimination against women . . . but to act, with the backing of his large majority in Congress, to secure the adoption of the pending Equal Rights Amendment."[9]

Paul believed that the Fourteenth Amendment failed in its purpose to protect the citizenship of African Americans and that it was an uncertain and time-consuming approach to women's equality. In addition, she and her supporters feared that linking sex and race equality would weaken the ERA campaign. For example, an NWP member who disliked Pauli Murray, a member of the president's commission, criticized her "preoccupation with the Negro problem" and claimed that "her primary purpose seems largely to be an attempt to hitch that wagon to our Equal Rights Amendment star."[10] She expressed her fear that southern states would no longer support the ERA if Murray's goals were successful and that it was best to keep the two issues separate. Though Paul avoided questions pertaining to her views on race equality, this letter and others like it are probably indicative of her viewpoint. On one level, she associated with African American women who supported the ERA but "has those prejudices" when dealing with African-Americans as a race.[11] She always presented her beliefs in a context of the movement for sex equality and remained silent about other campaigns for equal rights.

By pursuing sex equality, Paul and her supporters emphasized the importance of women's right to compete on the basis of merit with men in the workplace. The NWP considered the Civil Rights Act of 1964 as a great victory not because it ended employment discrimination on the basis of race, ethnicity, and religious beliefs, but because the law included sex in its provisions. Stating the NWP's position, the Research Committee argued that discrimination against women regardless of race, religion, or nationality was so rampant "that if an American woman of the white race and the Christian religion were denied the right to appeal to the Federal Employment Commission for protection, she would be unable to compete with women in special racial and religious groupings." Members also wrote that "the right to earn a living should not be confined to the masculine element of the population or to the women in government-favored religious and racial groups." The committee argued that white women were more exploited than all other workers and thereby ignored how race and gender were intertwined in a hierarchical system of labor.[12]

Paul's interpretation of women's equality was increasingly challenged in the late 1960s. Following the founding of the National Organization for Women (NOW) in 1967, she began to lose control of the ERA campaign. NOW built a coalition of women that was more diverse than the NWP, gaining support of former ERA opponents who changed their views following the implementation of Title VII. Nonetheless, Paul became a hero to many members of the second women's movement who remembered her militancy during the suffrage movement but ignored the controversy of the ERA.

Paul's leadership helped to keep women's equality on the national agenda throughout the twentieth century. Many studies, however, have not analyzed the critical aspects of her leadership. Though such scholarship has enhanced our understanding of the NWP, it has limited discussion of an elusive and perplexing woman, not to mention the problems of pursuing equal rights as a legislative goal. Criticizing Paul's career helps to trace the link between equal rights and constructions of womanhood from the early to late twentieth century. This approach will hopefully open dialogue on a central issue in women's history, social policy and politics that affect all women, but not in the same way.

NOTES

1. Alice Paul to Richard Mayer, March 19, 1922, folder 7, box 7, National Woman's Party Papers, Library of Congress (NWP–LC); Alice Paul to Izetta Jewell Brown, March 30, 1921, reel 7, National Woman's Party Papers (NWPP).

2. Alice Paul to Rebecca Hourwich, June 10, 1922, reel 15, NWPP.

3. Alice Paul, "Feminism One Hundred Years from Now," December 1922, reel 20, Alice Paul to Miss Katharine Fisher, April 10, 1922, reel 14, NWPP.

4. Alice Paul to Richard Mayer, March 19, 1922, folder 7, box 7, NWP–LC.

5. Alice to Mamma [summer 1909], folder 31, box 2, March 19, 1909; folder 159, box 11, October 22, 1909; folder 28, box 2, November 10, 1909, Alice Paul Papers.

6. Alice Paul, "The Legal Position of Women in Pennsylvania" (Ph.D. diss., University of Pennsylvania, 1912), 86–89, 93–94, 254, 262–263; Paul, "The Legal Position of Women in the United States" (D.C.L. thesis, American University, 1928), see Chapter 13 in draft form, folder 1030, box 77, Alice Paul Papers.

7. Alice Paul to Isabelle M. Allias, October 23, 1963, reel 108, NWPP.

8. Alice Paul to Mrs. Rita Redlich, September 1963, reel 109, NWPP.

9. Alice Paul, "The National Woman's Party Protects Conclusion of President's Commission on Status of Women on Equal Rights for Women Amendment," folder 1143, box 87, Alice Paul Papers; Emma Guffey Miller to Franklin D. Roosevelt, Jr., August 16, 1965, reel 109, NWPP. For a copy of the commission's recommendations, see October 11, 1963, reel 108, NWPP.

10. Miriam Y. Holden to Anita, February 16, 1963, reel 108, NWPP.

11. Amelia Fry, "Mabel Vernon: Organizer for Women's Rights, Petitioner for Peace" (Bancroft Library, Oral History Projects, 1978), 157–158; NWP Research Committee, "Present Day Discriminations against Women in the Field of Employment; The Necessity for the Same Protection for the Woman Worker as for the Worker Discriminated against on the Ground of Race, Color, Religion, or Country of Origin," folder 1024, box 76, Alice Paul Papers.

12. NWP Research Committee, "Civil Rights for Women," August 1964; "Present Day

Discrimination against Women in the Field of Employment," folder 1024, box 76, Alice Paul Papers.

WORKS BY ALICE PAUL

"The Woman Suffrage Movement in Great Britain." *Annals of the American Academy of Political and Social Science*, Supplement 27 (May 1910): 2627.
"The Legal Position of Women in Pennsylvania." Ph.D. diss., University of Pennsylvania, 1912.
"Towards Equality: A Study of the Legal Position of Women in the United States." D.C.L. thesis, American University, 1928.

WRITINGS ON ALICE PAUL AND HER WORK

Becker, Susan. "An Intellectual History of the National Woman's Party." Ph.D. diss., Case Western Reserve University, 1975.
———. *The Origins of the Equal Rights Amendment: American Feminism between the Wars.* Westport, CT: Greenwood Press, 1981.
Cott, Nancy. *The Grounding of Modern Feminism.* New Haven, CT: Yale University Press, 1987.
Ford, Linda. *Iron-Jawed Angels: The Suffrage Militancy of the National Women's Party, 1912–1920.* Lanham, MD: University Press of America, 1991.
Irwin, Inez Haynes. *Alice Paul and the Story of the National Woman's Party.* Fairfax, VA: Denlinger's, 1921.
Kirkby, Diane. *Alice Henry: The Power of Pen and Voice.* New York: Cambridge University Press, 1991.
Leach, William. *Land of Desire: Merchants, Power and the Rise of a New American Culture.* New York: Vintage Books, 1993.
Lunardini, Christine. *From Equal Suffrage to Equal Rights: Alice Paul and the National Woman's Party, 1910–1928.* New York: New York University Press, 1986.
O'Leary-Archer, Lynne. "The Contentious Community: The Impact of Internecine Conflict on the National Woman's Party, 1920–1947." Ph.D. diss., University of Southern California, May 1988.
Patten, Simon. *The New Basis of Civilization.* Cambridge: Belknap Press of Harvard University Press, reprint, 1968.
Rosen, Andrew. *Rise Up Women!: The Militant Campaign of the Women's Social and Political Union, 1903–1914.* Boston: Routledge and Kegan, 1991.
Rupp, Leila, and Verta Taylor. *Survival in the Doldrums: The American Women's Rights Movement.* New York: Oxford University Press, 1987.
Sklar, Kathryn Kish. "Why Were Most Politically Active Women Opposed to the ERA in the 1920s?" *Rights of Passage: The Past and Future of ERA.* Ed. Joan Hoff-Wilson. Bloomington: Indiana University Press, 1984.
———. *Florence Kelley and the Nation's Work: Women's Political Culture, 1830–1900.* New York: Cambridge University Press, 1991.
Strachey, Ray. *The Cause: A Short History of the Women's Movement in Great Britain.* Port Washington, NY: Kennikat Press, 1928; reprinted 1969.

Oral History

Fry, Amelia R. "Conversations with Alice Paul: Woman Suffrage and the Equal Rights Amendment." Suffragists Oral History Project, University of California, Berkeley, 1973.
———. "Mabel Vernon: Organizer for Women's Rights, Petitioner for Peace." Suffragists Oral History Project, University of California, Berkeley, 1978.

Archival Collections

Records of the National American Woman Suffrage Association, Cornell University.
Papers of the National Woman's Party, 1913–1974, Library of Congress.
National Woman's Party Papers, 1913–1974, Microfilm.
Alice Paul Papers, Schlesinger Library, Radcliffe College.

ANNA QUINDLEN
(1952–)

Carolyn Kitch

Pulitzer Prize-winning journalist and novelist Anna Quindlen was born in Philadelphia on July 8, 1952, the oldest of five children in a Roman Catholic, Italian-Irish family. Her father, Robert Quindlen, was a management consultant, and her mother, Prudence Pantano Quindlen, was a homemaker. Despite the fact that she eventually had three young brothers, Anna was pushed to succeed "by a man who swore his firstborn would be a boy and never changed his mind" (quoted in Williams 1994, 64).

During her childhood, the family lived in Drexel Hill, Pennsylvania, and Wheeling, West Virginia, where Quindlen attended Catholic schools. When she was a teenager, they moved to Kendall Park, New Jersey, where she went to a public high school. After a year at Barnard College in New York, she returned to Kendall Park to nurse her mother through the final stages of ovarian cancer.

Prudence Quindlen's illness and death in 1972, when Anna was nineteen years old, would inspire her daughter's second novel twenty-two years later. At the time, it gave Anna a chance to think about her mother's conventional past and her own future. "I figured either life was going to be considerably different for me than it was for my mother, or I was going to be angry all the time," she later remembered (Quindlen, 1988, 193).

Quindlen chose journalism as her way to that different life. "In journalism, you could do all the things good girls were not supposed to do," she once explained. "You were obligated to ask rude questions. They made you go to strangers' homes; they made you ask how much money people earned. . . . it was like a dream come true." Quindlen had begun her career the summer she was eighteen, working as a copy girl and reporter at the daily New Brunswick, New Jersey, *Home News*. While she completed her English degree at Barnard, she sold a short story to *Seventeen* magazine and had another summer reporting job at the *New York Post*.

When she graduated from college in 1974, she was hired by the *Post* and

worked there as a reporter for two years. Then, in February 1977, she moved to
the paper at which she would rise to stardom, the venerated *New York Times*.
Quindlen was the direct beneficiary of a class-action, sex-discrimination lawsuit
filed that year against the *Times* by six of its female employees. She was initially
surprised at getting hired:

I was in no way a *Times*man, being twenty-four, relatively inexperienced, and, of course,
a woman. And then at some point I got it; I realized that that was exactly why I had
gotten hired in the first place—because I was a woman. That fact . . . shaped my life at
the *Times*. . . . [it] affected the responsibilities I [felt] toward my colleagues, toward the
paper and its readers. (Quindlen, 1993, xxiii)

Quindlen had several jobs in her early years at the *Times*. She covered City
Hall from 1977 to 1981, and she wrote the "About New York" column, a regular
feature on urban life, from 1981 to 1983. For the latter work, she won the Meyer
Berger Award from Columbia University for the best writing about New York
City in 1983. The same year, she was promoted to deputy metropolitan editor.

As she was building a career, Anna Quindlen was also building a family with
Gerald Krovatin, an attorney she married in 1978. Their first child, Quin, was
born in 1983. After a second son, Christopher, arrived in 1985, Quindlen left
her staff job but continued to freelance. A year later, after several of her essays
had appeared in the *Times*' "Hers" column, she received an offer from a rival
newspaper to be a columnist. Executive editor Abe Rosenthal responded by offering Quindlen her own column in the *Times*.

Thus began "Life in the 30's," a series of personal essays she wrote each week
from 1986 to 1988. She described this work as being "a reporter of my own life"
(*New York Times*, December 1, 1988, C1). Though she also wrote on public
issues such as obscenity and capital punishment, much of the material for the
column came straight out of her own family life. By the time her daughter, Maria,
was born in 1988, Quindlen had done enough self-revelation. In her final column, she explained, "Sometimes it is time to examine your life. And sometimes
it is time to just live it" (*New York Times*, December 1, 1988, C1).

Her voice did not remain out of the *Times* for long. In 1990, she was offered
something only two other women had ever had: a regular spot on the paper's op-
ed page. (The others were Anne O'Hare McCormick and Flora Lewis.) For the
next four years, she wrote "Public and Private," a semiweekly column that was
syndicated in more than fifty newspapers and that won the 1992 Pulitzer Prize
for commentary.

As its title implied, "Public and Private" was a way for Quindlen to merge the
personal and the political, to build on the feminist tradition of insisting that the
personal *is* political. Her subjects ranged from abortion, to job loss in middle-
management America, from gay rights, to domestic abuse. She wrote from a
mother's perspective about the Persian Gulf War, surrogate motherhood, and

AIDS. She stressed the personal consequences of political issues for women—
for women in the news, as well as for women reading the news.

During these years, Quindlen was also publishing fiction. Her first two novels
were both inspired by her own life: *Object Lessons* (1991) was a coming-of-age
story about a Catholic teenage girl, and *One True Thing* (1994) told the story of
a young woman who returns to live in her childhood home when her mother is
dying of cancer.

By 1994, Quindlen was considered a role model by other women on the *Times*
staff and was widely assumed to be in line for a top management job at the paper.
Therefore, it came as something of a shock to many in the media community—
and to many feminists—when she announced in September of that year that she
was leaving journalism to spend more time working on her fiction and being with
her three children in their Hoboken, New Jersey, home. She called this choice
"perhaps the most difficult decision I've ever made" (*New York Times*, September
10, 1994, A15).

From a feminist perspective, Quindlen's career is remarkable for at least two
reasons: the nature and content of her journalism and her decision to remove
herself from contention for a top spot at the *Times*. The latter received considerable press attention and was seen as a symbolic move for women in the 1990s.
Upon leaving the *Times*, Quindlen explained, "If I had two distinct lives to lead,
one of them would be led trying to help lead the *New York Times* into the twenty-
first century. But it would be very difficult to spend as much time as I'd like to
spend with my kids and be in a management position at the *Times* and do it
well" (*Washington Post*, September 10, 1994, C1).

What did this mean for the career potential of other working mothers? com-
mentators asked in publications ranging from the *Wall Street Journal* to *People*
magazine. "*Times* history is filled with golden boys, but the Pulitzer Prize-winning
Quindlen was its first true golden girl," wrote media critic Jon Katz in *New York*
magazine. "If she couldn't pull off the career-family balancing act, then who
could? And if the *Times* couldn't make *her* happy, what chance was there for her
women colleagues?" (Katz 1994, 22).

These are questions worth asking—especially in light of the high visibility of
Quindlen's decision—yet they overshadow the meaning of her career so far.
What she did during her seventeen years in the field has helped to transform the
field itself. Quindlen is significant not only for being (or having been) a candidate
for top editorial management at the *Times* but also for her success at convincing
that management to redefine "serious journalism" to include the details of everyday life, of women's lives. She connected the personal with the political in America's most elite and masculine newspaper, its "newspaper of record."

Quindlen—who once claimed that "real life is in the dishes" (Steinberg 1991,
41)—used domesticity as a lens through which to see the rest of the world and
its larger issues. She wrote in 1993, "When I hear about a little boy who has
been beaten to death by his mother, I respond on many levels, but one of the
most important, and the truest, is as the mother of little boys myself, little boys

whose injuries routinely break my heart" (Quindlen 1993, 79). This rhetorical strategy was hardly new in newspaper journalism (female reporters had been using it for a century), but it was unusual in the *New York Times*, and it was unprecedented in the masculine domain of the op-ed page.

Quindlen assessed the bottom-line, personal consequences of political moves. Writing about Anita Hill, the law professor who accused Supreme Court nominee Clarence Thomas of sexual harassment, she praised Hill's courage and saw her as a role model for women, yet she also saw the discouraging implications for other women. The ultimate message of the story of Thomas' confirmation hearings, Quindlen wrote, was intimidation. "The lesson we learned, watching the perfect victim, is that all of us imperfect types, with lies in our past or spotty job histories, without education or the gift of oratory, should just grin and bear it, and try to stay out of the supply closet" (*New York Times*, October 16, 1991, reprinted in Quindlen, 1988, 144–145).

Quindlen's attention to the details of women's lives—the criteria by which women are judged more harshly than men in public life—provided a framework within which she could discuss issues of class and race as well. In one of her best-known columns, she contrasted how her own paper had handled two high-profile rape cases, that of the "Central Park jogger," who remained anonymous in the press, and that of the woman the *Times* named when she accused a member of the politically prominent Kennedy family:

In the face of what we did in the Central Park case, the obvious conclusion was that women who graduate from Wellesley, have prestigious jobs, and are raped by a gang of black teenagers will be treated fairly by the press. And women who have "below average" high school grades, are well known at bars and dance clubs, and say that they have been raped by an acquaintance from an influential family after a night of drinking will not. (*New York Times*, April 21, 1991; reprinted in Quindlen 1993, 74)

Quindlen tried to find the common feminist themes in seemingly disparate news events. In one column, she wrote: "History repeats herself. Many of the members of the Senate treated Professor Hill's accusations the way the officials at Dow Corning treated the pain of women whose implants had gone haywire. Hysterics. Complainers. Crybabies. Women who get beaten up by their husbands can tell you about this phenomenon" (*New York Times*, February 23, 1992; reprinted in Quindlen 1993, 274–275).

Primarily through domestic detail, Quindlen has mapped out broader themes in her fiction. "I can't think of anything to write about except families," she has admitted. "They are a metaphor for every other part of society" (Steinberg 1991, 40). Novelist Anne Tyler wrote that Quindlen's *Object Lessons* was "laced with acute perceptions about the nature of day-to-day family life" (Tyler 1991, 7); in the *Times* itself Maureen Howard praised Quindlen's "sharp eye for details of class and manners," as well as her "ardent reading of domestic lives" (Howard 1991, C19).

That ardent reading is evident in Quindlen's journalism as well. Especially in her "Life in the 30's" columns, she wrote about the public meanings of motherhood and family ties, and she used personal anecdotes to frame her commentary on public issues. Some of this writing was overtly emotional.

The domestic nature of Quindlen's style alienated some feminists. Karen Lehrman called Quindlen a "remorseless sentimentalist who ends up trivializing matters of considerable importance" by reducing all issues to lessons based in everyday experience (Lehrman 1991, 38). Marjorie Williams called Quindlen's editorial voice "timidly girlish" and accused her of retreating to "the moral high ground" when discussing political issues (Williams 1994, 60, 64). Others have called Quindlen's style "mommy journalism."

Quindlen defends her style and choice of subject matter, maintaining that they are not a retreat from feminism but rather the logical extension of the women's movement within journalism:

In our determination during the seventies to be treated equally, we wanted to be sent to cover the White House, the Supreme Court, the wars. But as time went by we began to feel freer to discuss differences within the context of being treated fairly and equitably. We began to admit that some of what we had once covered about home and hearth still moved us as reporters, that we believed writing about those matters was as important for readers as the world events we had been offering them on page one. (Quindlen 1993, xxiv)

Moreover, she considers emotion a feminist issue. "In public discourse," she has said, "it's implied that emotions are suspect—yet people make personal and even policy decisions on the basis of them all the time. I think the devaluing of emotional content is basically a devaluing of women" (Hubbard 1994, 108).

In response to the charge that she does "mommy journalism," Quindlen has replied, "The truth is that 90 percent of the work I do is motivated by being a mother" ("A Woman," 1994, 28). Becoming the mother of a daughter was what reaffirmed her commitment to feminism. In a 1990 column, she wrote:

When I look at my sons, it is within reason to imagine all the world's doors open to them. Little by little some will close, as their individual capabilities and limitations emerge. But no one is likely to look at them and mutter: "I'm not sure a man is right for a job at this level. Doesn't he have a lot of family responsibilities?" Every time a woman looks at her daughter and thinks, She can be anything, she knows in her heart, from experience, that it's a lie. . . . My daughter is ready to leap into the world, as though life were chicken soup and she a delighted noodle. . . . Today is her second birthday and she has made me see fresh this two-tiered world, a world that, despite all our nonsense about post-feminism, continues to offer less respect and less opportunity for women than it does for men. (*New York Times*, November 22, 1990; reprinted in Quindlen 1993, 286–287)

A few years earlier, in one of her "Life in the 30's" columns, Quindlen had suggested that liberal feminism had failed. What women needed, she wrote, was not a string of individual achievements but rather "a root change in the way things work: in the way everyone approached work, in the way everyone approached the care of children, in the way everyone, male or female, approached the balance of life and work and obligations and inclinations" (Quindlen 1988, 195).

In her both writing and her career path, Anna Quindlen has tried out new approaches and tried to readjust the balance of women's obligations. To some extent, her successes have changed what it means to be a woman and a journalist in the late twentieth century. More significantly, they have also—in a limited, but very visible, forum—transformed how women are represented in the media, how they become news, and how American readers understand the meaning of women's lives.

WORKS BY ANNA QUINDLEN

Journalism

"Life in the 30's." Weekly column, *New York Times* (1986–1988).
Living Out Loud. New York: Random House, 1988. [Collection of "Life in the 30's" columns.]
"Public and Private." Semiweekly op-ed page column, *New York Times* (1990–1994).
Thinking Out Loud. New York: Random House, 1993. [Collection of "Public and Private" columns.]

Fiction

Object Lessons. New York: Random House, 1991.
The Tree That Came to Stay [children's book]. New York: Crown, 1992.
One True Thing. New York: Random House, 1994.
Black & Blue: A Novel. New York: Random House, 1998.

WRITINGS ON ANNA QUINDLEN AND HER WORK

Abcarian, Robin. "Anna and the Boys of the N.Y. Times." *Los Angeles Times*, October 30, 1994, E1, E5.
Adkins, Rose A. "Reporting the Details of Life." *Writer's Digest* (March 1993): 35–37.
Alter, Jonathan. " 'This Is What I Want to Do.' " *Newsweek* (September 19, 1994): 54.
Beck, Melinda. "Living the Examined Life." *Newsweek* (April 4, 1988): 65.
Conant, Jennet. "Of Love and Loss." *Redbook* (October 1994): 81–86.
Duffy, Martha. "The Girls of Summer." *Time* (April 8, 1991): 76.
Howard, Maureen. " 'Life in the 30's,' the Novel: Westchester Adolescence" [book review]. *New York Times*, April 18, 1991, C19.
Hubbard, Kim. "Her Own True Thing." *People* (October 17, 1994): 107–110.
Katz, Jon. "Is Anna Quindlen a Martyr?" *New York* (September 26, 1994): 22–23.
Kurtz, Howard. "Quindlen Quits N.Y. Times." *Washington Post*, September 10, 1994, C1.

Lamb, Chris. "A 'Public and Private' Talk with a Columnist." *Editor and Publisher* (November 30, 1991): 32–34.

Lehrman, Karen. "She the People." *The New Republic* (June 10, 1991): 38–41.

Morrisroe, Patricia. "Laureate of Real Life: Anna Quindlen Brings a New Voice to the *Times* Chrome-Domed Op-Ed page." *New York* (December 24–31, 1990): 100–102.

"1992 Pulitzer Prize Winners and Their Works in Journalism and the Arts." *New York Times*, April 8, 1992, B6.

"Quindlen Leaving the Times to Be a Full-Time Novelist." *New York Times*, September 10, 1994, A15.

Shellenbarger, Sue. "Quindlen Decides Having Some Is Enough." *Wall Street Journal*, September 21, 1994, B1.

Steinberg, Sybil. "*PW* Interviews: Anna Quindlen." *Publishers Weekly* (March 15, 1991): 40–41.

Tyler, Anne. "Object Lessons" [book review]. *New York Times Book Review* (April 14, 1991): 7, 9.

Williams, Marjorie. "All about Anna." *Vanity Fair* (September 1994): 60–76.

"A Woman for the Times." *Psychology Today* (September–October 1994): 26–30.

Young, Virginia. "Anna Quindlen." *Women on Deadline: A Collection of America's Best.* Ed. Sherry Ricchiardi and Virginia Young. Ames: Iowa State University Press, 1991, 117–134.

ADRIENNE RICH
(1929–)

Sioban Dillon

Adrienne Rich's work includes poetry, scholarly social criticism, teaching, and activism. Growing up in a middle-class suburb of Baltimore, Rich benefited from having parents who encouraged her to read and write in her youth; she published two plays and a group of poems by age twelve. Shortly after graduating from Radcliffe College in 1951, she married Alfred Conrad, a teacher in economics at Harvard University, and bore three sons between 1955 and 1959. Rich remembers this time as a maddening period of her life (possibly marked by an eight-year gap between publications). When her husband began teaching at City College of New York, they moved to New York City. There Rich formed her seminal relationships with Audre Lorde and June Jordan. Included on the roster of schools where Rich has taught are Swarthmore College, Columbia University, Brandeis University, and City College of New York (after her husband died in 1970, Rich continued to teach at Brandeis and in New York City). Among her many prizes and awards is the prestigious National Book Award for Poetry in 1974, which she rejected for herself but accepted with cowinner Audre Lorde in the name of all women. Since 1976, Rich has lived with her partner Michelle Cliff, a writer and historian. She currently spends much of her time in California.

Rich's major contributions to feminist theory break down into two divisions: her poetry and her essays, yet to fix Adrienne Rich within a specific theory of feminism is a difficult task. The categories lesbian-feminist, Jewish-feminist, materialist-feminist, and woman-centered race/class theorist are all partially apropos, but her eclectic essays, poetry, and musings exceed the bounds of these definitions. Her work unifies different "schools" of feminist thought in order to explore the common concerns different oppressions share without negating those differences. Of all the terms Rich utilizes—"lesbian," "race," and "identity" occur repeatedly in her prose—the figure of woman and real women form the core from which she draws her authority to speak out against global injustices. Adrienne Rich never forgets the relentless economic hardships faced by the majority of the world's population under a system of patriarchal domination. This burden, she argues, has crippling effects on the spiritual, emotional, and intellectual growth of women in particular.

In her early years, Adrienne Rich adopted traditional poetic conventions in her meter, stanzas, and rhymes that, in retrospect, enabled the poet to subdue growing internal conflicts through rigid artistic structures: "In those early years formalism was part of the strategy—like asbestos gloves, it allowed me to handle materials I couldn't pick up barehanded" (Rich 1993a, 171). *A Change of World* (1951) and *The Diamond Cutters* (1955) are both exemplary of a crafted poise and the ideal of an emotionally restrained, detached voice Rich inherited from the master poets.

Her training as a poet in the academy served her well before she underwent a "turning." In 1951, Rich's *A Change of World* was selected for the Yale Series of Younger Poets. This distinction, awarded, in part, for Rich's poetic "good manners," earned her a place among the inner circles of the academic elite, but Rich would eventually perform a scathing analysis of the male-controlled mechanisms that elevated her to such rarefied heights. Years later Rich would rail against "so diminished a scope for poetry" (Rich 1993b, 192).

After winning literary success within the modern poetic tradition established by T. S. Eliot, Ezra Pound, William Yeats, and other revered male artists, Rich's next collection of poems signaled a watershed in her thinking. *Snapshots of a Daughter-in-Law* (1963) demonstrates Rich's new awareness of what it means to be a woman in Western culture, that is, to be stifled by the masculine imagination. But her consciousness was far from fully constituted as feminist since she continued to distance herself from her female poet-speakers. Rich retrospectively notes that she "hadn't found the courage yet to do without authorities, or even to use the pronoun 'I'—the woman in the poem is always 'she.'" Yet here the influence of alternative authorities is clearly visible in the echoes of Emily Dickinson's poetry and the writings of Simone de Beauvoir. Perhaps the timing of this collection, appearing squarely at the center of an American trend away from rigid poetic structures and objectivity toward free forms and experimental self-reflection, in conjunction with the prevalent social restlessness among left-leaning intellectuals of the era, partly accounts for Rich's textual resistance to inherited paradigms. The first sections of the title poem trace the complex and often soul-crushing entanglements women pass on to one another under patriarchal dominance: "all the old knives/that have rusted in my back, I drive in yours." This first poetic effort to record woman's experience is characterized as Rich's attack on her "own patterns of consciousness and the social and cultural structures that uphold them" (Du Plessis 1975, 203).

The process of institutional deconstruction in which Rich participated through her writing and activism during the 1960s resulted in the concept of "re-vision" she continues to utilize today, defined by Rich as "the act of looking back, of seeing with fresh eyes, or entering an old text from a new critical direction" (Rich, "When We Dead Awaken," *On Lies*, 35). *Necessities of Life: Poems 1962–*

1965 (1967), *Leaflets: Poems, 1965–1968* (1971), and *The Will to Change* (1971) show a gradual extension of Rich's thought beyond a strictly Western-feminist discourse into the territory of local and global politics, adding a materialist-feminist perspective to her writing. Rich acknowledges the racism she herself was brought up to adopt and the assimilationist strategies her Jewish family practiced in order to fit into a conformist, Anglo-American social network. Her attention to language may rightly be seen as the next logical step in her exploration of cultural values. During this period, themes of female sexuality, the body, and consciousness in Rich's writing coalesce as a resistant, emancipatory discourse that enables a poetic rebellion against the dominant (masculine) mode of destructive thinking. Describing herself as "an instrument in the shape/of a woman" trying to translate pulsations/into images," she tells us elsewhere that "this is the oppressor's language/yet I need it to talk to you" (Rich, 1993a, 39, 41). As in all her work, in *Diving into the Wreck* (1973) Rich measures the loss and despair to which women are subject under an oppressive social system; cheated of opportunity, they embody "the drowned face always staring/toward the sun."

While Rich writes on a wide range of topics—including rape, pedagogy, and history—she inevitably draws us back to what Marilyn Farwell in *College English* (1973) calls the "Western symbology" dividing male and female principles. Like her poetry and prose, the diverse topics she treats are always inextricably linked to planetary male domination as "the venereal disease that lives alike in the crimes of Vietnam and the myth of sexual liberation" (194). This persistent analysis of the world in terms of sexual divisions has often set her at odds with her early supporters. I cannot estimate what role her "coming out" as a lesbian played in the ambivalent reception of her more polemical texts during the 1970s and 1980s, including the controversial *Of Woman Born* (1976) and "Compulsory Heterosexuality and Lesbian Existence" (1980). In these works Rich explores the damage wrought by two "foundations" of women's identity, namely, motherhood and woman's presumed natural bond with men. Nevertheless, *Twenty-One Love Poems* (1977) stands as a commercially successful volume of lesbian poetry. It is important to remember, however, that one of Rich's most significant phrases, "lesbian continuum," includes a variety of "woman-identified experience, not simply the fact that a woman has had or consciously desired genital sexual experience with another woman" (Rich 1993a, 217).

More recently, critics have reshaped their own characterizations of Rich's project from strictly lesbian-feminist to what we now call postcolonial. Anne Herzog describes "Rich's framing of the question of language . . . as a colonialist issue" (Herzog 1989). Rich has cited James Baldwin, Franz Fanon, and Caribbean poet/activist Aime Cesaire as important authors to her development. In *Blood, Bread, and Poetry: Selected Prose 1979–1986* (1986), Rich's meditations on personal location sharpen her original engagement with differences among women in *On Lies, Secrets, and Silence* (1979). An earlier essay, "Disloyal to Civilization," raises issues of accountability and responsibility—analogous perhaps to the motif of shame that arises frequently in her poetry—because she observes that "the concept of racism itself is often intellectualized by white feminists" (Rich 1979, 303) and therefore expropriates the unique subject positions from which women of color speak. In *Blood*, she pushes the scope of her critical inquiry further, asking: "How do we actively work to build a white Western feminist consciousness that is not simply centered on itself, that resists white circumscribing?" (Rich, *Blood* 1986, 219). The progression from *The Dream of a Common Language: Poems, 1974–1977* (1978) to *Your Native Land, Your Life* (1986) is similarly noted by Mary S. Strine as "a shift in emphasis from the problems of feminine self-identity *per se* to constructive dialogic engagement with the social and historical circumstances from which that self-identity emerges" (Strine 1989, 33).

Adrienne Rich's two latest books, *What Is Found There: Notebooks on Poetry and Politics* (1993) and *Dark Fields of the Republic: Poems, 1991–1995* (1995), challenge the North American literary assumption that the commingling of poetry and politics produces inferior writing. She returns to this Western dilemma throughout the text, foregrounding her own experience as a female author trying to incorporate both "poles" in her art: "[I]t's not a matter of dying as a poet into politics, or of having to be reborn as a poet on the other side of politics (where is that?), but of something else—finding the relationship" (Rich 1993b, 21). *Notebooks*, like her other prose collections, blends personal, feminist narrative (verging on the fictional at times) with current political commentary and poetry by a wide range of writers. Peter Erickson reformulates Rich's reconciliation of art and activism: "[A]lthough poetry cannot itself be social change, it is capable of arousing the desire for such change," and therefore "the articulation of desire in a poem is not the equivalent of its realization in society, but it may well be an indispensable precondition" (Erickson 1995, 113). In *Dark Fields*, Rich opens the way for such an arousal by returning to the Marxist/socialist writers of twentieth-century Europe. Citing the poet Osip Mandelstam, essayist Rosa Luxemburg, and playwright Bertolt Brecht, Rich reexplores questions of the state, justice, compassion, and guilt through the eyes of a North American woman fifty years after World War II. As in all her work, the *figure* of woman (not necessarily biological woman) provides a fulcrum on which her political/poetic project rests. Women occupy a central place in Rich's ongoing dialogic poetry, revealing the expansive web of human relations: "[T]he sex of the women our bodies entire/ molten in purpose each body a tongue/each body a river and over and over" (Rich 1995, 67). Here Rich's poet-voice unites economic, sexual, and cultural analysis. Hence, Rich ultimately suggests that poetic language empowers us to resuscitate the ethical imperative of historical action: "[P]oetry means refusing/ the choice to kill or die."

WORKS BY ADRIENNE RICH

Poetry

A Change of World. Foreword by W. H. Auden. New Haven, CT: Yale University Press, 1951a.

Poems. New York: Fantasy Press/Oxford University Poetry Society, 1951b.

The Diamond Cutters, and Other Poems. New York: Harper, 1955.

The Knight, after Rilke. Privately printed, 1957.

Necessities of Life. New York: Norton, 1967a.

Selected Poems. London: Chatto and Windus, 1967b.

Snapshots of a Daughter-in-Law: Poems, 1954–1962. New York: Harper, 1963; revised, New York: Norton, 1967c.

Leaflets: Poems, 1965–1968. New York: Norton, 1969.

The Will to Change: Poems. New York: Norton, 1971b.

Diving into the Wreck: Poems, 1971–1972. New York: Norton, 1973.

Adrienne Rich's Poetry: Texts of the Poems, The Poet on Her Work, Reviews and Criticism. Ed. Barbara Charlesworth Gelpi and Albert Gelpi. New York: Norton, 1975; revised as *Adrienne Rich's Poetry and Prose*, 1993a.

Twenty-one Love Poems. Emeryville, CA: Effie's Press, 1977.

The Dream of a Common Language: Poems, 1974–1977. New York: Norton, 1978, 1993.

A Wild Patience Has Taken Me This Far: Poems, 1978–1981. New York: Norton, 1981, 1993.

Sources. Woodside, CA: Heyeck Press, 1983.

The Fact of a Doorframe: Poems Selected and New, 1950–1984. New York: Norton, 1984, 1994.

Your Native Land, Your Life. New York: Norton, 1986, 1993.

Time's Power: Poems, 1985–1988. New York: Norton, 1989.

An Atlas of the Difficult World: Poems, 1988–1991. New York: Norton, 1991.

Collected Early Poems, 1950–1970. New York: Norton, 1993, 1995.

Dark Fields of the Republic: Poems, 1991–1995. New York: Norton, 1995.

Nonfiction

Of Woman Born: Motherhood As Experience and Institution. New York: Norton, 1976, 1995.

Women and Honor: Some Notes on Lying. Pittsburgh: Motherroot/Pittsburgh Women Writers, 1977; San Francisco: Cleis, 1990.

On Lies, Secrets, and Silence: Selected Prose, 1966–1978. New York: Norton, 1979, 1995.

"Compulsory Heterosexuality and Lesbian Existence." *Signs* 4 (1980): 631–660.

Blood, Bread, and Poetry: Selected Prose, 1979–1985. New York: Norton, 1986.

What Is Found There: Notebooks on Poetry and Politics. New York: Norton, 1993b, 1994.

Translations

With Aijaz Ahmad and William Stafford. *Poems by Ghalib*. Ed. Aijaz Ahmad. New York: Hudson Review, 1969.

Reflections. By Mark Insingel. New York: Red Dust, 1973.

De amor oscoro/Of Dark Love. By Francisco Alarcon. Santa Cruz: Moving Parts, 1991.

WRITINGS ON ADRIENNE RICH AND HER WORK

Carter, Nancy Corson. "Claiming the Bittersweet Matrix: Alice Walker, Sandra Cisneros, and Adrienne Rich." *Critique* 35 (Summer 1994): 195–204.

Church, Jennifer. "Rethinking Dichotomies: Reflections on Adrienne Rich's What Is Possible." *Women's Studies* 17, nos. 3/4 (1990): 289–302.

Dennis, Helen. "Adrienne Rich: Consciousness Raising as Poetic Method," and Davidson, Harriet. " 'In the Wake of Home': Adrienne Rich's Politics and Poetics of Location." *Contemporary Poetry Meets Modern Theory.* Ed. Anthony Easthope. Toronto: University of Toronto Press, 1991.

DuPlessis, Rachel Blau. "The Critique of Consciousness and Myth in Levertov, Rich, and Rukeyser." *Feminist Studies* 3, nos. 1–2 (1975): 199–221.

Erickson, Peter. "Singing America: From Walt Whitman to Adrienne Rich." *The Kenyon Review* 17 (Winter 1995): 103–19.

Erkkila, Betsy. "Dickinson and Rich: Toward a Theory of Female Poetic Influence." *American Literature* 56 (December 1984): 541–559.

Farwell, Marilyn. "Toward a Definition of the Lesbian Literary Imagination." *Sexual Practice, Textual Theory: Lesbian Cultural Criticism.* Ed. Susan Wolfe. Cambridge, MA: Blackwell, 1993.

Greenwald, Elissa. "The Dream of a Common Language: Vietnam Poetry as Reformation of Language and Feeling in the Poems of Adrienne Rich." *Journal of American Culture* 16 (Fall 1993): 97–102.

Hamill, Sam. "A Poetry of Daily Practice: Adrienne Rich, S. J. Marks, Dorianne Laux." *The American Poetry Review* 21 (July/August 1992): 35–38.

Hedley, Jane. "Surviving to Speak New Language: Mary Daly and Adrienne Rich." *Hypatia* 7, no. 2, (Spring 1992): 40–62.

"The Hermit's Scream." *PMLA* 108, no. 5 (October 1993): 1157–1164.

Herzog, Anne. "Adrienne Rich and the Discourse of Decolonization." *The Centennial Review* 33, no. 3, (Summer 1989): 258–277.

Kennard, Jean. "Ourself behind Ourself: A Theory for Lesbian Readers," and Schweickart, Patrocinio. "Reading Ourselves: Toward a Feminist Theory of Reading." *Gender and Reading: Essays on Readers, Texts, and Contexts.* Ed. Elizabeth Flynn. Baltimore: Johns Hopkins University Press, 1986.

Kinzie, Mary. "Weeds in Tar." *The American Poetry Review* 14, no. 4 (July/August 1985): 43–46.

Kirby, Kathleen. "Thinking through the Boundary: The Politics of Location, Subjects, and Space." *Boundary* 20, no. 2 (Summer 1993): 173–189.

Langdon, Hammer. "Art and AIDS; or, How Will Culture Cure You?" *Raritan* 29 (March 1996): 57–77.

Lowell, Robert, Peter Taylor, and Robert Penn Warren, eds. *Randall Jarrell, 1914–1965.* New York: Farrar, Straus, 1967.

Matson, Suzanne. "Talking to Our Father: The Political and Mythical Appropriations of Adrienne Rich and Sharon Olds." *The American Poetry Review* 18 (November/December 1989): 35–41.

Miller, Nancy. "Changing the Subject: Authorship, Writing and the Reader." *Feminist Studies: Critical Studies.* Ed. Teresa de Lauretis. Bloomington: Indiana University Press, 1986.

Montenegro, David. "Adrienne Rich: An Interview by David Montenegro." *The American Poetry Review* 20 (January/February 1991): 7–14.

"Notes for a Magazine: What Does Separatism Mean?" *Sinister Wisdom* 18 (Fall 1981): 83–91.

Nowik, Nan. "Mixing Art and Politics: The Writings of Adrienne Rich, Marge Piercy, and Alice Walker." *The Centennial Review* 30, no. 2, (Spring 1986): 208–218.

Ostroff, Anthony, ed. *The Poet as Critic*. Boston: Little, Brown, 1965.

Runzo, Sandra. "Adrienne Rich's Voice of Treason." *Women's Studies* 18, nos. 2/3 (1990): 135–151.

Stimpson, Catherine. "Adrienne Rich and Lesbian/Feminist Poetry." *Parnassus* 12–13 (Spring–Winter 1985): 249–268.

Strine, Mary. "The Politics of Asking Women's Questions: Voice and Value in the Poetry of Adrienne Rich." *Text and Performance Quarterly* 9, no. 1 (January 1989): 24–41.

Templeton, Alice. "Contradictions: Tracking Adrienne Rich's Poetry." *Tulsa Studies in Women's Literature*. 12 (Fall 1993): 333–340.

———. "The Dream and the Dialogue: Rich's Feminist Poetics and Gadamer's Hermeneutics." *Tulsa Studies in Women's Literature* 7 (Fall 1988): 283–296.

The Tribute of His Peers: Elegies for Robinson Jeffers. New York: Tor House Press, 1989.

INTERVIEWS

Montenegro, David. *Points of Departure: International Writers on Writing and Politics*. Ann Arbor: University of Michigan Press, 1991, 5–25.

Trinidad, David. "Adrienne Rich Charts a Difficult World." *Advocate* 31 (December 1991): 82–84.

FAITH RINGGOLD
(1930–)

Ann Lee Morgan

Born in Harlem, where she has lived nearly all of her life, Faith Ringgold was the youngest of three children in a churchgoing, working-class family that valued self-respect and education. Although her parents separated before she was of school age, her father remained involved with his children and supported them financially. A housewife in the years that Ringgold was growing up, her mother, Willi Posey, later achieved considerable success as a fashion designer and dress-maker.

Ringgold was asthmatic as a child and consequently was often restricted in her activities, but she filled much of her time making art. She was educated in the public schools, and, following her graduation from high school in 1948, she entered New York City College to study art. She recalls in her memoirs that the painter Robert Gwathmey was one of her best teachers there. After two years, her progress was interrupted by marriage to musician Robert Earl Wallace, her teenage sweetheart. In January and December 1952 she gave birth to two chil-dren: Michele Wallace, today a professor of English, cultural critic, and promi-nent feminist writer, and Barbara Wallace, a linguist who currently teaches elementary school. Ringgold separated permanently from her husband in 1954 (she blames Wallace's drug addiction), and the marriage was subsequently an-nulled. In 1962 she married Burdette Ringgold, a longtime friend and automobile factory worker.

Ringgold received her college diploma in 1955, followed by a master's degree, also from City College. In the fall of 1955 she began her teaching career in the New York City public schools, where she remained until 1973. Beginning in 1970, she also taught courses at Pratt Institute, Wagner College, and the Bank Street College of Education, all in New York City. In the mid-1970s she began an extensive, nationwide program of lecturing and demonstrating her art, mainly in colleges and universities. Since the mid-1980s, she has been a professor at the University of California at San Diego, where she teaches each winter. In 1992 she moved to Englewood, New Jersey, just across the George Washington Bridge from upper Manhattan.

Demonstrating that Ringgold is a born storyteller, her career has expanded into writing in the 1990s, with the publication of several illustrated children's books and her autobiographical memoir, *We Flew over the Bridge.*

One of the first artists of her generation to incorporate issues of social and racial justice into her work, Faith Ringgold has been a force since the early 1960s in the New York art world. Her involvement in the 1960s with African American issues prepared her to address similar problems of fairness, equality, and power for women. Ringgold served as a leader in the early 1970s glory days of the women's movement, and she has since exemplified tireless commitment to the creative expression of women's concerns within a broadly humanitarian context.

When she was young, like nearly all serious artists of the 1950s and early 1960s, Faith Ringgold saw no place for social issues in art. By 1963, when she first began to look for gallery representation in order to present her work professionally, her paintings, as she describes them in her memoirs, "were colorful and well defined. Their subjects were flowers, landscapes, and trees painted in the French Impressionist manner"(Ringgold 1995). That summer, however, during a lengthy stay at Oak Bluffs on Martha's Vineyard, she began to produce paintings that herald her mature work. Working now with dramatically simplified forms painted in flat colors, Ringgold aspired to "make a statement in my art about the Civil Rights Movement and what was happening to black people in America at that time." This ambition resulted eventually in the American People series of more than twenty paintings that focus on relationships between black and white Americans.

In 1966 Faith Ringgold debuted as an artist in a group show, *Art of the American Negro*, the first such show to be held in Harlem since the prewar years. Soon she was invited to join a cooperative gallery called Spectrum, where she was the only black person and one of only a handful of women. There, in 1967, she had her first one-person exhibition, which featured the final paintings in the American People series. These three large canvases directly addressed the tensions of the civil rights era: *The Flag Is Bleeding, U.S. Postage Stamp Commemorating the Advent of Black Power*, and *Die*, a shocking evocation of recent race riots. Darkened color harmonies unified the Black Light series featured in her next solo show, early in 1970. These paintings also brought into her art for the first time two themes that she later found fruitful: imagery based on African motifs and written words as part of the compositional structure. The most powerful of these works was *Flag for the Moon: Die Nigger*, which responded to the 1969 American moon landing, widespread anger toward the U.S. government during this period of the Vietnam War, and the sorry state of American race relations. Playing on the form of the American flag, Ringgold incorporated the word "die" among the stars and made the stripes from the stylized forms of the word "nigger."

In the meantime, Ringgold had begun to take the activist stance that soon made her a leading public figure in the New York art world. In late 1968, when the Whitney Museum of American Art mounted a major review of American painting and sculpture from the 1930s without a single black artist, Faith Ring-gold spearheaded a demonstration outside the museum. Soon she became in-volved with the Art Workers Coalition (AWC), a large, but loosely structured, artists' organization that supported artists' rights and greater access to museums. Ringgold was among the leaders of an AWC group that pressed the Museum of Modern Art for improved representation of black artists; in the end, relatively little was gained, but the issues were given a public airing.

During her activist phase, Ringgold also participated late in 1970 in a large protest exhibition, the *People's Flag Show* at the Judson Memorial Church in Greenwich Village. In the aftermath, Ringgold and two white male artists were arrested as members of the organizing committee charged with desecrating the flag. The "Judson Three" became an art world cause célèbre, defended by the American Civil Liberties Union. Some months later they were found guilty and fined.

The women's movement first came to Ringgold's attention early, in 1967, through a personal friend, the civil rights lawyer Florynce Kennedy. However, Ringgold herself, like so many others, did not become involved until 1970. In May 1970, Ringgold and her daughter Michele Wallace formed Women Students and Artists for Black Art Liberation (WSABAL) in response to an AWC ex-hibition mounted to protest American participation in the Venice Biennale and, more generally, to register displeasure with American policies regarding Vietnam, racism, and repression. WSABAL was successful in opening the counterexhibi-tion to all who wished to participate—including large numbers of African Amer-ican women and men and white women.

A few months later, critic Lucy Lippard and artist Poppy Johnson asked Ring-gold to join them in founding what became known as the Ad Hoc Women's Group. Through picketing, press releases, and other tactics, this loose association of women successfully pressured the Whitney Museum into increasing the num-ber of women included in its next annual survey (these are now biennial) of American art. Although she quickly became a leader in seeking rights for women artists, Ringgold's position as a black woman was problematic. Many blacks saw the women's movement as divisive to the cause of African Americans, who, it was argued, should put race ahead of gender as an issue. Although Ringgold's work testifies to her refusal to make this choice, she did not remain on the feminist front lines for long, feeling that the predominantly white feminist move-ment failed to address her personal situation. She tried to organize black women artists into a network, or at least a support group, but without success. In the 1980s she worked for progressive change through the national Women's Caucus for Art, and in 1987 she was instrumental to the organization of Coast to Coast, which promotes the interests of all American women artists of color.

While she was engrossed in the politically oriented activities of the years around 1970, Faith Ringgold started to make posters to support her activist in-tentions. To convey their messages, posters obviously called for language in con-junction with images, thereby furthering that aspect of her work. About the same time, she produced her first major work clearly focused on the lives of women: a 1971 mural for the Women's House of Detention on Rikers Island in New York. In eight sections, it shows women, both black and white, involved in a variety of traditional and unconventional occupations.

In the summer of 1972, a trip to Europe—her first since an introductory tour in 1961—provided a hiatus in Ringgold's public activism on behalf of justice for people in marginalized groups. It also led her to a discovery that would deeply affect the nature of her creative output. In Amsterdam she encountered a display of Tibetan and Nepalese paintings on cloth. What particularly caught her imagination was their presentation, surrounded by brocaded cloth frames. Upon her return she began to frame her own paintings in this way, which made them easily portable because they could be rolled up. Moreover, this new interest in cloth and its uses as an expressive medium ultimately allowed her to move directly into original forms of both two- and three-dimensional art.

Painted in the months after her return, her first cloth-framed works—also her first in acrylic—constituted the Feminist Landscape series. These are painted landscapes inscribed in gold paint with statements from black women historically important to feminism, including Sojourner Truth, Harriet Tubman, and the only living exemplar, Shirley Chisholm. Soon Ringgold was at work on another series, the Slave Rape series, for which her mother made the cloth frames, initiating the collaboration that continued until Willi Posey's death nearly a decade later. Ringgold credits her mother with subtly transforming the Tibetan tradition into an African American form of expression.

In 1973 Ringgold moved into three-dimensional work with a series of masks, based loosely on African prototypes. Soon the masks were supplied with clothing, often conceived and executed by Ringgold's mother. At the time this work was done, the very notion of using cloth, often beaded and/or stuffed, frequently adorned with embroidery, raffia, or other offbeat materials, seemed outside the boundaries of fine art. Along with many other women artists who felt that their concerns could not be adequately expressed within the traditional artistic media, Ringgold pushed the limits of art to accommodate materials and forms formerly relegated to craft.

Ringgold's experimental work with cloth structures and sewn or appliquéd decoration led directly into two new interests: soft sculpture and costumes to be used in performance work. The soft sculptures of the mid-1970s encompassed a variety of types: evocations of personal friends, whimsical portraits of celebrities such as basketball player Wilt Chamberlain, and imaginary characters based on various social types. Eventually, the narrative implications inherent in such creations led Ringgold to performance. In 1976 she presented *The Wake and Resurrection of the Bicentennial Negro*, her first multimedia masked performance, which told a tale of tragedy and spiritual transcendence. Ringgold expanded the meaning of the piece for many young people by having local students play the roles under her direction when she visited their colleges. In the later 1970s,

Ringgold continued her sculptures with numerous figures, including those in the Woman on a Pedestal series and the Harlem series. In 1980 she began doing her own masked performances, in which she often addressed autobiographical issues.

For a retrospective exhibition in 1984 at Harlem's Studio Museum, her first one-person museum exhibition and her first solo show in New York since 1970, Faith Ringgold executed an ambitious quilt that provided yet another turning point in her career. Her first quilt, *Echoes of Harlem*, made in 1980, had been her last collaborative project with Willi Posey. Ringgold later had made a second, pieced quilt as a memorial to her recently deceased mother. However, *Who's Afraid of Aunt Jemima?* was the first story quilt; it tells a modern Jemima fable, which reinterprets the racist stereotype within the form of folk tale.

Subsequently, the story quilt has become Ringgold's preeminent form of expression. Drawing on traditional quilts as precedents for the form but expanding the approach with representational elements and text, these quilts embody complex narratives within their colorful and decorative designs. Many of the quilts belong to series, and some, such as the *Bitter Nest* group, also relate to performance pieces; *Bitter Nest* tells a fictional tale of life during the Harlem Renaissance.

Ringgold's continuing commitment to feminism is borne out in the quilt stories by the pervasively female point of view embodied there. Most of her stories center on women, and the narrative voice is virtually always a woman's. Moreover, Ringgold has developed her quilts into a distinctly hybrid form, which may incorporate painting, photography, lithography, or other fine art techniques into a format that derives directly from, and continues to refer to, women's traditional creative practice (as opposed to the previously male-identified tradition of easel painting).

The 1990s French Collection series of story quilts is the most charming and sophisticated so far. These incorporate portraits of the great French modernists, including Matisse and Picasso, their signature masterpieces, and the subversive figure of a young black woman who inserts herself into their milieu. In this series of witty images, Ringgold reconsiders her heritage in art history from the vantage point of a woman of African descent and emphasizes the legitimacy of her own quest as a fine artist. During a career that now encompasses nearly forty years, Faith Ringgold has only rarely produced overtly confrontational or didactic work. Yet, themes of gender and racial justice are at the heart of nearly all her creative endeavors. Her unconventional art appeals to a broad audience through effective use of humor, candor, novel approaches to materials and techniques, decorative vivacity, and imaginative storytelling.

WORKS BY FAITH RINGGOLD

We Flew over the Bridge: The Memoirs of Faith Ringgold. Boston: Little, Brown (Bulfinch Press), 1995.

WRITINGS ON FAITH RINGGOLD AND HER WORK

Flomenhaft, Eleanor, et al. *Faith Ringgold: A Twenty-Five Year Survey*. Hempstead, NY: Fine Arts Museum of Long Island, 1990.

Gouma-Peterson, Thalia, and Kathleen McMannus Zurko, eds. *Faith Ringgold: Painting, Sculpture, Performance*. Wooster, OH: College of Wooster Art Museum, 1985.

Lippard, Lucy, and Michele Wallace. *Faith Ringgold: Twenty Years of Painting, Sculpture, and Performance (1963–1983)*. New York: Studio Museum, 1984.

ROSEMARY RUETHER
(1936–)

Beth Blissman

Rosemary Radford Ruether is a strong feminist woman in a long line of strong, independent, and intellectual women. Her upbringing was influenced a great deal by her mother and her mother's friends, whom she describes as deeply affected by the very first wave of feminism in this country in the late nineteenth and early twentieth centuries. "These women were an important reference group for me in my development. Vigorous, intellectually active, and socially concerned into their late eighties and even nineties, they provided me a sense of roots for what I was doing" (Ruether, *Disputed Questions* 1989, 22).

Ruether's cultural roots are also complex and varied. She was born on November 2, 1936, in St. Paul, Minnesota. Her father, Robert Armstrong Radford, was from an aristocratic line of Virginia and Mississippi gentry. Religiously, Rosemary described him as "an Anglican of the twice-a-year variety." (Ruether, "Beginnings" 1925, 35). Her mother, Rebecca Cresap (Ord) Radford, was a devout, but independent-minded, Catholic who descended from an English family that came to the United States in the early nineteenth century and pioneered in California and Mexico. Rosemary spent much of her early childhood in the Georgetown area of Washington, D.C., and attended a private Catholic school. She describes her early influences as supportive of women and somewhat insulated from the larger, more sexist, and parochial church and society. Even though her father's family and her mother's paternal relatives held very conservative views about the role and place of women, Ruether notes that she did not encounter oppressive male figures on a daily basis "until it was far too late for me to change my assumptions" (Ruether, *Disputed Questions* 1989, 12). From 1947 to 1949, her family lived in Greece for a time, where her father died suddenly in 1948 due to pneumonia. A few years later Rosemary moved with her mother and her two older sisters to California, near her mother's childhood home, and finished high school at a public school in La Jolla, California.

Rosemary Ruether then went on to Scripps College in Claremont, California, for her bachelor's degree. As a teenager, she had wanted to be an artist, but in college her interests turned to the classics, particularly to the origins, rise, and triumph of Christianity. This interest carried her through both her master's in classics and Roman history and Ph.D. in classics and patristics, both completed at the Claremont Graduate School. At the end of her junior year at Scripps, Rosemary married Herman Ruether, and in the next six years she gave birth to two daughters and a son while finishing graduate work. Only with a Ph.D. in hand did she realize that, although her male professors had supported her intellectual journey, they had never really taken seriously the idea that she, as a woman, would consider going on to an academic career. They "neglected to introduce us to such mundane topics as power, prestige and promotion in academe." (Ruether, *Disputed Questions* 1989, 28). This betrayal by her academic mentors helped to set the stage for Rosemary's future feminist analysis, which started tentatively in the late 1960s.

Ruether's first academic appointment was at the Howard University School of Religion in Washington, D.C. She taught there from 1966 to 1976, with the exception of two visiting lectureships in feminist theology at Harvard Divinity School (1972–1973) and Yale Divinity School (1973–1974). Since 1976, she has been the Georgia Harkness Professor of Theology at Garrett Evangelical Seminary in Evanston, Illinois.

Ruether's most significant contributions to the feminist movement include the development of the field and conceptual methodology for feminist theology. Her numerous articles, essays, and books cover so many aspects of theology and religious thought that an adequate bibliography of her works would fill a text in and of itself. However, several texts speak of the breadth of her work.

Since she had been trained in the classics, Ruether's method was to use the classics as a context for understanding Christianity and religion in general. Her strong interest in religion, coupled with an emerging social consciousness, gave her a unique theoethical perspective. The social justice issues that influenced her work included cognitive dissonance with the larger culture and church (especially before Vatican II began in 1963) and the civil rights movement. In the summer of 1965, she worked in Mississippi as a Delta Ministry volunteer, doing community organizing to help people provide support and better educational alternatives for their children. This experience in the heart of the southern black community widened her perspectives about religion and racism, as well as the need to ground theory and theology in real-life situations (Ruether *Disputed Questions* 1989, 78–81). As Ruether began her academic career at Howard, she focused mainly on continuing to explore the Christian tradition and the ways in which theological ideas have been used to justify social injustices (Ruether 1967, 1972).

This exploration of social injustices also included a sensitivity to anti-Semitism. Rosemary admits that her uncle David (a Jewish man from New York who had married into the family) may have helped to create such a sensitivity, but it was also nourished by the absolute invisibility of Jewish history in her courses on Western civilization (Ruether, *Disputed Questions* 1989, 43–46). As she explored the origins of Christianity and the history of Judaism in greater depth, Ruether began to articulate the liberatory option expressed there, namely, the "critical, transformative alternative in the prophetic tradition of Hebrew Scripture and the New Testament" (Ruether "The Development of My Theology" 1989 2). The curiosity generated by her findings and her concern with Western anti-Semitism rooted in Christianity sparked continuing academic work (Ruether, *Faith and Fratricide*, 1974; Ruether with Ruether 1989). Ruether's interests have since grown to embrace the theological and social aspects of Palestinian oppression and liberation as well (Ruether with Ellis 1990).

As her career continued, Ruether's voice became ever stronger as an advocate for women, yet within the context of justice and liberation for *all* of the oppressed. In one of her early works, *Religion and Sexism* (1974), she explored the roles, treatment, and images of women in the Jewish and Christian traditions. Ruether then spent more time clarifying the interrelationship of sexism with other structures of oppression (*New Woman/New Earth*, 1975) and developing a comprehensive work of feminist theology (*Sexism and God-Talk: Toward a Feminist Theology*, 1983). The theology she is interested in developing goes beyond a simple reform of Christianity yet does not let go of the tradition altogether. Instead, Ruether seeks to preserve the prophetic tradition of Hebrew and Christian Scriptures, because it speaks of a vision "where humans live justly with one another and in harmony with nature" (Ruether, "The Development of My Theology 1989, 3). This visionary approach goes far beyond liberal feminism, thus, most of Ruether's struggles within the feminist movement have been centered around a focus on women's liberation within the larger context of oppression. She has been one of the most eloquent speakers in reminding us that patriarchy is a system, and this system of domination and deceit oppresses not only women but many others as well. She has been in the process of developing methodologies that creatively weave together all of her concerns: racism, sexism, classism, environmental destruction, heterosexism. Ruether's goal is to point out a new direction, not as a reformist or a separatist but "a prophetess who is also priestess leading us into new temples, temples filled with a God who goes with us into this exodus from the old to the new" (Chopp 1989, 10).

When addressing the practical issues associated with taking Christianity beyond reformation to transformation, Ruether invites women and interested men to go on an exodus from patriarchy into small, feminist, liturgical communities to explore new ways of living our foundational convictions. In fact, with theological and theoretical support from Ruether and other feminist theologians such as Elisabeth Schussler-Fiorenza, a grassroots movement called Women-Church emerged in 1975 to creatively explore new ways of being church. Originally titled the Women of the Church Coalition, the Women-Church movement can best be described as a loose-knit organization of groups or small communities interested in an experience of church that is inclusive and liberating for all who participate. The coalition's focus quickly shifted from pressuring the Catholic

Church to ordain women in the 1970s to working for a larger cultural and institutional transformation in the 1980s (Ruether, *Women-Church* 1985, 64–66).

Ruether fully supported the development and growth of the Women-Church movement by publishing numerous essays and then two texts in 1985: *Women-Church: Theology and Practice of Feminist Liturgical Communities* and *Womanguides: Readings toward a Feminist Theology*. These texts have been a great resource for feminist women and supportive men to be able to critique and transform outdated ways of expressing their commitment to the liberatory tradition of Jesus Christ. The theological and practical standpoint of the Women-Church movement, especially as evidenced through liturgy, stemmed from an ecclesiological stance viewing church as *spirit-filled community*, always in the process of reform and open to change (Ruether, *Women-Church* 1985, 66–67). Although tension still exists within the movement about the degree to which an individual or a church should stray from more traditional structures, the focus of the movement now has now shifted toward macroecumenism, as evidenced by the 1993 Women-Church convergence theme: "Women-Church: Weavers of Change." At this gathering six different cultures were the foci of all the sessions and liturgies. As women gathered to discuss weaving the future, spirituality, and religion, the threads included the voices of Latinos, African Americans, Native Americans, Asian Americans, lesbians/bisexuals, and Euro-Americans. Thus, the Women-Church movement has traveled a great distance already, from origins in the Catholic Church, to a view of not only ecumenism but macroecumenism, in the effort to bring together women who are discovering their voices and many gifts on a journey of faith. Ruether has acted as a key voice in this movement to articulate strategies for the long and demanding exodus from patriarchy.

Ruether's strong commitment to contextual diversity across culture, race, and religion also extends to other forms of life and nature itself. For several decades now, she has spoken out as an advocate for social *and ecological* justice in the United States and abroad. In 1992, Ruether published *Gaia and God: An Ecofeminist Theology of Earth Healing*. Here she puts forth a strong argument against ecofeminists who would prefer to cut all ties with the prophetic tradition of historical Christianity yet also takes an honest look at the oppressive history of the Christian tradition via historical analysis and social critique of the patriarchal systems and worldviews promoted by Western Christianity and its influence on modern science. She draws the connections among the current military industrial complex and economic systems and the oppression of women, nature, and indigenous peoples. Calling the current manifestations of oppression "systems of domination and deceit," Ruether tries to put forth options for new paradigms of healing and interrelationship by proposing a greater focus on the living interdependency of all things (Ruether 1992, 115–204, 251).

In her most recent effort, *Women Healing Earth: Third World Women on Ecology, Feminism and Religion*, she again brings forth an important collection of stories and critical reflections, this time told by the women who have experienced the daily struggles of survival in the so-called Third World. She also takes the opportunity to include an instructive overview of ecofeminism in the First and Third World contexts in the Introduction, which serves as an excellent intro- ductory resource for those who would like to learn more about ecofeminism. Ruether deftly typologizes and critiques the literature that has emerged so far and situates the current contributions of *Women Healing Earth* in the need for ongoing dialogue about our common ecological crisis.

Finally, there is a growing amount of literature about this fine thinker for those who wish to learn more about Rosemary Radford Ruether and her work. For a quick overview of her theology and its impact on the feminist movement, consult the review essay in the January 1989 issue of *Religious Studies Review* (Chopp 1989; Rabuzzi 1989). Articles by Rebecca Chopp, Kathryn Allen Rabuzzi, and Ruether herself situate her work within a feminist spectrum. Also, two excellent autobiographies of Ruether and her intellectual and personal journeys exist. The first is her *Disputed Questions on Being a Christian*, first published in 1982 by Abingdon Press and then again in 1989 by Orbis Books. The second autobio- graphical reflection is entitled "Beginnings: An Intellectual Autobiography" and can be found in the book *Journeys: The Impact of Personal Experience on Religious Thought*. Rosemary Ruether is one of the most significant contemporary feminists in religious studies, indeed, in all of academe. Her search for new ethical para- digms and new forms of human and biotic community is part of a revolution of consciousness, an effort to move through and beyond Greek dualistic thinking that has undergirded Western Christian society and into the less absolute, yet more life-centered, possibilities of what might happen if and when we actually believe in our interconnectedness. In her own words: "[O]ur revolution is not just for us, but for our children, for the generations of living beings to come. What we can do is to plant a seed, nurture a seed-bearing plant here and there, and hope for a harvest that goes beyond the limits of our powers and the span of our lives" (Ruether 1992, 274).

WORKS BY ROSEMARY RUETHER

The Church against Itself. New York: Herder and Herder, 1967.

Liberation Theology: Human Hope Confronts Christian History and American Power. New York: Paulist Press, 1972.

Ed. *Religion and Sexism: Images of Women in the Jewish and Christian Traditions*. New York: Simon and Schuster, 1974.

Faith and Fratricide: The Theological Roots of Anti-Semitism. New York: Seabury Press, 1974.

"Beginnings: An Intellectual Autobiography." *Journeys: The Impact of Personal Experience on Religious Thought*. Ed. Gregory Baum. New York: Paulist Press, 1975a, 34–56.

New Woman/New Earth: Sexist Ideologies and Human Liberation. New York: Seabury Press, 1975b.

Sexism and God-Talk: Toward a Feminist Theology. Boston: Beacon Press, 1983.

Womanguides: Readings toward a Feminist Theology. Boston: Beacon Press, 1985a.

Women-Church: Theology and Practice of Feminist Liturgical Communities. San Francisco: Harper and Row, 1985b.

With Herman J. Ruether. *The Wrath of Jonah: The Crisis of Religious Nationalism in the Israeli-Palestinian Conflict.* San Francisco: Harper and Row, 1989.

"The Development of My Theology." *Religious Studies Review* 15 (1989a): 1–4.

Disputed Questions on Being a Christian. Maryknoll, NY: Orbis Books, 1989b, 22.

Ed., with Marc H. Ellis. *Beyond Occupation: American Jewish, Christian, and Palestinian Voices for Peace.* Boston: Beacon Press, 1990.

Gaia and God. San Francisco: Harper, 1992.

Ed. *Women Healing Earth: Third World Women on Ecology, Feminism and Religion.* Maryknoll, NY: Orbis Books, 1996.

WRITINGS ON ROSEMARY RUETHER AND HER WORK

Chopp, Rebecca S. "Seeing and Naming the World Anew: The Works of Rosemary Radford Ruether." *Religious Studies Review* 15 (1989): 8–11.

Rabuzzi, Kathryn Allen. "The Socialist Feminist Vision of Rosemary Radford Ruether: A Challenge to Liberal Feminism." *Religious Studies Review* 15 (1989): 4–8.

JOANNA RUSS
(1937–)

Jeanne Cortiel

Joanna Russ is one of the most consistent radicals among feminist science fiction writers. Reaching far beyond the scope of the genre, her work has influenced both feminist fiction and theory. The story of Russ' childhood, as projected in interviews and the scattered biographical material on her, introduces the major themes in her career as a writer and feminist critic. Russ was born on February 22, 1937, in New York City. She grew up in an exclusively Jewish neighborhood in the Bronx. Her mother loved literature, and her father had an avid interest in popular science. Nonreligious and committed to socialism, both parents were teachers and eager to share their knowledge and enthusiasm with their only child. In 1949, Russ was accepted to the Bronx High School of Science, in the first year it admitted female students. However, Russ chose not to attend, possibly not a willing decision since she attributes it to "family insanity" (Holt 1982, 483). In her senior year of high school, in 1953, she became one of the ten top finalists in the Westinghouse Science Talent Search. Yet her interest in literature and writing was at least equally strong. Her first published work, two poems, appeared when she was fifteen in *Epoch*. Even then, her writing rang with the courage and willingness to confront, which is such a marked characteristic of all her work. In "Not for Years but for Decades" (1985) she recollects writing a wistful lesbian short story in high school that, not surprisingly, mortified her teacher.

Thus, the tensions between literature, science, and the effective exclusion of women from both fields played an important role in Russ' early development. The image of the closet emerges as another major presence in her life story. In an interview with Donna Perry in 1993 she states, "I had kind of come out at the age of eleven and a half and gone in a few years later" (Perry 1993, 295). This tension with the closet, which for her, one could argue, stands for possibility rather than disguise, also structures Russ' fictional work as well as her development as a writer.

Russ' higher education and professional career permanently set the emphasis on language and literature rather than science. When she was twenty, in 1957, she graduated from Cornell University with distinction and high honors in English. Two years later, as a student of playwriting and dramatic literature at the Yale School of Drama, she inaugurated her science fiction career with the short story "Nor Custom Stale" (1959). In spite of her training and her love for the theater, Russ chose narrative rather than the "bare art" of drama for her writing: "Too much of what I write is internal" (Perry 1993, 293). In 1963, she married, but she separated from her husband only four years later. Since 1966, she has supported herself teaching speech, literature, and creative writing. Following the emergence of feminism's second wave, Russ thoroughly claimed its politics for herself and has, since then, continuously contributed her radical voice to the discourses of late twentieth-century American feminism.

Russ' health became one of the central concerns in her adult life. In the 1970s, she struggled with severe back pain, which was only partially relieved by an operation in 1978. For years, writing was a physical ordeal, since she could work only standing up, writing by hand. Moreover, in 1990, a debilitating disease diagnosed as chronic fatigue immune deficiency syndrome forced her to quit teaching at the University of Washington in Seattle, where she had been working since 1977. Although Russ continued to write letters and criticism, her most recent published fictional work, "Excerpts from a Forthcoming Novel," came out in 1986. Her back pain forced her to discontinue working on this project, which she had planned as a response to the television series *Star Trek*. In January 1994, Russ moved to Tucson, Arizona, for its dry and sunny climate. In spite of these tremendous health problems, however, she completed a monumental critical work on the intersections between socialism, feminism, and antiracism, *What Are We Fighting For? Sex, Race, Class, and the Future of Feminism*, published in 1997.

Russ' significance for feminism stems from both her critical and her fictional work. Fiercely materialist, partially essentialist, and joyfully deconstructive, Russ' work derives its momentum from the tensions among these positions. Yet there are other such dynamic contradictions in Russ' work, such as the tension between convention and its destruction, as well as between the assertion of lesbianism and its dissolution. These multilayered networks of tension between elements simultaneously present in the text produce the complexity and the explosive dynamic of Russ' fiction. Although feminism and lesbianism are not the only concerns of Russ' work, the two do structure her development as a writer. Her texts' disruptive representations of gender, sexuality, and female authorship unfold in three chronological stages, which could be labeled "pre-" or "protofeminist," "explicitly feminist," and "critically feminist," respectively. Each new stage does not, however, represent a complete paradigm transformation but rather a partial critique and development of earlier texts.

Russ' early fiction is characterized by first experiments with genre conventions and gender expectations. The themes that later texts develop as fully feminist, such as women's agency, intergenerational relationships between women, and the disruption of gender, already permeate her writing. The vampire story "My Dear Emily" (1962), which is among her finest early work, is a case in point. The story is set in the first half of the nineteenth century and fully utilizes the subversive potential of the vampire trope. Emily's nongenital sexual relation to the vampire Martin Guevara is finally displaced by her own desire for her female friend Charlotte's blood.

A different type of gender insubordination is the hallmark of Russ' popular sword-and-sorcery heroine Alyx, the unruly protagonist of a series of short stories and Russ' first novel, *Picnic on Paradise* (1968). Alyx constituted a major breakthrough both for Russ as a writer and for science fiction/fantasy in general. Russ says about creating the stories about Alyx: "It was one of the hardest things I ever did in my life. . . . [B]efore writing the first I spent about two weeks in front of my typewriter shaking, and thinking of how I'd be stoned in the streets, accused of penis envy, and so on (after that it is obligatory to commit suicide, of course)" ("Reflections" 1975, 42). Alyx boldly takes center stage. She runs away from her husband and saves a young woman from an arranged marriage. She joins a band of pirates, kills a powerful magician, and survives in the eternal ice of Paradise. She has passionate sex with men but remains independent of her lovers, forming primary relationships with women. The strategy in these stories is to recombine traditional plot patterns of quest and romance, reinterpreting them to make space for a female hero and agent in her own right.

Toward the end of the 1960s, Russ' fiction moves characters out of the closet. "Scenes from Domestic Life" (1968), a nongenre short story that has unjustly been neglected to date, is Russ' first published text that explicitly explores lesbian sexuality. Formally close to a play, the story has its only two characters, Miss Jones and Miss Edward, act out parodic roles of romance. With these two women, "Scenes" introduces a model for intimate relationships that becomes prominent in Russ' later work. In this model, one of the women is either literally an adolescent or plays that role vis-à-vis the other, older woman. The more experienced woman carves out a safe narrative space for the younger to create her own stories of self-determination. While the Alyx sequence avoids explicit sexuality in these intergenerational relationships, sexuality becomes the primary site for the younger woman's growth as an individual in Russ' later work.

Russ' second novel, *And Chaos Died* (1970), continues Russ' displacement of science fictional conventions. In contrast to "Scenes from Domestic Life," *And Chaos Died* experiments with gender and sexuality rather than with age to disrupt the heterosexual plot of romance. Although Jai Vedh, the protagonist, claims he is homosexual, a female genetic surgeon effortlessly seduces him when he is shipwrecked on the planet of her telepathic community. Since most of the plot takes place in his mind, his body remains supremely unstable. These instabilities, which relate Jai to the other "J's" in Russ' oeuvre, invite a reading of this character as "lesbian woman."

After these tentative beginnings, Russ' work enters explicit feminism with a flourish in the early 1970s. *The Female Man* (1975), completed three years before its publication, is Russ' most influential and most critically acclaimed novel. Its feminist, all-female utopia Whileaway had been introduced in the award-winning short story "When It Changed" (1972b), which went a few steps further than the Alyx sequence to revolutionize the genre. *The Female Man* increases the explosiveness of the short story's utopian vision by juxtaposing Whileaway to three other worlds that exist on parallel timelines. Again, Russ uses conventional science fictional tropes, weaving them into radically new combinations. *The Female Man*, as the title may suggest, explores new ways to express the separation of sex from gender and of gender from sexuality. The novel's conceptual complexity and multilayered narrative not only anticipated but also influenced later developments in feminism. Feminist science fiction as well as feminist cyberpunk drew crucial clues from Russ' work in general and *The Female Man* in particular.

Joanna Russ continued to develop her major themes in subsequent novels. *We Who Are About To . . .* (1975) interrogates the science fictional trope of survival and colonization of an alien planet. *Kittatinny* (1978) is a complex and fantastic rewriting of time-honored fairy tales, in which, for example, Sleeping Beauty has become a vampire because life was drained from her by her enforced virginal sleep. In *The Two of Them* (1978), Irene, a transtemporal agent from a quasi-egalitarian society, encounters a starkly misogynist culture on the planet Ka'abah. She ends up killing her male partner and lover to rescue the precocious and rebellious girl Zubeydeh, taking her back to her own home earth. The dreamlike final section of the novel encodes hope for change in a Blakeian apocalyptic vision. Russ' "coming out" novel, *On Strike against God* (1980) explores the possibilities of lesbian love and desire as well as individual selfhood.

Russ' exuberant and varied imagination is most amply expressed in her short stories. Many of these stories, which originally came out in such magazines as *The Magazine of Fantasy and Science Fiction*, were collected in the two volumes *The Zanzibar Cat* (1983) and *The Hidden Side of the Moon* (1987). The two collections together constitute a rich compendium of Russ' short fiction, spanning her career as an experimental science fiction and fantasy writer from 1959 to the mid-1980s. In the 1980s, Russ continued to critique the feminist tradition she had helped to create. The short story sequence or episodic novel *Extra(Ordinary) People* (1984), which contains the award-winning story "Souls," intensifies her interrogation of categories such as "woman" and "lesbian." The authorial voice's sex, clearly female in her earlier work, becomes uncomfortably ambiguous. The narrators lose reliability. Furthermore, a commentating computer voice questions the stories' glimpses of utopia, without, however, completely invalidating them.

Like so many writers in the genre, Russ is also a critic. Yet her criticism reaches far beyond science fiction to form a solidly radical cultural critique informed by materialist feminism as well as constructivism. Her essays "The Image of Women in Science Fiction" and "What Can a Heroine Do? or Why Women Can't Write" (winner of the Florence Howe Criticism Award) helped shape early feminist literary criticism in the 1970s (Russ 1995, 79–93). Since the late 1960s, Russ has also participated in creating feminist lesbian fiction and theory.

One of the central concerns of Russ' critical work is to analyze the ways in which women have existed in the "chinks" of literature, as characters and narrators as well as authors. In *How to Suppress Women's Writing* (1983) Russ identifies strategies with which the dominant culture has silenced women as writers. *Magic Mommas, Trembling Sisters, Puritans and Perverts: Feminist Essays* (1985) collects critical work on lesbianism and sexuality. In these six essays, aspects of which she herself characteristically critiques in the Introduction, Russ articulates her own coming out, representations of lesbian sexuality, and her stance in the infamous lesbian "sex wars" between the "Puritans" and the "Perverts." Without taking either side, she criticizes the opponents of sexual deviation for their simplistic biologism and their prescriptive concept of "feminine-ist" sexuality. Her most recent collection, *To Write like a Woman: Essays in Feminism and Science Fiction* (1995), brings together some of her finest critical work and includes scholarly essays as well as letters and book reviews.

Joanna Russ' fiction and criticism trouble comfortable feminist simplifications. Acknowledging the complexity of phenomena and the arbitrariness of causal links between events, Russ' work never lapses into monolithic affirmations of any one political dogma or strategy. Still, her work is always deeply political and moved by materialist feminist theory. Although her work always expresses a concern with women's material lives, it never settles on a conclusive definition of "Woman." Thus, her essentialism is more than merely strategic: although her texts utilize and acknowledge the political power of deconstructing language, they do not espouse the *absolute* contingency of material being. Keeping her affiliations both radical and contingent, Russ makes these paradoxes politically productive.

WORKS BY JOANNA RUSS

"Nor Custom Stale." *Magazine of Fantasy and Science Fiction* 17, no. 3 (1959): 75–86, reprinted in *The Hidden Side of the Moon*. London: The Women's Press, 129–137.
"My Dear Emily." *The Magazine of Fantasy and Science Fiction* (July 1962), reprinted in *The Zanzibar Cat*, New York: Baen, 1983.
Picnic on Paradise. New York: Ace, 1968a.
"Scenes from Domestic Life." *Consumption* 2, no. 1 (1968b): 22–33.
And Chaos Died. New York: Ace, 1970.
"The Image of Women in Science Fiction." *Images of Women in Fiction: Feminist Perspectives*. Ed. Susan Koppelman Cornillon. Bowling Green: Bowling Green University Press, 1972a, 79–94.
"What Can a Heroine Do? or Why Women Can't Write." *Images of Women in Fiction*, 1972b, 3–20.
The Female Man. New York: Bantam, 1975a.
We Who Are About To . . . New York: Dell, 1975b.
Kittatinny: A Tale of Magic. New York: Daughters, 1978a.
The Two of Them. New York: Berkley, 1978b.
On Strike against God. Trumansburg, NY: Out and Out Books, 1980; reprinted London: The Women's Press.

The Adventures of Alyx. New York: Simon and Schuster, 1983a.

How to Suppress Women's Writing. Austin: University of Texas Press, 1983b.

The Zanzibar Cat. New York: Baen, 1983c.

Extra(Ordinary) People. New York: St. Martin's Press, 1984.

Magic Mommas, Trembling Sisters, Puritans and Perverts: Feminist Essays. Crossing Press
     Feminist Series. Trumansburg, NY: Crossing Press, 1985a.

"Not for Years but for Decades." In *Magic Mommas, Trembling Sisters, Puritans and Perverts:
     Feminist Essays.* Crossing Press Feminist Series. Trumansburg, NY: Crossing Press,
     1985b, 17–42.

"Excerpts from a Forthcoming Novel." *The Seattle Review* 9, no. 1 (1986); 51–58.

The Hidden Side of the Moon. New York: St. Martin's Press, 1987.

To Write like a Woman. Essays in Feminism and Science Fiction. Bloomington and Indian-
     apolis: Indiana University Press, 1995.

What Are We Fighting For? Sex, Race, Class, and the Future of Feminism. New York: St.
     Martin's Press, 1998.

WRITINGS ON JOANNA RUSS AND HER WORK

Brownworth, Victoria. "Battling Back." *Lambda Book Report: A Review of Contemporary
     Gay and Lesbian Literature* (November/December 1994): 6–7.

Cortiel, Jeanne. *Demand My Writing: Joanna Russ/Feminism/Science Fiction.* Liverpool,
     U.K.: Liverpool University Press, forthcoming.

Delany, Samuel. "Orders of Chaos: The Science Fiction of Joanna Russ." *Women World-
     walkers: New Dimensions of Science Fiction and Fantasy.* Ed. Jane B. Weedman.
     Lubbock: Texas Tech Press, 1985, 95–123.

Gardiner, Judith Kegan. "Empathic Ways of Reading: Narcissism, Cultural Politics, and
     Russ's *Female Man.*" *Feminist Studies* 20, no. 1 (1994): 87–111.

Garland, Barbara. "Joanna Russ." *Dictionary of Literary Biography*, Vol. 8, *Twentieth Century
     American Science Fiction Writers.* Ed. David Coward and Thomas L. Wymer. De-
     troit: Gall Research, 1981, 88–93.

Hacker, Marilyn. "Science Fiction and Feminism: The Work of Joanna Russ." *Chrysalis*
     4 (1977): 67–79.

Holt, Marilyn J. "No Docile Daughters: A Study of Two Novels by Joanna Russ." *Room
     of One's Own* 6, nos. 1–2 (1981): 92–99.

———. "Joanna Russ." *Science Fiction Writers: Critical Studies of the Major Authors from
     the Early 19th Century to the Present Day.* Ed. E. F. Bleiler. New York: Charles
     Scribner's, 1982, 483–490.

Law, Richard. "Joanna Russ and the 'Literature of Exhaustion.' " *Extrapolation* 25 (1984):
     146–156.

Lefanu, Sarah. *In the Chinks of the World Machine: Feminism and Science Fiction.* London:
     Women's Press, 1988, Chapter 14, "The Reader as Subject: Joanna Russ."

McCaffery, Larry. "An Interview with Joanna Russ." *Across the Wounded Galaxies: Inter-
     views with Contemporary American Science Fiction Writers.* Ed. Larry McCaffery.
     Urbana and Chicago: University of Illinois Press, 1990, 176–210.

McClenahan, Catherine. "Textual Politics: The Uses of the Imagination in Joanna Russ's
     The Female Man." *Transactions of the Wisconsin Academy of Sciences, Arts, and
     Letters* 70 (1982): 114–125.

Murphy, Patrick. "Suicide, Murder, Culture, and Catastrophe: Joanna Russ's *We Who Are About To . . .*" *State of the Fantastic: Studies in the Theory and Practice of Fantastic Literature and Film.* Ed. Nicholas Ruddick. Westport, CT: Greenwood, 1992, 121–131.

Perry, Donna. "Joanna Russ." *Backtalk: Women Writers Speak Out.* Ed. Donna Perry. New Brunswick, NJ: Rutgers University Press, 1993, 287–311.

Platt, Charles. "Joanna Russ." *Dream Makers.* Ed. Charles Platt. Vol. 2. New York: Berkley Books, 1983.

"Reflections on Science Fiction: An Interview with Joanna Russ." *Quest: A Feminist Quarterly* 2 (1975): 40–49.

Rosinsky, Natalie. "A Female Man? The Medusan Humor of Joanna Russ." *Extrapolation* 23, no. 1 (1982): 31–36.

Shinn, Thelma J. "Worlds of Words and Swords: Suzette Haden Elgin and Joanna Russ at Work." *Women Worldwalkers: New Dimensions of Science Fiction and Fantasy.* Ed. Jane B. Weedman. Lubbock: Texas Tech Press, 1985, 207–222.

Spector, Judith A. "Dr. Jekyll and Mrs. Hyde: Gender-Related Conflict in the Science Fiction of Joanna Russ." *Extrapolation* 24 (1983): 370–379.

Spencer, Kathleen L. "Rescuing the Female Child: The Fiction of Joanna Russ." *Science Fiction Studies* 17, no. 2 (1990): 167–187.

Walker, Paul. "Joanna Russ." *Speaking of Science Fiction: The Paul Walker Interviews.* Ed. Paul Walker. Oradell, NJ: LUNA, 1978, 242–252.

PATRICIA SCHROEDER
(1940–)

John R. Nealis

Patricia Schroeder retired from her post as the longest-serving woman in the U.S. House of Representatives in December of 1996. She represented the First Congressional District of Colorado, having been first elected to that post in 1972 and subsequently reelected eleven times. She was referred to as the "ultra-liberal's ultra liberal" (Spencer 1995, 15) and as a maverick. Schroeder was an outspoken leader within the Democratic party and a national leader on subjects as far ranging as gun control, education, foreign policy, disarmament, women's economic equity and health, constitutional rights, and national policies affecting children, women, and families. Her service on Congressional committees included first female member of the Armed Services Committee, member of the House Judiciary Committee, and chair of the House Select Committee on Children, Youth, and Families. In this last role she was only the fourth woman this century to chair a House Committee. She has also been a Democratic whip since 1978.

One of Patricia Schroeder's most important contributions to the women's movement was as founder and co-chair of the Congressional Caucus for Women's Issues, a group that has grown, through Schroeder's influence, to number 150 members of Congress and to serve as a significant lobbying force. Often critical of sexist traditions in Congress, Schroeder commented that "women are still outside the 'Boy's Club' Congress" and that she and her female colleagues "have not been let into the 'Billionaire Boys' Club' yet" (Ferraro, July 1, 1990). Nevertheless, regardless of the odds against her as a woman in politics, Patricia Schroeder has left a strong presence in the Congress and shaped many national policies through legislative change. Her key bills dealt with women, family issues, and civil rights, and included the significant Family and Medical Leave Bill.

In addition to her long tenure in the House, Schroeder made her mark by running for President of the United States in 1987. Gender was a key issue in this brief and exploratory campaign. Schroeder noted later, "There was a tendency, from the very beginning, for the press to categorize me as a 'women's candidate.' Would the country see me that way or view me as a presidential candidate who happens to be a woman? I did not want my gender to block my message" (Schroeder 1989, 5). But since gender is often a factor in politics, Schroeder is always ready to address it. Often rebuked for "running as a woman," she has her now customary reply: an elaborate and well-staged shrug and the quip, "Do I have a choice?"

The legendary and searing Schroeder wit can "vaporize her opponent in the 15 seconds suitable for a sound bite" (Ferraro 1990, 13). It was she who labeled Ronald Reagan the "Teflon President" and who called defense contractors the "welfare queens" of the 1980s. During her first Congressional campaign, when asked how she could be both a mother and a Congresswoman, she snapped, "I have a brain and a uterus and I use both" (Ferraro 1990, 13).

Behind the scenes, though, the witty Schroeder does a surprising amount of homework and displays a "shrewd, even lethal political savvy" (Ferraro 1990, 14). It is a fitting tribute that Patricia Schroeder was inducted into the Women's Hall of Fame for her passage of legislature helping women and families. For twenty-four years in Congress, she became "part of the Establishment without sacrificing either the family issues she stands for or her independent style, both of which have always set her at odds with it" (Ferraro 1990, 14).

Clearly, Patricia Schroeder has evidenced her commitment to women's and family issues and her powerful drive to change systems she feels are unjust and discriminatory. Perhaps her most important contribution to the feminist movement is that she has "almost single-handedly wrenched family issues—child care and education, pension reform for widows and former spouses, flextime in the work place for parents and women's economic equity—out of the dim peripheries of campaign rhetoric and into the political mainstream" (Ferraro 1990, 15).

Patricia Scott Schroeder's background reads like a handbook for becoming an independent thinking, courageous, and dedicated legislator. She was born in Portland, Oregon, in 1940, and recalls being introduced to important social and political issues at an early age. Born to parents who had a strong sense of political participation and actively taught their children to be informed and to discuss issues, she recalls dinner table debates and being encouraged to "argue both sides of an issue" (Jerry and Spangle 1994, 396). Schroeder's family made numerous moves and to these she attributes her ability to be spontaneous and develop an easy conversational manner—a trait that became a keystone of her campaign and speaking style (Jerry and Spangle 1994, 396).

By the age of three, she learned how to make friends: she lined up her toys on the sidewalk and told her mother, "This ought to get 'em." "I was always the one trying to get in," she says. "But in a way, it's one of the things people struggle with all their lives—to define themselves. If you move a lot, then you define yourself." (Ferraro 1990, 13)

Schroeder's effectiveness as a contemporary feminist and outspoken social critic was also shaped, in part, by her family environment. Her parents encouraged her to believe that there was nothing she could not achieve. The woman known for her conspicuous smile often quotes advice her father gave her: "Never frown at your enemies. Smile—it scares the hell out of them" (Ferraro 1990, 13). She has also been deeply influenced by her family's "tradition of independent women," several of whom served as role models for her (Jerry and Spangle 1994, 396). This family tradition was brought home to her when her own mother, a teacher and " 'spunky' defender of working women" (Jerry and Spangle 1994, 396), decided to continue her career during World War II and put her daughter into daycare. Patricia Schroeder, carrying on the tradition, earned a pilot's license at age 15, graduated magna cum laude and Phi Beta Kappa from the University of Minnesota (1961), and was one of only nineteen women in her class of 554 at Harvard Law School (1964).

Patricia Schroeder's personal convictions and personal life, as well as her political and legislative victories, have placed her in the front ranks of the women's movement. Her life is a study in triumph over gender challenges. One of her first blatant experiences with sexism, which she has often related, concerns her graduation from Harvard Law School in 1962.

At Harvard, when I was ready to graduate, I went to the personnel office and they said, "Look, you know nobody wants to hire young women. First of all, you're married. You will probably want to have babies and they just aren't going to be interested. We only try to put our students out that we feel really have some chance." And I said, "I have been paying you guys for this degree for three years. What am I supposed to do with it—hang it over the sink?" They kind of laughed and said, "Guess so." (Jerry and Spangle 1994, 396)

Schroeder did not allow such bias to stop her. She began her career working as a field attorney for the National Labor Relations Board–CO-WY-UT, from 1964 to 1966, and as a lecturer at the University of Colorado, Denver–Regis College from 1969 to 1972. Simultaneously, she was the hearing officer for the Colorado Personnel Department from 1971 to 1972. The frantic pace of this legal career, however, did not stop her from also having children and developing her long-held and sincere convictions about women's equity, child care, and family issues from an experiential as well as an intellectual viewpoint.

During a second pregnancy that ended after seven months, Schroeder lost twins and came to grips with the appropriation of women's rights by the male dominated medical profession. The pregnancy had been problematic and Schroeder repeatedly told her doctor that something was wrong; he insisted she was simply "high strung." "Most of all I was angry at myself. . . . Here I was, a trained lawyer, letting a doctor convince me I had no right to question his judgment about my pregnancy and my baby. He intimidated me and made me feel powerless" (Ferraro 1990, 13). Years later, responding to the socioeconomic stresses brought to bear on the contemporary American family, Schroeder championed the cause of family medical leave. Her Family and Medical Leave Act provides both male and female workers with at least a minimum amount of job protection while they are out of work on unpaid leave at the birth of or adoption of a child, or for serious but temporary family illness. Schroeder took the child care issue directly to the voters and lobbied for it in Congress. When President Bush said he would veto "any kind of maternity leave bill," she accused him of "coming out against motherhood" (Ferraro 1990, 15). In 1990, the bill passed in the House 287 to 187, and the companion bill passed in the Senate four days later.

Schroeder also became adept at linking domestic issues with those of foreign policy and defense spending. In 1990 she pressed for a $300 billion cut over the following five years with at least half of that amount going to the deficit and the remainder going to education.

Patricia Schroeder combines public and personal assessments of life in contemporary American society in her 1989 book, *The Great American Family*. The work provides needed insight into Patricia Schroeder: Schroeder the Congressional leader, Schroeder the ardent feminist, and Schroeder the family member. She presents a clear rationale for her actions, convictions, and policies, but more importantly she offers a full "position paper," a blueprint for the ongoing Schroeder agenda.

At a book promotion in 1989 at the Ritz-Carlton in Boston, the author prefaced her comments about her book with these words. "When I grew up, every woman was looking for a prince and every man was looking for a mommy . . . The dream husband was going to have the money to give his wife things. My problem was I wanted wings" (Christy 1989, 33). Speaking on a more realistic level she states, "My husband is remarkable in that he has his ego under control. . . . There's no goal post in our home. We don't keep score of each other" (Christy 1989, 33). The tone of *The Great American Family* is as direct, personal and conversational as is her speaking and debating style. There is an engaging, confident, and informed voice to be heard in her writing. Especially crucial reading are the chapters entitled "The Serious Matter of Motherhood," "Child Care," and "Every Mother Is a Working Mother." These are vividly illustrated with personal experience, Congressional investigation, and plans of action.

As Patricia Schroeder presents the women's movement with a legacy of progress and challenge, she places the responsibility for continued reform upon women themselves. "If women remain ignorant of their role in history, they may be reluctant to participate in debates that will dictate the future of their children and their country" (Schroeder 1989, 22). Part of the challenge facing the equality of and empowerment of women in the United States is the continued propagation of the stereotypical male breadwinner and woman-wife myth, which Schroeder believes "continues to have a strong hold on some policy makers, educators and corporate executives" (Schroeder 1989, 22). According to Schroeder there are still outrageous policies that discriminate against women in the workplace and destroy their economic security. The time has come to cast off the mythical image of the American family. "I think we need to take back the traditional definition of the family . . . and get on with reinforcing it" (Schroeder 1989, 22).

In the chapter "A National Family Policy," Schroeder argues that a national family policy should have three basic goals: "to acknowledge the rich diversities of American families; to protect the family's well-being; and to provide families with flexible ways to meet their economic and social needs." She helps educate policymakers about the many kinds of American families and the diverse strengths and needs they have. "An understanding of this diversity is essential," she writes, "if we are to avoid creating government policy that penalizes families that don't fit a particular mold" (Schroeder 1989, 174).

Women's groups, labor groups, children's rights groups, and various religious groups have all, at times, spoken out on "family issues" when it has been politically expedient to do so. But Schroeder argues that no one group can "own" the American family. "The new family constituency should be a combination of these groups, not specifically the property of any one of them" (Schroeder 1989, 174). Rather than creating separate "camps" an effective "family constituency" must develop its own identity and a specific agenda. "The goal should be how to improve how the American family functions" (Schroeder 1989, 175). Schroeder cites the major problems facing families today: family violence, alcoholism, teen suicide, and drug abuse. What we do not need, she argues, is another "Just say no" approach; Schroeder sees the Select Committee on Children, Youth, and Families as an important force for research and progress.

During her career thus far, Patricia Schroeder has been a powerful force behind women's and family issues. One hallmark of her approach has been to bring so-called periphery issues to the forefront. "She has taken numerous topics previously dismissed as women's issues and recast them as family issues or, what's even more significant, as society's issues" (Jerry and Spangle 1994, 403). She has worked during her entire career to bring the voices and needs of real American women and American families out from the shadows. For example, the term "women and children," shibboleths of the patronizing male establishment, has been appropriated since our nation's founding to block real empowerment of women and to muddy the language of equality. Schroeder has used her own rhetorical expertise to clarify and expose such political manipulation. Speaking of defense budget cuts, the former Congresswoman updates the usage of "women and children." "Everything that is purchased for the military is bought in the name of protecting women and children. Maybe women would be safer if we had more battered women's shelters and fewer missiles" (Jerry and Spangle 1994, 403).

Again and again, through her political work, her wit, and her writing, Patricia Schroeder explores the realities and explodes the myths of life in the contemporary United States. She advocates for and models positive political changes. "Our government and our people should step out together and make a strong moral and practical commitment to the Great American Family. It is our country's future that is at stake" (Schroeder 1989, 176).

WORKS BY PATRICIA SCHROEDER

The Great American Family. New York: Random House, 1989.

Selected List of Major Speeches and Interviews

"Great Expectations: From Abigail Adams to the White House." Address for the Alfred
     M. Landon Lectures on Public Issues. Kansas State University. March 19, 1984.
"Is America Better Off?" Address, National Press Club. September 23, 1987.
"Education and Family Issues Facing America." Speech to the Conference of the Coalition
     of Higher Education Assistance Organizations. January 19, 1988.
"Address For the Great American Family Tour." Columbia, S.C. February 23, 1988.
Interview on Abortion Rights. "MacNeil/Lehrer News Hour," July 3, 1989. Trans. No.
     3506.
"Leadership Death." Address, National Press Club. June 25, 1991.
"Women in Politics." "Listening to America with Bill Moyers." PBS. May 19, 1992.
"Interview with Family Values." "CNN Newsmaker Saturday." May 23, 1992. Trans. No.
     114.

WRITINGS ON PATRICIA SCHROEDER AND HER WORK

"Bring Our Troops Back Home—And Save Four Billion." *Washington Post,* June 24, 1990,
     Sec. C: 5.
Cantor, Dorothy W., and Tony Bernay. *Women in Power: The Secrets of Leadership.* Boston:
     Houghton Mifflin, 1992.
Christy, Marian. "Schroeder Without Tears." *Boston Globe,* February 26, 1989, 33.
Congressional Directory: 103 Congress. Washington D.C.: U.S. Government Printing Of-
     fice, 1994.
"Dean of Women in Congress to Retire." *U.S.A. Today,* November 30, 1995, Sec. A: 1
Ferraro, Susan. "The Prime of Pat Schroeder." *New York Times Magazine,* July 1, 1990,
     12–15.
Jerry, E. Clair, and Michael Spangle. "Patricia Schroeder." In *Women Public Speakers in
     the United States: 1925–1993.* Ed. Karlyn Kohrs Campbell. Westport, CT: Green-
     wood Press, 1994, 395–408.
"Pat Schroeder." *Citizen's Toolbox: U.S. News Online.* U.S. News & World Report, Inc.
     (AGT).
"Schroeder, Wirth Back Pro-Choice Bill." *Denver Post,* November 18, 1989, Sec. A: 2.
"Schroeder To Lead Panel on Children, Families." *Denver Post,* March 1, 1989, Sec. A:
     22.
"Schroeder Hails Vote for Women in Combat." *Denver Post,* May 9, 1991, Sec. A: 9.
"Schroeder Hails Gains on Issues For Women." *Denver Post,* December 3, 1993, Sec. A:
     14.
Spencer, Gil. "Standing Pat in Congress." *Denver Post,* June 25, 1995, Sec. E:1+.
Summers, Anne. "Pat Schroeder: Fighting for Military Moms." *Ms.* 1 (May/June 1991):
     90–91.

"Three Put Assault Weapons on Hit List." *Denver Post*, January 19, 1994, Sec. B: 2.
"To Cut Abortions, Cut Unwanted Pregnancies." *Atlanta Journal Constitution*, February 10, 1990, Sec. A: 22.
"U.S. Must Not Condone Abuses Against Women Elsewhere." *Atlanta Journal Constitution*, March 30, 1990, Sec. A: 11.
"Women's Hall of Fame Gains New Members, Calls For More Progress." *Christian Science Monitor*, October 16, 1995, 14.

ELEANOR SMEAL
(1939–)

Pat Murphy

"Until justice is ours": a rallying cry for feminists and Eleanor Smeal. A self-described "full time troublemaker for the [rights of] women since 1970" (Miller 1994), Smeal's activism, energy, and vision focus on justice for all women. Over the last quarter century she has been at the forefront of every major civil rights battle for women. Whether organizing against anti–affirmative action Proposition 209 in California, lobbying to bring the drug RU 486 into the country, encouraging feminists to run for office, fighting for the Equal Rights Amendment (ERA), or integrating Little League baseball, Smeal has been at the front line.

Smeal, a former three-term president of the National Organization for Women (NOW), is current president of the Fund for the Feminist Majority (FFM). The 1993 *World Almanac* selected Smeal as one of the most influential women in America. *Time Magazine* named her one of the "fifty faces for America's future," and *U.S. News and World Report* listed her as one of Washington's most influential lobbyists.

Eleanor Marie Cutri Smeal grew up with three older brothers, the daughter of first-generation Catholic Italian Americans. Her mother "always felt like she had been cheated and encouraged me to do everything" (Smeal in Koeppel 1995, 32). She attended public schools in Erie, Pennsylvania, because her mother wanted her exposed to the diversity of students there. Her father was a champion for the underdog, giving her a sense of justice (*Ms.* 1978).

Like many second wave feminists, her progressive activism started in the 1960s civil rights movement. As an undergraduate she realized how racially segregated Duke University was and fought to integrate the school, using many of the techniques that would characterize her later feminist activism. She picketed, supported pro-integration candidates, and voted for integration (Meyers 1995). Dissuaded from law school by professors who told her women didn't practice law, she later pursued graduate studies in political science at the University of Florida, receiving her M.A. in 1963. There she met Charles Smeal, marrying him on April 27, 1963.

In 1971 she began research on women's attitudes toward women in politics at the University of Pittsburgh (Koeppel 1995). Almost a quarter century ago, her research indicated that 80 percent of women wanted more women running for office (Smeal 1984a). She herself was on the board of the local League of Women Voters and from 1968 to 1972 served as secretary/treasurer of the Allegheny County Council.

Smeal has recognized the problems all women, especially mothers, face. She spent some time as a stay-at-home mom with her son Tod and daughter Lori. A back ailment forced her to spend a year of complete bed rest. She used the time to read about historical and contemporary feminism. Eventually, she wanted to go back to school and finish her Ph.D. Concerned about the lack of day-care availability, she founded the South Hills NOW Day Nursery School in 1971, enrolling Lori in the first class. She also served as its administrator (Davis 1991).

Later, under Smeal's presidency, NOW sponsored the National Assembly on the Future of the Family. In her address she demanded that women and men stop discriminating against wives and mothers like herself. "Women have been society's built-in, unpaid house workers, caring for the very young, the sick, elderly, disabled—those for whom society is unwilling to provide" (Reuters n.d.).

Eleanor Smeal joined NOW with her husband in 1970. She became president of the local Pittsburgh NOW chapter, and her phone became a NOW hot line where calls about job discrimination and violence against women poured in (Davis 1991). From that point on, women's rights became the outlet for her civic and intellectual energy. In 1972, she became president of Pennsylvania NOW, then chair of the national NOW board in 1975. In 1977 she became the first paid NOW national president, serving from 1977 to 1982. During that time she directed the Equal Rights Campaign and founded the NOW Political Action Committee, raising funds for feminist candidates. She became president again of NOW from 1985 to 1987. In 1987 she cofounded FFM with Peg Yorkin and serves as president.

Smeal defines feminism broadly. She is an advocate of increasing girls' sports participation. She won a lawsuit against the state of Pennsylvania for its policy that no female could practice or compete with a male in the state's secondary schools (Miller 1994). She picketed the Little League World Series to open baseball to girls. She has organized on college campuses such as Brown University, supporting their Title XI bias suit (Miller 1994). During the 1996 Olympics, FFM highlighted discrimination against women athletes on their World Wide Web page, pointing out how many countries have no women team members and how Iran officially prohibits women from Olympic participation, an action contrary to the Olympics' charter. Information was publicized, and links enabled people to e-mail the International Olympic Committee or print out and send petitions (http://www.feminist.org/action/action22.html 1996).

Smeal is perhaps best known for her leadership in the ERA campaign. When she assumed the presidency of NOW in 1977, the ERA deadline was eighteen months away. Smeal analyzed the voting record of the fifteen nonratified states and concluded that ratification before the deadline was impossible (Davis 1991). Two NOW members in law school proposed to Smeal that NOW ask Congress to extend ERA's ratification deadline, based on the fact that no previous amendment had had a time limit (Carabillo, Meuli, and Csida 1993). Smeal then strategized to "take it to the streets" and organized a massive march with the theme of "A Passion for the Possible" in Washington on July 9, 1978. In August, Congress passed a resolution by Elizabeth Holtzman and extended the deadline to June 30, 1982. Smeal's leadership galvanized grassroots activists, increasing NOW membership. However, without ERA supporters in the legislatures the ratification failed, in spite of popular support. Smeal later said that "at every step of the ERA fight we felt women were regarded as politically expendable" (Davis 1991, 418).

NOW in general and Smeal in particular are criticized for advocating white, middle-class feminism. During the ERA campaign, NOW tried to increase ERA support by organizing in minority neighborhoods, a tactic that some argue ignored the need and priorities of African American and minority women. In 1979 NOW elected an all-white group of officers for the second term in a row. Smeal was criticized for failing to support Sharon Parker, the only black woman running for national office (Buechler 1990). Following a 1995 speech at Northeastern University, African American women criticized the feminist movement for leaving them out. In response, Smeal answered that "we shouldn't allow this country to divide us by race . . . when that happens, nobody wins" (Irons 1995). She does, however, frequently work in coalitions on issues that cross racial and class lines. For example, in 1996 she organized extensively with Dolores Huerta on the campaign to counteract Proposition 209, which abolished affirmative action in California. The Feminist Majority was one of the largest providers of resources and staff in the drive to defeat that initiative. Smeal sees the nationwide attacks on affirmative action as an opportunity to unite women across racial and class lines.

The ERA loss led Smeal to the realization that women need political power to achieve justice and equality. In a 1980 issue of the *National NOW Times*, Smeal noted in a headline that "Women Vote Differently than Men . . . Feminist Bloc Emerges in 1980 Elections" (*National NOW Times*, 1980). This was the first article to note and name the "gender gap" in electoral politics. Smeal announced a strategy to elect feminist candidates in Florida and Illinois, two states where the ERA was bitterly contested. NOW members reminded the anti-ERA legislators that "we'll remember in November."

Barred by NOW bylaws from a third term as president, she wrote *Why and How Women Will Elect the Next President: The Gender Gap: What It Is and What It Means to You*. The book outlines the importance of voting and offers a step-by-step guide to getting organized, raising funds, and running for office. Smeal argues that if you elect feminists into the system, you can transform it. At the

1984 national NOW conference Smeal authored a resolution that if a woman
was not on the Democratic presidential ticket, NOW would take the nomination
to a floor fight at the convention. While this decision and NOW's prenomination
endorsement of Mondale have been criticized because of its movement away from
bipartisanship, the candidacy of Geraldine Ferraro for the vice presidency of the
United States permanently changed the face of politics and paved the way for
NOW support of Pat Schroeder's (D–CO) run for the presidency in 1988.

Smeal returned to NOW's presidency in 1985. NOW had been led for three
years by moderate Judy Goldsmith, whom Smeal had supported in the 1982
election over the more radical Sonia Johnson. Smeal felt by 1986 that, given the
impact of the Reagan presidency, the time had come for more militant leadership.
NOW's membership had dropped from 230,000 in 1983 to 150,000 in 1986.
Smeal favored returning to a confrontational style. Smeal remarked, "It's time
to put a lot more heat on the right wing and the reactionary policies of the right
wing. I intend to raise a little more hell" (Carabillo, Meuli, and Csida 1993,
116). Under her leadership, NOW organized the largest march for woman's rights
in U.S. history in Washington, D.C., on March 9, 1986. NOW also campaigned
for the Vermont ERA and narrowly lost.

After leaving the presidency of NOW in 1987, Smeal cofounded FFM with
Peg Yorkin. While NOW is a grassroots organization, with numerous local chapters and an emphasis on consciousness-raising, education, and activism, the FFM
is more centralized and activist. The FFM argues that the majority of citizens are
feminists and need to be empowered and integrated into governing structures.
This is accomplished by getting women involved and active in feminist political
struggles, especially as elected officials, and by working on state-level initiatives.
The first action taken by FFM was the "Feminization of Power Campaign" in
eight states and thirty-nine cities to increase the number of women running for
office.

The FFM focuses on diverse issues and utilizes a range of technologies and
strategies. One of the first issues Smeal focused on was abortion. To counter
antichoice activists, FFM produced videos: *Abortion for Survival* and *Abortion
Denied, Shattering Young Women's Lives*. The videos dramatize the impact of illegal abortion on women worldwide and on young women like Becky Bell, who
died as a result of an illegal abortion. These videos are educational and organizing
tools for college campuses and states where abortion restrictions are being debated. Smeal recruited Bell's parents to testify in states where parental-consent
abortion bills were proposed. Smeal worked to bring RU 486 into the United
States, first going over personally to meet representatives of Roussel Uclaf, the
manufacturer, and later returning with a scientific delegation. Under her direction, the FFM became expert trainers in clinic defense and successfully prevented
many abortion clinic blockades. In the fall of 1991, FFM and rock band L7
founded Rock for Choice, mobilizing music fans to organize for reproductive
freedom and register voters.

Smeal envisions equal representation of women in governance. In addition to encouraging women to run for office, Smeal has pressed to get more women appointed to positions at all levels of government. The goal is gender balance, a fifty-fifty representation, by the year 2000 (Carabillo, Meuli, and Csida 1993).

Aware of the importance women's perspectives bring to social policy, Smeal pushed integration of one of the most male-dominated professions, policing. Following the Los Angeles riots, the FFM launched the National Center for Women and Policing and sponsored a national conference on women and policing to increase the numbers of women in law enforcement (*Fund* 1995). Smeal argued that more women in policing would improve domestic violence victims' rights.

Smeal devotes significant time to college campus campaigning and organizing. She sees young people as vital to the growth and continuation of the women's movement. In addition to speaking on campuses, she meaningfully integrates students into the FFM. She sponsors internships and made college students an integral part of FFM's "Expo '96 for Women's Empowerment." This conference developed an agenda for the feminist movement and publicized the movement's diversity (FFM, "First-Ever" 1996). Smeal used the conference's energy to "hook" the young feminists. Free lodging was exchanged for volunteer labor during the conference, thus getting young women involved in the work of the feminist movement and rewarding them for their labor. During the conference students were recruited for "Freedom Summer 1996," an effort to register voters and build opposition to California's Proposition 209. The action was patterned after the 1964 Freedom Campaign in Mississippi.

Smeal wants feminism's message disseminated to the largest number of people possible. The large marches on Washington increased membership, motivated activists, and publicized NOW. While women's rights organizations, particularly NOW, were slow to utilize growing computer technology, Smeal seized upon the Internet as a significant organizing tool.

On August 26, 1995, Women's Equality Day, the Feminist Majority Foundation, the FFM's educational arm, announced their World Wide Web site. Smeal announced that "this is a major effort to . . . increase the number of women internet users. . . . This technology levels the playing field for women" (FFM, "Feminist Majority Foundation" 1995). Smeal argues, "We have the opportunity to organize with people across the world as if they were right next door. . . . Technology is like the wind at our backs; we must use it to bring justice to more people" (Pindak 1995). The site contains practical information, and each page has links enabling users to respond to policymakers.

For a quarter century Eleanor Smeal has determined the agenda of major women's rights organizations. Her focus includes traditional feminist issues such as abortion, violence against women, lesbian rights, and equal rights and contemporary ones like access to the Internet. The women's movement and she have been criticized for their championing of issues that mainly appeal to white, middle-class/professional women. To some extent this criticism is valid. Her move to take her organizing to the Internet privileges those with the resources to utilize it. Poor, minority, inner-city women will not have the same access as professionals. Likewise, her organizing on college campuses reaches only some young women, not all. Yet the issues around which she organizes and her focus on the importance of the gender gap stress the common experiences and interests of women, experiences that transcend race and class.

The issues on which Smeal organizes ultimately benefit all women. The use of RU 486 will make abortions more accessible and less expensive, increasing their availability to women who live where there is no abortion provider, predominantly poor, rural women. Educational equity also benefits all girls. Increasing the representation of women in positions of governance and leadership will ultimately ensure that the women's voices and needs are addressed. At that time justice will be ours.

WORKS BY ELEANOR SMEAL

And Audrey Wells. "Women's Attitudes toward Women in Politics: Survey of Urban Registered Voters and Party Committeewomen." *Research on Women in Politics*. Ed. Jane Jaquette. Towson, MD: Goucher College, 1977.

National Organization for Women Address. Videocassette. City Club Forum, Cuyahoga Community College Learning Resources Program, November 17, 1978.

"Eleanor Smeal Reacts as President of NOW to Defeat of the ERA in Illinois." Sound reel. ABC-TV, June 19, 1980.

"Equal Rights Amendment." *Feminist Articles and Leaflets*. Pittsburgh: KNOW, 1981.

Eleanor Smeal Report. Washington, DC: Eleanor Smeal and Associates, 1983–1990.

Maximizing the Women's Vote '84: A Study Prepared for the Democratic National Committee: Final Report. Washington, DC: Eleanor Smeal Associates, 1984a.

Why and How Women Will Elect the Next President. New York: Harper and Row. 1984b.

"Smeal Address." Recording. National Press Club. Washington, DC: National Public Radio, September 5, 1985.

"The Feminization of Power." Recording. National Press Club. Washington, DC: National Public Radio, July 8, 1987.

Abortion for Survival. Videocassette. Los Angeles, CA: Feminist Majority, 1989.

Abortion Denied: Shattering Young Women's Lives. Videocassette. Los Angeles, CA: Feminist Majority, 1990a.

Election Results Effect on Women. Videocassette. Purdue University Public Affairs Video Archives. C-SPAN, November 7, 1990b.

Supreme Court Nomination of David Souter. Videocassette. Tape 4. U.S. Senate Judiciary Committee, September 18, 1990c.

"Comment: RU 486: The Moral Imperative." *Chemistry and Industry*, no. 18 (September 21, 1992a).

"Empowering Women in Iowa; The Fight for Equal Rights." University Lecture Series, Iowa State University, April 15, 1992b.

"Viewpoint." *Glamour* 93 (October 1995): 148.

Carabillo, Toni, Judith Meuli, Eleanor Smeal, and Jennifer Jackman. *Teach Women's History Teacher's Guide*, 1995. [http://www.feminist.org/news/research/teach1.html].

"From Gender Gap to Gender Gulf: Abortion, Affirmative Action and the Radical Right."
   National Press Club Address. February 13, 1997 [http:///www.feminst.org/news/pr/
   pr021397.html].

WRITINGS ON ELEANOR SMEAL AND HER WORK

Buechler, Steven M. *Women's Movements in the United States: Woman Suffrage, Equal Rights and Beyond*. New Brunswick, NJ: Rutgers University Press, 1990.

"Eleanor Smeal." *Current Biography*. New York: H. W. Wilson, 1980.

Bond, Stephanie. "A Rhetorical Analysis of Eleanor Smeal and Judy Goldsmith." Thesis, Colorado State University, 1995.

Carabillo, Toni, Judith Meuli, and June Bundy Csida. *The Feminist Chronicles, 1953–1993*. Los Angeles: Women's Graphics, 1993.

Davis, Flora. *Moving the Mountain*. New York: Simon and Schuster, 1991.

Donovan, Josephine. "Eleanor Smeal." *Encyclopedia of World Biography: 20th Century Supplement*. Vol. 15. Palatine, IL: Jack Heraty and Associates, 1987, 329–330.

"Eleanor Smeal." *Ms.* (February 1978).

Fund for the Feminist Majority. *Feminist Majority Report*. Arlington, VA: Feminist Majority, 1988–.

———. "Feminist Majority Foundation Announces Major WWW Site on the Internet." FFM Press Release, August 30, 1995.

———. "Demand That the International Olympic Committee Respect the Olympic Charter's Anti Discrimination Provisions." FFM Online, 1996a [http://www.feminist.org/action/action22.html].

———. "First-Ever National Feminist Exposition to Be Held in Washington, DC." FFM Press Release, January 17, 1996b.

———. Feminist Majority Foundation Homepage. [http://www.feminist.org] 1996–.

Irons, Meghan. "Smeal: Women Must Unite." *Northeastern Voice* (December 7, 1995): 2. [http://155.33.212.105/voice/951207/feminist.html].

Koeppel, Barbara. "Eleanor Smeal: The Progressive Interview." *The Progressive* 15 (November 1995): 32–34.

Mitogen, Timothy. "FI Interview: Eleanor Smeal on Feminism Present and Future." *Free Inquiry* 15 (Spring 1995): 21–23.

Meyers, Mandora. "Feminist Leader Ellie Smeal Speaks on Tough Issues." *The Phoenix Online* (November 10, 1995) [http://www.sccs.swarthmore.edu/or/phoenix/arch/95/11/10/front/speaker.html].

Miller, Marshall. "Eleanor Smeal Discusses Title IX." *Brown Daily Herald*, February 4, 1994.

Multimedia Entertainment. *ERA: Pro and Con*. Videocassette. A Phil Donohue Show Presentation, 1979.

National Organization for Women. *Do It NOW: Monthly Action Newsletter of the National Organization for Women*. Chicago: NOW, 1968–1977.

———. *National NOW Times*, Washington, DC, 1977–.

———. *NOW's the Anniversary Show*. Videocassette. Los Angeles, CA: Peg Yorkin Productions, 1986.

———. NOW Homepage. [http://www.now.org].

Pindak, Kasha. "Feminist Majority Head Issues U. Wake-up Call." *Brown Daily Herald*, November 17, 1995, 1.

Reuters. "Feminists Tackle Bias against Wife–Mother Role," n.d. Reuter online [http://www.bconnex.net/~SPCC/daycare/tackle.html].

BARBARA SMITH
(1946–)

Jaime M. Grant

One of the most significant founding mothers of black feminist theory and practice in the United States, Barbara Smith has spent thirty years "making a way out of no way" as a scholar, activist, and teacher. Smith came of age in the thick of the civil rights and antiwar struggles, the imprint of these movements evident in her refusal to separate writing from teaching, theory from action, and feminist struggle from antiracist and class struggle. Having developed radical ideas through right action, Smith's life work has long posed a challenge to academics and activists rooted in a rarefied or single-issue praxis.

Smith was born in the segregated North in 1946 into a thriving black community in Cleveland, Ohio. Her family had come to Cleveland amid great masses of rural, southern blacks who migrated to northern cities in search of a better life. Smith notes that her activism is steeped in the reality of those times:

What I saw (the women in my family) endure at the hands of the outside world politicized me long before I became part of any movement. My mother died at age thirty-four from a disease that might not have been fatal if she had been born middle-class and white and I learned then all that I would need to know about injustice and the poison of anger that has no useful outlet. (Smith, July 1997 interview)

In high school in the early 1960s, Smith became active in school desegregation efforts and worked as a volunteer with the Congress of Racial Equality (CORE). During this period, she attended several speeches by Dr. Martin Luther King, Jr., and met Mississippi activist Fannie Lou Hamer on one "unforgettable night" following a civil rights rally. In 1965, she became one of a handful of black students who desegregated Mount Holyoke's campus and was swept up by the budding black power movement and antiwar activism. In 1968, she spent a year at the New School for Social Research, a pivotal year in which Dr. King and

Robert Kennedy were assassinated and in which she took part in the antiwar demonstrations at the Chicago Democratic National Convention.

Moving into graduate school directly after college, in the wake of four years of intense activism, Smith felt caught in the rigidity of black nationalist views of black women. She remembers:

I found the rigid sex roles that Black women were expected to play intolerable; this, combined with my hidden lesbian feelings, made me very much an outsider. I was aware of the newly forming women's movement, but despite my ability to identify with many of the issues, I was not motivated to join because the movement seemed so monolithically white. (Smith, July 1997 interview)

In the early 1970s, Smith was reenergized by the emerging black feminist movement. In 1972, she audited a course on Black Women Writers given by then-largely-unknown writer/activist Alice Walker. In class, Smith was able to discuss and shape her early feminist thinking on black women's lives. Then in 1973, she went to the first eastern regional meeting of the National Black Feminist Organization (NBFO), organized by Ms. magazine editor Margaret Sloan in New York City. From her first moments at the conference, Smith "knew I was home."

For more than twenty years following her first NBFO gathering, Smith has been both a definer and a champion of black feminism at the academy and community levels. In the early 1970s, she cofounded the Combahee River Collective, a group of black feminists who did pro-labor, antiracist, feminist organizing around a multiplicity of issues facing Boston's black community in an era that saw the violent desegregation of the Boston public schools. Combahee's "Black Feminist Statement" served as an early manifesto for identity politics, presenting a theory hewn out of their black feminist practice:

We are actively committed to struggling against racial, sexual, heterosexual, and class oppression and see as our particular task the development of integrated analysis and practice based upon the fact that the major systems of oppression are interlocking. The synthesis of these oppressions creates the conditions of our lives. As Black women, we see Black feminism as the logical political movement to combat the manifold and simultaneous oppressions that all women of color face. (In Smith, Home Girls 1982, 272)

In 1979, when more than a dozen black women were killed in Boston's contiguous black neighborhoods in the space of four months, the Combahee River Collective was able to act as a bridge between white feminist, mainstream black, and feminist of color communities to mobilize resistance to the violence. In the context of the severe racial polarization following Boston's public school desegregation, the collective's activism set a standard for coalition politics that would take up the imagination of feminist scholars and activists throughout the 1980s and beyond.

On the academic front, Smith spent the mid-1970s bringing black feminist theory and practice to white-dominated women's studies programs and male-dominated black studies programs through a series of talks on college campuses. In 1974, she served as the first woman of color on the Modern Language Association's Commission on the Status of Women, eventually shaping the association's first panels on black women's literature at its annual conference in 1975. At that time, she began work on *All the Women Are White*, the nation's first black women's studies anthology, recruiting poet Gloria T. Hull and social scientist Patricia Bell Scott as coeditors.

Smith describes the importance of black feminist studies as a basis for activism:

On an academic level, the work gives you a great deal of inspiration and hope—because you can look at history, you can look at how people before you came out of desperate condition. You realize that you're working for a kind of society that you may indeed never see. You try not to let stitches drop. (Smith, July 1997 interview)

In 1976, Smith met poet/activist Audre Lorde at a Modern Languages Association conference in which Lorde remembered Smith's standing up and saying, in effect: I'm a black, lesbian feminist; how am I going to survive? Lorde thought to herself—I've got to get my work out there more; this beautiful young woman has got to know there's a way! So their sixteen-year relationship began, an intense personal, professional, and political friendship that would profoundly impact them both.

In 1980, Smith, Lorde, and writer/activist Cherríe Moraga founded Kitchen Table: Women of Color Press, which remains the sole women of color-directed press in the nation. Kitchen Table books, including Smith's *Home Girls: A Black Feminist Anthology*, have since transformed the conversation on racism, sexism, and homophobia in classrooms and in movement settings for the past fifteen years. As the harbingers of identity politics, Kitchen Table writers have emerged as some of the most important feminist academics and activists of color of their time, including Gloria Anzaldúa, Donna Kate Rushin, Cheryl Clarke, and Merle Woo.

From 1980 to 1994, Smith served as the publisher and primary engine for Kitchen Table Press. In doing so, she forfeited many of the benefits that her peers accrued in that time: consistent paychecks, professorships, time and space to research and write. She also managed to produce an impressive array of reviews, critical essays, and lectures.

Smith's particular contribution as a trailblazing, black, lesbian feminist has been to challenge heterosexual women and men about the diversity of sexual expressions within a black context. Simultaneously, she has raised the issue of racism within the lesbian and gay movement, creating an expanded definition of lesbian and gay issues and politics. Perhaps most importantly, in taking up this work, she has provided a generation of black lesbian, gay, bisexual, and trans-gendered people visible, uncompromising leadership.

A winner of numerous awards, including the Stonewall Award for outstanding service to lesbian and gay communities and the Lambda Award for excellence in publishing, Smith is finally doing the work she loves best, researching and writing. Her current project is a history of African American gay, lesbian, bisexual, and transgendered people in the United States. Like most of Smith's work, she is creating a manuscript that has no predecessors, creating the work she herself needs to survive.

WORKS BY BARBARA SMITH

Home Girls: A Black Feminist Anthology. New York: Kitchen Table: Women of Color Press, 1982.

All the Women Are White, All the Blacks Are Men, But Some of Us Are Brave: Black Women's Studies. Ed. Gloria T. Hull, Patricia Bell Scott, and Barbara Smith. Old Westbury, NY: Feminist Press, 1982.

With Elly Bulkin, Minnie Bruce Pratt, and Barbara Smith. *Yours in Struggle: Three Feminist Perspectives on Anti-Semitism and Racism.* Ithaca, NY: Firebrand Books, 1984.

With Wilma Mankiller, Gwendolyn Mark, Marysa Navarro, and Gloria Steinem, eds. *The Reader's Companion to the History of American Women.* Boston: Houghton Mifflin, 1998.

WRITINGS ON BARBARA SMITH AND BLACK FEMINISM

Collins, Patricia Hill. *Black Feminist Thought: Knowledge, Consciousness, and the Politics of Empowerment.* Boston: Unwin Hyman, 1990.

Grant, Jaime. "Who's Killing Us?" *Femicide.* Ed. Diana E. H. Russell. New York: Twayne Press, 1992.

Lorde, Audre. *Sister Outsider: Essays and Speeches.* Trumansburg, NY: Crossing Press, 1984.

GLORIA STEINEM
(1934–)

Ann Mauger Colbert

Gloria Steinem, pioneer feminist magazine publisher and activist in the modern feminist movement, is known for her early journalism, including a humorous "undercover" foray into the Playboy Bunny Club in 1963 that was turned into a movie, for her campaigns to help women professionally and economically, and for her continuous efforts to successfully publish a magazine that would address the real concerns of women of all classes. A spokesperson for the women's movement of the 1960s, she seems to be asking herself most recently how and why she became the voice for the movement (Steinem 1993). This central question to her identity is also taken up by Carolyn Heilbrun in a recent biography. To what degree was Steinem's role constructed by the media she represented? Was she treated fairly, or did the continuous remarks about her physical appearance underplay the significance of her accomplishments? How much of a spokesperson has she been?

Steinem, born in Toledo, Ohio, on March 25, 1934, had an unconventional life that has been recounted with poignancy by Steinem herself and by others. Indeed, her childhood seems to have placed her in the role of "mother" to her own mother. Because her parents were divorced, and her mother was mentally ill, she was forced to be the responsible one while still a child. At the age of ten, with her sister at college and her parents separated, young Gloria Steinem began to take care of her mother. They moved to Toledo and into the house that her mother had inherited. The house, located in a slowly deteriorating, working-class neighborhood, offered some security, but when Steinem attempted to write about these experiences in *Revolution from Within*, she writes that nausea assaulted her. As she puts it, as a child she had lain in her upper bunk waiting for her mother to allow her to be sick and to take care of her; when she realized that no help could come, that her mother was always to be the sicker one, she climbed down and coped (Steinem 1983, 134; Steinem 1992, 35–38).

Steinem writes of what has been described by biographers as brutal, ugly childhood poverty; she recalls that keeping her toes under the covers was a protection from being bitten by rats. While the stories of her poverty have been questioned, a letter to a Toledo paper from another person who resided there corroborates many details (Heilbrun 1995, 25). Clearly, as her mother's illness got worse, the poverty and details of their life in a ramshackle, upstairs room got worse. Nevertheless, the experiences somehow gave her a strength and an open-mindedness about possibilities for women. The young Gloria apparently tried to keep in her mind the stories of her mother's early life, during which she earned a master's degree in history and worked as a journalist writing under a male pseudonym. In fact, her mother had had a secret desire to go to New York and work there as a journalist, a desire that was to play itself out in Gloria Steinem's own life. Positive experiences with an unconventional father also added to her ability to move beyond both the poverty and the solidly middle-class expectations of the times.

Steinem often found herself in the role of guardian to a mentally ill parent. Certainly, she found herself reacting to circumstances over which she felt she had to exercise control, even as other girls her age were able to enjoy their girlhoods. Her young life included dancing for money and entering a beauty pageant during her high school years. She was "rescued" at the end of her junior year in high school, when her father agreed to care for her mother for a year. Heilbrun writes that the rescue came at the point when Steinem's life might otherwise have become a disaster (1995, Heilbrun 1995, 32).

After graduating from high school, Gloria Steinem attended Smith College, from which she received a B.A., magna cum laude, in 1956. The money for college came from scholarships and from her mother's selling of the deteriorated Toledo house, scene of so much pain and poverty for them both. Later, when Steinem wrote of these times, she described her fear at leaving her mother alone. The older woman did not always remember where Steinem had gone; sometimes she called the police, and other times she walked through snowy streets waiting for Gloria's return.

Her opportunity to attend an eastern women's college must have seemed like the reward she had finally earned for continuing to function amid the personal chaos of her life with a mentally ill mother. At Smith, Steinem faced new challenges. Mixing with many students from the upper class, she confronted real differences with her peers. She found herself surprised at many of the attitudes of her classmates and developed an interest in upper-class women's lives that has continued to this day. In fact, in her future writings she would speculate that upper-class women were more trapped by a male elite than those from lower economic or racial strata (Steinem 1983, 128; Steinem 1992, 181–182). What she found most strange was her classmates' lack of appreciation for their opportunities.

After her graduation, Gloria Steinem received a Charles Bowles Asian Fellowship and was hence able to do graduate study at the University of Delhi and University of Calcutta, India, 1957–1958. Her time in India allowed her to continue studies in political science. She described life there as easy for her to adjust to, largely because English was the common language. One pivotal event in her stay occurred when she had the opportunity to visit people living in the countryside. As she was to explain later, her experiences gave her a deep sympathy for all poor as well as an enduring love for India and its people.

Steinem was able to work as a freelance writer while in India, and upon her return she began developing what was to become a wide-ranging journalistic career. Professionally, her positions have been varied and impressive. She won the Penney-Missouri Award for her article on black power in 1970, and she has been director, Independent Research Service, Cambridge, Massachusetts, and New York City, 1959–1960; contributing editor, *Glamour* magazine, New York City, 1962–1969; cofounder and contributing editor, *New York* magazine, 1968–1972; cofounder and editor, 1972–1987, columnist, 1980–87, consulting editor, 1987, *Ms.* magazine, New York City; contributing correspondent to NBC's *Today* show; and editorial consultant to Condé Nast, 1962–1969, Curtis Publishing, 1964–1965, and Random House, 1988–present. Her national memberships include PEN, National Press Club, Society of Magazine Writers, Authors Guild, Authors League of America, American Federation of Television and Radio Artists, National Organization for Women, Women's Action Alliance (cofounder; chairperson, beginning 1970), National Women's Political Caucus (founding member; member of national advisory committee, beginning 1971), Ms. Foundation for Women (cofounder; member of board, beginning 1972), Coalition of Labor Union Women (founding member), Voters for Choice (cofounder), Phi Beta Kappa. Steinem was named Woman of the Year by *McCall's* magazine in 1972; received a doctorate of human justice from Simmons College in 1975; was a Woodrow Wilson International Fellow in 1977; and has received the Ceres Medal, the Front Page Award, and the Clarion Award.

Steinem's experiences in India provided the focus for some of her early freelance writing, but her best-known article from her early career came in 1963, when *Show* magazine asked her to cover the opening of the Playboy Club in New York City. For her Bunny piece, Steinem received "training" in the arts related to dressing in scant Bunny clothes and working to serve the male customers. The Bunny article received raves: it was called "hysterically funny" and powerful. But to a *Los Angeles Times* writer Steinem acknowledged that the Bunny experience had been more humiliating than she had expected. Certainly, having to have a pelvic examination by the Playboy Club's doctor would have added to this reaction (Steinem 1983, 29).

In a recent collection of essays (Steinem 1993) Steinem recalls the dearth of assignments available to a "girl reporter" when she started out and the gap between what she cared about and the assignments she had been given. During the second half of the 1960s, she was a celebrity date, as well as a prominent figure in reform politics in the Democratic Party. A 1965 article in *Newsweek* talks about her dating Ted Sorensen and Mike Nichols and quotes Nichols' compli-

menting her mind and her looks. In fact, this business of her beauty continues
to be both boon and bane; biographer Heilbrun mentions Steinem's good looks
in many contexts.

In 1968, the year Chicago policemen attacked demonstrators and members of
the press, Steinem was in a group of aides to George McGovern. The same year,
she got her first chance to write extensively on politics, in *New York Magazine*.
Her column, "The City Politic," brought her in touch with George McGovern,
Martin Luther King, Jr., John Lindsay, Nelson Rockefeller, and even visitors to
the city like Ho Chi Minh.

As a journalist with talent for spotting hypocritical poses and as a writer with
an unusual ability for clear, honest prose, Gloria Steinem moved into the seemingly glamorous New York magazine world. Her efforts resulted in her cofounding
two magazines—*New York* in 1968 and *Ms.*, in 1972. Both were publishing successes despite the continuing problems finding an advertising base for *Ms.* She
describes the decision to sell *Ms.*, after years of begging advertisers to consider
women a prospective market, in "Sex, Lies, and Advertising," one of the articles
reprinted in *Moving beyond Words* (1993). As she puts it, ever since Sarah Josepha
Hale's efforts for *Godey's Lady's Book* in the nineteenth century, the relationship
between advertising and women's magazines must be understood as both social
and economic controls on the magazine itself. As Steinem describes her efforts
to explain the importance of *Ms.* to potential advertisers, the reader is taken into
a somewhat seamy world of manipulation and editorial compromise.

The first issue of *Ms.* provided a turning point for Steinem, who suddenly went
from journalist-about-town to editor of a successful monthly magazine. She is
quoted in the *Chicago Tribune* as having said that, even though she felt that there
should be a feminist magazine, she didn't want to start it herself. She wanted to
be a freelance person and said she had thought she'd turn the editorship over to
someone else as soon as it was on its feet. However, with *Ms.*, Steinem became
one of the leading proponents of feminism in the United States.

Steinem's most recent collection of articles, *Moving beyond Words*, includes a
"Doing Sixty" essay, which seems to be an exercise in examining what "kind"
of movement she helped instigate thirty years earlier, as well as speculating—
still with some wonder—about how she became a central voice for that movement. One of her characteristics, continually noted by former colleagues and by
those who have interviewed her, is a natural modesty. To those who belong to
a younger generation of feminists, the trait has been suspect, but to all who have
known her well, the modesty and self-deprecation are real. In addition to examining her past and its links to feminism, she has examined what her present
role should be in encouraging and sustaining various forms of feminism. Her
thoughts are reflective, sometimes addressing questions she must have been asked
in innumerable interviews. "I'm not sure feminism should require an adjective,"
is one typical comment, reminding readers that she has used that same thinking
to debunk the way language undercuts gender and race distinctions. Anytime a

writer uses "black" or "woman" before a noun, she has argued, the process of gender or racial equity has been stalled (Steinem 1993, 270).

Some of the comments that address an early radicalism seem almost too easy, critics have suggested. Steinem was not part of the suburban housewife reaction triggered by Betty Friedan's "mystique." Indeed, her unconventional, sometimes poverty-ridden girlhood and her college education at Smith appear to have combined to form an almost classless ability to examine women's lives from a variety of perspectives. Despite this basic orientation, her arguments most frequently resonate from a working-class perspective; her interest in middle- and upper-middle-class women and their problems can seem almost childlike in its innocence. Perhaps it is simply her journalistic stance of the observer, not the participant, that has led her to some of her positions. Indeed, as a person who began as the observer-writer, the shift to polemic must have been difficult.

Despite the limitations to the observer-writer stance of the journalistic tradition, Steinem's anger at systemic limitations of women is clear. That she tries to maintain some distance is clear from the ways she develops a clever approach. "If Men Could Menstruate," for example, suggests that women's "curse" would become a symbol of power with multiple "show-you" aspects if it were something men, alone, did (Steinem 1983, 337). In this piece, as in "I Was a Playboy Bunny," Steinem writes terse, humorous reportage. But her more recent examinations of age and race and economic status are more polemic and appear to be more accepted by both feminist theorists and academics looking at the social implications of issues. Her early writing is sprightly, even fun-filled. "I Was a Playboy Bunny," for example, has been described by more than one critic as a romp. But this same sense of fun and journalistic bravado—while reminiscent of the Nellie Bly tradition—has been criticized by theorists who would push Steinem into the role of thinker, quite possibly because journalists have used her as friendly source.

Her actions might be considered more revolutionary than her words, a contradiction that must be bothersome to those who would talk but not act. Her attempts to understand the rich woman and the sex symbol have been criticized. Indeed, the feminist, cautionary tale of the life of Marilyn Monroe, described later, might be best understood as an attempt at empathy, a writer's effort to create understanding between women who have been quick to judge women like Marilyn Monroe or Linda Lovelace. What she tries to tell us is that these women are victims of patriarchy as surely as the battered wife. Indeed, in both cases, the clear line of fear and abuse is drawn.

Outrageous Acts and Everyday Rebellions (1983) was the title of her first collection of essays. Here is the Bunny story once again, along with a few other pieces of journalism that Angela Carter calls "far more persuasive . . . than are the lay sermons reprinted from *Ms.*" (*Contemporary Literary Criticism*, 381), a hint that the journalist-observer role that seemed to come to her naturally was, in fact, the role that gave her credibility in a movement noted for its purely personal politics.

Marilyn, a biography written to accompany photographs by George Barris, was published in 1986 and received mixed responses. It provides a counterpoint to an earlier piece by Norman Mailer, called by Julian Barnes the "long, brawling amour he never had with the actress (luckily for her)." By comparison, Barnes observes, Steinem's Marilyn is an attempt to rescue and understand this "constructed" sex object, this victim of desire (*Contemporary Literary Criticism*, 285). Diana Trilling, however, calls the work thoughtful and absorbing and writes that Steinem "for the most part admirably avoids the ideological excess that we have come to associate with the women's movement" (*Contemporary Literary Criticism*, 387).

Revolution from Within: A Book of Self-Esteem (1992) has been criticized as New Age, as too tied up with psychological, self-help jargon. But Steinem provides criticism herself of the New Age terminology. She extends her analysis of support by adding groups like Pakistani village women doing communal clothes washing. Her own travels provide a metaphor, as she proposes that men and women unlearn artificial selves and journey back to truer understandings of the self. Lauren Glen Dunlap, in the *Seattle Times*, writes that Steinem's prose is thoughtful and authentic and does not represent a "wrong turn" for the women's movement (*Contemporary Literary Criticism*, 282).

By 1995 Gloria Steinem had been described as an icon by L.A. Winokur of *The Progressive* and Molly O'Neill in the *New York Times*. Indeed, she has become both symbol and working theorist of the modern women's movement. In addition to her advocacy of women, Gloria Steinem has written extensively about the contrasts between wealth and poverty and has worked in coalition with others fighting for civil rights, against the Vietnam War, and for justice for migrant workers. Steinem has said she lived her first fifty years externally, reacting and being much too nice. But about her mother and her mother's mental illness, she has been honest. That she doesn't blame her father and wrote of him with an appreciation of his unconventional life and personal charms is another important clue to her basic ability to state her own philosophy. She has written of her parents with pride as well as with despair and confusion. Carolyn Heilbrun has written that Steinem's life might challenge us all to redefine the functional family, that despite poverty and heavy responsibility, Gloria Steinem's childhood produced a passionately engaged and loving human being.

SELECTED WORKS BY GLORIA STEINEM

The Beach Book. New York: Viking, 1963.
With G. Chester. *Wonder Woman*. New York: Holt, 1972.
Outrageous Acts and Everyday Rebellions. New York: Holt, 1983.
"I Was a Playboy Bunny." *A Bunny's Tale* (television movie), 1985.
Marilyn: Norma Jean. New York: Holt, 1986; London: Golancz, 1987.
Bedside Book of Self-Esteem. Boston: Little, Brown, 1989.

Revolution from Within: A Book of Self-Esteem. Boston: Little, Brown, and London: Blooms-
     bury, 1992.
Moving beyond Words. New York: Simon and Schuster, 1993; London: Bloomsbury, 1994.
With Wilma Mankiller, Gwendolyn Mark, Marysa Navarro, and Barbara Smith, eds. *The
     Reader's Companion to the History of American Women.* Boston: Houghton Mifflin,
     1998.

WRITINGS ON GLORIA STEINEM AND HER WORK

Heilbrun, Carolyn. *The Education of a Woman: The Life of Gloria Steinem.* New York: Dial
     Press, 1995. (A list of Steinem's early journalism is included in Heilbrun's exten-
     sive bibliography.)
"Steinem, Gloria." *Contemporary Literary Criticism.* Ed. Roger Matuz. Vol. 63. Detroit:
     Gale Publishers, 1991, 378–388.

MARGO ST. JAMES
(1937–)

Diane L. McKay

Margaret Jean St. James was born September 12, 1937, in Bellingham, Washington. As the oldest of three children on her father's dairy farm, Margo was expected to participate fully in a physically demanding daily routine. Before and after school, she drove tractors, cleaned gutters, harvested crops, and milked cows. In the scant leisure time afforded her, she developed an interest in outdoor sports, including long-distance running. Yet, despite her demonstrated athletic ability, Margo was denied a position on her high school's all-male track team. In response, she registered what she now identifies as her first "feminist" protest against sexual discrimination: she organized the young women in her class into a block vote, electing all females to class office.

By age fifteen, the rebellious Margo had grown tired of what she viewed as her father's exploitative reliance on her labor. She decided to leave his farm to live in town with her mother, who was working as a secretary in Bellingham. She finished high school, then, at seventeen, married a man who worked in a local fish house and gave birth to a son that same year. But once again, she began to chafe against the obligations and restrictions of domestic life. In 1958, at twenty-one, she divorced her husband and left her son, migrating first to Seattle and then to San Francisco, where she landed a job in an after-hours club. Though these clubs were often frequented by prostitutes, St. James herself remained "straight"; as a B-girl, her duty was simply to make money for the club by encouraging men to spend freely on drinks. In 1961, she secured a slightly more lucrative position as a cocktail waitress, which enabled her to move to a larger apartment in the hip North Beach neighborhood.

St. James reveled in the beatnik atmosphere of San Francisco in the early 1960s, and her home quickly became a hangout for young people. The constant flow of traffic in and out of the "St. James Infirmary," as her apartment was known, soon caught the attention of the local vice squad, which sent an undercover officer to her apartment in an attempt to engage her in a cash-for-sex transaction. Although she refused his attempt, she was nonetheless arrested and formally charged with "soliciting in prostitution" and "keeping or residing in a house of ill fame" in 1962. The inexperienced lawyer hired to represent her chose to waive a jury trial, which would have allowed her to present her case before a more diverse (and perhaps sympathetic) group of peers. Instead, she wound up inadvertently incriminating herself when she testified on her own behalf before the judge, by declaring that she had never "turned a trick in her life." According to her account, the judge observed that "anyone who speaks the language is obviously a professional" and found her guilty on both counts (St. James 1980a, 197).

Stunned and angered by this judgment, St. James began to educate herself about prostitution and the law. During a stint as an employee in a bail bonds office, she cultivated a network of acquaintances among attorneys and law enforcement officials. She took and passed the California College Equivalency exam in 1963; later that year, she applied and was accepted to Lincoln University's night law school program, where she studied for two years. She decided to appeal her conviction on the grounds that the statutes under which she been arrested were unconstitutional. Her challenge was successful, and the conviction was overturned. But St. James discovered that this legal victory did very little to change the way others perceived her. Though she had cleared herself of criminal charges, she could not disburden herself of the charge that she was a "whore"— the label inflicted upon any woman, prostitute or nonprostitute, whose sexual behavior fails to conform to strict societal standards and prohibitions. This social stigma made it extremely difficult for St. James to secure "legitimate" work. She reasoned that she might as well become a prostitute, since she had already been branded as such (St. James 1980a, 198). She therefore entered the sex work industry with the intention of reaping the benefits it offered, namely, financial independence and sexual freedom.

Actually, St. James was an active prostitute for a relatively brief period of time. She "hooked" often enough to pay her bills, drifting out of the business altogether in a few years. In the late 1960s, she moved to Marin County, where she spent her days working for her own domestic cleaning service; during her off-hours, she often baby-sat for other women while they attended local "rap groups" and consciousness-raising meetings. Although Elsa Gidlow, a lesbian poet who lived next door, shared with her the literature of the early women's liberation movement, a couple of years passed before St. James began to attend these local meetings herself, often held at the home of black feminist lawyer and activist Florynce Kennedy. The women who met at Kennedy's home were deeply divided over the issue of prostitution. Recognizing the need for dialogue between prostitute and nonprostitute women, who seemed unable to recognize their common struggles and goals, St. James organized WHO (Whores, Housewives, and Others) in 1972, the culmination of a three-year period of feminist politicization. Although the group met only a few times, it was a forerunner to another sex workers' rights and education organization, COYOTE (Call Off Your Old Tired Ethics), which St. James launched on Mother's Day 1973.

With the help of several start-up grants and other resources from contributors ranging from the Glide Memorial Church to the Playboy Foundation, St. James campaigned tirelessly for reform and support among influential San Franciscans and prostitutes alike. COYOTE called its first prostitutes' convention in July 1974, and in October of that year, it sponsored the first of what would become its most successful fund-raising events—the Annual Hookers' Masquerade Ball. As the primary spokesperson for COYOTE, St. James manufactured an astonishingly high profile for the group and for herself. Within the first year of its formation, COYOTE claimed a membership of over 1,000; by 1979, that number had jumped to 20,000. Though many of its members were nonprostitutes, COYOTE served as a model for a several sister organizations that appeared across the United States and abroad.

In 1976, Florynce Kennedy founded the Victoria C. Woodhull Memorial Foundation, a nonprofit corporation designed to be a funding clearinghouse for the decriminalization of prostitution and related issues. Along with Priscilla Alexander, St. James directed the activities of one of the foundation's ad hoc committees, the National Task Force on Prostitution (NTFP), charged with establishing national and international networks of support for sex workers. St. James refocused her energy on this international effort and moved to Europe in 1985, founding the Amsterdam-based International Committee for Prostitutes' Rights (ICPR) with Gail Pheterson. During these years, St. James was a vital presence at a number of conferences on women and women's rights, starting with the 1975 and 1980 United Nations Decade of Women conferences in Mexico City and Copenhagen, respectively; and the 1976 Tribunal on Crimes against Women in Brussels. Along with other feminist activists, including Jennifer James, she has lobbied women's groups (e.g., NOW) to concretely address the issue of sex workers' rights.

In 1993, St. James moved back to the United States and married San Francisco journalist Paul Avery. She resumed her local political efforts on behalf of sex workers, serving on the San Francisco Task Force on Prostitution. In 1996, she ran for the office of supervisor of the city of San Francisco, including in her platform a call for the repeal of prohibition of prostitution. Although she did not win the election, she established a broad base of support for her campaign and she intends to run again.

As the founder of COYOTE, which remains one of the most active and visible sex workers' organizations, St. James is widely recognized as the architect of the modern prostitutes' rights movement in the United States. When COYOTE emerged in 1973, women's rights groups had not considered issues relating to prostitution with any sustained interest or commitment. Most importantly, St. James observes, no one was speaking about these issues from the perspective of prostitutes themselves ("COYOTE/National Task Force" 1979, 291). If feminists were unable to perceive prostitutes as self-determining agents, those outside the movement were even less likely to do so. Indeed, the very prohibition COYOTE still seeks to repeal effectively denies prostitutes any legal recourse in the face of widespread civil rights violations, physical abuse, and economic exploitation. An ex-prostitute, St. James was able to represent the concerns of this invisible constituency with a relative degree of both safety and authenticity.

Part of St. James' function as a spokesperson for workers in the sex industry has been to educate the public by demystifying prostitution. In several essays and interviews, she appeals to historical accounts of prostitution in order to demonstrate that its criminalization has taken place only recently, in the first decades of the twentieth century; until that time, she suggests, women successfully managed their professional affairs as prostitutes with far less interference from moralists and lawmakers (St. James 1987, 81; St. James 1980, 191). She refutes the myth that prostitutes pose a menace to public health by citing statistics that show lower rates of venereal disease and AIDS among prostitutes than in other populations, attributing this difference to the better knowledge and caution with which prostitutes approach their work (St. James 1987, 84). In response to those who argue that prostitution is the result of the sexual and economic victimization of women, St. James insists that most women choose to work as prostitutes—"the only job for which women are paid more than men" (St. James 1980, 192)—and that to deny them their right to work is to deny them their civil rights: "In private the whore has power. She is in charge, setting the terms for the sexual exchange and the financial exchange. In public, of course, she has absolutely no rights—no civil rights, no human rights" (St. James 1987, 82).

Arguing that most of the problems associated with sex work are the result of prohibition, COYOTE, under the leadership of St. James, defined its earliest political mission as the reform of laws relating to prostitution. The prohibition or criminalization of prostitution, St. James notes, has been ineffective in eliminating the existence of prostitution. Resources spent enforcing laws against prostitution—generally a victimless crime, St. James contends—might be put to better use elsewhere. Moreover, de facto legalization of establishments like massage parlors and escort services puts all economic and legal control in the hands of third-party managers ("pimps") and law enforcement officials, inviting corruption from entrapment to extortion. Women who, in an effort to exert control over their mobility and private activity, choose to work outside this male-controlled system of "legalized" prostitution wind up streetwalking, where they are even more vulnerable to arrest and physical assault.

To alleviate these problems, St. James advocates decriminalization, or the repeal of all criminal codes against consensual adult sexual activity (commercial or noncommercial). Unlike legalization, which merely transfers the balance of power from law enforcement officials and third-party management to government agencies, the decriminalization of all aspects of voluntary adult prostitution would confer complete autonomy to prostitutes by ensuring the right to work, as well as the rights of freedom of association and travel. Indeed, the notion of prostitution as work is central to St. James' vision for legislative reform, which recasts prostitution as a labor issue rather than a sexual issue. Women in the sex industry are punished not for having sex but for asking for money—or for "interfer[ing] with the male control of cash and commodities" (McClintock 1993, 1). The point of legislative reform, then, is to secure for women more power in the marketplace. Prostitution should be subject to standard business regulations, from contracts, to zoning, to taxation, and prostitutes should have the right to bargain for higher pay and better working conditions.

From the outset, St. James has linked the campaign for prostitutes' rights to one of the fundamental principles of the feminist movement: that women have the right to control their own bodies, whether the issue is prostitution, reproductive rights, or sexual preference. Shaped by the rhetoric of the women's liberation movement of the late 1960s and 1970s, St. James' public discussion of prostitutes' rights emphasizes her belief that a woman's freedom depends on her sexual autonomy. "As a woman-whore," she explains, "I feel equality will never be achieved until women's sexuality ceases to be the source of their shame: until men are forced to abandon their pussy patrols" (St. James n.d., 9). One of the recurrent themes of her essays has been the double standard, whereby women are punished for behavior that society accepts and even expects from men. In "The Reclamation of Whores," a 1985 address delivered at a Toronto conference of feminists and sex workers, St. James noted that this double standard is obvious in statistics on arrests for prostitution: only 30 percent of those arrested are men, and only 10 percent of that 30 percent are "johns," or male clients of female prostitutes (St. James 1987, 82). Such discriminatory enforcement victimizes women who choose to sell sexual services while ignoring the men who buy these services.

Part of St. James' strategy in forging an alliance between feminists and prostitutes has been to show how the stigma attached to sex work affects all women, regardless of whether or not they are actually engaged in sex work. Calling a woman a "whore" or a "slut" is a way to exert social control over her, "to remind her of what she can be reduced to" (St. James 1978, 12). In "What's a Girl like You . . ?" St. James theorizes that the "whore" label is a mechanism by which men discipline women. Men use it to justify physical violence against women who "act like whores" and to intimidate "respectable" women into a state of emotional and financial dependence. Prostitutes become "legitimate victims—society's scapegoat—while they function as an overt lesson to the rest of the female population that they had better mind their Ps and Qs, and continue working in the home for free, and in the job market for less than men" (St. James 1980, 192). By placing all women on the "whore/Madonna sliding scale"—dividing them into "bad girls" and "good girls"—the "patriarchal ruling class" pits women against each other "for the sake of a man's attention and resources" (St. James 1978, 12). Elsewhere, St. James has provocatively argued that all women—not just prostitutes—are forced to trade on their sexuality all the time, no matter what they do. The "hooker" and the "housewife" occupy parallel markets:

"[K]eeping the one that pays the most money illegal, and the other poor-paying but respectable, insures the economy a surplus labor force" (St. James 1978, 12). In an unpublished manuscript, St. James concludes that feminists and prostitutes must learn to speak to each other in order to achieve their common goals: "[O]nly when women can stop pointing fingers at their whore sisters will they have the unity and strength to stop the intimidation, the rising rape rate, the sexual harassment on the job, and the general exploitation of themselves" (St. James 1980b, 4).

Despite St. James' success in initiating a dialogue between feminists and prostitutes, feminists remain deeply divided over the issue of sex work. Not all women who work on behalf of prostitutes agree with her analysis of the problems inherent in the sex industry and her proposed solutions. As Priscilla Alexander notes, prostitutes' rights organizations tend to take one of three different ideological approaches (Alexander 1987, 17). Groups like COYOTE argue from what might be called a pro-sex or civil libertarian stance, which holds that there is nothing inherently wrong with sex work and that women have the right to do whatever they want with their own bodies. They deplore any restrictions placed upon a woman's sexual behavior and see the prohibition of prostitution as such a restriction. Other groups, like the U.S. Prostitutes' Collective (U.S. PROS), see prostitution as a class issue. According to this account, women are forced into prostitution because they have few viable economic choices; their goal is to eliminate prostitution by working to obtain better employment options for women. Finally, groups like Women Hurt in Systems of Prostitution Engaged in Revolt (WHISPER) operate from a highly protectionist stance, viewing all prostitutes as victims of an oppressive and exploitative institution "created by patriarchy to control and abuse women" (Alexander 1987, 17). They claim that no woman ever chooses to work as a prostitute and that commercial sex, from pornography to prostitution, is "the vehicle by which men sexualize women's chattel status" (Wynter 1987, 268).

The extent of women's agency continues to fuel much debate among feminists. Yet despite our different positions, few of us would argue with St. James' assertion that prostitution, located at the junction of capitalism and patriarchy, is "the barometer of the oppression of women" (St. James 1979, 2). In moving prostitutes from the margins to the center of feminist awareness, by insisting that their struggles are, in fact, the struggles of all women, St. James reminds us that women's solidarity is essential to women's freedom.

WORKS BY MARGO ST. JAMES

"Does Good Pay Make Women Bad?" COYOTE Howls 5, no. 1 (Spring 1978), COYOTE holdings, Schlesinger Library.

"Editorial." NTFP News (September/October), COYOTE holdings, Schlesinger Library, 1979.

"Prostitute, Police, Pimp, Patron, and Prohibition." COYOTE holdings, Schlesinger Library, 1980b, unpublished.

"What's a Girl like You . . . ?" *Prostitutes—Our Life*. Ed. Claude Jaget. Bristol, England: Falling Wall Press, 1980a, 191–201.

"The Reclamation of Whores." *Good Girls/Bad Girls: Feminists and Sex Trade Workers Face to Face*. Ed. Laurie Bell. Seattle: Seal Press, 1987, 81–87.

"Preface."*A Vindication of the Rights of Whores*. Ed. Gail Pheterson. Seattle: Seal Press, 1989, xvii–xx.

"Prostitutes as Political Prisoners." *The Realist*, n.d., COYOTE holdings, Schlesinger Library.

Website: *http://www.creative.net:80/-penet/margo.shtml*

WRITINGS ON MARGO ST. JAMES AND HER WORK

Alexander, Priscilla. "Why This Book?" *Sex Work: Writings by Women in the Sex Industry*. Ed. Frederique Delacoste and Priscilla Alexander. Pittsburgh: Cleis Press, 1987, 14–18.

COYOTE holdings. Schlesinger Library at Radcliffe College, Cambridge.

"COYOTE/National Task Force on Prostitution." *Sex Work: Writings by Women in the Sex Industry*. Ed. Frederique Delacoste and Priscilla Alexander. Pittsburgh: Cleis Press, 1979, 290–296.

Jenness, Valerie. *Making It Work: The Prostitutes' Rights Movement in Perspective*. New York: Aldine de Gruyter, 1993.

Leigh, Carol. "Prostitutes' Education Network." Website. Available at *http://www.creative.net:80/-penet/*

McClintock, Anne. "Sex Workers and Sex Work: Introduction." *Social Text* 37 (Winter 1993): 1–10.

Styron, Ann. "Margo St. James: Growing Up Wild" (Interview). Pamphlet by the American Women's Himalayan Expedition. COYOTE holdings, Schlesinger Library, 1978.

Wynter, Sarah. "Whisper: Women Hurt in Systems of Prostitution Engaged in Revolt." *Sex Work: Writings by Women in the Sex Industry*. Ed. Frederique Delacoste and Priscilla Alexander. Pittsburgh: Cleis Press, 1987, 266–270.

ALICE WALKER
(1944–)

Angela Cotten

Born on February 9, 1944, in Eatonton, Georgia, Alice Malsenior Walker was the eighth child of two sharecroppers, Minnie Tallulah Grant and Willie Lee Walker. Moving from one farm to the next, Walker grew up witnessing how the women of an economically exploited race not only mustered strength to survive but developed an untouchable spiritual interior to resist being consumed by an alienating culture. Walker remembers that her mother's art of cultivating flowers and her grandmother's quilting operated as aesthetics of resistance to the dehumanizing structures of a racist patriarchal society (Walker 1983, 241).

Walker began her education at Spelman College but later transferred to Sarah Lawrence after traveling to Africa in 1964. She discovered that she was pregnant during her senior year, and, unable to confide in her parents and receiving no sympathy from her siblings, she became deeply depressed and contemplated suicide. With the help of a friend, however, Walker emerged from the depths of despair to choose life and the attendant struggles that are involved in any black woman's attempt to objectify her desire into creative art forms. After graduating from college, Walker worked on a number of civil rights projects in Georgia and Mississippi, published her first short story, "To Hell with Dying" (1965), and wrote a number of poems for her first volume of poetry, *Once: Poems* (1968).

Partly out of her frustration of not having heard "one word about early black women writers" in college and partly due to her feminist ethics, Walker developed and taught the first courses on black women writers at Wellesley College and the University of Massachusetts-Boston in the early 1970s (Walker 1983, 9). Continuing on a prolific track for the next two decades, Walker became a contributing editor to *Ms.* magazine and published five novels, two short story collections, the first Zora Neale Hurston reader, two collections of essays, and five volumes of poetry. While writing in a variety of genres, Walker presents a wide spectrum of black women characters and the complex social network of their oppression. One of her greatest gifts to contemporary feminist and black struggles for freedom is her womanist analyses and aesthetic of resistance, that is, her portrayals of the complex ways in which structural axes of economic, gender, and racial subjugation work in tandem to thwart the full blossoming of black women's visions and the creative forms of resistance they fashion to "survive whole" (Walker 1983, 250). While her portrayals of these forces in black women's lives reveal the patriarchal politics that are inherent in black (masculinist) praxis of resistance, they also interrogate the class and racial myopia of early feminist analyses of women's oppression.

Like Zora Neale Hurston, Walker works in several genres to dissect the nexus of gender, racial, and economic subjugation and portray the ways in which individuals resist mental-spiritual colonization by rejecting racist-sexist cultural forms and drawing upon "the specific forms of black humanity" of folk wisdom to affirm their selfhood and forge relationships of mutual responsiveness (Harris 1981, 51). Central to Walker's explorations of these complexities are black women whose art of making a way out of no way constitutes a womanist aesthetic of resistance: "I am preoccupied with the spiritual survival, the survival *whole* of my people. But beyond that, I am committed to exploring the oppressions, the insanities, the loyalties, and the triumphs of black women" (Walker 1983, 250). As with Hurston, Walker's work has been criticized by some male writers for her explorations of incest, colorism, lesbian desire, and domestic abuse in black communities—problems on which black women have been silenced under the tutelage of a duplicitous and totalizing rationality that has defined black solidarity as devoid of ideological difference, feminism, and same-gender sexuality. What Barbara Christian (1984) and other feminist critics have identified in Walker's writings as a willingness to excavate forbidden areas of black life that are constituted by a dual politics of race-sexuality in order to arrive at another level of complex truths, many black male critics have labeled as threatening to "the black struggle." Examples of Walker's analyses are necessary before considering her womanist aesthetic.

The short story "Really, Doesn't Crime Pay" (1973) is about the marital difficulties of a southern, black, middle-class couple, Myrna and Ruel. Myrna enjoys writing and wants Ruel's encouragement, but he refuses to take her seriously. He cannot bear to listen to Myrna and is condescendingly discouraging of her, suggesting that she shop, play with her cosmetics, or think of having a baby whenever she mentions her writing to him (15). Myrna has an affair with a wandering writer, Mordecai Rich, because he praises her short stories and encourages her to write. One day, however, he disappears and publishes one of her stories in his own name. Added to Ruel's dismissiveness, Mordecai's betrayal sends Myrna over the edge. Ruel has her committed to an insane asylum after she attempts to kill him. Upon returning home, she finds that Ruel is still obsessed with her getting pregnant. As a way of thwarting his desire and guarding her relative independence, Myrna secretly ingests birth control pills, leaving Ruel perplexed as to why she does not conceive.

In this story, Walker foregrounds the dialectic of gender subjection in black heterosexual relationships and demonstrates the ways in which economic and racial oppression structures its internal logic. Myrna deceives Ruel not because she is ethically weak but because she intends to treat Ruel in the identical way that he has treated her; she thwarts his desire for a child in the same way that he has refused her her desire to write. As Myrna's character follows the logic of identity in this dialectic of denial, Walker demonstrates that moral decay in black heterosexual relationships is inevitable when men will not recognize women on women's own terms, preferring, instead, to see and relate to women through patriarchal constructions of women's roles. Yet, Walker foregrounds an additional dimension to Myrna and Ruel's circumstances: the ways in which the politics of racial resistance structure gender politics in black heterosexual relationships. Ruel's desire for Myrna to play the role of southern belle reflects not only his belief in patriarchal conventions but also his reactionary politics to white men's economic subjugation of black people and racial-sexual degradation of black women. In Barbara Christian's words:

To have a wife who is a visual representation of one's financial achievement, or to protect and keep pure the black woman, despite the white man's often successful attempts to drag down the race, are goals essential to their view of themselves as [black] men. Racism then has the effect, not only of physically and economically restricting these men, but also of reinforcing their need to imitate the oppressor's conventions in order to match his worth. (Christian 1985, 38)

In the praxis of racial-economic resistance by some black men like Ruel, black women foot the bill in the form of gender subjection. Walker not only lays bare the dialectics of sexism but also demonstrates the ways in which black people's historical endurance of racial and economic oppression determines the course of black women's subjugation differently from white women's within the context of racial resistance. Myrna has a room of her own where she writes freely, but her talents cannot fully blossom because the encouragement that Ruel should give her is deferred by his interest in debunking racist myths about black people as "low-class degenerates" and black women as "Jezebels."

In this same collection, a similar deteriorating trajectory occurs in the marriage of Jerome and his wife in the story "My Sweet Jerome." A black revolutionary, Jerome is so taken up with his books and conferences that he is scarcely aware of his wife's existence except for the household labor that she performs—a labor that makes it possible for him to read books on the revolution. It is significant that her character fulfills the duties and image of "Mammy"—the black, domestic Aunt Jemima look-alike whose only desire is to satisfy that of the white Other. Strategically, Walker does not give her a name, for, like Myrna, Jerome's wife is merely a being in the service of his desire. Like Ruel, Jerome refuses to recognize her as a being-for-her-self with desires of her own—one of which is for his affection. Here again Walker demonstrates how gender politics for black women is charged with additional racial currents by foregrounding the ways in which the antiracist discourse of black power and racist iconographic significations of black women work interdependently to assign black women to an inferior existential category of being-for-the-black-male-Other's freedom. Jerome's revolutionary praxis is inherently contradictory; his commitment to a politics of black freedom excludes his wife's desire, an exclusion that is made possible by his acceptance (perhaps unwitting) of a racist figuration of her as "Mammy." Walker shows that Jerome's neglect of his wife is not merely sexist but also racist. Moreover, in her profiles of the ways in which racial and class politics complicate Myrna's and Jerome's wife's gender subjections, Walker also interrogates the racial and class myopia of early feminist analyses of women's oppression and extends that conception to include specific problems that black women face.

Although these stories display the ways in which the politics of race and class complicate the dynamics of chauvinism in heterosexual relationships, Walker does not absolve black men of their responsibility to step beyond the overlapping dialectics of racial, gender, and class oppression and forge new ways of being-in-relation to black women and children. The transformative trajectory of the black sharecropper, Grange Copeland in Walker's 1970 novel, *The Third Life of Grange Copeland*, best illustrates Walker's moral challenge to black men, particularly to those who justify their abuse of black women as a logical outcome of black men's oppression.

That Myrna and Jerome's wife go insane points to another current in Walker's work: both women perish because they lack the support of other spirited black women and are isolated in their frustration and despair. Walker stresses the necessity of bonding among black women (that is sometimes sexual) across social locations and generations as crucial to their survival and self-development (Walker 1983, 81). In her 1982 novel, *The Color Purple*, the dehumanized protagonist Celie could not know her self as beautiful without her lover, Shug Avery: Shug mirrored the beauty of Celie's being back to her. Writing about the significance of her experience at the 1974 National Black Feminist Organization conference, Walker explains:

I realized at the . . . conference that it had been much too long since I sat in a room full of black women and, unafraid of being made to feel peculiar, spoke about things that matter to me. We sat together and talked and knew no one would think, or say, 'Your thoughts are dangerous to black unity and a threat to black men.' Instead, all the women understood that we gathered together to assure understanding among black women, and that understanding among women is not a threat to anyone who intends to treat women fairly. (Walker 1983, 273)

I use the term "womanist aesthetic of resistance" to refer to the convergence of three traditions of criticism and deconstruction—U.S. black feminism, poststructural French philosophy, and the black aesthetic—that constitute an ethics that accounts for the ways in which black women resist the cultural forms of "Mammy," "Jezebel," "mules of the world," "Sapphire," and "Welfare Queen" and re-create themselves as subjects through the dehiscence of their desire. It is a *practique de soi* (self-forming activity) by which Walker's black women characters regard their subjected body-selves as works of art and engage in a sequence of exercises by which each transfigures that body-self into one that is radically other to those through which she has been discursively and iconographically constructed. This aesthetic is spirited by the audacious will that Walker finds characteristic of "womanish" behavior (Walker 1983, xi), since for a black woman to look upon her body-self as a work of art is a defiant act when considering that the "black female body, as a repository of otherness, is the site selected for dis-identification" among nonblack female artists and intellectuals (Allan 1993, 144).

Only in her relationship with Shug is Celie awakened to her repressed desire, and the substance of Celie's interiority is mirrored by another black woman who sees not only the Queen Anne's lace but also its purple heart. If female bonding is crucial to Walker's womanist aesthetic, the art of women's forebears is equally significant to resistant practices—an example of which is the impact that Zora Hurston's life and work have had on Walker. Walker's mother's gardens display the importance of black women's knowledge of their forebears' lives and the strategies—both dialectical displacement and self-affirming—that they deployed in surviving a racist capitalist patriarchy. What makes their art pertinent to contemporary women's struggles is the implicit notion of self-valuation in the act of creating beauty to adorn the surroundings of one's existence. Walker remembers that her mother "adorned with flowers whatever shabby house we were forced to live in . . . She planted ambitious gardens . . . with over fifty different varieties of plants. . . . She is involved in work her soul must have. Ordering the universe in the image of her personal conception of Beauty" (Walker 1983, 241). At times Walker's womanists objectify their desire, adorning and transforming the environment of their corporeality; at other times, they transform internalized negativity into beautiful creations—an example of which is Celie's sublimation of her animosity toward Albert into sewing colorfully patterned pants.

Characterized as a bildungsroman, Alice Walker's second novel, *Meridian* (1976), displays two womanist tenets: the significance of matrilineal heritages and of female support to the development of a young black woman's consciousness (McDowell 1981, 262). Walker also criticizes the repressive effects that black motherhood as an institution and black nationalist and assimilationist politics have on Meridian's maturation. Meridian's *teleology* (the kind of being to which she aspires) is the Revolutionist, but in young adulthood her morality has yet to take form: she accepts that she could die for the revolution, but she is uncertain if she could kill for it.

Meridian's mother's brand of Christianity and traditional beliefs about women's "duties" belong to a different era and are too constraining for Meridian. After a few months of marriage, Meridian discovers the social contradiction of motherhood—that women are "honored" as mothers and devalued and degraded as second-class gendered citizens (Christian 1985, 220–221)—a contradiction that Walker represents in the character of Mrs. Hill, as negating of women's selfhood and desire. Where Mrs. Hill had little choice but to personify "Black Motherhood" (Walker 1976, 96), Meridian lives in the midst of social transformations; after 80 years, black Americans are saying no to Jim Crow. Instead of capitulating to conventional roles of "Obedient Daughter," "Devoted Wife," and "Adoring Mother" (Walker 1976, 19), Meridian ventures on an antithetical path to become a subject of her own desire, giving up the baby and marriage and choosing to pursue a formal education at the local women's college, Saxon.

No sooner does Meridian arrive at Saxon than she confronts more constraints: the stultifying effects of Saxon's assimilationist politics and the emergence of guilt from having given up her baby. Saxon insists that students acquire the cultural accoutrements of "ladyhood," which precludes their learning the survival skills and art of their foremothers like Louvinie, a slave woman after whom the campus' largest magnolia tree, the Sojourner, is named (Walker 1976, 42–44). Whereas elsewhere Walker has criticized black nationalists' search for African origins as effecting a historical erasure of black women's resistance (Korenman 1994, 144), here she levels a similar critique of black assimilationist politics. However, the Saxonists' strivings not only efface the black maternal tradition. As Walker demonstrates through the college president's and dorm mother's callous disregard of an orphan for whom Meridian cares, they also negate the womanist practice of communal child care: when black people take on the bourgeois values of the dominant culture, they affirm an ethic of individualism that excludes womanist ethics of communal responsibility.

During Meridian's first year at Saxon, her guilt from having given up her baby reemerges to consume her conscience and flesh. But Meridian's guilt is not simply about her sense of failure as a mother and failing her own mother's wishes. As Walker points to the significance of racial history and politics, the intensity of Meridian's guilt is also owed to the history of slave mothers' powerlessness to keep their children (Walker 1976, 122) and the respondent ways in which discourses of racial resistance have ideologically charged black motherhood as both a privilege and obligation of black women. Because Meridian is a black woman, she not only lives the existential contradiction of motherhood that all mothers endure in a patriarchal society but also faces the additional difficulties that race introduces into that subject position for black women. Given the history of slave mothers' deprivation, according to black male prescriptive politics, Meridian should *want* her child; yet, she desires to be a warrior in the black struggle for liberation—an existential category whose duties are represented as antithetical to maternal obligations. Unable to resolve this second contradiction, spiritually and corporally consumed by guilt, Meridian approaches insanity. However, unlike Myrna and Jerome's wife, Meridian is saved by the school's organist, Miss Winter, who functions as a surrogate mother and releases Meridian from her self-consuming guilt for having failed her mother and the "desire" of black mothers historically (Walker 1976, 125).

Having worked through various dilemmas, Meridian arrives at a truth concerning her moral quandary about killing for the revolution: that there is no definitive universal morality but only decisions that are determined by their existential specificity (Walker 1976, 200). More important to Meridian than killing or dying for a movement is the role that she darns for herself to play in "just" causes: the role of the poet of History—the one who recites truths about the complexity of Being in poetic verse to the People and kindles the fire of universal freedom (Walker 1976, 201). Given the womanist analyses and aesthetics in both her fiction and nonfiction, the poet of History aptly characterizes Alice Walker's dual role in contemporary feminist and black struggles for freedom.

WORKS BY ALICE WALKER

Once: Poems. New York: Harcourt Brace Jovanovich, 1968.
The Third Life of Grange Copeland. New York: Harcourt Brace Jovanovich, 1970.
Revolutionary Petunias and Other Poems. New York: Harcourt Brace Jovanovich, 1971.
Five Poems. Detroit: Broadside Press, 1972.
In Love and Trouble: Stories of Black Women. New York: Harcourt Brace Jovanovich, 1973.
Langston Hughes, American Poet. New York: Crowell, 1974.
Meridian. New York: Harcourt Brace Jovanovich, 1976.
Good Night Willie Lee, I'll See You in the Morning: Poems. New York: Dial, 1979a.
I Love Myself When I Am Laughing . . . And Then Again When I Am Looking Mean and Impressive: A Zora Neale Hurston Reader. Old Westbury, NY: Feminist Press, 1979b.
You Can't Keep a Good Woman Down: Stories. New York: Harcourt Brace Jovanovich, 1981.
The Color Purple. New York: Harcourt Brace Jovanovich, 1982.
In Search of Our Mother's Gardens: Womanist Prose. New York: Harcourt Brace Jovanovich, 1984.
Horses Make a Landscape Look More Beautiful: Poems. New York: Harcourt Brace Jovanovich, 1984.
Living by the Word. New York: Harcourt Brace Jovanovich, 1988.
The Temple of My Familiar. New York: Pocket Books, 1989.
Possessing the Secret of Joy. New York: Harcourt Brace Jovanovich, 1992.
The Same River Twice. New York: Scribner, 1996.

WRITINGS ON ALICE WALKER AND HER WORK

Allan, Tuzyline J. "A Voice of One's Own: Implications of Impersonality in the Essays of Virginia Woolf and Alice Walker." *The Politics of the Essay: Feminist Perspectives.* Ed. R. B. Joeres and E. Mittman. Bloomington: Indiana University Press, 1993.
Christian, Barbara. *Black Women Novelists: The Development of a Tradition, 1892–1976.* Westport, CT: Greenwood Press, 1980.
———. "Alice Walker: The Black Woman Artist as Wayward." *Black Women Writers.* Ed. Mari Evans. New York: Doubleday, 1984, 457–477.
———. *Black Feminist Criticism: Perspectives on Black Women Writers.* New York: Pergamon Press, 1985.
Courington, Cella. "In Search of Common Gardens: Virginia Woolf and Alice Walker."

Virginia Woolf: Emerging Perspectives. ed. M. Hussey and V. Neverow. New York: Pace University Press.

Harris, Trudier. "Three Black Women Writers and Humanism: A Folk Perspective." *Black American Literature and Humanism*. Ed. R. B. Miller. Lexington: University Press of Kentucky, 1981, 50–74.

———. "On *The Color Purple*, Stereotypes, and Silence." *Black American Literature Forum* 18 (1984): 155–161.

Howard, Lillie P. *Alice Walker and Zora Neale Hurston: The Common Bond*. Westport, CT: Greenwood Press, 1993.

Korenman, Joan S. 1994. "African-American Women Writers, Black Nationalism, and the Matrilineal Heritage." *Journal of College Language Association* 38 (1994): 144.

McDowell, Deborah E. "The Self in Bloom: Alice Walker's *Meridian*." *Journal of College Language Association* 24 (1981): 262.

REBECCA WALKER
(1969-)

Jennifer Kohout

Rebecca Walker was born in Jackson, Mississippi, in November 1969. Her parents, white civil rights lawyer Mel Levanthal and black novelist Alice Walker, married in the face of Mississippi's antimiscegenation laws and worked together during the civil rights movement of the 1960s. Rebecca, born at the end of that tumultuous decade and coming into a world already politically charged, had the benefit of parents who were already questioning issues of race, class, and gender at the time of her birth. Her godmother is Gloria Steinem, one of the foremost members of the liberal feminist movement both currently and at the time of Walker's birth. Rebecca Walker comes from a dynamic tradition of political change and activism.

Walker credits that kind of open and loving environment for making her adolescent transition into embracing her female sexuality and feminism an easy one. In her article "Lusting for Freedom," Walker discusses her first sexual experience at eleven and her subsequent experiences in her teenage years with a variety of men, trying on a variety of roles:

Because my common sense and experience of nonabusive love led me to decent men, my relationships consisted of relatively safe explorations of sex that were, at the time, fulfilling physically and emotionally. I also began to play with different kinds of strength. While I learned about my partners' bodies, I learned that I had the power to make them need me. While I learned how much of myself to reveal, I learned how to draw them out. While I learned that they were not "right" for me, I learned that I was more than what they saw. (Walker 1995d, 98)

She also came to realize that "I wanted more pleasure and more freedom, and I intuitively knew I deserved and could get both" (Walker 1995d, 96). Ultimately, Walker recalls that she came to the realization that "I deserve to live free of shame, my body is not my enemy, and pleasure is my friend and my right," a realization that she believes is contradicted by much of the public information young women get about sex (Walker 1995d, 98).

Walker is one of the leading feminists speaking about issues that affect young women. This group of young feminists has been called the third wave, with the woman suffrage movement of the nineteenth and early twentieth centuries designated as the first wave and the feminist movement of the 1960s and later designated the second wave. For this group of young feminists, Walker envisioned an organization called Third Wave, an idea that came to Walker while watching the Clarence Thomas Senate confirmation hearings involving Anita Hill's allegations of sexual harassment. She writes about this experience in "Becoming the Third Wave." Walker felt those hearings represented much of the backlash against women in the United States. "Thomas's confirmation, the ultimate rally of support for the male paradigm of harassment, [sent] a clear message to women: 'Shut up! Even if you speak, we will not listen.' " She continues by remarking that "while some may laud the whole spectacle for the consciousness it raised around sexual harassment, its very real outcome is more informative. He was promoted. She was repudiated. Men were assured of the inviolability of their penis/power. Women were admonished to keep their experiences to themselves" (Walker 1995a, 215).

Working through this anger, Walker began to crystallize her idea of feminism and the kinds of feminist action she would participate in:

To be a feminist is to integrate an ideology of equality and female empowerment into the very fiber of my life. It is to search for personal clarity in the midst of systemic destruction, to join in sisterhood with women when often we are divided, to understand power structures with the intention of challenging them. While this may sound simple, it is exactly the kind of stand many of my peers are unwilling to take. So I write this as a plea to all women, especially the women of my generation: Let Thomas's confirmation serve to remind you, as it did me, that the fight is far from over. Let this dismissal of a woman's experience move you to anger. Turn that outrage into political power. Do not vote for them unless they work for us. Do not have sex with them, do not break bread with them, do not nurture them if they don't prioritize our freedom to control our bodies and our lives. I am not a postfeminism feminist. I am the Third Wave. (Walker 1995a, 217–218)

In the midst of such transition and development, Walker attended Yale University and graduated in 1992. After graduation she teamed up with colleague Shannon Liss, and the two planned the 1992 Freedom Summer Riders Project. This project, with its 125 participants, was a twenty-three-day bus tour that covered twenty-one cities across the United States with the goal of registering inner-city and underrepresented voters. By the end of the tour the group had registered 20,000 voters, and a new young feminist organization, Third Wave, had been born (Walker 1996b).

Third Wave is a national, multicultural organization designed to meet the needs of young feminists, offering them information and venues for action. It has an open, general membership, and its purpose is to create a "community in which members can coalesce, network, strategize, and ultimately take action around issues that affect us all." The organization planned two Freedom Summer Riders Projects: the first in 1992 and a second in 1996; sponsored Literacy Plus, Third Wave's literacy program; cosponsored the Third Wave Film Festival with New York University's Film School; began work on a traveling Third Wave Multi-Media Festival; and published a general newsletter to keep members up-to-date. With Walker as its president, Third Wave has become a model organization for feminists everywhere, using a paradigm of community and action (Third Wave).

The organization has also become part of a larger effort in the feminist community to include younger feminists. With the 1997 National Women's Studies Association's conference on girls and the 1997 Girls Conference, which took place in New York City in January 1997, the larger feminist community, which is still heavily influenced by leaders from feminism's Second Wave, has been more inclusive of, and influenced by, its younger members. The Third Wave organization has become an effective voice for those members.

In 1995, Walker compiled her book *To Be Real: Telling the Truth and Changing the Face of Feminism*, a collection of essays by young feminists from a variety of backgrounds working to find their place in the feminist movement as well as defining how they want that movement to be. The variety and diversity of the contributors to the volume are an accurate reflection of the current feminist movement itself. From Donna Minkowitz's article about pornography, violence, and arousal, to Eisa Davis' examination of her relationship with hip-hop even in its most misogynistic forms, to Jennifer and David Allyn's journey into reshaping heterosexual notions of marriage, the book is a mirror of what is happening in the feminist movement outside its pages. There the debates about feminism range from the feminist philosophy of Gloria Steinem, to the impact of women like bell hooks in bringing racism in the movement to light, to Elizabeth Fox-Genovese's critique of feminism, *Feminism Is Not the Story of My Life*, to the overnight success of Ellen Fein and Sherrie Schneider's *The Rules: Time Tested Secrets for Capturing the Heart of Mr. Right*. The feminist movement is undergoing monumental changes, which feel confusing and contradictory, at best, for many young women.

Walker herself came to *To Be Real* feeling like her life was "a feminist ghetto." She explains: "Every decision I made, person I spent time with, word I uttered, had to measure up to an image I had in my mind of what was morally and politically right according to my vision of female empowerment. Everything had a gendered explanation, and what didn't fit into my concept of feminist was 'bad, patriarchal, and problematic' " (Walker 1995b, Introduction). She was not alone in her distress about what being a feminist meant. Walker found through her speaking engagements and other activist projects that "many of the young women who came to my talks responded most to my suggestions that they stop trying to measure up to an ideal of feminism that makes them feel ashamed of some of their thoughts or actions" (Walker, 1995f). Many young women have seen the second wave and the feminism that came from it as uniform and concrete, not personal and malleable. Young women have then struggled, reworking their mothers' feminism in an attempt to mold it to fit their lives and expectations. Walker's response to such feelings was to try to create an awareness that the movement could have room for all of those views and feelings, that the feminist movement did not have to be a set of rigid rules that everyone had to follow. With this in mind, the book was designed to reflect Walker's commitment "to make room for people, and to encourage them not to stop acting for change because they feel they don't have all the right words or beliefs" (Walker, 1995f). In her Introduction of *To Be Real*, Walker explains:

Young women coming of age today wrestle with the term [feminist] because we have a very different vantage point on the world than that of our foremothers. . . . For many of us it seems that to be a feminist in the way that we have seen or understood feminism is to conform to an identity and way of living that doesn't allow for individuality, complexity, or less than perfect personal histories. We fear that the identity will dictate and regulate our lives, instantaneously pitting us against someone, forcing us to choose inflexible and unchanging sides, female against male, black against white, oppressed against oppressor, good against bad. This way of ordering the world is especially difficult for a generation that has grown up transgender, bisexual, interracial, and knowing and loving people who are racist, sexist, and otherwise afflicted. . . . For us the lines between Us and Them are often blurred, and as a result we find ourselves seeking to create identities that accommodate ambiguity and our multiple personalities. (Walker 1995b, Introduction)

Walker chose the contributors to her book out of their dynamic variety, including voices from all aspects in the wide spectrum of feminism. Like many feminists before her, Walker rejects dualistic thinking:

These voices are important because if feminism is to continue to be radical and alive, it must avoid reordering the world in terms of any polarity, be it female/male, good/evil, or, that easy allegation of false consciousness which can so quickly and silently negate another's agency: evolved/unconsciousness. It must continue to be responsive to new situations, needs, and especially desires, ever expanding to incorporate and entertain all those who wrestle with and swear by it, including those who may not explicitly call its name. (Walker 1995b, Introduction)

Reflective of this situation, Walker found that

the concept of a strictly defined and all-encompassing feminist identity is so prevalent that when I read the section in my talk about all the different things you can do and still be a feminist, like shave your legs everyday, get married, be a man, be in the army, whatever, audience members clap spontaneously. This simple reassurance paves the way for more openness and communication from young women and men than anything else I say. (Walker 1995b, Introduction)

Yet, all this has not been accomplished without some criticisms. In the introduction of *To Be Real*, Gloria Steinem kindly reminds readers that many of the ideas and themes examined in the book have been part of the feminist movement for years. Steinem remembers her own generation tackling questions of motherhood and work, sexuality and power, superwoman versus victim status. As she herself remarks, "I want to remind readers who are younger or otherwise new to feminism that some tactical and theoretical wheels don't have to be reinvented. You may want to make them a different size or color, put them on a different wagon, use them to travel in a different direction, or otherwise make them your own—but many already exist" (Walker 1995b, Introduction). Steinem's attitude, a gentle reminder that the third wave should be in close contact with the second, is the recurring message that comes from voices outside third wave feminism. It is this bridge that Walker is attempting to negotiate with her book and her feminism.

Rebecca Walker has also been busy working on her latest project—testing her success as a young entrepreneur with the opening of her coffee bar/bookstore/cyberlounge/Afroscene, Kokobar, which opened in Brooklyn, New York, in January 1996. Again with work for the community in mind, Walker and her partner, Angel Williams, noticed that Brooklyn did not have the kind of cyber-friendly shops and stores that the Soho and Manhattan districts did, and so they created Kokobar with Brooklyn clients in mind. Brooklynites have responded most positively, keeping Walker and Williams very busy.

With her responsibilities as president of Third Wave, as well as her speaking engagements, political activism, and dynamic writing career, Walker continues her work of opening the gates of feminism to those who dream of an equitable society for everyone.

Rebecca Walker has been a contributing editor to *Ms.* magazine since 1991. Her work has also appeared in *Cosmopolitan*, *Essence*, and the *Utne Reader*, as well as the anthologies *Listen Up: Voices from the Next Feminist Generation*, *Testimony*, and *A Voice of Our Own: Leading American Women Celebrate the Right to Vote*.

WORKS BY REBECCA WALKER

Review of *Yearning: Race, Gender, and Cultural Politics*, by bell hooks. Ms. (January/February 1991a): 62–63.

"A Day in the Life." *Ms.* (July/August 1991b): 106–107.

"The Fight Is Far from Over." *Utne Reader* (January 1993): 59–60.

"The Initiate's Journey." *House and Home: Spirits of the South.* Ed. Max, Belcher, Beverly Buchanan, and William Christenberry. Seattle: University of Washington Press, 1994, 1–20.

"Becoming the Third Wave." *Testimony.* Ed. Natasha Tarpley. Boston: Beacon Press, 1995a, 215–218.

Ed. and "Introduction." *To Be Real: Telling the Truth and Changing the Face of Feminism.* New York: Anchor Books, 1995b.

"Lusting for Sexual Freedom." *Cosmopolitan* (August 1995c): 94–96.

"Lusting for Freedom." *Listen Up: Voices from the Next Feminist Generation*. Ed. Barbara Findlen. Seattle: Seal Press, 1995d, 95–101.

Review of *Outlaw Culture: Resisting Representations*, by bell hooks. Ms. (January/February 1995e): 71–72.

"Dear Editor/Producer." Unpublished letter. November 1995f.

"Changing the Face of Feminism." *Essence* (January 1996a): 123.

"Finding America." *A Voice of Our Own: Leading American Women Celebrate the Right to Vote*. Ed. Nancy M. Newman. San Francisco: Jossey-Bass, 1996b, 12–18.

WRITINGS ON REBECCA WALKER AND HER WORK

Burgher, Valerie. "Better Latte Than Never." *Village Voice*, February 27, 1996, 6.

Danquah, Mari Nana-Ama. "Keeping the Third Wave Afloat." *Los Angeles Times*, December 6, 1995, E1, E4.

"Doing the Third Wave." *Ms.* (September/October 1992): 87.

Friend, Tad. "Yes." *Esquire* (February 1994): 48–56.

"Hot Picks." *Mother Jones* (January 1996): 86.

Kaminer, Wendy. "Feminism's Third Wave: What Do Young Women Want?" *New York Times Book Review* (June 4, 1995): 3–23.

Third Wave. Membership Information. Third Wave, 185 Franklin Street, 3rd Floor, New York, NY 10013.

Van Biema, David. "Tomorrow." *Time* (December 5, 1994): 65.

"What's the 411 on Phone Sex?" *Essence* (April 1996): 76.

MICHELE WALLACE
(1952–)

Viki Soady

Postcolonial critic of black feminism, culture, art, and literature and their relationship to the dominant discourse, Michele Wallace is the author of three books
that track her personal, theoretical process from the alterity of an angry young
black feminist in *Black Macho and the Myth of the Superwoman* (1979), to the
assurance of a conveyor of voice for black women in *Invisibility Blues: From Pop
to Theory* (1990), to the activism of a designer of "a politics of resistance" for
black culture (Collins 1993, 730) in the anthology *Black Popular Culture* (coedited with Gina Dent, 1993). As creative writer, teacher, and cultural commentator, Wallace's feminist project is to find a theoretical basis for the voice of
black women that neither essentializes them nor subordinates them within the
narratives of black men or white culture. Of the fetishism and stereotyping of
the semiotic of the black female both as persona and as body she describes, in
Invisibility Blues, the "high visibility" of black women in our culture but, paradoxically, their almost "total lack of voice" (Burford 1990, 39).

Wallace heard the feminist voices of her mother and other New York-based
feminist and artistic associates from her own cosmopolitan, privileged location
as "a black American princess in the Harlem of the 50s and 60s" (Wallace 1996a,
35). This daughter of musician Robert Earl Wallace and "ambitious, fiercely
militant" feminist activist Faith Ringgold describes herself as "an inveterate
mama's girl right through my early twenties" (Wallace 1996a, 35). In fact, Wallace still appears at conferences with her mother, as they did at the Feminist
Generations Conference at Bowling Green State University early in 1996, but
offers, at this point, a far more independent critique of her mother's work.

About her introduction to feminism, Wallace writes: "My family specialized
in superwomen of various sorts and women who just couldn't cope on almost
any level. . . . From an early age, you were expected to declare which you would
be. I always thought that Faith and I came to feminism at the same time, but I
now suspect that I was following her lead in the way that a child can without

being aware of it" (Wallace 1996a, 35). Activist causes were part of her daily life as she joined her mother in the antiracist, antiwar, anti-imperialist artistic movements of the 1960s and 1970s. With assistance from her mother, Wallace founded Women Students and Artists for Black Art Liberation, which offered a powerful critique of the establishment art world while undertaking vigorous demonstrations and protests at the Metropolitan, where they once occupied the offices of Thomas Hoving, the Whitney, and other prominent museums. Of this time in her life, she writes: "I remember the Redstockings visionary Shulamith Firestone and the Minimal artist Robert Morris visiting our apartment in Harlem. Sometimes I had the sense that we were making history. I certainly thought that we were on the verge of a revolution" (Wallace 1996a, 35).

While attending City College of New York, from which she received her B.A. in English in 1974, she was sent by Teresa Schwartz of the *New York Element* to cover the famous Panther convention in Washington, D.C., where Huey Newton and Jane Fonda made prominent appearances. At City College, she recalls reading her own black feminist poetry at sessions with Audre Lorde and other prominent poets. Graduation brought a sense of letdown, even depression, but Wallace was well on her way to a successful literary career.

While working as a book review researcher for *Newsweek*, she was able to move into feature stories that allowed her to contact other feminists such as Erica Jong and Toni Morrison. With her mother and "the usual suspects," she founded the National Black Feminist Organization. In addition to sponsoring arts festivals and exhibitions, by 1977 or so, this group was meeting regularly at Alice Walker's house in Brooklyn to discuss what stance or stances black women writers should take about feminism. Within this artistic, social, and political context *Black Macho and the Myth of the Superwoman* (1979) took its revolutionary and revelatory shape.

The book is a true artifact of the 1960s, which Wallace now asserts, in "Memoirs of a Premature Bomb-Thrower," was "one of those manuscripts that was never supposed to see print. [It was] the result of an unhappy alliance between a perfectionist aesthete (book editor Joyce Johnson) and a young, nihilistic, black-feminist militant, half-crazed, and sexually frustrated maniac" (Wallace 1996a, 36). In spite of this hypercritical self-assessment, Wallace states that she still supports the basic truths of the work, which describes in two parts the destructive effects of slavery and racism on the interpersonal relations of black women and men. Black men are characterized as taking power by the only means available to them, the exercise of sexual dominance over white women, to the exclusion of black women, who thus are doubly oppressed by both sexual barriers and social barriers. Concomitantly, while, in fact, the black woman is powerless and voiceless both inside her own race and within white hegemonic orders, she is mythologized, by Patrick Moynhihan and others, as a "superwoman," whose strength has served to emasculate and disempower black men. Thus, black women are blamed for the faults of their race and lack of social conformity with white paradigms. Not surprisingly, Wallace concludes, black women distrust feminism as a possible source of support or remedy both because it operates primarily from a white, middle-class perspective and partly because the black women have internalized the myth of themselves as independent superwomen who do not need help.

Black Macho offended feminists, both black and white, as well as black men and some white men. June Jordan, for example, criticized the book for the fact that it drew its examples from literary representations of black men and women, in American cultural history pre–Civil War and forward. She complained that "there is not a direct quotation from an interview that she conducted with a living black man or woman in the entire book" (1979, Jordan 15). Jordan also accused Wallace of reducing the entire civil rights movement and the issue of black nationalism to a problem of "interracial dating" and not showing a complete understanding of the women's liberation movement. Positive reviewers, however, could see that the book represented a serious effort to put forward an explanatory psychosocial examination of the location of the black race within the oppressive fabric of white-dominated American culture. In 1990, Verso Press asked to republish the book along with other iconic works of the 1960s by Eldridge Cleaver, Angela Davis, Susan Brownmiller, Robin Morgan, and others. Wallace agreed because she felt that its inclusion among such works of those "heady times" was entirely appropriate. Concerning the experience of having written the book and then having lived out the consequences of its reception, Wallace recently stated: "Did I have doubts, then and later, about *Black Macho*? Sure. About its grace and wisdom, certainly, although not about its essential, upsetting truth. But I never stopped believing that it is better to blurt truth even in a headlong way than it is to keep silent for the sake of peace. That's what much of Women's Liberation was about: breaking our patient, fearful silence" (Wallace 1996a, 36).

With the publication of *Invisibility Blues* (1990b), Wallace revealed her continued determination to find voice for black women and for black artistic expression generally within the broader fabric of a revised and inclusive American culture. In the twenty-four essays that constitute the book, black artists, filmmakers, and entertainers are encouraged to give voice and interpretation to their creative directions in an effort to remedy the problem of the invisibility of the black aesthetic. From shared art and understanding among constituencies within a culture can flow resistance to racism and sexism. In like manner, *Black Popular Culture* (1993) contains essays by such diverse black intellectuals as Cornel West, bell hooks, Henry Louis Gates, Jr., Marlon Riggs, and Angela Davis, each exploring in his or her own thoughts the social construction and representation of blackness in American popular culture. In both books, Wallace focuses upon the relationship between blackness and power in postcolonial terms, demanding that art be "flexible, free-wheeling, indeterminate and polyvocal" (Wallace 1995a, 8).

Wallace's perspective is neither separatist nor assimilationist. She can be equally critical of the leftist, separatist leanings of bell hooks (Wallace 1995a,

8), which she fears tend to reinforce essentialism and therefore the white dis-cursive structure, and the potential for the obfuscation or erasure of race as a category in the theories of such black thinkers as Cornel West and Henry Louis Gates, Jr. In "Art for Whose Sake?" Wallace deals harshly with black luminaries who shape their theories to fit the frame of white, patriarchal "mainstream" values and definitions: "Given the array of opportunistic Sapphires (and King-fishes) on the lecture circuit gravy train, this difficult job must start somewhere, especially now that hooks seems to be steering toward the same mainstream to which Cornel West and Skip Gates and a lot of other names too painful to mention have already retreated" (Wallace 1995a, 8).

Wallace's own philosophical views are closer to those of Patricia Hills Collins, who envisions an alignment of enlightened others who can respect differing epistemological locations within the polyvocality of postmodernism and yet come together to oppose such socially discriminatory evils as racism. On this subject, in her review of *Black Popular Culture*, Collins writes: "Correspondingly, those black intellectuals who refuse to wall themselves off in quasi-nationalist, essen-tialist views of Black culture . . . expand an existing poetic of responsibility for black people to work in coalition with antiracist whites . . . to achieve resistance to racism" (Collins 1993, 730).

Michele Wallace's larger cultural project concerns power relationships within the decentered flux of postmodern life and the persistent, deforming influence of racism upon the black struggle for recognition and legitimacy within American culture. In "Pictures Can Lie," while addressing the subject of the representa-tional reduction of the black male to a highly visible sexual commodity, she describes the immediate advantages of "invisibility":

I as a black feminist have come to see invisibility as not just a handicap but also a strategic necessity for blacks who would be intellectuals, artists, or just any ole body who wants to get something accomplished within the confines of racism. The ideal would be to mix visibility with invisibility—success in the dominant discourse with the metaphorizing folk wisdom of black oral traditions—in just the right balance. Too much visibility of the wrong kind, and at the wrong time, can not only be dangerous to your health but also to the general well-being of blacks as a class. (Wallace 1996c, 25)

In common with many radicals of the 1960s and 1970s, Wallace's wit and straightforward style convey tireless conviction and boundless optimism that change is a good thing and here to stay, even if slowly realized. In describing the "agonizingly slow" social process of the *New York Times* on issues such as femi-nism, gay rights, AIDS, race, and the homeless, Michele Wallace reveals a great deal about her own brand of optimistic activism, which will doubtless continue for many years to come: "Increasingly, I believe that the only life worth living is one lived in the expectation of progress and improvement on certain funda-mental issues and social problems. In the absence of any concrete evidence of progress, supposition, speculation and even fantasy will do. Whatever it takes to remain reasonably positive is justified because from the moment you nut out on the end-game scenario, you're useless" (Wallace et al. 1995e, 15).

WORKS BY MICHELE WALLACE

Black Macho and the Myth of the Superwoman. New York: Verso, 1979.

And Arthur E. Thomas, eds. *Teacher's Guide: Like It Is, Arthur E. Thomas Interviews Leaders on Black America.* New York: Central State University: E. P. Dutton, 1981.

All the Women Are White, All the Blacks Are Men, But Some of Us Are Brave: Black Women's Studies. Old Westbury, NY: Feminist Press, 1982.

"Baby Faith." *Ms.* 16, no. 1 (July 2, 1987a).

"Sexism Is the Least of It." *New York Times Book Review* (March 15, 1987b).

"Who Dat Say Dat When I Say Who Dat?" *Village Voice* 33, no. 15 (April 12, 1988).

"Invisibility Blues: Michele Wallace on Doing the Real Thing (the Portrayal of Women in *Do the Right Thing*)." Artforum 28 (October 1989a).

"Variations on Negation and the Heresy of Black Feminist Creativity (As Seen in Black Women Writers)." *Heresies* 6, no. 4 (1989b).

"Arts: Women Rap Back." *Ms.* 1, no. 3 (November 1990a).

Invisibility Blues: From Pop to Theory. New York: Verso, 1990b.

"Beyond Assimilation." *Village Voice* 36, no. 38 (September 17, 1991).

And Gina Dent, eds. *Black Popular Culture.* Seattle: Bay Press, 1992.

"*Boyz N the Hood and Jungle Fever*" and "Afterword: 'Why Are There No Great Black Artists?' The Problem of Visuality in African-American Culture." *Black Popular Culture.* Ed. Michele Wallace and Gina Dent. Seattle: Bay Press, 1993a.

"Race, Gender and Psychoanalysis in Forties Film: Lost Boundaries, Home of the Brave and The Quiet One." *Black American Cinema.* Ed. Diawara Manthia. London: Routledge, 1993b.

Et al. "Roundtable: Sexuality in America after Thomas/Hill." *Tikkun* 7, no. 1 (January 1993c).

"A Fierce Flame (on Marlon Riggs)." *Village Voice* 39 (April 26, 1994).

"Panther: The Hollywood Version of Black Power." *Ms.* 5, no. 6 (1995b).

"Review of Harlem on My Mind: Cultural Capital of Black America, 1900–1968, by Allon Schoener." *Village Voice* 40, no. 35 (August 29, 1995c).

"Art for Whose Sake?—Review of Art on My Mind: Visual Politics by bell hooks." *Women's Review of Books* 12, nos. 10–11 (July 1995a).

Et al. "Engaging and Escaping." *Women's Review of Books* 12, nos. 10–11 (1995e): 13–15.

"Review of Killing Rage: Ending Racism by bell hooks." *Voice Literary Supplement* 140 (November 1995d): 19.

"Memoirs of a Premature Bomb-Thrower." *Village Voice* 41, no. 7 (February 13, 1996a, 35–36).

"Out of Step with the Million Man March." *Ms.* 6, no. 4 (1996b).

"Pictures Can Lie." *Village Voice* 41, no. 14 (April 2, 1996c): 25.

"The Prison-House of Culture: Why African Art? Why the Guggenheim? Why Now?" *Black Renaissance* 1, no. 2 (1997a): 162–176.

"Review of Sexing the Watermelon film by Cheryl Dunye." *Village Voice* 42, no. 9 (March 4, 1997b).

WRITINGS ON MICHELE WALLACE AND HER WORK

Alexander, Karen. "Review of Invisibility Blues." *Sight and Sound* 1 (June 1991): 36.

Boorstein, Karen. "Beyond Black Macho: An Interview with Michele Wallace." *Black American Literature Forum* 18, no. 4 (Winter 1984).

Braun, Janice. "Review of Invisibility Blues." *Library Journal* 115 (December 1990): 146.

Burford, Barbara. "Review of Invisibility Blues." *New Statesman and Society* 3 (November 1990): 39.

Collins, Patricia Hill. "Review of Black Popular Culture." *Signs* 20, no. 3 (Spring 1993): 728–731.

Jordan, June. "Review of *Black Macho and the Myth of the Superwoman*." *New York Times*, March 18, 1979, 15.

McCluskey, Audrey Thomas. "Am I Not a Woman and a Sister? Reflections on the Role of Black Women's Studies in the Academy." *Feminist Teacher* 8, no. 3: 105–111.

Spillers, Hortense. "From Pop to Theory by Michele Wallace: Reviews of Black Popular Culture/Black Macho and the Myth of the Superwoman/Invisibility Blues." *African American Review* 29, no. 1 (Spring 1995): 123–126.

Video Data Bank. Michele Wallace Interview. Chicago, 1991.

SARAH WEDDINGTON
(1945–)

Susan L. Patnode

While the *Roe v. Wade* case reflected the politically charged atmosphere of the women's movement in the 1970s, it was in no way a calculated effort on the part of a national organization. Had it been, it is unlikely that Sarah Weddington, just out of law school and never having argued in a court of law, would have been chosen to appear before the U.S. Supreme Court.

Some people are driven from their very beginnings to be agents of change. They seem from birth to boldly assert their right to leadership and assume the center of attention. As in all significant social movements, there have been many larger-than-life figures in the feminist movement, activists whose personalities seemed at times to overshadow their politics on the way to making history. But there have also been others who did not seem to consciously set out to turn the tide. Yet somehow, a series of experiences, circumstances, and coincidences can combine to propel an otherwise traditional person into the radical political arena. For some, this political actualization may be short-lived. For others, like Sarah Weddington, it can lead to a lifelong political commitment.

As a twenty-five-year-old, inexperienced attorney, Weddington successfully argued the 1973 milestone case *Roe v. Wade* before the Supreme Court, and she continues twenty-five years later to devote her life to women's reproductive freedom. Her early life, however, was hardly an indicator of the impact she would have on the lives of generations of American women. Personal circumstances and public events caused her to become one of the most significant change agents for women in this century.

Sarah Ragle Weddington was born on February 2, 1945, in Abilene, Texas, to Herbert and Lena Ragle. Her father was a Methodist minister, and consequently her family lived in various west Texas towns during her childhood. As a minister's child she grew up in a very traditional setting, singing in the church choir and serving as an officer in the Methodist Youth Fellowship. From her high school position as president of Future Homemakers of America, there was little

indication of the significant role she was eventually to play in breaking constitutional ground for women.

An excellent student, Sarah Weddington completed high school two years
early and went on to attend McMurry College in Abilene. In 1965, she earned
her baccalaureate degree magna cum laude. Directly following her years at
McMurry, she enrolled in law school at the University of Texas. She made the
decision to study law at a time when women were actively discouraged from
being lawyers, partly motivated by an adviser who told her law school was far
too difficult for women students. When she entered law school, she was one of
five women in her class of 125.

During her final year at law school a series of unforeseen events occurred,
events that would, in every way, influence the future course of Weddington's
private and public life. Involved at the time in a relationship with the man she
would later marry, Sarah found herself pregnant. Both she and Ron Weddington
were serious students who did not wish to suspend their schooling to begin a
family. Abortion, although illegal in Texas, appeared to be the obvious choice.
With the help of friends, they made arrangements to visit a clinic in the nearby
Mexican border town of Piedras Negras. Although the procedure went smoothly,
Weddington, writing in her 1992 book, A Question of Choice, claims she will
never forget the intense feelings of fear: fear that she would die and fear that
friends and family would find out.

For the decade of the 1960s, it has been estimated that over 1 million illegal
abortions were performed each year. Illegal in every state, abortion was one of
the most compelling issues facing the second wave of the women's movement in
America. Feminists considered changing state laws a top priority. What evolved
was a strong position on the part of women activists that the government did
not have the right to regulate women's bodies.

In 1967, Sarah Weddington received her juris doctorate from the University
of Texas. Although she finished in the top quarter of her class, she was unable
to find a position in a law firm and worked briefly assisting a former professor
reviewing the American Bar Association's Canon of Professional Ethics. While
Sarah worked on this project, Ron Weddington was still working to complete
his law degree. The two married in 1968.

During this time Sarah Weddington met and became active in a women's
consciousness-raising group. These early feminists were part of the political community in Austin associated with the underground newspaper called the Rag.
Among other topics, the group discussed a prepublication mimeograph of the
groundbreaking book Our Bodies, Ourselves. Before long, this small-town minister's daughter found herself part of a larger activist circle pressing for social
change.

In time these feminists began to have a greater voice in both the publication
of the newspaper and its editorial policies. The paper began to consistently address issues of birth control and women's health, providing public service articles
educating women about safe and unsafe abortions. This work led to the organi-

zation in October 1969 of an abortion referral group that chose as its official name the Women's Liberation Birth Control Information Center. The group investigated and established safety criteria for clinics in nearby Mexico. In addition to the abortion information hot line, the organization provided education about birth control and sexually transmitted diseases. Sarah Weddington consistently did legal research for the referral project and was also available as a speaker on women's legal issues. As the group's work became more overt, public scrutiny increased. Many volunteers began to feel they were under surveillance while they tried to raise badly needed funds from garage sales. As she did research, Weddington uncovered much about the early abortion laws in the United States. The Texas abortion law was among the most restrictive in the nation.

Fascinated to find that abortion was not a crime in the early years of the United States, Sarah Weddington learned that as the growing male medical profession began to establish itself in the mid-1850s, it was determined to do away with midwives and their services to women, including abortion. By 1900, abortions in the United States had become a completely underground activity.

In the course of her research she came upon the significant 1965 Supreme Court case *Griswold v. Connecticut*, wherein the Supreme Court overturned a law that made the sale of contraceptives to married women illegal. The issue in that case was the right to privacy. Her legal research also led her to state decisions overturning abortion laws. As she amassed more and more information, she continued to share what she learned with the abortion referral project.

Some members of the referral project wondered if the existing Texas abortion law could be challenged in federal court. If so, they felt strongly that the case should be presented by a woman lawyer, and Sarah Weddington was the only woman attorney they knew. At first Weddington was extremely reluctant. She had never done any trial work or even appeared in court. However, she eventually agreed to file a federal lawsuit challenging the constitutionality of the Texas statute. Although she had support from law students and professors, it was clear that she needed another attorney on the team. Weddington approached former law school classmate Linda Coffee, who worked in a law firm and was knowledgeable about federal procedure. Coffee agreed to join her.

An existing statute cannot simply be challenged; it requires a plaintiff who has been affected by the statute to make the challenge. Weddington and Coffee set out to find appropriate plaintiffs, and they found two. The first was Norma McCorvey, who was to become famous as Jane Roe. The poverty and hardship she had faced in her young life, her unwanted pregnancy, and her willingness to participate made it clear to the two attorneys that they had found an appropriate plaintiff. A second set of plaintiffs was found in a married couple. The wife had a medical condition that made pregnancy a danger, and, therefore, if she became pregnant, abortion would be a logical choice for her to consider. This couple was referred to in the case as plaintiffs John and Mary Doe.

Upon finding the plaintiffs, on March 3, 1970, two suits were filed in federal court against Henry Wade, Dallas County district attorney. This was the marking of the official beginning of what were to be enormous changes for all women in America. Successive court appearances occurred in the following months. Weddington and Coffee amended the original complaints to include class-actions. Since these statutes affected far more people than Jane Roe or John and Mary Doe, the lawyers decided a class action suit was appropriate. In her memoir of the period, *A Question of Choice*, Sarah Weddington acknowledges the support and assistance that were available throughout this arduous process.

The case was first heard on May 22, 1970, at the Dallas Federal Courthouse, before a three-judge panel. On June 17, the court released its decision. The judges had agreed that the current abortion laws in Texas were unconstitutional. According to the opinion, "freedom to choose in the matter of abortions had been accorded a status of a 'fundamental' right" (Weddington 1992, 68). For Weddington and Coffee, this was a significant victory.

The decision, however, was only a partial victory. The court's opinion did not order the district attorney to refrain from prosecuting physicians who performed abortions. In addition, the district attorney and the attorney general both appealed the court's decision. The district attorney's decision to enforce the abortion law that had been declared unconstitutional afforded the two women attorneys a procedural break. Instead of appealing to the federal court's Fifth Circuit, the case was allowed to be filed directly with the U.S. Supreme Court. Once the case was filed, *Roe v. Wade* began to attract national attention.

Concurrently, the Weddingtons had moved to Fort Worth, where Sarah was offered a position as assistant city attorney. She and Linda Coffee communicated regularly about their case. At this time many abortion cases were being filed in the high court. A network of attorneys and groups working on abortion cases developed, whereby help, advice, and research were shared.

While the Supreme Court reviews thousands of cases each year, it chooses to actually hear only a very few. It was quite remarkable, then, when, on May 21, 1971, the Supreme Court announced that *Roe v. Wade*, along with an abortion case from Georgia, *Doe v. Bolton*, would be heard. Sarah Weddington's first contested case, then, was to be argued before the U.S. Supreme Court.

Although Sarah Weddington had been satisfied with her position as an attorney for the city of Fort Worth, apparently the controversy over the abortion case did not sit well with her employer. Weddington recalls in her memoir that she was called into his office and handed a note that read, "No more women's lib. No more abortion" (Weddington 1992, 83). With that, she left the job and moved back to Austin to open a private law practice with her husband.

Among supporting groups offering help to prepare for the Supreme Court argument was the James Madison Constitutional Law Institute in New York City. Its president, Roy Lucas, described the institute as specializing in abortion cases and offered Weddington a part-time position in the summer of 1971. She moved to New York to work with Lucas and his staff on the brief that had to be prepared for filing.

When deadlines loomed closer, and actual work on the brief seemed a low priority for Lucas, Ron Weddington joined Sarah in New York. With the assistance of many efficient and committed people, work progressed toward the August 17 deadline. Financial support came from philanthropic sources, and the project managed to remain afloat. In addition to those working or contributing directly to the specifics of *Roe v. Wade*, there was a loosely organized, effective coalition of attorneys and organizations around the country preparing parallel supporting documents. An "amicus brief" is a brief prepared in support of a pending case. Amicus briefs in this case were filed by attorneys, individuals, and groups around the country. Sarah Weddington found herself in the company of thousands of women, from all walks of life, united on this single historic case.

At summer's end, Sarah and Ron Weddington returned to Texas, and Sarah began to prepare for the formidable oral argument ahead. The case was scheduled for December 13, and the court requested the name of the attorney who would argue the case. Since the James Madison Constitutional Law Institute had been involved in the background preparation, Roy Lucas assumed he had the right to argue this important case. Legions of women supporters insisted that this was uniquely a women's issue and should therefore be argued by a woman. The final word, however, was the decision of the clients. Jane Roe, John and Mary Doe, and attorney Linda Coffee all agreed that Sarah Weddington should argue the case.

In Washington, several days in advance, Sarah Weddington reflected on the enormous responsibility she carried. The future of all American women would be affected by her success or failure. The argument was scheduled to last only thirty minutes, but these would be thirty minutes of far-reaching consequences.

The months that followed the argument were ones of change for Sarah Weddington, both personally and professionally. In the wake of the excitement of the preparation and argument, her marriage began to fail. As she and her husband grew apart, she became more active in politics as a way to address women's issues. Still in her twenties, she was convinced by friends to run for the state House of Representatives. Running against three other candidates, Weddington's was a grassroots campaign with minimal funding. Volunteer efforts were strong, and Ann Richards, later to become governor of Texas, was a committed supporter. Women who had worked with Weddington lobbying the state legislature on abortion issues joined her campaign.

In the midst of organizing her campaign, Sarah Weddington received word that *Roe v. Wade* was scheduled for reargument that fall. The process of submitting papers, a decidedly arduous task, began anew. The second argument, on October 11, 1972, proceeded without crisis but with no hint of how the justices would decide. Several weeks later, Weddington was elected the first woman from her district to the Texas House of Representatives. The final months of 1972 were ones of continuing distance between her and her husband. On January 9, 1973, Weddington was sworn in as one of five women in the state legislature. On January 19 she filed her first proposed legislation outlining changes to state laws governing abortion.

On January 22, 1973, Weddington learned from a *New York Times* reporter that she had won her Supreme Court argument. The immediate response from people around the country confirmed the fact that for all women in America, enormous change had been realized. Justice Blackmun's majority opinion affirmed the points in Weddington's argument. The Court, in *Roe v. Wade*, found that a woman's decision, in consultation with her physician, to terminate a pregnancy was protected by the right of privacy extended in the earlier case, *Griswold v. Connecticut*. According to the Court, the decision in the first trimester of pregnancy was left to the woman and her physician. In the second trimester, the state could regulate abortion if the woman's health was at risk. After viability, or approximately the third trimester, the state could regulate abortion to protect the health of the woman or the potential life of the fetus.

The Court's decision was greeted with controversy on both sides. Although pleased with the progress for women generally, feminist legal scholars felt that to gain the right to reproductive choice based on a principle of privacy, rather than the more obvious principle of gender equality, diminished the victory. On the other side, antiabortion groups were understandably outraged and began intense mobilization.

In Weddington's memoir, she is quick to point out that the decision did not provide pregnant women with immediate access to abortion services. Many physicians lacked equipment, and hospitals were reluctant to take responsibility. Even more critical, legal abortions were available only to women with substantial money to pay for the procedure and care.

At the time of the *Roe v. Wade* decision, Sarah Weddington was active in bringing other changes for women in Texas. In 1972, Texas included an Equal Rights Amendment in the state constitution, passed legislation ensuring that pregnant teachers would not lose their jobs, and also passed the Texas Equal Credit Act, assuring women equal credit rights.

While Weddington expected opposition to the decision from within the American legal community, she claims to have been unable to imagine the enormity of opposition that would emerge and continue to grow among antiabortion groups. These groups typically employed shock tactics, such as oversize posters depicting aborted fetuses or audiotapes of aborted fetuses' alleged cries. Antiabortionists, with the support and funding of primarily the Roman Catholic Church, worked tirelessly to end the legality of abortion. Sarah Weddington was deeply troubled by what she viewed as direct opposition to the principle of separation of church and state.

Following the Supreme Court victory, Weddington became active in NARAL (the National Association for the Repeal of Abortion Laws) and served for a time as its executive director. Post-*Roe v. Wade*, the organization kept the acronym but changed its name to the National Abortion Rights Action League. The enduring goal of the organization is the protection of women's rights to access to abortion. The Human Rights Amendment, proposed in Congress by Senator Jesse Helms, sought to establish the definition of life as beginning at conception. This and other similar proposed legislation did not prove successful but did keep activist groups like NARAL constantly working to challenge them. In September 1974, Sarah and Ron Weddington were divorced. She cites her public success and busy schedule as major factors ending the marriage.

In November 1976, Weddington was elected to her third term in the Texas House of Representatives. In that same month the country elected Jimmy Carter president. Among other issues, that presidential campaign marked the first official Republican platform on abortion, supporting an amendment for right to life for unborn children. With both pride and reluctance Weddington accepted in 1977 the offer of a position in the Carter administration. She was to serve as general counsel of the U.S. Department of Agriculture. With regret, she left her legislative office and good friend and assistant Ann Richards to move to Washington.

Once in Washington, she voiced her opposition to Carter's policy opposing federal funding of abortions for poor women. In spite of their disagreement, she was offered a White House position as special assistant to the president in 1978. One of her main responsibilities was investigative: finding qualified women for federal positions and women to include in White House events. In 1979, she was named assistant to the president and chair of the Interdepartmental Task Force on Women. The attention to women and women's issues in the Carter administration was unprecedented. Many from the fundamental Christian Right, however, who had supported Carter, were disappointed that he did not defend their stand on issues such as abortion and the Equal Rights Amendment. In 1980, the Reagan/Bush Republican victory ended Weddington's White House position, as well as any substantial White House interest in women's issues, for years to come.

Sarah Weddington began, at this time, to accept a series of teaching positions at various universities. From 1980 to 1981, she was a visiting professor at Wheaton College in Norton, Massachusetts. From 1982 to 1983, she served as the Carl Hatch Professor of Law and Public Administration at the University of New Mexico at Albuquerque. From there she went on to join the Texas Women's University faculty as a lecturer until 1993. Concurrently, since 1986, she has also been a lecturer at the University of Texas at Austin.

During the Reagan/Bush years the antiabortion activists escalated their action. They targeted the National Abortion Rights Action League as well as individual clinics and doctors. There were, and continue to be, threats, harassment, fires, and bombings. One of the more recent incidents, an abortion clinic bombing on January 15, 1997, in Atlanta, Georgia, injured six people.

The Republican Party platform officially supported the banning of abortion, and the administration went on to make conservative Republican Supreme Court appointments. As Supreme Court hearings challenging the *Roe v. Wade* decisions came forward, national pro-choice organizations mobilized to voice their opposition. Sarah Weddington became a key figure, speaking at national events concerning the critical importance of commitment to choice.

In subsequent years since the Bush administration, Weddington joined with countless women and witnessed one after another Supreme Court case chip away at the rights that had been granted in the 1973 decision. The *Roe v. Wade* decision had ruled that a woman's decision to terminate a pregnancy was a constitutionally protected right. In intervening years, however, several cases, most notably *Webster v. Reproductive Health Services* in 1989 and *Planned Parenthood of Southeastern Pennsylvania v. Casey* in 1992, have allowed states more latitude to regulate abortions. Weddington also witnessed the new Supreme Court appointments that were certain to change the climate of the Court that had decided *Roe v. Wade*.

In September 1991, Weddington was included on a panel with Kate Michelman, the executive director of NARAL; Faye Wattleton, director of Planned Parenthood; and Vermont's former governor Madeline Kunin. This panel testified in Senate hearings opposing the Supreme Court appointment of Clarence Thomas. Weddington, in her memoir, expresses hope that the Thomas appointment will act as a mobilizing force for women, that their anger and determination will work to reverse the backward turn in reproductive rights for all American women. To this end, she continues to be a tireless public speaker across the country, particularly on college campuses, where she feels the audience is most vulnerable. She has received numerous awards and has been granted honorary doctoral degrees from several colleges and universities. In 1990, she was named Lecturer of the Year by the National Association for Collegiate Activities.

According to Flora Davis, writing in *Moving the Mountain: The Women's Movement in America since 1960*, "Feminists have made progress by seizing chances where they found them" (Davis 1991, 11). A series of events placed before Sarah Weddington the chance to effect an enormous change for generations of American women. She seized the chance, and amazing progress was made. Since that historic moment, Weddington has continued to work with skill and dedication to preserve and improve the reproductive rights of all women.

WORKS BY SARAH WEDDINGTON

Primary writings consist of volumes of legal documents prepared for *Roe v. Wade*, as well as other cases and legal issues. These documents are a part of official court records.

A Question of Choice. New York: G. P. Putnam and Sons, 1992.

Texas Women's University Archives. Denton, Texas. Sarah Weddington's Personal Papers: Reports, Articles, Journals, Newspaper Clippings, Ephemera.

Jimmy Carter Presidential Library. Oral History Project. Sarah Weddington contributed twenty-two pages to this project as a member of the Carter White House Staff.

SELECTED WRITINGS ON SARAH WEDDINGTON
AND *ROE V. WADE*

Books

Davis, Flora. *Moving the Mountain: The Women's Movement in America since 1960.* New York: Simon and Schuster, 1991.

Faludi, Susan. *Backlash: The Undeclared War against American Women.* New York: Crown, 1991.

Faux, Marian. *Roe v. Wade: The Untold Story of the Landmark Supreme Court Decision That Made Abortion Legal.* New York: Macmillan, 1988.

Joffee, Carol. *Doctors of Conscience: The Struggle to Provide Abortion before and after Roe v. Wade.* New York: Beacon Press, 1995.

O'Connor, Karen. *No Neutral Ground: Abortion Politics in an Age of Absolutes.* Boulder, CO: Westview Press, 1996.

Petchesky, Rosalind P. *Abortion and Women's Choice: The State, Sexuality and Reproductive Freedom.* New York: Longman Press, 1984.

Radl, Shirley L. *Over Our Live Bodies: Preserving Choice in America.* New York: Longman Press, 1984.

Reagan, Leslie J. *When Abortion Was a Crime: Women, Medicine, and Law in the United States, 1867–1973.* Berkeley: University of California Press, 1997.

Schneir, Miriam. *Feminism in Our Time: The Essential Writings, World War II to the Present.* New York: Random House, 1994.

Staggenborg, Suzanne. *The Pro-Choice Movement: Organization and Activism in the Abortion Conflict.* New York: Oxford University Press, 1991.

Articles, Reviews, and Interviews

Berringer, Felicity. "Abortion Clinics Preparing for More Violence." *New York Times,* March 12, 1993.

Bragg, Rick. "Six Hurt in Abortion Clinic in Atlanta." *New York Times,* January 17, 1997.

Garrow, David. "Review of *A Question of Choice.*" *New York Times,* September 27, 1992.

Haylor, Barbara. "Abortion." *Signs* 5, no. 2 (1979).

MacKinnon, Catharine. "The Male Ideology of Privacy: A Feminist Perspective on the Right to Abortion." *Radical America* 17, no. 2 (1983).

Petchesky, Rosalind. "Fetal Images: The Power of Visual Culture in the Politics of Reproduction." *Feminist Studies* 13, no. 2 (1987).

———. "Reproductive Freedom: Beyond a Woman's Right to Choose." *Signs* 5, no. 3 (1980).

Stearns, Nancy. "Roe v. Wade: Our Struggle Continues." *Berkeley Women's Law Journal* 4, no. 1 (1989).

Taylor-McGhee, Belle. "One on One: An Interview with Sarah Weddington." *NARAL News* 27, no. 3 (1997).

VanGelder, Lawrence. "Cardinals Denounce Decision; Other Leaders' Reaction Mixed." *New York Times,* January 23, 1973.

Weaver, Warren. "High Court Rules Abortion Legal the First Three Months." *New York Times,* January 23, 1973.

"What Is Right and Wrong with Roe v. Wade? The View from Friends of the Court." *New York Times*, April 23, 1989.
"Abortion and the Court." *Newsweek* (May 1, 1989).

U.S. Supreme Court Cases

Griswold v. Connecticut, 381 U.S. 479 (1965)
Roe v. Wade, 410 U.S. 113 (1973)
Doe v. Bolton, 410 U.S. 179 (1973)
Webster v. Reproductive Health Services, 492 U.S. 490 (1989)
Planned Parenthood of Southeastern Pennsylvania v. Casey, 113 S. Ct. 2791 (1992)

ELLEN WILLIS
(1941-)

Deborah J. Gepner Salvaggio

Journalist, professor, author, activist, rock critic, social commentator, and self-described radical feminist, Ellen Willis has been called "one of the primary architects of the women's liberation movement" (Hess 1981). Through her writing and active participation, Willis helped frame the discussions and define the terms of debate that allowed women to recognize their own oppression and work toward freedom during what has now been dubbed the "second wave of feminism."

Born into a working-class family in New York City, Willis was educated in the New York City public school system. She earned a scholarship to Barnard College and earned a B.A. in English in 1962. Willis describes her parents (Melvin, a New York City police officer, and Miriam, a housewife) as "college-educated, literary-minded, and politically liberal" (1981a, 263). Despite this description, Willis terms her class origins as "lower middle-class" and cites the discrepancy between the values instilled by her upbringing and those she was exposed to during her years at Barnard as the basis of her sensitivity to the inherent class differences within the women's liberation movement. Ever the skeptic, Willis' keen understanding of the diversity of experience, particularly in terms of class differential, informed her understanding of the position of women within U.S. society.

After graduate school at the University of California at Berkeley, Willis returned to New York City and began her career as a journalist, a career that includes editorial positions at *Village Voice, Rolling Stone, Ms.,* and *New Yorker* magazines, as well as freelance writer, reviewer, and reporter for numerous other publications, including *Newsday* and *The New York Times Book Review.*

In 1968, Willis joined New York Radical Women, a group established primarily by women involved in leftist politics. From that association, Willis went on to form, with Shulamith Firestone, the Redstockings, a radical feminist organization that separated itself from male-centered, leftist politics and focused on the situation of women in patriarchal society. For the next few years, the

Redstockings would significantly impact the entire women's liberation movement, redefining the discussion in terms of woman-centered experience from both economic and personal standpoints.

When asked about her own process of becoming a feminist, Willis stated, "As long as I can remember, I was aware that women were subordinate.... The big revelation of the movement for me was that this wasn't just cultural benightedness, it was political and could be opposed collectively" (Interview 1996).

Despite her appeal to collective action and her work within collective groups, it is clear from her writing that Willis' underlying morality lies in the freedom of the individual. In that collective organizations can often work successfully toward such freedom, she has been a major force within the feminist movement. This sensibility, however, has often put her at odds with the movement itself, and, through her constant questioning of the position of individual rights within any given platform, she continues to be a controversial, sometimes divisive, and always respected and influential voice in the women's movement. "When Ellen Willis's pieces appear in New York's *Village Voice* or in *Rolling Stone*, they are something of an event—debated and discussed, sometimes ridiculed, often admired" (Denby 1981).

Today, Willis is an associate professor of journalism at New York University. She continues to write for numerous publications. Willis lives in New York City with Stanley Aronowitz and their daughter, Nona Willis-Aronowitz.

Willis' influence in the women's movement began when she joined the New York Radical Women. A student of leftist politics, Willis believed in fighting for a free society. As part of that belief, however, Willis began to question definitions of freedom in terms of women and more particularly the role of feminism as part of leftist politics. The Left's concept of a "free society" might address the oppression of the classes, but it did not address the oppression of women as a class. Not just the state but the relationship between men and women oppressed women and needed changing. As she states in the introduction to her first collection of essays, *Beginning to See the Light*, "The suppression of sexuality and the subjugation of women raise the question of freedom in the most direct and inescapable way . . . there is no task more radical, more in keeping with a vision of a free society, than changing sexual relations" (Willis 1981a, xix).

From this understanding of the oppression of women, Willis became one of the first feminist leaders from the Left to urge for a separate, autonomous, radical women's group rather than fighting for a greater role within leftist politics. In her essay "Radical Feminism and Feminist Radicalism" (1984), she describes this distinction as "the politico-feminist split":

The "politicos" . . . saw capitalism as the source of women's oppression. . . . I sided with the feminists, who at some point began calling themselves "radical feminists." We argued that male supremacy was in itself a systematic form of domination. . . . And since the male-dominated left would inevitably resist understanding or opposing male power, the radical feminist movement must be autonomous, create its own theory and set its own priorities.

In early 1969, Willis, along with Shulamith Firestone, founded the radical feminist group Redstockings. The political foundation of this group stemmed from leftist politics in its class-based interpretation of women's oppression, but it also incorporated an absolutely personal and individual sensibility in its recognition of the position of women in patriarchal society, a sensibility previously absent from the women's liberation dialogue. The Redstockings began from a "pro-woman" stance and viewed the conditions of the world through that perspective. The Redstockings were to become a defining force in the women's liberation movement, a force whose actions and dialogue would help shape the way women throughout the United States experienced the events of the late 1960s and early 1970s.

The Redstocking Manifesto, published in the summer of 1969, outlined the basic beliefs of the members with shocking directness; it was a combination of political theory and basic female reality that shook the very roots of the women's movement. Rather than blame institutions or social constructs, as did many women's organizations, including the National Organization for Women (NOW), the *Redstocking Manifesto* declared that men were the root of women's oppression: "We identify the agents of our oppression as men. Male supremacy is the oldest, most basic form of domination. All other forms of exploitation and oppression (racism, capitalism, imperialism, etc.) are extensions of male supremacy: men dominate women, a few men dominate the rest" (Morgan 1970, 533).

The Redstocking Manifesto renounced the idea that institutions or women themselves are the cause of women's oppression. Instead, it proclaimed, "Women's submission is not the result of brainwashing, stupidity, or mental illness but of continual, daily pressure from men. We do not need to change ourselves, but to change men." This groundbreaking declaration was in direct conflict with most other women's groups of the time; rather than telling women how they must change their own lives and beliefs in order to be free of oppression, the Redstockings were saying that men, not women, needed to change. The manifesto, in fact, took this line one step further and stated, "In fighting for our liberation we will always take the side of women against their oppressors. We will not ask what is 'revolutionary' or 'reformist,' only what is good for women."

Though the "pro-woman" line would come under strong attack from other women's groups as stifling and victimizing, and even Willis herself has noted that it was "simplistic," the importance of this approach was in its validation of personal experience. Whether or not all women should be supported in all of their positions may be debated, but the basis of this as a starting point provided a validity to the woman, first and foremost, as an oppressed being fighting for freedom. This recognition would change the discussion of women's liberation, not only in the discussion groups of New York's bohemia but in nascent women's groups all over the country, groups comprising women who dealt with the reality of oppression during every waking moment while raising children, grocery shopping, and running households.

According to *The Redstocking Manifesto*, the group's first goal was to "develop female class consciousness through sharing experience and publicly exposing the sexist foundation of all of our institutions." This goal was to be met primarily through the formation of "consciousness-raising groups": discussion groups in which women (and only women) would share their personal experiences and together discover the underlying sexual oppression that shaped those experiences. Though not a new concept, the phenomenon of consciousness-raising took the women's liberation movement and the country by storm. Suddenly, women did not have to join a political movement or study abstract theory to take part in the discussion of their own liberation. Women all over the country began to meet, both in public and in private, to ask the questions that no one had asked them before.

The Redstockings distributed guidelines for these discussions. The questions they asked were vital to the definition of women's lives but had never before been articulated or investigated by the theoretical community in terms of actual individual experience. Questions included: "How did you learn what feminine meant?" "What is a nice girl?" "How do you feel about your body?" "Did you consider having children a matter of choice?" The outpouring of emotion, recognition, and demand for change that was sparked by someone's finally asking women these questions and valuing their answers was incredible; it provided the momentum for the extraordinary amount of activism that would take place in the early years of the second wave of feminism. Willis, as cofounder of the Redstockings, was a major force in these events.

For a brief time, through the momentum of the consciousness-raising groups, as well as the work of many women's organizations throughout the country, the female solidarity for which the Redstockings declared such a need did exist, though never without internal problems. In addition to the arguments that this approach to activism was too emotional and static, that it was easy for a consciousness-raising group to devolve into a "bitch session" with no active outcome, and that it was itself contradictory because women's experiences are framed by patriarchal attitudes, the very nature of the exercise in terms of group dynamics and individual personalities made the consciousness-raising forum one that could very easily dissolve into an oppressive environment itself. In later years, many women would describe the groups as repressive and flawed in their assumption of equality among women. The "pro-woman" approach, which validated all women's experience, did not account for the differences between women; though all women were oppressed, the experience of that oppression was vastly different for those from different classes and races.

None of this was a surprise to Willis. Her sensitivity to class differences and, later ethnic distinctions as well, informed her recognition of the inevitability of these divisions. In her article "Radical Feminism and Feminist Radicalism," Willis cites the basic individual differences among women as the obstacle to any universal women's movement but, in doing so, also notes that these differences exist among men as well, and, despite the differences, collective groups can and have made a difference (Willis 1984). Throughout her writings, there is a telling recognition of the tenuousness of the solidarity of any women's movement, and introspection and skeptical questioning that are characteristic of Willis' understanding of the world. She is ever aware of the bourgeois nature of the counter-culture and of the women's liberation movement and of the class and race distinctions that many radical feminists denied.

An offshoot of the consciousness-rasing concept was the "speak-out," a tactic used extensively by the Redstockings. Willis was active in organizing these public demonstrations in which women spoke publicly about their own experiences, especially those related to abortion. Willis herself helped frame the debate over abortion, and in her writing and speaking on the subject she defined the position of reproductive rights as inherent human and individual freedoms and separated the issue from any moral or religious debate. She helped organize the demonstration against the so-called expert Abortion Reform Hearings in the New York State legislature and the subsequent Redstockings' public "Abortion Hearings" held by women, the real experts. These activities set the tone for much of the abortion activism in the women's movement.

Willis' contribution to the abortion debate has been an exacting and continued discussion that reinforces the idea that abortion is only one of many rights women are and should be fighting for. She has framed the discussion of abortion in the context of "reproductive rights" rather than moral dilemmas and, by doing so, helped to expand the discussion to a larger struggle for individual freedom. In "Villains and Victims: Sexual Correctness and the Repression of Feminism," she asserts, "Feminist passion about abortion rights . . . has never been just about abortion, but about the larger struggle to redefine women as subjects rather than vessels" (Willis 1996, 47).

Willis has also been a strong voice in the pornography debate within the feminist community. She considers herself an adamant "pro-sex feminist" and as such wrote, spoke, and organized extensively in opposition to the antipornography faction within the feminist community. Willis' position on the issue is based, again, on individual freedom and, more specifically, on women's individual freedom. Female sexuality, she argues, has been controlled by others throughout history; any support of the repression of female sexual freedom is in direct opposition to everything the women's liberation movement has fought for. To Willis, the antipornography campaign, spearheaded by Andrea Dworkin and Catharine MacKinnon, reinforces patriarchal notions of sexuality and the fear of female sexuality. She was also one of the first to point out the inherent trap of personal judgment and censorship in this approach and the suspect similarity between feminist antipornography rhetoric and the pro-family position of the far Right, a position that defined women as passive, in need of protection, and ultimately powerless. Outraged by what she saw as a conservative backlash to the freedom gained by women in the 1970s, Willis fought hard to counter the popularity of the antipornography movement within the feminist community.

As a member of the planning committee for the now-famous Barnard Sexuality Conference of 1982 and through her action and her writings, Willis helped develop a pro-sex opposition to feminist antipornography politics.

Willis' arguments have appealed to many feminists who were uncomfortable with the implied antiheterosexuality of the antipornography movement but were wary of the concept of sexual freedom (remembering the "sexual revolution" of the 1960s and its lack of freedom for women). In articles such as: "Feminism, Moralism and Pornography" (1979), "Lust Horizons: Is the Women's Movement Pro-Sex?" (1981), "Nature's Revenge" (a scathing review of Andrea Dworkin's *Pornography* and Susan Griffin's *Pornography and Silence*) (1981), and "Toward a Feminist Sexual Revolution" (1982) Willis examined, dissected, and attacked the basis of the antipornography movement and argued for sexual freedom for all people.

Throughout her career, Ellen Willis has helped define the terms by which our society has come to understand women's liberation. Her intelligent, often skeptical analyses of the position of women within patriarchal society and her unfailing call for the recognition of personal experience and personal freedom have continued to challenge feminist and political thought. Her writing continues to be informed as well by an overriding belief in the possibility of change. As she stated in her first compilation of articles in 1981, "In one way or another, my pieces on such apparently diverse subjects as rock-and-roll and feminism, radical politics and religion reflect my belief in the possibility of a genuinely democratic culture-community based on the voluntary cooperation of equals" (Willis 1981). Willis' ability to connect feminist and leftist political theory with female reality, though, has made the greatest impact on the women's movement. She will be remembered for her articulate and inclusive calls for fairness, equity, and personal freedom for all women.

WORKS BY ELLEN WILLIS

Books

Beginning to See the Light: Sex, Hope and Rock and Roll. Hanover: Wesleyan University Press (originally published by Knopf, 1981a).
No More Nice Girls: Countercultural Essays. Hanover: Wesleyan University Press, 1993.

Selected Book Chapters

"Radical Feminism and Feminist Radicalism." *The Sixties without Apology.* Ed. Sohnya Sayres et al. Minneapolis: University of Minnesota Press, 1984.
Foreword to Alice Echols, *Daring to Be Bad: Radical Feminism in America.* Minneapolis: University of Minnesota Press, 1990.
"Let's Get Radical (Why Should the Right Have All the Fun?)." *Radical Democracy.* Ed. David Trend. New York: Routledge, 1996a.

"Villains and Victims." *Bad Girls/Good Girls*. Ed. Nan Bauer Maglin and Donna Perry. New Brunswick: Rutgers University Press, 1996b.

Selected Articles

"Up from Radicalism: A Feminist Journal." *US* (October 1969).
"Women and the Myth of Consumerism." *Ramparts* (1970).
"Economic Reality and the Limits of Feminism." *Ms.* (June 1973).
"Feminists vs. Freud: Round Two." *Ms.* (July 1974).
"Rape on Trial." *Rolling Stone* (July 28, 1975).
"Abortion Backlash: Women Lose." *Rolling Stone* (November 3, 1977).
"Feminism, Moralism and Pornography." *Beginning to See the Light: Sex, Hope and Rock and Roll*. New York: Knopf, 1981.
"Lust Horizons: Is the Women's Movement Pro-Sex?" *Village Voice* (June 17, 1981).
"Nature's Revenge." *New York Times Book Review*, July 12, 1981.
"Betty Friedan's 'Second Stage': A Step Backward." *Nation* (November 14, 1981).
"Sisters under the Skin? Confronting Race and Sex." *Village Voice Literary Supplement* (June 1982).
"The Politics of Dependency." *Ms.* (July 1982).
"Toward a Feminist Sexual Revolution." *Social Text* 6 (Fall 1982).
"The Politics of Abortion." *In These Times* (June 15, 1983).
"Putting Women Back into the Abortion Debate." *Village Voice* (July 16, 1985).
"Looking for Mr. Good Dad" (the fallacies of "pro-life feminism"). *Village Voice* (September 3, 1985).
"From Forced Pregnancy to Forced Surgery: The Wrongs of Fetal Rights." *Village Voice* (April 11, 1989).
"Aborting Freedom" (on the Webster decision). *Village Voice* (July 11, 1989).
"Is Motherhood Moonlighting?" *Newsday* (March 12, 1991).
"Feminism without Freedom." *Dissent* (Fall 1991).
"Unholy Alliances" (on Pornography Victims Compensation Act). *Newsday* (February 25, 1992).
"Why I'm Not 'Pro-Family.'" *Glamour* (October 1994).
"Season of the Bitch." *Village Voice* (January 24, 1995).
"Porn Wars" (on Wendy McElroy's XXX). *Times Book Review* (September 1995).
"Sex, Truth and Politics." *Village Voice* (September 26, 1995).
"Interview with Deborah J. Gepner Salvaggio," 1996.

WRITINGS ON ELLEN WILLIS AND HER WORK

Bauer Maglin, Nan Perry, and Donna Perry, eds. *Bad Girls/Good Girls: Women, Sex and Power in the Nineties*. New Brunswick, NJ: Rutgers University Press, 1996.
Cohen, Marcia. *The Sisterhood: The True Story of the Women Who Changed the World*. New York: Simon and Schuster, 1988.
Denby, David. "The Promised Land of Feminism" (review of *Beginning to See the Light*). *The New Republic* (June 20, 1981): 36–37.
Hess, Elizabeth. "Captain of Consciousness" (review of *Beginning to See the Light*). *Ms.* (June 1981): 34–35.

Morgan, Robin, ed. *Sisterhood Is Powerful: An Anthology of Writings from the Women's Liberation Movement.* New York: Vintage, 1970.

Tanner, Leslie B., ed. *Voices from Women's Liberation.* New York: Plume and Meridian Books, 1971.

Wandersee, Winifred D. *On the Move: American Women in the 1970s.* Boston: Twayne, 1988.

SELECTED BIBLIOGRAPHY

Abbott, Sidney, and Barbara Love. *Sappho Was a Right-on Woman: A Liberated View of Lesbianism*. New York: Stein and Day, 1972.

Albrecht, Lisa, and Rose M. Brewer. *Bridges of Power: Women's Multicultural Alliances*. Philadelphia: New Society, 1990.

Allen, Pamela. *Free Space: A Perspective on the Small Group in Women's Liberation*. Washington, NJ: Times Change Press, 1970.

Anzaldúa, Gloria, ed. *Making Face, Making Soul: Haciendo Caras: Creative and Critical Perspectives by Women of Color*. San Francisco: Aunt Lute Books, 1990.

Asian Women United of California. *Making Waves: An Anthology of Writings by and about Asian American Women*. Boston: Beacon Press, 1989.

Babcox, Deborah, and Madeline Belkin, eds. *Liberation Now: The Writings of the Women's Liberation Movement*. New York: Dell, 1971.

Baehr, Ninia. *Abortion without Apology: A Radical History for the 1990s*. Boston: South End Press, 1990.

Beauvoir, Simone de. *The Second Sex*. New York: Knopf, 1953.

Bell Scott, Patricia. *Life Notes: Personal Writings by Contemporary Black Women*. New York: W. W. Norton, 1994.

Berry, Mary Frances. *Why ERA Failed*. Bloomington: Indiana University Press, 1986.

Blee, Kathleen M. *No Middle Ground: Women and Radical Protest*. New York: New York University Press, 1997.

Boston Women's Health Book Collective. *Our Bodies, Ourselves*. New York: Simon and Schuster, 1973. Also available, *The New Our Bodies, Ourselves*. New York: Simon and Schuster, 1992, 1998.

Brown, Elaine. *A Taste of Power: A Black Woman's Story*. New York: Pantheon, 1993.

Brownmiller, Susan. *Against Our Will: Men, Women, and Rape*. New York: Simon and Schuster, 1975; reprint, Greenwich, CT: Fawcett, 1993.

———. *Femininity*. London: Hamish Hamilton, 1984.

Bunch, Charlotte. *Passionate Politics: Feminist Theory in Action*. New York: St. Martin's Press, 1986.

Butler, Judith. *Gender Trouble: Feminism and the Subversion of Identity*. New York: Routledge, 1990.

Cade, Toni. *The Black Woman: An Anthology*. New York: Signet, 1970.

Cannon, Katie. *Black Womanist Ethics*. Atlanta: Scholars Press, 1988.

Caraway, Nancie. *Segregated Sisterhood: Racism and the Politics of American Feminism*. Knoxville: University of Tennessee Press, 1991.

Carson, Clayborne. *In Struggle: SNCC and the Black Awakening of the 1960s*. Cambridge: Harvard University Press, 1981.

Castro, Ginette. *American Feminism: A Contemporary History*. New York: New York University Press, 1990.

Collins, Patricia Hill. *Black Feminist Thought. Knowledge, Consciousness, and the Politics of Empowerment*. New York: Routledge, 1990.

Cook, Joanne, Charlotte Bunch-Weeks, and Robin Morgan, eds. *The New Woman: An Anthology of Women's Liberation*. Greenwich, CT: Fawcett, 1970.

Crawford, Vicki L., Jacqueline Rouse, and Barbara Woods, eds. *Women in the Civil Rights Movement: Trailblazers and Torchbearers, 1941–1965*. New York: Carlson, 1990.

Crow, Barbara A. *Radical Feminism: A Documentary History*. New York: New York University Press, 1997.

Cruikshank, Margaret. *The Gay and Lesbian Liberation Movement*. New York: Routledge, 1992.

Daly, Mary. *Gyn/Ecology: The Metaethics of Radical Feminism*. Boston: Beacon Press, 1979.

Davis, Angela. *Women, Race, and Class*. New York: Vintage Books, 1983.

———. *Women, Culture, and Politics*. New York: Random House, 1989.

Davis, Flora. *Moving the Mountain: The Women's Movement in America since 1960*. New York: Simon and Schuster, 1991.

Douglas, Susan J. *Where the Girls Are: Growing Up Female with the Mass Media*. New York: Times Books, 1994.

Dworkin, Andrea. *Woman Hating*. New York: E. P. Dutton, 1974.

———. *Letters from a War Zone: Writings 1976–1989*. New York: E. P. Dutton, 1989.

———. *Pornography: Men Possessing Women*. New York: Putnam, 1981.

Echols, Alice. *Daring to Be Bad: Radical Feminism in America, 1967–1975*. Minneapolis: University of Minnesota Press, 1989.

Eisenstein, Zillah, ed. *Capitalist Patriarchy and the Case for Socialist Feminism*. New York: Monthly Review Press, 1978.

Evans, Sara. *Personal Politics: The Roots of the Women's Liberation Movement in the Civil Rights Movement and the New Left*. New York: Knopf, 1979.

Faderman, Lillian. *Odd Girls and Twilight Lovers: A History of Lesbian Life in Twentieth-Century America*. New York: Penguin, 1991.

Faludi, Susan. *Backlash: The Undeclared War against American Women*. New York: Crown, 1991.

Ferree, Myra Marx, and Patricia Yancey Martin. *Feminist Organizations: Harvest of the New Women's Movement*. Philadelphia: Temple University Press, 1995.

Ferree, Myra Marx, and Beth B. Hess. *Controversy and Coalition: The New Feminist Movement across Three Decades of Change*. New York: Twayne, 1994.

Findlen, Barbara. *Listen Up: Voices from the Next Feminist Generation*. Seattle: Seal Press, 1995.

Firestone, Shulamith. *Dialectic of Sex*. New York: Bantam, 1970.

Firestone, Shulamith, and Anne Koedt, eds. *Notes from the Second Year: Women's Liber-*

ation, the Major Writings of the Radical Feminists. New York: New York Radical Women, 1970.

Fox-Genovese, Elizabeth. *Feminism Is Not the Story of My Life: How Today's Feminist Elite Has Lost Touch with the Real Concerns of Women.* New York: Nan A. Talese, 1996.

Freeman, Jo. *The Politics of Women's Liberation: A Case Study of an Emerging Social Movement and Its Relation to the Policy Process.* New York: David McKay, 1975.

Friedan, Betty. *The Feminine Mystique.* New York: W. W. Norton, 1963.

———. *It Changed My Life.* New York: Dell, 1991.

Fritz, Leah. *Dreamers and Dealers: An Intimate Appraisal of the Women's Movement.* Boston: Beacon Press, 1979.

Frye, Marilyn. *The Politics of Reality: Essays in Feminist Theory.* Trumansburg, NY: Crossing Press, 1983.

Garcia, Alma M., and Mario T. Garcia, eds. *Chicana Feminist Thought: The Basic Historical Writings.* New York: Routledge, 1997.

Giddings, Paula. *When and Where I Enter: The Impact of Black Women on Race and Sex in America.* New York: William Morrow, 1984.

Gordon, Linda. *Woman's Body, Woman's Right: A Social History of Birth Control in America.* New York: Grossman, 1976.

Gornick, Vivian, and Barbara K. Moran, eds. *Women in Sexist Society.* New York: Signet, 1972.

Gould, Jane S. *Juggling: A Memoir of Work, Family, and Feminism.* New York: Feminist Press, 1997.

Greenberg, Cheryl Lynn, ed. *A Circle of Trust: Remembering SNCC.* New York: New York University Press, 1998.

Greer, Germaine. *The Female Eunuch.* New York: McGraw-Hill, 1970.

Guy-Sheftall, Beverly, ed. *Words of Fire: An Anthology of African-American Feminist Thought.* New York: New Press, 1995.

Haywood, Leslie, and Jennifer Drake, eds. *Third Wave Agenda: Being Feminist, Doing Feminism.* Minneapolis: University of Minnesota Press, 1996.

Hirsch, Marianne, and Evelyn Fox Keller, eds. *Conflicts in Feminism.* New York: Routledge and Kegan Paul, 1990.

Hole, Judith, and Ellen Levine. *Rebirth of Feminism.* New York: Quadrangle, 1971.

———. *Women Power: The Movement for Women's Liberation.* New York: Tower, 1970.

hooks, bell. *Ain't I a Woman: Black Women and Feminism.* Boston: South End Press, 1981.

———. *Feminist Theory: From Margin to Center.* Boston: South End Press, 1984.

———. *Talking Back: Thinking Feminist, Thinking Black.* Boston: South End Press, 1989.

———. *Yearning: Race, Gender, and Cultural Politics.* Boston: South End Press, 1990.

Hull, Gloria, Patricia Bell Scott, and Barbara Smith, eds. *All the Women Are White, All the Blacks are Men, But Some of Us Are Brave: Black Women's Studies.* New York: Feminist Press, 1982.

Johnston, Jill. *Lesbian Nation: The Feminist Solution.* New York: Simon and Schuster, 1973.

Joseph, Gloria I., and Jill Lewis. *Common Differences: Conflicts in Black and White Feminist Perspectives.* New York: Doubleday, 1981.

Kahn, Karen, ed. *Frontline Feminism 1975–1995: Essays from Sojourner's First 20 Years.* San Francisco: Aunt Lute Books, 1995.

Kaplan, Laura. *The Story of Jane: The Legendary Underground Feminist Abortion Service.* Chicago: University of Chicago Press, 1995.

Kennedy, Florynce. *Color Me Flo: My Hard Life and Good Times.* Englewood Cliffs, NJ: Prentice-Hall, 1976.

Kimball, Gayle, ed. *Women's Culture.* Metuchen, NJ: Scarecrow Press, 1981.

King, Mary. *Freedom Song: A Personal Story of the 1960s Civil Rights Movement.* New York: William Morrow, 1977.

Koedt, Anne, Ellen Levine, and Anita Rapone, eds. *Radical Feminism.* New York: Quadrangle, 1973.

LeGates, Marlene. *Making Waves: A History of Feminism in Western Society.* Toronto: Copp Clark, 1996.

Lorde, Audre. *Zami: A New Spelling of My Name.* Watertown, MA: Persephone Press, 1982.

————. *Sister Outsider: Essays and Speeches.* Trumansburg, New York: Crossing Press, 1984.

MacKinnon, Catharine A. *Feminism Unmodified: Discourses on Life and Law.* Cambridge: Harvard University Press, 1987.

Maglin, Nan Bauer, and Donna Perry, eds. *"Bad Girls"/"Good Girls": Women, Sex, and Power in the Nineties.* New Brunswick, NJ: Rutgers University Press, 1996.

Mansbridge, Jane. *Why We Lost the ERA.* Chicago: University of Chicago Press, 1986.

Maran, Meredith. *Notes from an Incomplete Revolution: Real Life since Feminism.* New York: Bantam Books, 1997.

Millett, Kate. *Sexual Politics.* New York: Avon, 1971.

Mitchell, Juliet, and Ann Oakley, eds. *Women's Estate.* New York: Pantheon, 1971.

————. *What Is Feminism? A Re-Examination.* New York: Pantheon, 1986.

Mohanty, Chandra, Ann Russo, and Lourdes Torres, eds. *Third World Women and the Politics of Feminism.* Bloomington: University of Indiana Press, 1991.

Moraga, Cherríe, and Gloria Anzaldúa, eds. *This Bridge Called My Back: Writings by Radical Women of Color.* Watertown, MA: Persephone Press, 1981.

Morgan, Robin. *Going Too Far: The Personal Chronicle of a Feminist.* New York: Vintage Books, 1968.

————, ed. *Sisterhood Is Powerful: An Anthology of Writings from the Women's Movement.* New York: Vintage, 1970.

Morrison, Toni, ed. *Race-ing Justice, En-gendering Power: Essays on Anita Hill, Clarence Thomas and the Construction of Social Reality.* New York: Pantheon, 1992.

Murray, Pauli. *Proud Shoes: The Story of An American Family.* New York: Harper and Row, 1956.

Myron, Nancy, and Charlotte Bunch, eds. *Lesbianism and the Women's Movement.* Baltimore: Diana Press, 1975.

Reed, Evelyn. *Problems of Women's Liberation.* New York: Pathfinder Press, 1969.

Reid, Inez. *"Together" Black Women.* New York: Emerson-Hall, 1971.

Rich, Adrienne. *Blood, Bread, and Poetry: Selected Prose, 1979–1985.* New York: W. W. Norton, 1986.

Robinson, Jo Ann Gibson. *The Montgomery Bus Boycott and the Women Who Started It.* Knoxville: University of Tennessee Press, 1987.

Rupp, Leila J., and Verta Taylor. *Survival in the Doldrums: The American Women's Rights Movement, 1945 to the 1960s.* New York: Oxford University Press, 1987.

Ryan, Barbara. *Feminism and the Women's Movement.* New York: Routledge, 1992.

Sargent, Lydia, ed. *Women and Revolution: A Discussion of the Unhappy Marriage of Marxism and Feminism.* Boston: South End Press, 1981.

Smith, Barbara, ed. *Home Girls: A Black Feminist Anthology*. Latham, NY: Kitchen Table: Women of Color Press, 1983.

Snitow, Ann, ed. *Powers of Desire: The Politics of Sexuality*. New York: Monthly Review Press, 1983.

Spelman, Elizabeth. *Inessential Woman: Problems of Exclusion in Feminist Thought*. Boston: Beacon Press, 1988.

Swerdlow, Amy. *Women Strike for Peace: Traditional Motherhood and Radical Politics in the 1960s*. Chicago: University of Chicago Press, 1993.

Tanner, Leslie, ed. *Voices from Women's Liberation*. New York: Signet, 1970.

Thom, Mary. *Inside Ms.: 25 years of the Magazine and the Feminist Movement*. New York: Henry Holt, 1997.

Thompson, Mary Lou, ed. *Voices of the New Feminism*. Boston: Beacon Press, 1970.

Tobias, Sheila. *Faces of Feminism: An Activist's Reflection on the Women's Movement*. Boulder, CO: Westview Press, 1997.

Vaid, Urvashi. *Virtual Equality: The Mainstreaming of Gay and Lesbian Liberation*. New York: Anchor Books, 1995.

Walker, Alice. *In Search of Our Mothers' Gardens: Womanist Prose*. San Diego: Harcourt Brace Jovanovich, 1983.

———. *Living by the Word: Selected Writings, 1973–1987*. San Diego: Harcourt Brace Jovanovich, 1988.

Walker, Rebecca, ed. *To Be Real: Telling the Truth and Changing the Face of Feminism*. New York: Anchor Books, 1995.

Wallace, Michele. *Black Macho and the Myth of the Superwoman*. New York: Dial, 1979.

Wandersee, Winifred. *On the Move: American Women in the 1970s*. Boston: Twayne, 1988.

Weddington, Sarah. *A Question of Choice*. New York: Putnam, 1992.

West, Guida. *The National Welfare Rights Movement: The Social Protest of Poor Women*. New York: Praeger, 1981.

Whittier, Nancy. *Feminist Generations: The Persistence of the Radical Women's Movement*. Philadelphia: Temple University Press, 1995.

Wing, Adrien Katherine. *Critical Race Feminism: A Reader*. New York: New York University Press, 1997.

INDEX

Page numbers in **bold type** refer to main entries in the sourcebook.

ABOUT THE EDITOR AND CONTRIBUTORS

JENNIFER SCANLON is Associate Professor and director of women's studies at Plattsburgh State University in New York. She is the author of *Inarticulate Longings: The Ladies' Home Journal, Gender, and the Promises of Consumer Culture* (1995), coauthor of *American Women Historians, 1700s–1990s: A Biographical Dictionary* (Greenwood, 1996), and author of numerous articles on feminist pedagogy and women's relationship to popular and consumer culture. For the 1998–1999 academic year she is a Fulbright Scholar at the University of the West Indies, Trinidad and Tobago.

AMY BETH ARONSON is currently coediting a new edition of Charlotte Perkins Gilman's *Women and Economics*. She teaches humanities and writing at New York University and has previously taught in the Department of Journalism and Media Studies at Rutgers University and the New School for Social Research.

BEATRIZ BADIKIAN-GARTLER was born in Buenos Aires, Argentina, and now lives in Chicago. She is the author of *Mapmaker*, a collection of poetry, as well as *Akewa Is a Woman*, a chapbook of poetry, now in its second edition. Her work has been published in *Spoon River Quarterly*, *Hammers*, *The Americas Review*, *Third Woman*, *Emergence*, *Lucky Star*, *Tonantzin*, *Ruptures*, *Imagine*, and other publications. Her poetry has also been translated and published in India, Greece, and Canada. Badikian coauthored *Naming the Daytime Moon*, an anthology of Chicago women writers, and is a contributor to the minianthology *Emergency Tacos*. Badikian-Gartler teaches literature and writing in Chicago.

BETH BLISSMAN is a doctoral candidate in religion and social change at the Iliff School of Theology and the University of Denver. She has many interests, including lesbigay ecotheology, the environmental justice movement in the

United States, the invisibility of whiteness, Catholic communities of women religious, and service learning in universities and seminaries.

EILEEN BRESNAHAN has been a radical feminist activist for more than a decade. Bresnahan was formerly a collective member, editor, and writer of *Big Mama Rag Feminist Newsjournal*; collective member, editor, writer, and reader of "Women Everywhere" Feminist Radio Collective; and a founding member of the Denver Feminist Organizing Committee, all in Denver. She was also a founding member and member of the Board of Directors at the University of South Florida Women's Center. Bresnahan has been employed as a postal worker, printing press operator, taxi driver, and hospital worker. She is currently Assistant Professor of political science and women's studies at the University of Utah in Salt Lake City.

AMY BUTLER received her bachelor's degree from UCLA in 1988 and her Ph.D. in American history from Binghamton University, SUNY, in 1997. She is currently working on a biography of Ethel M. Smith of the National Women's Trade Union League.

SUSAN BUTLER is a Professor of American history at Cerritos College, located in southern California. Since coming to the school in the fall of 1995, she has reestablished women's history in the core curriculum and is working with the administration to establish a women's studies program. She is currently working on an intellectual biography of Mary McCarthy, which is an outgrowth of her dissertation.

ANN MAUGER COLBERT is the Journalism Coordinator at Indiana Purdue University at Fort Wayne. She has been a professional journalist and has written for magazines and newspapers; her writing has received two writing awards. Her recent work is with women and journalism, primarily in the area of historical narrative.

JEANNE CORTIEL is an assistant to the chair of American literature and culture at the University of Dortmund in Germany. She has written a book on Joanna Russ, *Demand My Writing: Joanna Russ/Feminism/Science Fiction*. Her research interests include feminist fantasy/science fiction and the cultural specificities of American feminist, lesbian, and queer theories.

ANGELA COTTEN is a student in the Institute of Liberal Arts at Emory University. Her areas of research and writing are poststructuralism/postmodernism, women's and queer studies, and the history of black political thought.

JULIE A. DAVIES is a teaching associate at the State University of New York at Plattsburgh, in both the women's studies program and the Canadian studies program. Her academic work and her work as a visual artist show her interest in investigating the impact of borders and borderland on women's lives.

DANIELLE DeMUTH is a Doctoral Candidate in English at the University of Toledo, where she also teaches in the women's studies program. Her other research interests include women's studies interdisciplinary curriculum design and feminist pedagogy.

LARA E. DIECKMANN is currently an Instructor in the Theatre Arts and Dance department at California State University, Los Angeles.

SIOBAN DILLON is a graduate student in the English department at Binghamton University, SUNY. Her interests include women's studies, American literature, and cultural studies.

STACEY DONOHUE is an Assistant Professor of English at Central Oregon Community College in Bend, Oregon. She has published essays on Mary McCarthy and Mary Lavin and is currently writing a book on Irish American women writers.

UCHE EGEMONYE is a dual degree student at Emory University. Her research interests are black women in the Reconstruction and Progressive Era.

ANNE F. EISENBERG is currently in the department of sociology at the University of Iowa. Her research interests include issues associated with gender, technology, and science. She agrees with Dr. Keller, the subject of her work here, that the academy needs to recognize other voices in the field and in the laboratory.

MARY L. ERTEL is an Associate Professor of sociology at Central Connecticut State University. She teaches courses in gender, power, deviant behavior, family, social problems, and women's studies. Her current interests include power in gendered communication; uses of humor, with special reference to sociological, power, and gendered aspects of humor; and feminist issues in pornography. She recently wrote a position paper, "It's Not Just about Sex! Flynt, Hate, Porn, and Free Speech."

KAREN GARNER is an Assistant Professor of history at Alma College in Alma, Michigan, where she teaches U.S. Women's History, U.S. Foreign Relations, and Modern China and Japan and cochairs the Women's Studies Program. She is currently writing a biography of foreign policy activist Maud Muriel Russell.

NANCY McCAMPBELL GRACE is an Associate Professor of English at the College of Wooster in Wooster, Ohio. She directs the College's Writing Center and teaches courses in women's studies, James Joyce, literature of the beat generation, and journalism. She is the author of *The Feminized Male Character in*

Twentieth-Century Fiction (1995), which features chapters on Joyce, Hemingway, Kerouac, and Bellows.

JAIME M. GRANT is a lesbian writer/activist whose work has spanned feminist, antiracist, and queer liberation movements. Currently, she serves as director of the Union Institute Center for Women, the only academic women's center in the nation dedicated to building coalitions between scholars and activists.

MARINA KARIDES is a graduate student in sociology at the University of Georgia. Presently, she is researching the interaction of race, class, and gender in the informal economy. Her areas of interest are political economy and feminist theory.

CAROLYN KITCH is an Assistant Professor of magazine journalism at the Medill School of Journalism at Northwestern University. She is a freelance writer and a former articles editor for *McCall's* and *Good Housekeeping*.

JENNIFER KOHOUT is a doctoral candidate in English at the University of Toledo and co-editor of *The Mark: A Literary Journal*.

NEREA A. LLAMAS is currently the Minority Fellow at the University of California, Santa Barbara, and serves as collection manager for women's studies, French, and English.

MARGARET R. LaWARE has been an Assistant Professor in the Department of Communication at Plattsburgh State University in New York since 1993. She is presently a visiting Assistant Professor in the Department of English at Iowa State University in Ames, Iowa. Her areas of research include rhetorical theory, rhetorical criticism, feminist theory, gender and communication, and visual communication.

DIANE L. McKAY is a graduate student and instructor in the English department at Duke University. She also teaches in Duke University's women's studies program.

JOYA MISRA is an Assistant Professor of sociology at the University of Georgia. Her work primarily stresses feminist approaches to political economy, including a focus on the welfare state in a number of countries. Her recent work has begun addressing the "race-ing" and gendering of U.S. welfare policy since the turn of the century.

ANN LEE MORGAN, an art historian and critic, is working on a book about American women artists in the 1960s and 1970s. The author of a monograph on Arthur Dove, she has also edited several other books. Her articles and reviews have appeared in *Art in America, Afterimage, New Art Examiner, American Book Review, Art Journal*, and elsewhere.

PAT MURPHY is an Assistant Professsor of sociology at SUNY, Geneseo, where she also teaches in the women's studies program. From 1986 to 1990 she was president of the National Organization for Women in New Hampshire. From 1990 to 1994 she served on the National NOW Board.

GWENN BROWN NEALIS lives in the Catskill Mountains and has taught high school English classes since 1974.

JOHN R. NEALIS currently teaches at Delaware Academy in New York state. He has also taught at Hofstra University, Dowling College, and the State University of New York Colleges at Delhi and Oneonta.

JENNIFER OLDHAM is a staff writer for the *Los Angeles Times*, where she covers telecommunications and technology for the business section. Her involvement in feminism includes drafting newsletters for Planned Parenthood, sitting on the board of L.A. List, a nonpartisan fund-raising organization, and analyzing women's health programs for the Colorado Women's Agenda and the Eastside Neighborhood Health Center. She lives in Studio City, California.

LINDA ROHRER PAIGE, Associate Professor of English at Georgia Southern University, Statesboro, serves as vice president of the Popular Culture Association in the South. With articles appearing in such journals as *Papers on Language and Literature, The Literature/Film Quarterly, Studies in Short Fiction*, and *The Journal of Popular Film and Television*, Paige's scholarly interests lie primarily in drama, film, popular culture, and women's studies.

SUSAN L. PATNODE is an attorney practicing in Plattsburgh, New York. She is also a teaching associate at the State University of New York at Plattsburgh in the women's studies program.

ANNMARIE PINARSKI has taught English and women's studies at Bowling Green State University. She is currently a law student at Rutgers Law School in Newark, New Jersey.

GÖNUL PÜLTAR is a member of the English Department at Bilkent University (Ankara, Turkey), the vice-president of the American Studies Association of Turkey, a member of the International Committee of the American Studies Association, and the founding editor of the *Journal of American Studies in Turkey*. Her written works include *Technique and Tradition in Beckett's Trilogy of Novels* (1996) and the novels *Ellerimden Su İçsinler* (Let Them Drink Water from My

Hands, forthcoming) and *Dünya Bir Atlikarinca* (The World Is a Merry-Go-Round, 1979).

MICHAELA CRAWFORD REAVES currently teaches women's studies at California Lutheran University. With several articles to her credit, she is currently working on a book about the Grange in California during the 1870s.

JUDITH RICHARDS is a lecturer in the department of Spanish and Portuguese at the University of Kansas. Her research areas are Latina and Latin American women writers, women's autobiographical writing, and feminist critical theory and analysis. She participated in the 1996 National Endowment for the Humanities (NEH) Summer Seminar on Feminist Epistemologies at the University of Oregon, during which she wrote the introductory chapter for her present book project, *Revolting Developments: Fiction and Autobiography in Contemporary Mexican Women's Writing*.

CHERYL RODRIGUEZ is an Assistant Professor of Africana studies and anthropology at the University of South Florida. She teaches courses on black women in America and applied research in African American communities. Her research focuses on economic development for low-income women and black women's grassroots activism.

DEBORAH J. GEPNER SALVAGGIO is currently an Adjunct Professor of English and women's studies at the College of New Jersey. She is former editor of the Trenton State College *Women's Studies Newsletter* and a contributing editor to *The Reader's Encyclopedia of Women's Literature*.

NIKKI SENECAL is a doctoral candidate in English at the University of Southern California. She is currently working on a project that examines women's violence in the work of Margaret Atwood, Toni Morrison, and Joyce Carol Oates, tentatively titled *Violent Femmes: Feminism and the Problem of Women's Literary Violence*.

LISA SIGEL is visiting Assistant Professor at Carnegie Mellon University. She works in the fields of the history of sexuality and the history of gender. She is currently writing a history of nineteenth-century British pornography provisionally entitled *Sexual Imaginings*.

GRACE SIKORSKI is a Ph.D. candidate in The Pennsylvania State University's English Department. She is an Americanist with a specialization in women's literature, literary theory, and queer theory.

FREDERICK J. SIMONELLI is currently Assistant Professor of history at Mount St. Mary's College in Los Angeles.

VIKI SOADY, after a long career at Brock University in Ontario, where she received the Alumni Teaching Award, is now director of women's studies at Valdosta State University in Valdosta, Georgia. Her interests include feminist ethics and women in history.

TRACY WAHL is a doctoral candidate in political science at the University of Wisconsin, Madison. She is also a freelance journalist in Washington, D.C., where she produces radio features for National Public Radio and Pacifica Network News.

LINDA WONG is a graduate student in educational policy and administration at the University of Minnesota. Her concerns lie in the role Asian American women play in domestic policies and international development policies in Asia.

ISBN 0-313-30125-5

90000>

EAN

9 780313 301254

HARDCOVER BAR CODE